WITHDRAWN

THE VOCAL SONGS IN THE
PLAYS OF SHAKESPEARE

THE
VOCAL SONGS
IN THE PLAYS OF
SHAKESPEARE

A CRITICAL HISTORY

Peter J. Seng

HARVARD UNIVERSITY PRESS

CAMBRIDGE, MASSACHUSETTS

1967

Distributed in Great Britain by Oxford University Press, London

Publication of this book has been aided
by a grant from the Hyder Edward Rollins Fund

Library of Congress Catalog Card Number: 66–18256

Made and printed in Great Britain by
William Clowes and Sons, Limited, London and Beccles

Book design by David Ford

ACKNOWLEDGMENTS

The Bodleian Library, Oxford—for permission to reproduce the song-lyrics of MS. Don. c. 57 (fol. 78); by permission of the Keeper of Western Manuscripts.

The British Museum, London—for permission to reproduce extracts from Brit. Mus. MSS. Egerton 2711, Add. 15,117, 17,492, and 27,879. By permission of The Trustees of the British Museum.

Brown University Press, Providence, R. I.—for permission to reproduce extracts from Andrew J. Sabol's *Songs and Dances for the Stuart Masque*, 1959.

Cambridge University Press, Cambridge, England—for permission to reproduce extracts from The New Cambridge Edition of Shakespeare, ed. Sir Arthur Quiller-Couch and John Dover Wilson: *As You Like It*, 1926; *Twelfth Night*, 1930; from *The Pepysian Garland*, ed. Hyder E. Rollins, 1922; from *The Complete Works of George Gascoigne*, ed. J. W. Cunliffe, 1907–1910.

The Clarendon Press, Oxford—for permission to reproduce extracts from Richmond Noble's *Shakespeare's Use of Song*, 1923; and from *Ben Jonson*, ed. C. H. Herford, Percy and Evelyn Simpson, 1925–1952; by permission of the Clarendon Press, Oxford.

J. M. Dent & Sons, Ltd., London—for permission to reproduce extracts from W. Robertson Davies' *Shakespeare's Boy Actors*, 1939.

Dover Publications, Inc., New York—for permission to reproduce extracts from Frederick W. Sternfeld, *Music in Shakespearan Tragedy*, Dover Publications, Inc., New York, 1963. Reprinted through permission of the publisher.

Explicator—for permission to reproduce extracts from Edward F. Nolan's "Shakespeare's 'Fear No More the Heat o' th' Sun'," *Explicator XI*, item no 4, 1952; copyright by the publishers of *Explicator*, University of South Carolina, Columbia, S.C. Also by permission of the author, Edward F. Nolan.

Faber and Faber, Ltd., London—for permission to reproduce extracts from "Music in Shakespeare." © Copyright 1957 by W. H. Auden. Reprinted from *The Dyer's Hand* by W. H. Auden, by permission of Faber and Faber, Ltd.

Harvard University Press, Cambridge, Mass.—for permission to reproduce extracts from the following editions by Hyder E. Rollins: *A Handful of Pleasant Delights*, 1924; *Tottel's Miscellany*, 1928–1929; *The Pepys Ballads*, 1929–1932; *A Poetical Rhapsody*, 1931–1932; *England's Helicon*, 1935; from *Catullus, Tibullus, and Pervigilium Veneris*, ed. F. W. Cornish, The Loeb Classical Library, [1912], 1939; and from The New Arden Shakespeare: *The Tempest*, ed. F. Kermode, 1954, 1958.

Leslie Hotson, Sorrento, Me.—for permission to reproduce extracts from *The First Night of Twelfth Night*, Macmillan and Co., New York, 1954.

Methuen & Co., Ltd., London—for permission to reproduce extracts from the Arden and New Arden Shakespeares: *The Tempest*, ed. M. Luce, 1926; ed. F. Kermode, 1954, 1958; *Othello*, ed. H. C. Hart, 1928; *Twelfth Night*, ed. M. Luce, 1929.

Modern Language Association of America, New York—for permission to reproduce "Carol 3" from "The Bradshaw Carols," *PMLA*, 1966, 81: 309–310; reprinted by permission of The Modern Language Association; also by permission of the editor, Rossell Hope Robbins, and the owners of MS. Add. 7350, Cambridge University Library, Cambridge, England.

Music and Letters, London—for permission to reproduce extracts from John P. Cutts, "Music and the Supernatural in *The Tempest*," *Music and Letters*, 1958, 39: 347–358; by permission of the editor.

The New York Public Library—for permission to reproduce an extract from MS. Drexel 4041; by permission of the Head of the Rare Book and Manuscript Collection, Music Division.

Mr. James M. Osborn, New Haven, Conn.—for permission to reproduce William Elderton's "The Gods of Love" from a privately owned manuscript, "The Braye Lute Book."

Oxford University Press, London—for permission to reproduce the lyrics of Thomas Ford's "Sigh no more, ladies," from *Four English Songs of the Early Seventeenth Century*, ed. Peter Warlock [i.e., Philip Heseltine], 1925.

Princeton University Press, Princeton, N.J.—for permission to reproduce extracts from Harley Granville-Barker's *Prefaces to Shakespeare*, Princeton University Press, 1947. Copyright 1947 by Princeton University Press.

Random House, Inc., New York—for permission to reproduce extracts from "Music in Shakespeare," © Copyright 1957 by W. H. Auden. Reprinted from *The Dyer's Hand* by W. H. Auden, by permission of Random House, Inc.

Routledge and Kegan Paul, Ltd., London—for permission to reproduce extracts from Frederick W. Sternfeld's *Music in Shakespearean Tragedy*, 1963.

Rupert Hart-Davis, Ltd., London—for permission to reproduce extracts from Leslie Hotson's *The First Night of Twelfth Night*, 1954.

The Sewanee Review, Sewanee, Tenn.—for permission to reproduce extracts from John Hollander's "*Twelfth Night* and the Morality of Indulgence," *The Sewanee Review*, 1959, 67: 220–239. Copyright by the University of the South, Sewanee, Tenn. Also by permission of the author, John Hollander.

The Shakespeare Association of America, New York—for permission to reproduce extracts from John P. Cutts' "The Original Music of a Song in 2 *Henry IV*," *Shakespeare Quarterly*, 1956, 7: 385–392; and from M. A. Shaaber's "*The First Rape of Faire Hellen* by John Trussell," *Shakespeare Quarterly*, 1957, 8: 439.

University of Florida Press, Gainesville, Fla.—for permission to reproduce extracts from *Shakespeare's Use of Music: A Study of the Music and Its Performance in the Original Production of Seven Comedies*, by John H. Long, published by the University of Florida Press, 1955; and *Shakespeare's Use of Music: The Final Comedies*, by John H. Long, published by the University of Florida Press, 1961. Used by permission.

University of Wisconsin Press, Madison, Wis.—for permission to reproduce extracts from John Robert Moore's "The Function of the Songs in Shakespeare's Plays," *Studies by Members of the Department of English of the University of Wisconsin*, 1916.

For My Father

PREFACE

Important scholarly research on the songs in Shakespeare's plays has been mostly a product of the present century. Seventeenth- and eighteenth-century editors of the plays made notational comments on the songs when explanation was egregiously called for, but on the whole they apparently preferred to deal with what they regarded as the more relevant cruxes, textual difficulties in the spoken dialogue. When the songs themselves began to draw attention in the nineteenth century, that interest came, as was to be expected, mostly from music historians. Yet these scholars were interested in Shakespeare's songs only as part of a larger pattern involving Renaissance music and the popular and broadside ballad. William Chappell's *A Collection of National English Airs* (1840), and his later reworking of much of the same material in his indispensable *Popular Music of the Olden Time* [1855–1859], reflect the concerns of the historian of music, not of the Shakespeare scholar.

Works in the nineteenth century which deal exclusively with Shakespeare's songs are either collections of musical scores or bibliographical listings of available music. In the former category are William Linley's *Shakespeare's Dramatic Songs* (1816), John Caulfield's extremely untrustworthy *A Collection of the Vocal Music in Shakespeare's Plays* [1864], and the anonymous *Shakespeare Vocal Album* (1864). Among the compilers of data on Shakespeare's songs were Alfred Roffe, *Handbook of Shakespeare Music* (1878), and J. Greenhill, W. A. Harrison, and Frederick J. Furnivall, *A List of All the Songs & Passages in Shakespeare Which Have Been Set to Music* (1884). At the very end of the century, as if anticipating the scholarship to come, J. Frederick Bridge published his *Songs from Shakespeare. The Earliest Known Settings* [1894?], material in part reproduced in his *Shakespearean Music in the Plays and Early Operas* (1923).

Since 1900 at least twenty scholars in music and literature have seriously concerned themselves with Shakespeare's use of music and song. Their researches, in the last twenty years alone, have turned up a surprising amount of new material. As a result, modern producers and stage directors can now avail themselves of reasonably authentic melodies; and rather than regarding the songs in Shakespeare's plays as mere divertisements from the dramatic action, they can begin to regard them as integral parts of the plays.

To raise questions, however, about the authenticity of the music, or about the dramatic functions of Shakespeare's songs, may seem pure antiquarianism to the reader of Shakespeare who may not understand what music and song meant to the playwright and his contemporaries. Whether they performed music themselves or hired trained musicians to perform it for them, the musical arts were an organic part of their lives. Renaissance Englishmen were a singing people; many of the songs and tunes they sang survive to attest the fact.

To say this much, however, is not to assert that "every domestic hearth was the scene of musical performance of a very high standard," or that "the art of singing was cultivated with equal zeal and discernment, in every grade of social rank." Renaissance England's "nest of singing birds" must also have included a goodly number of choughs, daws, magpies, and crows. And even among the educated classes there were the "godly" who regarded all secular music as profane; there were the *philosophes* who cited classical authorities to prove that cultivating the art of music was not worth the waste of time that could be spent in more profitable pursuits, and that certain kinds of music tended to enervate moral fiber. Finally, there were the arbiters of taste and social decorum like Elyot and Castiglione who argued that good manners would dispose a gentleman or lady to dissemble their musical abilities when in public. On no account, said the courtesy-book writers, should gentlefolk be forward to display their skills—certainly not if to do so would taint them in the eyes of commoners with the appearance of professionalism, or suggest that they were competing with "mechanicals" such as the hired musicians.

Yet for all such artificial strictures on the part music might be allowed to play in social intercourse, the habit of music and song in Renaissance England flourished. The attitudes of the upper classes are reflected in the handbooks of nurture and education for their offspring; nearly all of these books prescribe some training in musical skills, always with the proviso that it not be carried to excess. Hence the "affable remarks" of Thomas Morley at the beginning of his *Plaine and Easie Introduction to Practicall Musicke* (1597), implying that skill in performing music was important for social success, must certainly have been aimed at potential buyers of the book who could be persuaded by observation and experience that those remarks were true.

Once he understands the role that music played in the lives of Renaissance Englishmen, the modern reader of Shakespeare may perceive the considerable difference between himself and the playwright and his contemporaries with respect to the use of music on the stage. To the modern theatergoer music and song on the stage is a mere dramatic convention. Characters in a musical comedy sing because they are characters in a musical comedy. The spectacle behind the proscenium has little, if anything, to do with real life. But when an actor on Shakespeare's stage broke into song he was very likely regarded as doing just what was to be expected under the circumstances. The stage-lover who serenaded his mistress was functioning as he very well might have in real life.

Although systematic study of Shakespeare's songs did not flourish until the present century, most of the fruits of that research are still buried in scholarly periodicals. Discoveries by earlier researchers are even more hidden: they are lost in the footnotes of seldom-read eighteenth- and nineteenth-century editions of Shakespeare, or buried from sight in the learned or cultural journals of the time. This book endeavors to bring together all of the relevant material on the vocal songs in Shakespeare's plays; it aims to make available to the modern student a chronological history of the textual and analytical criticism of the songs, information about the original or early musical settings when these exist, and a critical examination of the dramatic functions of the songs within the plays.

A book such as this could not have been written without the help of numerous institutions and people. I am chiefly grateful to the Harvard College Library and to the Houghton Library of Harvard College for their generous cooperation over many years. A Dexter Fellowship from Harvard University in the summer of 1952 enabled me to work at libraries abroad. The Boston Public Library trustingly put at my disposal their four Shakespeare folios from the Barton Collection. The British Museum, the Bodleian Library, and the Cambridge University Library allowed me the use of their rare book and manuscript collections. A liberal grant from the Folger Foundation in Washington, D.C., enabled me to spend a summer as a Fellow of the Folger Shakespeare Library. The New York Public Library, particularly the Music Division, and the library of the University of Wisconsin-Milwaukee, helped me in my researches. Finally, I am grateful to Connecticut College for a number of financial grants which aided me in completing this book.

Among the persons who have helped me I am particularly indebted to Professor Herschel C. Baker of the English Department, Harvard University. At the very beginning of my study I was warmly encouraged— though he may not remember it—by John Robert Moore, now Emeritus Professor of English, Indiana University. Professor Frederick W. Sternfeld of the Faculty of Music, Oxford; Professor John Ward of the Harvard School of Music, and Professor Baker, have read my manuscript; I am grateful to them for their patience and counsel which have saved me from innumerable errors.

Miss Carolyn Jakeman of the Houghton Library and Miss Hazel Johnson of Palmer Library, Connecticut College, have both, on many occasions, generously given their time and effort to assist me with difficult bibliographical problems. Mr. James Osborn of New Haven, Connecticut, has allowed me to transcribe from a manuscript in his own collection the unique source of one of Shakespeare's songs. Four former students of mine cheerfully helped, at one time or another, in the dreary task of checking bibliographical details: Cecelia Holland, Robin Lee, Barry David Horwitz, and Carolyn Adkins Dohrmann.

This last place, a paragraph by himself, I have saved for Hyder Edward Rollins. There is no way of repaying the debt which I owe to him.

PETER J. SENG

CONTENTS

INTRODUCTION

The methodology of this study is modeled in part on the system used by the editors of the *New Variorum Edition of Shakespeare*. The texts of the songs from the earliest authoritative editions have been collated with all the sixteenth- and seventeenth-century editions, and significant variants are recorded in the textual notes. The texts of the songs have also been collated with the editions of twenty-four modern editors, beginning with the second edition of Nicholas Rowe (1709) and concluding with the edition by William Allen Neilson and Charles Jarvis Hill (1942). From these modern complete editions significant variants have likewise been recorded and, in addition, critical and textual comments have been freely extracted. Critical comments have also been taken from numerous individual editions of plays or poems down to 1963, and from books, articles, and manuscripts from the early sixteenth century down to 1966. The songs are numbered from 1 to 70 and are arranged in order as they appear in the plays; the chronology of the plays is the one given by E. K. Chambers in his *William Shakespeare. A Study of Facts and Problems* (1930).

The material for each song is arranged as follows:

1. A headnote giving the source of the text, the signature of its location in the early edition, and its location by act, scene, and line numbers in standard modern editions; also information about the typography of the song in the source, and about its stage direction, if any.

2. The text of the song exactly reproduced from the earliest authoritative edition.

3. General critical commentary arranged according to date. For some songs, however, special topics or problems have engaged the attention of critics or editors. In these instances the material on those topics has been segregated into a separate chronology so as to afford the reader an historical view of their critical treatment.

4. Textual commentary arranged according to date.

5. Information about music for the song.

6. Information about sources or analogues (if any), and about other relevant subjects.

7. Observations about the dramatic function of the song in the play.

All material in quotation marks, or in extract-type, or directly following a : is quoted, with an ellipsis [. . .] used to mark the omission of words, phrases, or sentences in the source from which the quotation is taken. The mark ✦ is used to end a direction quotation begun with the mark :. Everything within brackets, and all commentary otherwise unattributed, is the present editor's. In most instances quotations by the various commentators from earlier works than their own have been checked against the original sources (or modern scholarly editions of those sources), and silently corrected when necessary, or expanded when the added quotation seemed informative. The exact source of such quotations is recorded in brackets.

Because of the thousands of references made to other works in the course of this book, a special system of short-reference has had to be devised. The sources of works cited in this book are indicated by the last name of a given author or editor and, within parentheses, the date(s) of the work of his which is cited, and the location in his work of the citation. In instances of multiple authorship or editorship, only the name of the first author or editor is indicated in the text, though the full bibliographical reference is, of course, given in the Bibliography at the end of this book. Thus Greenlaw (1932–1949, I, 16) on p. 15, means Greenlaw, Edwin, Charles G. Osgood, and Frederick M. Padelford, eds., 1932–1949, *The Works of Edmund Spenser. A Variorum Edition*, 9 vols. in 10, The Johns Hopkins Press, Baltimore, Md., vol. I, p. 16. In the few instances where duplicate surnames of authors or editors, or duplicate dates for the same author or editor, would cause confusion, specifying initials or titles are also included in the short-reference.

A similar method is employed for references to modern editions of the works of Shakespeare. When the citation is made to one of the complete modern editions, the name of the editor or edition is given, followed by the date of the edition in parentheses. Thus Neilson (ed. 1942) refers to the edition listed in the Bibliography under that name and date in Works of William Shakespeare: II., Complete Editions Since 1709. The citation will be a note to the relevant song in that edition. When the edition cited is one of the individual modern editions, the parenthetical reference (ind. ed. 1958) will direct the reader to find the work under the appropriate play in Works of William Shakespeare, III: Individual Editions of the Plays or Poems. Once again the citation will be to a note on the relevant song.

For purposes of uniformity the name *Shakespeare* and the adjective *Shakespearean* have been regularized throughout the book. Unusual typographical forms like the long *s* [ſ] are usually normalized, except in the text of Shakespeare's songs. The same is true of manuscript abbreviations which would require special fonts or superscript letters for exact reproduction. References to the plays by act, scene, and line are to the edition by Kittredge (1936); most of the quotations from Shakespeare's works made by the present editor are also from this edition, though occasionally it has been useful to quote from an original quarto or folio text.

There are so many lyrics of various kinds embedded in the texts of Shakespeare's plays that I have found it necessary to define the meaning of "song" rather rigidly. By "song" is meant any lyric passage which was originally intended to be sung on the stage by the actor to whom it is assigned, that intention being manifested either by a stage direction (s.d.) in the original source, or by a clear reference to the lyric as a song or to the actor as a singer in the approximate context. Thus I have excluded recited verses (even when they appear in other books or manuscripts of Shakespeare's time as songs), songs for which no certain texts exist (*e.g.*, "Concolinel," in *Love's Labor's Lost*, III.i.3, and the Witches' Songs in *Macbeth*, III.v.33, IV.i.43), and songs from plays or parts of plays outside the generally accepted Shakespeare canon.

THE VOCAL SONGS IN THE
PLAYS OF SHAKESPEARE

The Taming of the Shrew

I

TEXT: Folio (1623), sig. T₃ (IV.i.143 f.).
TYPOGRAPHY: Unindented verse, roman face.

Where is the life that late I led?
Where are thofe? [. . .]

GENERAL COMMENTARY

Malone (ed. 1790) cites a poem in Clement Robinson's *A Handefull of pleasant delites*, 1584 (ed. Rollins, 1924, pp. 15 f.), titled "Dame Beauties replie to the Louer late at libertie: and now complaineth himfelfe to be her captiue, Intituled: Where is the life that late I led." The poem begins,

> The life that erst thou ledst my friend,
>   was pleasant to thine eyes:
> But now the losse of libertie,
>   thou seemest to despise.

Rollins' note (pp. 88 f.) sums up the known information about the lost song by Petruchio : The title of the ballad [in *A Handefull*] means "Dame Beauty's Reply to the Lover Who Wrote a Complaint Called 'Where is the life that late I led?'" [It] is, to repeat, a reply to a lost ballad that began as the snatch sung by Petruchio. . . . That the words of the second line omitted by Petruchio were "pleasant days" is indicated not only by the phrase, "pleasant to thine eies" [in l. 2 of the "Reply"], but also by Pistol's remark in *2 Henry IV* [V.iii.146 f.] . . .

> "Where is the life that late I led?" say they:
> Why, here it is; welcome these pleasant days!

This lost ballad was undoubtedly that registered by Richard Jones about March 1566 (Arber [1875], I, 308), as "a newe ballet of one who myslykeng his lybertie soughte his owne bondage through his owne folly." ¶ The facts just given furnish good evidence that . . . [the "Reply"] had appeared before the 1566 *Pleasant Sonnets* was compiled. That it had appeared before 1578 is certain, for it is imitated in the *Gorgeous Gallery of Gallant Inventions* [ed. Rollins, 1926, pp. 39–42] by a poem called

"The Louer wounded with his Ladies beauty craueth mercy. To the Tune of where is the life that late I led." ✦ [The facts cited by Rollins, the allusion, "Reply," and imitation, suggest that the original of Petruchio's song-fragment was a popular ballad, and that it may have been in existence almost thirty years before Shakespeare put it into his play. E.K. Chambers (1930, I, 270, 327) dates *The Taming of the Shrew* about 1593–1594. The ballad was popular until at least 1612 for "A Louer bewailing the absence of his Loue" in Thomas Deloney's *Strange Histories* (sig. L₄ᵛ) is "To the tune of Where is the life that late."]

MUSIC

The original tune for Petruchio's ballad-fragment is not known. Long (1961, p. 4) has set the first line alone to an old ballad "Lusty Gallant" from Gibbon (1930, p. 65), and remarks that "there is a half-hearted, casual quality about Shakespeare's treatment of music in *The Shrew* which suggests a degree of haste or lack of interest" not characteristic of Shakespeare's practice in earlier comedies. He notes that Shakespeare may have found music "uncongenial to the farce type. . . ."

An amusing development of Petruchio's ballad-fragment is to be found in Cole Porter's *Kiss Me, Kate*, 1948 (Spewack, 1953, pp. 105–108).

DRAMATIC FUNCTION

The dramatic function of this fragment—if such a term does not press it to death—is obviously comic irony. Another married man may once have mourned the carefree days of his bachelorhood to the words and tune of "Where is the life that late I led," but not Petruchio. He is clearly having the time of his life. If the original song was a popular ballad as the evidence suggests, the audience who had heard it lugubriously bawled in the streets would have been delighted by Petruchio's pretense that he was unhappy in marriage.

2

TEXT: Folio (1623), sig. T₃ (IV.i.148 f.).
TYPOGRAPHY: Unindented verse, italic and roman face.

It was the Friar of Orders gray,
As he forth walked on his way.

GENERAL COMMENTARY

Petruchio's scrap of song is apparently from a lost version of a ballad or carol, probably scurrilous in nature, and perhaps related to the analogues reproduced below. Bishop Percy in his *Reliques* (1765, I, 226) worked these lines along with others from Shakespeare's plays into a ballad of his own composition, "The Friar of Orders Gray." Numerous references are made to the (often unsavory) reputations of soliciting friars in *Measure for Measure* (see V.i.127, 131, 261 f., 267–269, and 307 ff.). A grey friar is a Franciscan.

MUSIC

The original tune for Petruchio's song cannot be known for certain since the fragment quoted in Shakespeare's play is too short to permit positive identification with the analogues, the tune for which is known. The similarity between the opening line of the Shakespeare song and that of the first analogue may be only coincidental—it seems a common enough beginning for a ballad or carol about a soliciting friar. Long (1961, p. 4) has set Petruchio's song-fragment to a 1599 "Coranto" tune by Thomas Morley. But the song can also be fitted to the popular old tune called "The Friar and the Nun," which may have been the tune to which the analogues, below, were sung. Versions of that tune are to be found in Chappell ([1855–1859], I, 146), Wooldridge (1893; reprinted 1961, I, 286), and C. Simpson (1966, p. 239). As Simpson points out (pp. 238 f.), the popularity of "The Friar and the Nun" is amply attested by the fact that it appears in all editions of John Playford's *The English Dancing Master* from 1651 to 1728, in his *Musick's Delight on the Cithren*, 1666, in Thomas D'Urfey's *Wit and Mirth*, 1719-1720, as well as in a number of ballad operas.

ANALOGUES

What may be an analogue or perhaps even the source of the lines sung by Petruchio is a carol recently edited by Robbins (1966, pp. 308–310) from Cambridge University Library MS. Add. 7350 (fol. 2). The text which follows is from his edition (pp. 309 f.):

Inducas Inducas
in temptacionibus

Ther was a frier of order gray
Inducas
which loued a Nunne full meny a day
In temptacionibus

This fryer was lusty proper and yong
Inducas
he offerd the Nunne to lerne her syng
in temptacionibus

Othe re me fa the frier her tawght
Inducas
Sol la this nunne he kyst full oft
in temptacionibus

By proper chaunt and Segnory
inducas
This Nunne he groped with flattery
in temptacionibus

The fryers first lesson was Veni ad me
Inducas
& ponam tollum meum ad te
in temptacionibus

The frier sang all by bemoll
inducas
Of the Nunne he begate a cristenyd sowle
in temptacionibus

The Nunne was taw3ght to syng depe
inducas
lapides expungnauerunt me
in temptacionibus

Thus the fryer lyke a pretty man
inducas
Ofte rokkyd the Nunnys Quoniam
in temptacionibus

ffinis short & swete

According to Robbins the above carol dates from about 1500 and is "a much expanded and more subtle version" of a later analogue dating from about 1550 printed in Richard Kele's *Christmas carolles newely Imprynted*, sigs. A₃–A₃ᵛ. The text following is from the edition of Kele's book by Reed (1932, pp. 19 f.):

Inducas inducas
In temptationibus.

The nunne walked on her prayer
 Inducas. &c.
Ther cam a frere and met with her
 In temptationbus. &c.
  Inducas inducas
  In temptationibus.

This nunne began to fall aslepe
 Inducas
The frere knelyd downe at her fete
 In temptationibus.
  Inducas inducas.
  In temptationibus.

This fryer began the nunne to grope
 Inducas
It was a morsell for the pope
 In temptationibus.
  Inducas inducas
  In temptationibus.

The frere & the nunne whan they had done
 Inducas
Eche to theyr cloyster dyd they gone
 Sine temptationibus
  Inducas inducas
  In temptationibus.

  Finis

DRAMATIC FUNCTION

A note by Reed (1932, p. 78) explains the appropriateness of Petruchio's snatch of song. He quotes Nicholas Udall as referring to "syngyng merie songes and rymes for makyng laughter and sporte at marryages, euen like as is nowe vsed to syng songes of the Frere and the Nunne, with other sembleable merie iestes, at weddynges, and other feastynges." Petruchio has dragged Kate away from her own wedding feast in Padua and brought her to his country house for the jejune repast he thinks fit for a shrewish bride. He calls to his servants to bring in food for himself and his bride, and then sings a customary "merie songe" to celebrate the wedding feast he will not allow Kate to taste. Shakespeare's audience, familiar with the customs of the marriage feast, and probably knowing by heart the song Petruchio sings, would have been delighted by the incongruity of the situation.

The Two Gentlemen of Verona

3

TEXT: Folio (1623), sig. C₅ (IV.ii.39–53).
TYPOGRAPHY: Indented verse, italic face; s.d., *Song.*

> *Who is Siluia? what is ſhe?*
> *That all our Swaines commend her?*
> *Holy, faire, and wiſe is ſhe*
> *The heauen ſuch grace did lend her,*
>   *that ſhe might admired be.*   5
> *Is ſhe kinde as ſhe is faire?*
> *For beauty liues with kindneſſe:*
> *Loue doth to her eyes repaire,*
> *To helpe him of his blindneſſe:*
>   *And being help'd, inhabits there.*   10
> *Then to Siluia, let vs ſing,*
> *That Siluia is excelling;*
> *She excels each mortall thing*
> *Vpon the dull earth dwelling.*
>   *To her let vs Garlands bring.*   15

GENERAL COMMENTARY

Noble (1923, p. 39) regards the song as casting satirical glances at the Renaissance passion for sonneteering : [Like *Love's Labor's Lost*, this comedy contains] topical literary criticisms, which would be above the heads of a popular gathering, but ... would be keenly enjoyed by products of the Renaissance, who would quite easily recognize the extravagance in their friends' sonnets. ... In caricature of the conventional sonnet *Who is Silvia* had its origin. [Noble attributes a super-subtle intention to a thoroughly conventional song. *Two Gentlemen* is one of Shakespeare's earliest plays and everywhere gives evidence of its author's green or hasty hand. E. K. Chambers (1930, I, 329–331) notes the confusion of persons and locale in the play and suggests hasty writing around 1594–1595. New Cambridge (ind. ed. 1921, pp. xiii–xix) calls attention to the awkward construction and the patchwork ending wherein Valentine hands over a speechless Silvia to her would-be ravisher. The poverty of this resolution, the utter conventionality of the characters and situations in *Two Gentlemen*, show it to be a play wholly lacking in the sophistication that pervades *Love's Labor's Lost*. Noble goes on to analyze the subtleties he finds in the song (pp. 41 f.)] Like the aubade to Imogen in *Cymbeline*, [it] is in behalf of a lover whose suit is foredoomed to fail. . . . Its attraction lies not in its prettiness but in its humour. Thurio has written, or has had written for him, a "sonnet" which a sentimentalist might describe as a "fragrant lyric." It is not acceptable, however, for its terms are extravagant, its compliments are bare and pointed, and the flattery by its obvious insincerity is insulting. . . . There is an impertinent use of Silvia's name in the first stanza, an impudent request for and assumption of her kindness in the second, and in the third an extolling of her excellence "in so high a style that no man living shall come over it." . . . The caricature is intentionally delicate; the grotesque would clearly have been out of place, for it would have broken down the action. The "sonnet" had to have sufficient appearance to induce Proteus to claim its fatherhood, it had to be capable of affecting Julia with grief, and yet it had not to have quality sufficient to transform Thurio's folly into wisdom. ✦ Arden (ind. ed. 1925) takes a plainer view : We need not suppose [the song is] Thurio's "sonnet" of III.ii.93, as from lines 7–15 [of IV.ii] much has evidently occurred since then, and this cannot be the first serenading of Silvia. In Lyly's *Endimion* [1591], IV.ii.24–27, we have a burlesque love-poem by a burlesque Sir Thopas, but neither here nor in Cloten's case (*Cymbeline*, II.iii.) does Shakespeare see need to sacrifice his opportunity for a pretty song. ✦ [That the song was *not* Thurio's sonnet seems clear from the closing lines of III.ii. where Proteus advises Thurio how to win Silvia's love. A lady should first be approached, he says, through "wailful sonnets" in which "You sacrifice your tears, your sighs, your heart." Only after a series of such "dire lamenting elegies" should the lover offer a serenade by night beneath her window. To the proffered advice Thurio replies that he will use both techniques, adding that he already has "a sonnet that will serve the turn To give the onset to thy good advice." The sonnet, then, is presumably dispatched to Silvia that same day. Thus Thurio reveals himself as a most uncourteous courtier. He will not write a sonnet to his mistress' eyebrow; he already has an old one that will "serve the turn."] Brooks (1948, pp. 234 f.) : On one level the song is an attempt to answer the question "What is Silvia?" and the answer given makes her something of an angel and something of a goddess. She excels each mortal thing "Upon the dull earth dwelling." Silvia, of course, dwells herself upon that dull earth, though it is presumably her own brightness which makes it dull by comparison. . . . Why does she excel each mortal thing? Because of her virtues . . . and these are the special gift of heaven. She is heaven's darling ("The heaven such grace did lend her,/That she might admired be"). Theologically considered, this is an odd motive for the bestowal of grace. . . . One is tempted to say that there is even an element of light-hearted and twinkling irony in this quite untheological use of "grace." But what follows is odder still, for the love that "doth to her eyes repair" is not merely Christian "Charity" but the little pagan god Cupid. . . . But if Cupid lives in her eyes, then the second line of the stanza takes on another layer of meaning. "For beauty lives with kindness" becomes not merely a kind of charming platitude ... [but] means also that the Love god lives with the kind Silvia and indeed has taken her eyes ... for his own. ¶ Is the mingling of pagan myth and Christian theology, then, an unthinking confusion into which the poet has blundered, or is it something wittily combined? The mingling is certainly not a confusion, and, if blundered into unconsciously, it is surely a happy mistake. But I do not mean to press the issue of the poet's self-consciousness (and with it the implication of a kind of playful irony). Suffice it to say that the song is a charming and delightful fusion. ... The touch is light and there is a lyric grace, but the structure is complex nonetheless. ◆ Sullivan (1948, pp. 164 f.) : Did Shakespeare intend the reader to think of actual, efficacious, or sanctifying grace, or should "grace" be understood more in the sense of "gracefulness"? ... Sylvia is a supremely beautiful girl physically and mentally, one to awe the admiring audience with her rare and delicate beauty. Consistent with this impression, "grace" suggests her poise of body, her stately walk, her graceful movements. ... ¶ The use of "swain" adds weight to the suggestion that "grace" is intended primarily in the physical and mental but not theological meaning of the word. It is hard to imagine a "swain" being very much concerned with more than the appearance (the "looks") of a girl. ... ¶ The "integrity" of the poem, then, is preserved when "grace" is not considered theologically ... and the artistic need for organic unity is fulfilled more readily if "grace" is construed in the sense in which the "swain" might understand it. ◆

Long (1953, pp. 90–93) calls attention to the parallel episode in Shakespeare's source, the *Diana* (1598) by Montemayor, and suggests a plan for a "replica staging" of the serenade. According to his proposal the song would be followed by instrumental music serving as a background to the lines spoken by Julia and the Host. He notes that the source makes use of instrumental music in addition to the song, and argues that Shakespeare would probably have followed his model in the original staging. He also contends that the band of musicians who accompany the serenade and provide the background instrumental music should be kept off-stage to avoid distracting the audience's attention from this complex scene. Long (1955, pp. 53–60) repeats the substance of his proposal for a "replica staging" of this episode, and adds : Turning to his source, Shakespeare perhaps noted that the Host would serve as a means by which Julia could reveal her discovery and to whom she could express her grief. Yet she must remain unrecognized; hence the meaning behind her words must not be intelligible to the Host, but must be understood by the audience. ... Earlier in the play [Shakespeare] had written a nineteen-line passage (I, ii, lines 79–98) for Julia and Lucetta, in which they discuss a love letter from Protheus in terms of music. If a similar play on words could be used between Julia and the Host—one meaning for the Host, another for the audience—the problem of by-passing the Host would be solved. And, if terms of music be again employed, an ironic parallel would be constructed between Julia's reactions ... in Act I and ... in Act IV. ◆

Auden (1957, p. 38) : Shakespeare shows us music being used [here] with conscious evil intent. ... Proteus, who has been false to his friend, has forsworn his vows to his girl and is cheating Thurio, serenades Sylvia while his forsaken Julia listens. ... Proteus knows exactly what he is doing. Through music which is itself beautiful and good, he hopes to do evil, to seduce Sylvia. ◆ Vyvyan (1960, p. 119) :

[In this scene we have] the musicians, the mandolins, and the moonlit serenade; and with them one of Shakespeare's lovely songs. . . . It is at this point that Julia steps into the fourth act—always, we must remember, the love-act, and when Shakespeare puts music, two heroines and moonlight on the stage at once we may be quite certain that the power of love is about to change discords into heavenly harmony. It may not succeed immediately, but the transmutation has begun. . . . Perhaps Shakespeare is seeing Silvia as Beauty at this point—the Platonic Beauty in the sense in which the Renaissance had re-interpreted the idea—while Julia is Love. ◆ [Vyvyan's critical judgement is ruled by the *idée fixe* that Shakespeare's love plays are to be read as allegories in the light of the *Roman de la Rose*; even their act structure, he insists, is allegorically schematized.]

B. Evans (1960, pp. 16 f.) holds that the song, "exquisite in itself," is transformed by its context : To Thurio . . . it seems that his own suit to Silvia is being forwarded. To Proteus . . . the song is a device for betraying everyone and winning Silvia for himself. To the Host . . . it is only a lovely song in the night. To Silvia, while the music plays, it is hardly more than a flattering serenade for which she thanks the unknown musicians. But when she hears Proteus speak, her quick wit catches the full import. . . . But . . . to Julia . . . the significance of the song . . . advises her of Proteus's treachery with jolting abruptness . . . and our realization of the effect of the song upon Julia is . . . the key factor in its effect upon ourselves. . . . Her discovery raises her abruptly to our level of awareness . . . and at the end of the scene [she] is quite ready . . . to use her advantage for victory: "Pray you, where lies Sir Proteus?" It is not she, but Proteus, suddenly the hunted rather than the hunter, who is now to be pitied. Fallen from the top place in the scheme of awarenesses, he is lost and does not know it. ◆ Vyvyan (1961, pp. 69 f.) : Silvia . . . is both a mortal woman and something more; and it is likely that a Renaissance audience would have seen at once that she is intended to reveal the celestial Love and Beauty. It is not Shakespeare's fault if we miss this point: he does his best—short of ruining the allegory by explaining it outright—to make it clear. This [song] is a salutation to a goddess. And who should this heavenly Silvia be, but the Uranian Aphrodite?

TEXTUAL COMMENTARY

2. **Swaines**] Denotatively, "young men," from its original meaning of "a young man attending on a knight." But the word early acquired a rustic connotation, probably from its use in pastoral poetry.

3. **wise is she**] Collier (ed. 1878) : wise as FREE. So the Corr. fol. 1632, instead of the blundering repetition *is she* of the old editions. ◆ [The emendation is spurious. Collier bases it on a manuscript insertion in the notorious "Perkins folio," an imperfect and sophisticated copy of the second folio (1632). For the use he made of this book with its manuscript forgeries see Collier (1853, p. 23), and for a complete account of the forgeries, Hamilton (1860).]

7. **For . . . kindnesse**] Johnson (ed. 1765) : Beauty without kindness *dies* unenjoyed, and undelighting. ◆ [This line expresses a proverbial notion. See Tilley (1950, D-410) and C. G. Smith (1963, no. 316).]

8. **To ... blindnesse**] Derived from the old proverb; see Tilley (1950, L-506) and W. G. Smith (1935, p. 279).

10–11. **Then ... excelling**] The motive of flattery becomes transparent in these lines.

14. **dull earth**] Malone (ed. 1790) cites *Venus*, 1593 (*Poems*, 1938, pp. 40 f., ll. 337–340),

> He sees her comming, and begins to glow:
> Euen as a dying coale reuiues with winde,
> And with his bonnet hides his angrie brow,
> Lookes on the dull earth with disturbed minde;

and Sonnet XXIX (*Sonnets*, 1944, I, 83):

> (Like to the Larke at breake of daye arising)
> From sullen earth.

MUSIC

The original tune for this song is unknown. A 1727 setting by Richard Leveridge is reprinted in the *Shakespeare Vocal Album* (1864, p. 100). A List (1884, pp. 70 f.) records seventeen other settings up to 1883, the most famous of which is certainly the music by Franz Schubert in 1826.

DRAMATIC FUNCTION

Two Gentlemen is a comparatively simple play in structure. Its single, conventional plot involves the fortunes of two pairs of lovers—Proteus and Julia, Valentine and Silvia—and comic divertisement is provided by the clowning episodes of Launce and Speed. Shakespeare was later to take up a similar plot in *Midsummer Night's Dream*, to develop it there with a more playful touch and with almost geometric precision.

The most obvious quality of the play is the conventionality of its characters and situations. While Shakespeare seems to be making some sort of attempt to deal seriously with the conflicting loyalties of *philia* and *eros*, his efforts in this direction come to a wretched end in the final scene when Valentine proposes to hand his lady over to her would-be ravisher, thereby demonstrating a love that not only passes the love of women, but passes understanding as well.

The dialogue is at one with the plot in its exposition of conventional love. Various characters consistently ring the changes on the commonplaces of a watered-down courtly love tradition. Even the clowns know the cant of love (cf. II.i.16–84), and the Duke of Milan himself assumes the pose of an infatuated lover in order to expose Valentine's planned elopement.

Among conventionalities such as these it would be surprising, indeed, to find a love song with the dew upon it. Quite the contrary, "Who is Silvia" is part and parcel of the play in which it is sung. Nothing in the song suggests that it is Shakespeare's composition—or that it is not. Its diction, imagery, and metaphors are the hackneyed stuff of most lovers' poetry. In short, it is a song that "will serve the turn."

Noble (1923, pp. 42 f.) accurately assesses the mechanical function of the serenade in the action of the play : Not only is the serenade here employed . . . to show how Proteus crossed by "some sly trick, blunt Thurio's dull proceeding," but also it is used as a covering device, whereby the end may be connected with the middle of the play. By its means Julia is made rationally to appear among the principals in Milan (it was the prospect of the Music being performed and his knowledge that Proteus would be there, that caused the Host to bring Julia to the spot) and at the same time it is a convenient method whereby she may be informed of Proteus's perfidy. ♦

If it is supposed that the music continues after the song has been completed, then the silence of Proteus and Thurio may be plausibly attributed to their attention to the music. At the same time the continuing music would serve to cover the aside conversation of the intruders, the Host and Julia, and give additional point to their musical quibbles. Finally, musical accompaniment to Julia's words in a stage presentation would heighten the pathos of the episode in which she is made to realize her lover's disloyalty.

Love's Labor's Lost

4

TEXT: Quarto (1598), sig. K$_2$ (V.ii.904–921).
TYPOGRAPHY: Indented verse, roman face; s.d., *The Song*.

When Dafies pied, and Violets blew,
And Cuckow-budds of yellow hew:
And Ladi-fmockes all filuer white,
Do paint the Meadowes with delight:
The Cuckow then on euerie tree,   5
Mocks married men; for thus finges hee,
Cuckow.
Cuckow, Cuckow: O word of feare,
Vnpleafing to a married eare.

When Shepheards pipe on Oten Strawes,   10
And merrie Larkes are Ploughmens Clocks:
When Turtles tread and Rookes and Dawes,
And Maidens bleach their fummer fmockes:
The Cuckow then on euerie tree,
Mockes married men, for thus finges he,   15
Cuckow.
Cuckow, cuckow: O word of feare,
Vnpleafing to a married eare.

GENERAL COMMENTARY

Stephens (1872, p. 368) reprints two stanzas of an analogous song from "a satirical pamphlet, called *The Welch Embassadour, [or the happie Newes his Worship hath brought to London*, 1643, sigs. A$_4$–A$_4^v$]." The song is entitled "Her Embassadors Message described, to the tune of the merry Pedler, &c":

12

> On a day when Jenkin
> Did walke abroad to heare
>   The Birds rejoyce,
>   With pleasant voyce,
> In Spring time of the yeare;
>   Proudly and loudly
> Her heard a Bird then sing,
>   Cuckoe, Cuckoe.
> The Cuckoe never lins,
> But still doth cry so mery merily,
> And Cuckoe Cuckoe sings.
>
> Her thought her had flouted
> Poore Jenkin with a jeere,
>   And told in scorne
>   That the Horne
> Should on her brow appeare;
>   Soundly and roundly
> This bird one note doth sing
>   Cuckoe, Cuckoe,
> The Cuckoe never lins;
> But still doth cry so merry merily,
> And Cuckoe Cuckoe sings. ✦

Noble (1923, p. 35) ꞉ [In the Cuckoo Song] everything is bright and gay, all except married men, whom the Cuckoo's call makes fearful of their freehold. The comic intent, in keeping with the play, is manifest. All the learned men's idealism of the meadow flowers, the shepherds' piping on oaten straws and the merry larks waking the ploughmen is dissipated by the fear of the woful tragedy which, as the cuckoo's habits remind them, married men are threatened in the Spring, when inclinations are supposed to be amorous and lovers heedless. ✦ Long (1955, p. 78)꞉ The language of the two stanzas assigned to Spring is marked by the frequent use of vowel tones and alliteration. When read aloud it has a light, melodious, and graceful quality. The imagery makes use of several pastoral subjects. . . . Yet the refrain lifts the cuckoo out of the pastoral context and associates him with a common subject for scorn and mockery. The subject matter . . . is certainly in the courtly tradition and forms a close parallel to the pastoral quality of the high comedy plot. ✦

TEXTUAL COMMENTARY

1. **Dasies pied**] *Bellis perennis*, the red, white and yellow English daisy to which Chaucer so often refers, not the white and yellow field daisy familiar to Americans. (See Chaucer's *Legend of Good Women*, ll. 41–43,

... of alle the floures in the mede
Thanne love I most these floures white and rede,
Swyche as men calle dayesyes in oure toun.

and the General Prologue to *The Canterbury Tales*, ll. 89 f. and 331–333.)

2. **Cuckow-budds**] Malone (ed. 1790) **:** Gerarde in his *Herbal*, 1597 [sig. N$_6$], says, that the flos cuculi, cardamine, &c., are called in English *cuckoo flowers*, in Norfolk *Canterbury bells*, and ... in Cheshire *ladie-smocks*. Shakespeare, however, might not have been sufficiently skilled in botany to be aware of this. ... Lyte in his *Herbal*, 1578 and 1579 [sig. L$_2$], remarks, that cowslips are in French, of some called *coquu*. ... This he thinks will sufficiently account for our author's *cuckoo-buds*. ... Whalley ... proposed to read *crocus* buds. The cuckoo-flower, he observed, could not be called *yellow*, it rather approaching to the colour of white ◆ New Arden (ind. ed. 1951) **:** Britten and Holland [1886, p. 134] ... give this name from North-ampton and Sussex to *Ranunculus bulbosus*, or Crowfoot, one of the first buttercups to bloom. In Co. Donegal (S.W.) the name "Cuckoo-flower" is applied to *Lotus corniculatus*, the Bird's-foot Trefoil. Hart [Arden, ind. ed. 1930] suggested that the "yellow hue" has a special force of jealousy, appropriate to the context; Nym's yellowness, in *Merry Wives of Windsor*, I.iii.lll, will be recalled. ◆

2–3. **And ... white**] Theobald (ed. 1740) first noted the obvious inversion of ll. 2 and 3, and his correction has been followed by all subsequent editors.

3. **Ladi-smockes**] New Arden (ind. ed. 1951) **:** The flowers of *Cardamine pratensis*, or Cuckoo-flower; probably a corruption of "Our Lady's smock," like "Lady's Mantle," "Lady's Bedstraw." A general provincial name. It occurs in Ben Jonson's *Pans Anniversarie* [1620; ed. Herford, 1925–1952, 7: 530]:

> Bring rich Carnations, Floure-de-Luces, Lillies,
> The chequ'd, and purple-ringed Daffodillies,
> Bright Crowne-imperiall, Kings-speare, Holy-hocks,
> Sweet *Venus* Navill, and soft Lady-smocks. ◆

[The popular epithet for the flower adroitly suggests another aspect of spring which is explicitly stated in l. 13: the maidens' smocks stretched on the shrubs to dry and bleach in the sun.]

4. **paint ... delight**] Warburton (ed. 1747) **:** This is a pretty rural song in which the images are drawn with great force from nature. But this senseless expletive of *painting with delight*, I would read thus, Do paint the meadows MUCH BEDIGHT, i.e., much bedecked or adorned, as they are in spring-time. The epithet is proper, and the compound not inelegant. ◆ [And the emendation is without authority.]

5–8. **The Cuckow ... feare**] Noble (1923, p. 35) **:** The song feigns seriousness in its conceits just like any of the pretty verse of the time, and naturally something like "Cuckoo, the Sweet Spring" might be expected to follow. Instead there is a fall from the sublime to the ridiculous. ...

> The cuckoo then on every tree
> Mocks married men; for thus sings he.

Then there is a long drawn out "Cuckoo," as is indicated by the full stop, followed by a couple of sly, echoing calls ... whereat the singer shivers in pretended fear and shakes his head at the impropriety of such a call being sounded in the presence of married men. A joke of such a kind was dear to Elizabethan hearts. ◆ [But the "joke" would perish so broadly manhandled. Noble's interpretation is in part due to his acceptance of the "rhetorical punctuation theory" advanced by Quiller-Couch and J. D. Wilson in the New Cambridge *Tempest* (ind. ed. 1921), pp. xxix–xxxix; see also P. Simpson (1911, *passim*) and Pollard (1917, pp. xv–xxxiii, 88–93.) The notion that a cuckoo's call is a threat to married men is commonplace. In *Merry Wives* (II.i.127) Pistol warns Ford about Falstaff's designs on Mrs. Ford by saying, "Take heed, ere summer comes or cuckoo birds do sing."]

7. **Cuckow**] Long (1955, pp. 76 f.) would remove this word from the text of the song and make it a stage direction for a bird-call that would be "sounded without interrupting the rhythm of the singers."

10. **Oten Strawes**] New Arden (ind. ed. 1951) **:** Compare T. Watson, *An Eglogve Vpon the death of . . . Walsingham*, 1590 [sig. C₁]:

> An humble stile befits a simple Swaine,
> my Muse shall pipe but on an oaten quill.

And Golding's *Ovid* [1567, sig. C₄]:

> . . . some good plaine soule that had some flocke
>   to feede
> And as he went he pyped still vpon an Oten Reede.

Spenser speaks of the shepherd's "oaten pipe" in *Shepheard's Calendar* for January (1579) [ed. Greenlaw (1932–1949, I, 16)]: "So broke his oaten pype, and downe dyd lye." ◆

12. **Turtles**] Turtledoves. *NED* notes the figurative application of the word to lovers or married persons in allusion to the turtledove's affection for its mate.

13. **bleach . . . smockes**] The reference is to the custom of washing and hanging clothes on shrubbery to dry and bleach in the sun. Thus the maidens' undergarments on the hedge are as much a homely emblem of spring as the birds and flowers. See song 56, l. 5. Such a custom it was which provided snappers-up of unconsidered trifles like Autolycus with a part of their revenue. So he says in *Winter's Tale* (IV.ii.23 f.), "My traffic is sheets. When the kite builds, look to lesser linen."

5

TEXT: Quarto (1598), sigs. K₂–K₂ᵛ; (V.ii.922–939).
TYPOGRAPHY: Indented verse, roman face; s.d., [*The Song*].

When Iſacles hang by the wall,
And Dicke the Sheepheard blowes his naile:
And Thom beares Logges into the hall,
And Milke coms frozen home in paile:
When Blood is nipt, and wayes be full,   5
Then nightly ſinges the ſtaring Owle
Tu-whit to-who.
   A merrie note,
   While greaſie Ione doth keele the pot.

When all aloude the winde doth blow,   10
And coffing drownes the Parſons ſaw;
And Birdes ſit brooding in the Snow,
And Marrians noſe lookes red and raw:
When roaſted Crabbs hiſſe in the bowle,
Then nightly ſinges the ſtaring Owle,   15
Tu-whit to-who.
   A merrie note,
   While greaſie Ione doth keele the pot.

GENERAL COMMENTARY

Noble (1923, pp. 35 f.) : In the first stanza romance is contrasted with reality, the picturesque with the disagreeable and, in the second, comic objects are cunningly interspersed among ordinary objects of natural history. Thus in the first ... we have the icicles hanging by the wall, and ... the nipped blood and muddy roads, and, in the second, we have the coughing drowning the parson's saw—the use of the word "saw" is good in itself—and the red and raw condition of Marian's nose. But the most disagreeable of all the sensations to be experienced in Winter is ... the sight and smell of the sluttish Joan keeling the pot, for she makes uncomfortable the farm kitchen, the only refuge from the inclemency of the season. The unmusical laughing hoot of the owl acts as a diversion where all else is depressing. Pastoral romance gives way to pastoral realism. ◆ [Nothing in the song supports the notion that Joan is sluttish or repulsive; Noble probably reads too much into the epithet *greasy*. See the note on this word, below.] Long (1955, p. 78) : In contrast to the Spring stanzas, the language of those assigned to Winter is marked by the use of strong consonants and a relative absence of alliteration. The general effect is one of ruggedness. Also in strong contrast to the imagery of the Spring stanzas, that of Winter is realistic and, in the refrain, even coarse. We find the images of the shepherd blowing his nails, Marrian's red and raw nose, the coughing which drowns out the Parson's sermon, and greasy Joan stirring the pot. The rustic and homely quality of the Winter stanzas forms a neat parallel to the realism in the low comedy plot of the play. It is significant . . . that the mocking twist given the Spring stanzas is absent from the Winter song. ◆ [But the "mocking twist" is not lacking; see Dramatic Function.]

TEXTUAL COMMENTARY

1. **by the wall**] Malone (ed. 1790) : i.e., from the eaves of the thatch or other roofing, from which in the morning icicles are found depending in great abundance, after a night of frost. So in *K. Henry IV* [actually, *Henry V*, III.v.23 f.]:

> Let us not hang like roping icicles
> Upon our houses' thatch. ◆

2. **Dicke**] A common name among the lower classes in Shakespeare's day, and so here intended to suggest humble origins. Berowne (V.ii.464) playfully refers to Boyet in this play as "Some mumble-news, some trencher knight, some Dick." For similar uses of the name in Shakespeare, see *Twelfth Night*, V.i.202, *1 Henry IV*, II.iv.9, *2 Henry IV*, IV.ii.27; and *Coriolanus*, II.iii.123.

blowes his naile] Halliwell (ed. 1853–1865) cites Anthony Nixon's *The Blacke yeare*, 1606 (sig. B₁), "Those that have no Mittens in Winter may blow their nailes by authoritie, for no man will pitie them that are needy," and William Browne's *Britannia's Pastorals* [1613], sig. L₁ :

> In witners [*sic*] time when hardly fed the flockes,
> And Isicles hung dangling on the Rockes;
> When *Hyems* bound the floods in siluer chaines,
> And hoary Frosts had candy'd all the Plaines;
> When euery Barne rung with the threshing Flailes,
> And Shepheards Boyes for cold gan blow their nailes. ◆

New Arden (ind. ed. 1951) offers an additional interpretation : Wait patiently while one has nothing to do. . . . To warm [one's] hands [is] an accidental property of the saying, arising out of idleness in cold. The expression occurs again as descriptive of listlessness in *3 Henry VI*, II.v.[1–4,

> This battle fares like to the morning's war,
> When dying clouds contend with growing light,
> What time the shepherd, blowing of his nails,
> Can neither call it perfect day nor night.

The above example, which Arden does not quote, seems ambiguous. Other examples he gives support his interpretation better. From *Doni's Philosophie*, 1570,

tr. Sir Thomas North, sig. 2D₄, Arden cites:] "hee was driuen to daunce atten-
daunce without doores and blowe his nailes"; [and from the *Merrie Conceited Iests
of George Peele*, 1607, sig. B₄ᵛ,] "who sat all this while with the porter blowing of his
nailes." . . . [From Cotgrave's *Dictionarie*, 1611, under the word *ceincture*, he quotes
the definition] "pull strawes, plucke daisies, picke rushes, or blow their fingers;
generally the phrase imports, an idle, and lazie fashion, or posture." . . . [But] in
verses by Campion from Davison's *Poetical Rhapsodie* [(1602), ed. Rollins, 1931–1932,
I, 215] cold is specified:

> But in their brests wher loue his court shuld hold,
> Poore *Cupid* sits, and blowes his nayles for cold. ◆

[To support the "while away the time" sense of the phrase one may also cite *The
Taming of the Shrew* (I.i.7–9), "Our love is not so great, Hortensio, but we may blow
our nails together and fast it fairly out." In this sense of idleness the phrase has
survived until fairly recent times. Sir Walter Scott in 1818 echoes it in *The Heart of
Midlothian* (1852, p. 218), "and sae we'll leave Mr. Sharpitlaw to whistle on his
thumb." Yet the imagery in Shakespeare's song of warmth withindoors and cold
outside makes it likely that the expression refers to Dick's attempt to warm his
frostbitten fingers.]

   5. **wayes be full**] The singular verb *be* with a plural subject is common in
Shakespeare. See Abbott (1884, p. 212). The First Folio corrects the orthography of
full to *fowle*. Modern editors have *foul*.

   6. **singes . . . Owle**] T. Y., (1850, p. 164), notes that the screech of the owl "is still
heard with alarm"; and he remains with us, as in Chaucer's days,

> The oule eke that of deth the bode bringeth.

[The owl is traditionally a bird of ill-omen, and its song is certainly not a "merrie
note." Long (1955, p. 77) is surely incorrect in emending l. 8 so as to make it a
stage direction for an "Owl call" in the midst of the song. He makes his emendation
to bring the spring and winter songs into metrical accord; but Capell (ed. [1767–
1768]) justified the two songs by entering "To-who" after ll. 6 and 15 to correspond
to the "Cuckoo" in the same places in the earlier song. The majority of modern
editors have accepted Capell's emendation. Acceptance of Long's requires the
addition of artificial bird-calls and a willingness to accept an owl's hoot as "a
merry note."]

   9. **greasie**] An unpleasant epithet to modern ears, but the word probably refers
not only to Joan's soiled appearance, the result of her kitchen labors, but to the
fact that she is stout and hence sweaty from her labors over the kitchen fire.
Shakespeare frequently applies the word to fat people. Falstaff in *Merry Wives*
(II.i.12) is "this greasy knight"; the scullery girl in *Comedy of Errors* (III.ii.94–96) is
called a "fat marriage" because she is "all grease"; and the Arden deer in *As You
Like It* (II.i.55) are described as "fat and greasy."

   Ione] A suitable name for a kitchen wench. It is used proverbially in this play
(III.i.207), "Some men must love my lady, and some Joan," and also in *King John*
(I.i.184).

   keele] Capell (ed. [1767–1768]) : [This term] is explained by no editor: the

Revisal inclines to *cool*, the sense of keel (it is said) in some northern counties; but this is going too far for it. . . . [There is] a fitter idea, more comic . . . namely—that of a cookmaid, twirling her *pot* about on its side, cleaning it with her dishclout, and singing at her employment. ◆ Malone (ed. 1790) **:** To keel the pot is to *cool* it . . . [by stirring] the pottage with a ladle to prevent the *boiling over*. . . . It is a common thing in the North for a maid servant to take out of a boiling pot a *wheen*, i.e., . . . a porringer or two of broth, and then to fill the pot up with cold water. The broth thus taken out is called the *keeling wheen*. In this manner greasy Joan keeled the pot. ◆ Steevens (ed. 1793) quotes Witlim (1760, pp. 276 f.) **:** The thing is, they mix their thickning of oatmeal and water, which they call *blending the litting*, and put it in the pot, when they set it on, because when the meat, pudding and turnips are all in, they cannot so well mix it, but 'tis apt to go into lumps. Yet this method of theirs renders the pot liable to boil over at first rising, and every subsequent increase of the fire, to prevent which, it becomes necessary for one to attend to cool it occasionally, by lading it up frequently with a ladle, which they call KEELING *the Pot*, and is indeed a greasy office. ◆ Collier (ed. 1878) **:** To "keel" means to *cool*, and sometimes to *skim*: either sense will here answer to the purpose. ◆ [The same term appears in John Marston's *Antonio and Mellida*, 1602, sig. H$_2$, "I wold haue you paint mee, for my deuice, a good fat legge of ewe mutton, swimming in stewde broth of plummes (boy keele your mouth, it runnes ouer)."]

11. **saw**] Hudson (ed. 1880–1881) **:** *Saw* is, properly, *saying*, of which it is an old corruption, or abbreviation; here put for *discourse* or *sermon*. Sometimes it means proverb or maxim, as in the passage [*As You Like It*, II.vii.156], "Full of wise saws and modern instances." ◆

14. **When . . . bowle**] Malone (ed. 1790) in a supplementary note in the last volume of his edition (X, 577) explains **:** The bowl must be supposed to be filled with ale; a toast and some spice and sugar being added, what is called *Lamb's* wool is produced. So, in [*The Famovs Victories of*] *Henry V*, 1598 [sig. C$_1$]:

> But Dericke, though we be so poore,
> Yet wil we haue in store a crab in the fire,
> With nut-browne Ale, that is full stale,
> Which wil a man quaile, and laie in the mire. ◆

14. **Crabbs**] Crab apples.

GENERAL COMMENTARY

[4–5]

Noble (1923, pp. 33 f.) **:** Shakespeare's satire was directed against an extravagant form of utterance, which had an existence quite independently of either Guevara or Lyly: he derided not only pedantic ornamentation of language but also the pseudo-pastoral romanticism which pervaded the dainty sonnets to whose composition courtiers and their imitators were addicted. Hence on the revival of [this] comedy in 1597, he very appropriately added two songs as Epilogues, wherein pretty pastorals and sententious verses are mercilessly ridiculed. ¶ The two songs

2*

help to clear the stage, and . . . to sustain, even in the end, the laughing character of the comedy. Evidently the play, in its original form, had ended with Berowne's "That's too long for a play." Not only was such an ending too abrupt and in-effective for clearing the stage, but also something had to be done to restore the spirit of comedy, banished by the news of the death of the Princess's father. . . . The announcement of the songs as a dialogue or debate between two birds was a sample of pedantry in itself, for it was meant to exhibit Armado's and Holofernes' scholarly knowledge of mediaeval minstrelsy wherein such academic exercises were of frequent occurrence. ◆ New Cambridge (ind. ed. 1923) : From its first page to its last [this play] is a poke-fun at pedantry, a gay rally of our nature against pompous artifice. . . . Its raillery ends by transposing (for fools) the call of Spring into a word of fear and the hoot of owl into a merry note. . . . After the solemn announcement of "the dialogue that the two learned men have compiled" these songs burst upon us with exquisitely ludicrous effect. The punctuation is beauti-fully expressive, and is undoubtedly Shakespeare's. ◆ [The final remark reflects the New Cambridge editors' one-time adherence to the "Rhetorical Punctuation Theory" of Shakespeare's plays (see commentary on ll. 5–8, song 4).] L. B. Wright, (1927, pp. 262 f.) : The comic epilogue songs . . . necessitating a return of the clowns to the stage, certainly left the audience laughing, but the relation between the songs and the preceding play is slight. The separation of the Princess from the King and his courtiers had made sufficiently easy the clearing of the stage. The comic implications of the "Cuckoo Song" are such as to produce laughter, but how they "sustain, even in the end, the laughing character of the comedy," as Mr. Noble maintains, I fail to see. Laughter followed the song, but it was in a different tone from that of the comedy. Surely Mr. Noble does not mean that laughter produced by any device would sustain "the laughing character of the comedy"? ◆ T. Spencer (1942, p. 90) : Just as the theme of the play dissipates illusion for reality, so does the language. . . . It is surely no accident that the most verbally artificial and metrically elaborate of all Shakespeare's plays should end with the most rustic, simple and countrified of all his songs. ◆ Granville-Barker (1947, II, 448) : For the end we have song and dance both. . . . The play finishes, as a play of merry-making should, with everyone ranged for our last look at them. The simplest sort of a thing will serve best. Pedantry, cleverness, set poses, nice speaking, are all dropped. Armado, the incorrigible, the votary still, will have it, of course, that we are to hear a dialogue by the two learned men. The two learned men are to be found but a moment later dancing a hay with the best. ◆ Bronson (1948, pp. 36 f.) : Granted that everything flowers to beauty for Shakespeare, is there no special reason for his introducing not merely an obvious contrast that sets song against song, but also, and more subtly poised, this further conflict of elements within each separate song? Reduced to logical propositions, the first song says, in part, "The sum of vernal delights but serves to remind husbands of their fears of infidelity in their wives"; and the second, "The sum of winter's annoyances but intensifies one's sense of well-being. . . ." It is, then, the age-old lesson of the imper-fect and paradoxical condition of human felicity that is resident in this anti-phony. . . . ¶ [Furthermore] I can hardly believe that the poet's humanity was so nice as to consider greasy Joan a repellent figure. . . . Rather, as I take it, the aim is to suggest hearty enjoyment, not irony nor burlesque. Moreover, if "merry" be taken ironically, we spoil the pretty opposition between the boding bird of spring and the comfortable bird of winter, which itself makes a delightful surprise and reversal of the traditional "debate" of the birds that Armado has led us to anticipate. Surely, part of the fun lies in this unexpected flouting of convention; and if the reversal is not completed, the point is lost. Again, if "merry" be not honest, the structural parallel and contrast with the spring song are both obliterated, and our pleasure in the artistry and logical neatness of the antithesis is correspondingly impaired. [Yet even for the sake of structural parallelism and "logical neatness" it is hard to see how the owl's winter note could ever be called "merry" in any literal sense; such an interpretation would seem to violate all literary and folklore tradition, not to mention natural experience. If "merry" is not ironic, then it seems meaningless.] ◆

G. W. Knight (1953, pp. 82 f.) finds these songs significant of the dramatic theme of the play : Henceforth romance is ever to be related to tragedy. No Shakespearean comedy sports in such golden fun at the start: none ends so sadly.... ¶ The final song is important. First we have Spring, and all its delights painted, with yet a suggestion of man's married infelicity.... Then Winter, freezing and cruel.... The order is most significant: spring, winter. And yet the song is, nevertheless, music. The pain is dissolved in music. ◆

Nosworthy (1958, p. 62) : The earliest comedies are sparing in their use of music, and offer little that is not entirely conventional. A change of purpose is perceptible in *Love's Labour's Lost*, where two songs at the very end cut across the fantastic artificiality of the action and substitute the everyday realities of Dick, Tom, Marian and greasy Joan, with an effect that is almost didactic in such a context. ◆ Barber (1959, pp. 113 f.) : The pageant and songs of summer and winter are the finale Shakespeare used instead of a wedding dance or a masque; and they are exactly right.... The songs evoke pleasures of the most traditional sort, at the opposite pole from facile improvisations. Nobody improvised the outgoing to the fields in spring or the coming together around the fire in winter. After fabulous volubility, we are looking and listening only; after conceits and polysyllables, we are told a series of simple facts in simple words.... The cuckoo and owl songs are ... a very high order of poetry and of imaginative abstraction.... These songs are not simply *of* the world they describe, not folk songs; they are art songs, consciously pastoral, sophisticated enjoyment of simplicity. Their elegance and humor convey pleasure in life's being reduced to so few elements and yet being so delightful. Each centers on vitality, and moves from nature to man. The spring song goes from lady smocks to the maidens' summer smocks ... from turtle cocks who "tread" to implications about people. The old joke about the cuckoo is made so delightful because its meaning as a "word," as a call to the woods, is assumed completely as a matter of course. In the winter song, the center of vitality is the fire.... Gathered together ... it is merry to hear the owl outside in the cold.... Even the kitchen wench, greasy Joan, keeling the pot to keep it from boiling over, is one of us, a figure of affection. ◆

Noble (1923, p. 37) : Who were the singers of the songs ? ... It is usually assumed that Moth is one of the singers, but for this assumption there is small support.... But Shakespeare about the time of this revival in 1597 had a singing boy capable of enacting a minor female part. . . . Might not the boy, who personated Jaquenetta, have been the singer of *The Owl Song*? ♦ Long (1955, p. 73) : The stage direction states, "Enter all," which evidently means all of those members of the cast not already on the stage. . . . If we omit the Forester, whose bit part was probably doubled, the "all" could only refer to Holofernes, Nathaniel, Moth, Costard, Dull, and Jaquenetta. It is apparently the "all" who sing the songs. . . . [Pp. 74 f.] If the six singers were equally divided, there would be three voices in each group. This suggests that the voices employed for each song were a treble, a mean (tenor), and a baritone or bass. . . . I would assign the first to Moth (treble), Nathaniel, and Holofernes, and the second to Jaquenetta, who was actually a boy (treble), Costard, and Dull. ♦ [The actual evidence of the play points only to Moth as a singer, for Armado calls on him for a song (never sung) at I.ii.130, and Moth is certainly the singer of "Concolinel" at III.i.3, whatever that may be. Finally, he is a patent forbear of Feste in *Twelfth Night*. Yet unless special singers were brought on the stage for the performance of the two songs, the solution proposed by Long is probably the correct one.]

THE TEXT

There are serious textual problems in the play, and these may have an important bearing on the songs at its end. The sole authority for the text is the First Quarto:

> [Ornament]/*A*/PLEASANT/Conceited Comedie/
> CALLED,/Loues labors lost./As it vvas presented
> before her Highnes/this last Christmas./Newly
> corrected and augmented/By *W. Shakespere.*/
> [Ornament]/Imprinted at London by *W. W.*/for
> *Cutbert Burby.*/1598.

From this was derived the First Folio version which adds a single line (V.ii.941) not found in Q_1: "You that way, we this way." This exit speech may have been a manuscript addition to a prompt copy used by the Folio compositor.

While Q_1 is badly printed, it also contains certain evidence either of rewriting or revision of an original play. The major cruxes are as follows: ll. 8–30 of Berowne's speech on sig. F_2^v (IV.iii.298–319) are in substance repeated and expanded in ll. 31 ff. (IV.iii.320 ff.) of sigs. F_2^v–F_3. The same holds true of ll. 1–6 of sig. K_1 (V.ii.826–831) which are elaborated in ll. 22 ff. (V.ii.846 ff.) of sig. K_1. These "duplicated speeches" may represent nothing more than carelessly canceled first drafts in the author's manuscript; or, if Q_1 was set up from a corrected copy of a hypothetical bad quarto, the doubled speeches may reflect bad quarto material mistakenly included by the compositor.

But a third possibility, and this one highly conjectural, has also been raised: that the duplications give evidence of a real revision of the play, years after its original composition, and prior to the presentation before Queen Elizabeth "this last Christmas." The revision hypothesis has been strongly supported by H. D. Gray (1918), and by J. D. Wilson in the New Cambridge edition of the play (1923). They call attention to some additional textual problems: the confusion surrounding the pairing-off of the lovers in the masking jest, sigs. C_1^v–C_2^v (II.i.114–214), which may just possibly be a rudimentary version of the far more successful tricking of the lovers by the masked ladies at sigs. G_3–H_1 (V.ii.127–264); the disproportionately long fourth and fifth acts, the inconsistent stage directions, speech prefixes, and character nomenclature; and the statement of the title page that the play is "Newly corrected and augmented."

It is not necessary to suppose a "revision" to explain these lesser cruxes. The mix-up of the lovers and ladies in II.i, since it depends on speech prefixes and easily confused single names, is what might be expected in a badly printed quarto. Nor is the repeated use of the masking trick especially significant: lovers who can be gulled once for an audience's amusement can probably be gulled a second time with even more hilarious effect. Since the quarto has no act divisions (these were apparently introduced for the first time by the Folio editors), and since the play, in any event, was probably acted through without a pause, the disproportion of "Acts 4 and 5" is of little consequence. Nor does the statement of the title-page need to be taken seriously. Q_2 of *Romeo* (1599) was also advertised on its title-page as "Newly corrected, augmented, and amended," and, like *Love's Labor's Lost* was also printed for Cuthbert Burby, being the only other extant Shakespeare quarto that bears his name. But the *Romeo and Juliet* quarto was issued to replace a bad quarto of 1597 printed by John Danter. The same may hold true for this play, though, if so, the bad quarto has been lost. The supposition that there was a bad quarto of *Love's Labor's Lost* is supported by the absence of a copyright-protecting initial entry for the play in the Stationers' Registers, and the nearness of the dates of the two plays. The remaining typographical errors—inconsistent speech pre-fixes, stage directions, and character-names—may simply reflect the author's carelessness or erratic manuscript changes from time to time in the prompt copy or other text (perhaps a corrected bad quarto) that came to the hands of the printer.

The best foundation for a theory of revision would be proof of an early date of original composition. Such proof has not been forthcoming. E. K. Chambers (1930, I, 335), a conservative critic, sees no evidence "for two dates, and no evidence for a very early date." He regards the play as the earliest of the "lyrical group" and places it with *Midsummer Night's Dream*, *Romeo and Juliet*, and *Richard II* around 1595.

If the late revision theory could be successfully demonstrated—the discovery of a lost bad quarto would probably go a long way toward settling the matter—one important difference between the two versions, if two ever existed, might be that one included songs and that the other dispensed with them. The quarto of 1598 bears *prima facie* witness that the songs were not essential to a performance. The only major songs in the play are tacked on rather lamely at the end where the audience in a public theater might expect the customary jig. They could just as easily be untacked if necessary, and the play could end some sixteen lines earlier with Berowne's "That's too long for a play," an exit line almost as palpable as the Folio's "You that way, we this way."

Even clearer evidence that something may have gone strangely awry with the musical side of this comedy is offered by the scene between Armado and Moth (I.ii.127–131) where a twice called-for song is never sung. Perhaps this passage bears witness to a performance of the play without songs, or without an actor-singer. Similarly, "Concolinel" (III.i.3) seems to mark a place where a song could be performed or omitted; no words are provided for this song (if it is a song), and none have been discovered.

MUSIC

No music of the period is known for either of these songs. The earliest extant setting, a single tune for both by Richard Leveridge, about 1725, is contained in a British Museum music album, press mark G.313/62. Most familiar of the later settings are those by Arne. Music for them is reprinted in the *Shakespeare Vocal Album* (1864, pp. 14 and 75). Long (1955, pp. 76 f.) borrows from Chappell ([1855–1859], I, 75) a tune from Ravenscroft's *Deuteromelia* (1609) which he says will fit both songs.

DRAMATIC FUNCTION

In composing these songs Shakespeare was infusing fresh content into old and traditional forms. The songs share features in common with both the medieval debate and the *reverdie*. Though they are announced as a debate "composed by the two learned men," they imply rather than use the debate form. One upholds the *al fresco* joys of the countryside in summer, the other the cheery comfort of the kitchen fireside in winter. If not strictly a debate, they at least have a long heritage of debate poems behind them, from the *Conflictus Veris et Hiemis* of Alcuin to the holly-ivy songs of the high Middle Ages. See Waddell (1935, pp. 82–87) and Robbins (1952, pp. 45–47). Only the "Cuckoo Song" with its catalogues of birds and flowers suggests the *reverdie*—nature rejoicing in the return of spring—but the "Owl Song" seems a deliberate attempt on the author's part to compose a parallel song for winter. The great charm of both songs is due to the freshness with which the old forms are treated. Diction, imagery, and poetic treatment all conduce to present glimpses not into the lives of a banished duke and his retainers in Arcadia, but into the world of Hob, Dick, and Robin Ostler.

In summer it is the common field flowers, shepherds, plowmen at their work, the love-making of ordinary country birds, and maidens bleaching their summer smocks in the sun (an activity suggesting that they, too, look forward to love), which dominate the scene. In winter it is the chores of the farm, grange, or farm-kitchen that vividly portray the life of the countryfolk. They may feel the bitter pinch of winter winds and weather, but they have a huddled social refuge in the long winter services of the country church, and in the kitchen of the farmhouse where the fruits of the harvest are enjoyed around a bowl of ale at the hearth no matter how cold the wind blows out of doors. What crowns all, of course, is the fact that the pot which Joan "keels" is filled to overflowing. Finally, the two songs are perfectly linked by the bird-calls of their refrains. The cuckoo is the traditional harbinger of spring, but by a playful twist his song is also made to suggest the perils that lie in wait for overconfident husbands when "Lenten ys come with loue to toune." Similarly, the owl, who usually bodes winter, death, or gloom, has his song ironically elevated to "a merry note," and is the only owl so honored in all Shakespeare.

To press a dramatic function on songs which could be easily omitted—and probably often were—is to weave a rope of sand. It is true that they clear the stage, but so would the lines "That's too long for a play" and "You that way, we this way." That they embody satire of "an extravagant form of utterance," or ridicule "pretty pastorals and sententious verses," as Noble contends, seems to weigh them down with literary clogs. The songs are certainly in sharp contrast with the tone and language of the rest of the play, and so perhaps represent a simple return to reality. Beyond this plain function they probably have no other, and L. B. Wright seems to be correct in his view that they are largely extraneous. Shakespeare was merely giving his audience what would please it; these songs have pleased many and pleased them long.

Romeo and Juliet

6

TEXT: Second Quarto (1599), sig. E₃ᵛ (II.iv.141–146).
TYPOGRAPHY: Unindented verse, roman face; s.d., First Quarto (1597),
sig. E₂ᵛ, *He walkes by them, and sings.*

An old hare hoare, and an old hare hoare is very good meate in
lent.
But a hare that is hore, is too much for a ſcore, when it hores ere
it be ſpent.

GENERAL COMMENTARY

Johnson (ed. 1765) **:** *Mercutio* having roared out, *so ho!* the cry of the sportsmen
when they start a hare; *Romeo* asks *what he has found.* And *Mercutio* answers, No
hare, &c. The rest is a series of quibbles unworthy of explanation, which he who
does not understand, needs not lament his ignorance. ◆ Hanmer (ed. 1770–1771,
p. vi) **:** Most of these passages are here thrown to the bottom of the page and
rejected as spurious, which were stigmatized as such in Mr. Pope's edition; and it
were to be wished that more had then undergone the same sentence. ◆ White
(ed. 1883) **:** Like most of its sort in these plays, this song appears to have been old
and popular. If the last two words ["hare hoar"] of the second line were printed
as they are to be understood, they would be very indecorous. ◆ New Variorum
(ind. ed. 1871) quotes Halliwell, who copies a jest from *Mirth in Abundance*, 1659,
sig. A₇ᵛ **:**

> A Wenching fellow having beene out all night, was asked where he had been?
> Who was answered, a hunting. A hunting quoth the other: where I prethee?
> marry in *Bloomsbury* Park replyed the fellow, how quoth his friend in *Bloomsbury*
> Park? that was too little purpose for I am sure there is ne're a Hare in it.

TEXTUAL COMMENTARY

1-2. **An ... lent**] Probably an allusion to the proverb "Hare is melancholy
meat"; see Tilley (1950, H-151) and W. G. Smith (1935, p. 131).

MUSIC

No music seems to exist for Mercutio's bawdy lyric. That it was sung is clearly indicated by the bad quarto (1597) with its (probably reported) stage direction, sig. E$_2$^{v}. A pirating reporter might mangle the lines he heard, but he is not apt to forget what he witnessed on the stage.

DRAMATIC FUNCTION

Mercutio's song is like the one by Silence in *2 Henry IV* (song 11, below). Both play on indecent meanings, and both may have been bawled out in the public houses in Shakespeare's time. Like Mercutio's speeches, his song characterizes him as an extrovert, tough-minded and cynical, but also raucously good-humored, a foil to the sentimental and greensick Romeo. The bawdry of the song is a part of the naturalistic undercurrent of sexual humor in the play, an undercurrent which is apparently intended to suggest that below the surface stream of young, idealistic, romantic love runs the cynical tide of self-gratification.

A Midsummer Night's Dream

7

TEXT: First Quarto (1600), sig. C₃ (II.ii.9–24).
TYPOGRAPHY: Indented verse, italic and roman face; s.d., *Fairies sing*.

You ſpotted Snakes, with double tongue,
Thorny Hedgehogges be not ſeene,
Newts and blinde wormes do no wrong,
Come not neere our Fairy Queene.
Philomele, with melody,   5
Sing in our ſweete Lullaby,
Lulla, lulla, lullaby, lulla, lulla, lullaby,
Neuer harme, nor ſpell, nor charme,
Come our louely lady nigh.
So good night, with lullaby.   10
　　1. *Fai.* Weauing Spiders come not heere:
Hence you long legd Spinners, hence:
Beetles blacke approach not neere:
Worme nor ſnaile doe no offence.
Philomele with melody, &c.   15
　　2. Fai. Hence away: now all is well:
One aloofe, ſtand Centinell.

GENERAL COMMENTARY

Noble (1923, p. 53) : If the reader examines the scene, he will observe how easily and naturally the song comes into being, how it relieves from awkwardness and makes interesting Titania's retirement, how it imparts to the whole a fairy-like atmosphere, how perfectly it is ended and the continuation provided for, and how it leads up to and facilitates Oberon's little plot. ◆

Patterson (1916, p. 442), commenting on Titania's request (II.ii.1) for "a roundel and a fairy song," remarks : A genuine *rondel* . . . consists of a lyric in which, among other characteristics, the first lines are used as a recurring refrain. The fairies' song is simply a round or dancing song, far removed from the more sophisticated *rondel*. ◆ Noble (1923, pp. 57 f.) **:** The stage direction is "Fairies sing," and they all approach singing, and then when they come to "Philomele, with melody" they circle round in quick racing movement after the manner of children's games. Then "1 Fairy" sings solo "Weaving spiders," the fairies taking up the refrain as before. . . . It is interesting to note that although the second stanza is sung solo its punctuation is considerably heavier than that of the first stanza which is sung in chorus. This is because the movement involved in the first stanza and chorus has taxed the breathing of the participants and consequently in the second stanza there is a lull in the movement, they are circling at no more than a walking pace and phrases are therefore deliberate. ◆ [This seemingly eye-witness account of an original performance is largely due to Noble's adherence to the "rhetorical punctuation theory" once espoused by the New Cambridge editors and by Alfred Pollard (see commentary on ll. 5–8, song 4). Even if that theory had merit it is hard to see how the punctuation of the song could be arranged to reflect the physical exertions of the singers and dancers.]

Davies (1939, p. 165) **:** Large numbers of children are needed in [this play] as fairies. . . . The circumstances under which . . . [it was] performed would ease the strain on the resources of the company. If, as has been suggested by . . . [E. K.] Chambers [1930, I, 359] . . . [it] was played at the wedding of Thomas Berkeley and Elizabeth Carey at Blackfriars on 19th February 1594, Sir George Carey's singing-boys would be available to serve as fairies. ◆ [Actually, Chambers considers another marriage-performance just as likely. See note on line 4, below.]

TEXTUAL COMMENTARY

2. **Thorny Hedgehogges**] Edward Topsell, *The Historie of Foure-Footed Beastes* (1607, sigs. 2B$_1$–2B$_1$^{v}) **:** They differ in place, or in habitation: some of them keepe in the mountaines and in the Woods or hollow trees, and other about Barnes and houses: in the Summer time they keepe neare vineyards and bushy places, and gather fruite, laying it vp against winter. It is about the biggnesse of a Cony, but more like to a Hogge, being beset and compassed all ouer with sharpe thorney haires, as well on the face as on the feete: and those sharpe prickles are couered with a kind of soft mosse, but when she is angred or gathereth her foode she striketh them vp by an admirable instinct of nature, as sharpe as pinnes or Needles. ◆

3. **Newts**] Edward Topsell, *The Historie of Serpents* (1608, sigs. T$_4$^{v}–T$_5$) **:** This is a little blacke Lyzard. . . . They liue in standing waters or pooles as in ditches of Townes and Hedges. The colour as we haue saide is blacke, and the length about two fingers, or scarce so long. Vnder the belly it is white, or at least hath some small white spots on the sides and belly. . . . The skinne is strong and hard, so as a knyfe can scarse cut the same, and beeing cut, there issueth out a kind of white mattery liquor, like as is in Salamanders. ¶ . . . The taile beeing cutte off, liveth longer then the body, as may be seene in euery dayes experience, that is, by motion giueth longer signes and token of lyfe. ¶ . . . There is nothing in nature that so much offendeth it as salt . . . for it byteth & stingeth the little beast aboue measure. . . . It doth not like to be without water, for if you try one of them, and

keepe it out of water but one day, it will be found to be much the worse. ¶ Beeing moued to anger, it standeth vpon the hinder legges, and looketh directlie in the face of him that hath stirred it, and so continueth till all the body be white, through a kind of white humour or poyson, that it swelleth outward, to harme (if it were possible) the person that did prouoke it. And by this is their venomous nature obserued to be like the Salamander, although theyr continuall abode in the water, maketh their poyson the more weake. ◆ [The creatures are, of course, perfectly harmless; but Topsell's account expresses not only the beliefs of the common people, but of the naturalists of Shakespeare's time.]

3. **blind wormes**] Edward Topsell, *The Historie of Serpents* (1608, sigs. A₆–A₆ᵛ) : Of the Slow-Worme. This Serpent was called in auncient time among the Graecians *Tythlops* and *Typhlines*, and *Cophia*, because of the dimnes of the sight thereof, and the deafnes of the eares and hearing.... It beeing most euident that it receiueth name from the blindnes and deafnes thereof, for I haue often prooued, that it neither heareth nor seeth here in England, or at the most it seeth no better then a Mole.... The colour is a pale blew, or sky-colour, with some blackish spots, intermixed at the sides.... It hath a smooth skinne without all scales.... They are in length about a spanne, and as thicke as a mans finger, except toward the tayle which is more slender.... If they be killed with the young in their belly, the little ones will instantly creepe out at their dammes mouth.... They loue to hide themselues in Cornefieldes vnder the rype corne when it is cut downe. It is harmelesse except being prouoked, yet many times when an Oxe or a Cow lieth downe in the pasture, if it chaunce to lye vppon one of these Slow-wormes, it byteth the beast, & if remedy be not had, there followeth mortalitie or death, for the poyson thereof is very strong. ◆ Singer (1852, p. 556) calls attention to *Cymbeline* (IV.ii.215–218) :

> Why, he but sleeps!
> If he be gone, he'll make his grave a bed;
> With female fairies will his tomb be haunted,
> And worms will not come to thee.

It should be remembered [he notes] that it was held that no noxious creatures would be found where fairies resort. ◆

4. **Fairy Queene**] Perhaps a complimentary allusion to Elizabeth I, who is certainly referred to earlier (II.i.158) as "a fair Vestal, throned by the West." These allusions may date performances of this play. Elizabeth was present at the marriage of William Earl of Derby and Elizabeth Vere at Greenwich on 25 January 1595, and she may have attended the nuptials of Thomas Berkeley and Elizabeth Carey at Blackfriars on 19 February 1596. According to E. K. Chambers (1930, I,358 f.), if this play was given a marriage-performance, either of these weddings may have been the occasion.

5. **Philomele**] The nightingale. Philomela, the ravished sister of Procne, was changed into a nightingale after the sisters revenged themselves on King Tereus by feeding him, unawares, the flesh of his son Itys. The story is told in Ovid, *Metamorphoses*, VI, 440 ff.

11. **Spiders**] Edward Topsell, *The Historie of Serpents* (1608, sigs. 2B₃ᵛ–[2]B₄) : All Spyders are venomous, but yet some more, and some lesse. Of Spyders that neyther doe nor can doe much harme, some of them are tame, familiar, and

domesticall, and these be commonly the greatest among the whole packe of them. Others againe be meere wilde, liuing without the house abroade in the open ayre, which by reason of their rauenous gut, and greedy deuouring maw, haue purchased to themselues the names of wolfes, and hunting-Spyders. ◆

16–17. **Hence ... Centinell**] Most of the editors since Capell (ed. [1767–1768]) made the change, have regarded these lines as dialogue, not as part of the song. Noble (1923, p. 58), curiously, remarks that these lines "although not strictly part of the song [,] ought to be sung." Yet even a cursory examination of the song indicates that it must certainly end with the second repetition of the refrain (ll. 5–10) which begins again at l. 15. The inclusion of ll. 16–17 is clearly a printer's error.

MUSIC

The original music for this lullaby appears not to have survived. Long (1955, pp. 86 f.) gives a setting to a "slightly altered" melody from a lullaby in Anthony Holborne's *Pavans, Galliards, Almains, and other short Æirs* (1599).

THE TEXT

The first quarto, though not so carefully printed as might be desired, is the sole authority for the text. From it was derived Q_2 which, though it bears the date 1600, was actually printed under suspicious—probably illegal—circumstances in 1619 by William Jaggard, the printer of *The Passionate Pilgrim* (1599). According to E. K. Chambers (1930, I, 358), the version of the play in the First Folio was copied from Q_2.

Q_1 is sparse in stage directions generally, a fact which may account for the slight confusions of solo and chorus in the song; but there seems little question about the intended arrangement of the song's parts: ll. 1–4 are solo, followed by ll. 5–10 as a refrain either by another voice or a chorus of voices, and ll. 11–14 are a second stanza sung solo, followed again by a similar refrain. The final two lines, though not typographically distinguished by the compositor of the quarto, are obviously intended to be spoken as dialogue.

There is no reason to suppose that the song is not Shakespeare's. It shares many features of tone and imagery in common with other fairy lyrics in the play (see II.i.2–13 and V.i.378–445), and even with other plays in the so-called lyrical group (cf. the "Queen Mab" speech in *Romeo and Juliet*, I.iv.53–94). Titania calls for "a roundel and a fairy song" (II.ii.1), but the dance could have preceded the song rather than accompanying it.

DRAMATIC FUNCTION

The use of music at this point probably meant more to an Elizabethan audience than it does to a modern audience. They believed that music had actual therapeutic value, that it could minister to a mind diseased, cure sickness, or induce sleep.

This song is more than a lullaby, or even a magic lullaby; it is a charm to ward off evils. Mere mortals who took Reginald Scot's charms and spells for warding off the *puka* or the nightmare more or less literally, and who were not very doubtful about the existence of Oberons and Titanias, would have no difficulty in crediting the efficacy of the fairies' charm for protecting their queen. Yet there is a delightful irony in the fact that while the song can protect her from "newts and blind-worms" and other natural evils, it does not preserve her from the preternatural magic of Oberon and his puck. While it may lull her to a deep and dreamless sleep, she will waken to a grotesque nightmare when the translated Bottom comes trudging along, singing out the misremembered lines of another song to show that he is not afraid.

8

TEXT: First Quarto (1600), sigs. D₂ᵛ–D₃ (III.i.128–131, 133–136).
TYPOGRAPHY: Unindented verse, roman face.

The Woofell cock, fo blacke of hewe,
With Orange tawny bill,
The Throftle, with his note fo true,
The Wren, with little quill.

.   .   .

The Fynch, the Sparrowe, and the Larke,   5
The plainfong Cuckow gray:
Whofe note, full many a man doth marke,
And dares not anfwere, nay.

GENERAL COMMENTARY

Patterson (1916, pp. 434 f.) : Another form of the medieval lyric of which we find more than a trace in Shakespeare, is the *reverdie* or nature song celebrating the coming of spring. The *reverdie* in its purest form is simply a song expressing the joy which birds, flowers, and trees find in the newly awakened earth; seldom, though, it fails to suggest that the joy of mere living has entered the poet's life. . . . [Close] to the *reverdie* in its narrowest sense, in that the names of various birds are woven into the lyric, is the song which Bottom sings. ♦ Moore (1916, p. 83) : At times the dramatist uses the song in by-play to secure the most humorous scenes, amusing not for buffoonery but for revelation of human nature. . . . The boisterous Bottom sings in the forest to show his skulking comrades that he is unafraid. [And (pp. 93 f.)] . . . song is frequently used to incite characters to or against action. [So] . . . Bottom's song to show his courage . . . serves as an effective introduction of the metamorphosed weaver to the enamored queen. ♦ Long (1955, p. 89) : There seems little doubt that here Bottom sings two fragments of a song. The completion of the song, to judge from the text, was probably a refrain. The song resembles a folk type such as would be appropriate for Bottom. The performance of the song was probably as crude as could be sung with any resemblance to music, since the humor of the situation is derived partly from the dainty Titania's delight in what was, no doubt, a far-from-angelic voice. ♦ Finney ([1962], p. 90) calls attention to Titania's reaction to Bottom's song (III.i.141–144),

Mine ear is much enamoured of thy note;
So is mine eye enthralled to thy shape;
And thy fair virtue's force (perforce) doth move me,
On the first view, to say, to swear, I love thee.

These words, she feels, are evidence of Shakespeare's "amused skepticism" about Ficino's notion that the three sources of love-inspiring beauty were music, shape, and virtue. She adds that "most serious Neoplatonists excluded music from the realm of beauty."

TEXTUAL COMMENTARY

1. **Woosell cock**] Malone (ed. 1790) : The *ouzel cock* is generally understood to be the cock-blackbird. ♦ Arden (ind. ed. 1930) : The male blackbird, *Turdus merula*. Cotgrave [*Dictionarie*] gives: Merle: m. *A Mearle, Owsell, Blackbird*. Merle noir. *The Blackbird, or ordinarie Owsell.* ♦

2. **Orange tawny bill**] Hudson (ed. 1880–1881) : [This] accords with what Yarrel says of the blackbird: "The beak and the edges of the eyelid in the adult male are gamboge yellow." ♦ [There is a similar reference in *The Knave in Graine, New Vampt* by J. D. (1640), sig. G₁ᵛ:

> . . . as sure as the black Ousell
> Has a yellow mouth, that whistles me awake.

Moreover, the color "orange-tawny" may have been a fad with Bottom since he uses it to refer to a beard at II.i.26.]

3. **Throstle**] Malone (ed. 1790) : It appears from the following passage in Thomas Newton's [*An*] *Herball to the Bible* [1587, sig. O₄ᵛ] that the *throstle* is a distinct bird from the thrush: "Like vnto this, is there also another sort of Myrte or Myrtle which is wilde, whose berries the Mauisses, Throssels, Owsells & Thrushes, delite much to eate." ♦ Arden (ind. ed. 1930) : The thrush, *Turdus musicus*. ♦ [According to *NED*, thrush is a generic name, and may refer to the *Turdus musicus*, or song thrush, also known as *throstle* and *mavis*, as well as to the less musical *Mistle-thrush*, known to ornithologists as *Turdus viscivorus*; and thence to other members of the genus *Turdus* or family *Turdidae*.]

4. **quill**] Arden (ind. ed. 1930) : Pipe, note; not . . . wing-feather. ♦ [So *NED*: A musical pipe, made of a hollow stem, 1567.]

6. **plainsong Cuckow**] Hanmer (ed. 1770–1771, Glossary) : That is, the cuckoo, who, having no variety of strains, sings in plain song, or in *plano cantu* . . . in opposition to *pricksong*, or variegated music sung by note. Skelton introduces birds singing the different parts of the service at the funeral of his favourite sparrow. . . . [*Phyllyp Sparowe*, n.d., sig. B₃]:

> But with a large and a long
> to kepe iust playne songe
> Our chanters shalbe ye Cuckoue
> The Culuer, the stockedoue. ♦

Arden (ind. ed. 1930) : Plain-song here probably refers to plain melody without any variation or accompaniment. . . . Harting . . . 1871, pp. 150 f., says:

> The cuckoo, as long ago remarked by John Heywood (*Epigrams* . . . 1587), begins to sing early in the season with the interval of a minor third; the bird then

proceeds to a major third, next to a fourth, then to a fifth, after which its voice breaks, without attaining a minor sixth. . . . From this bird has been derived the minor scale, the origin of which has puzzled so many; the cuckoo's couplet being the minor third sung downwards. . . . ◆

7-8. **Whose . . . nay**] The cuckoo's name and its call sound like the word *cuckold*. The name is supposedly derived from the cuckoo's custom of laying its eggs in another bird's nest; but in English the name is always applied to the husband of the unfaithful wife, not to her lover (see song 4, ll. 5–9).

MUSIC

The original tune for the song is not known. The earliest extant setting is one in Caulfield (n.d., I, 96). Long (1955, p. 90) has set the words to a contemporary tune called "Rowland" from the Fitzwilliam Virginal Book, as transcribed by Chappell ([1855–1859], I, 115). Professor John Ward has suggested "Wooddy-Cock" (Fuller-Maitland, 1894–1899, II, 138–145) as an apposite tune that could easily be fitted to the words. The original actor could have used almost any popular ballad-tune.

THE SOURCE

A single stanza in "A poeme of a Mayde forsaken," in Nicholas Breton's *The Arbor of amorous Deuises*, 1597 (ed. Rollins, 1936, pp. 8 f.) may have provided Bottom's inspiration and Shakespeare's source:

> The Larke, the Thrush and Nightingale,
> The Linnets sweete, and eke the Turtles true,
> The chattering Pie, the Iay, and eke the Quaile,
> The Thrustle-Cock that was so blacke of hewe.

In the poem all these birds sing a lament and dirge for the "Mayde forsaken." According to Rollins (*ibid.*, pp. xv f.) the poem may have been written by Richard Edwards, the author of other poems in *The Arbor*.

DRAMATIC FUNCTION

If "A poeme of a Mayde forsaken" is a partial source for Bottom's song, its literary inferiority is perhaps indicative of his lamentable taste. Like Quince (I.ii.26) he may favor poems about lovers who die "most gallant for love." Long (1955, p. 89) has pointed out that Bottom's taste in music is no better since in that art he is for "tongs and the bones" (IV.i.31).

Forsaken by his comrades in the forest, Bottom may be reminded of this "poeme of a Mayde forsaken"; on the basis of one line which he imperfectly remembers he composes or fakes words to fill out the balance. The catalogue of birds is easily dubbed in, and the mention of the cuckoo immediately suggests a time-honored jest which Bottom elaborates in the lines following the song. The song, indeed, is as good as the rustics' play of "Pyramus and Thisbe" which Bottom apparently has heard before and considers "a very good piece of work" (I.ii.14).

The Merchant of Venice

9

TEXT: First Quarto (1600), sigs. E₄–E₄ᵛ (III.ii.63–72).
TYPOGRAPHY: Unindented verse, italic and roman face; s.d., *A Song the whilst Baſſanio comments on the caskets to himſelfe.*

Tell me where is fancie bred,
Or in the hart, or in the head,
How begot, how nouriſhed?   Replie, replie.
It is engendred in the eye,
With gazing fed, and Fancie dies: 5
In the cradle where it lies
Let vs all ring Fancies knell.
Ile begin it.
Ding, dong, bell.
All. *Ding, dong, bell.*   10

GENERAL COMMENTARY

Hudson (ed. 1880–1881) : This song is very artfully conceived, and carries something enigmatical or riddle-like in its face, as if on purpose to suggest or hint darkly the way to the right choice. The clew, however, is such as to be seized only by a man whose heart is thoroughly right in the matter he goes about. *Fancy*, as here used, means, apparently, that illusive power or action of the mind which has misled the other suitors, who, as Portia says [II.ix.81], "have the wisdom by their wit to lose." And the illusion thus engendered in the eyes, and fed with gazing, dies just there where it is bred, as soon as it is brought to the test of experience by opening the wrong casket. The riddle evidently has some effect in starting Bassanio on the right track, by causing him to distrust such shows as catch the fancy or the eye. ✦

Hanford (1911, pp. 315 f.) calls attention to "the striking resemblance between Shakespeare's song .. and a poem which appeared in Davison's 'Poetical Rhapsody' (1602), signed with the initials W. R." He notes that the initials are supposed to stand for Walter Ralegh, and adds, "The possibility of a literary relation ...

between Sir Walter and his great contemporary is of considerable interest...."
The first three stanzas from W. R.'s poem (ed. Rollins, 1931–1932, I, 219) are as
follows:

> Conceipt begotten by the eyes,
> Is quickly borne, and quickly dies:
> For while it seekes our harts to haue,
> Meane while there Reason makes his graue:
> For many things the eyes approue,
> Which yet the hart doth seldome loue.
>
> For as the seedes in spring time sowne,
> Die in the ground ere they be growne,
> Such is conceipt, whose rooting failes,
> As childe that in the cradle quailes,
> Or else within the Mothers wombe,
> Hath his beginning, and his tombe.
>
> Affection followes Fortunes wheeles;
> And soone is shaken from her heeles;
> For following beautie or estate,
> Hir liking still is turn'd to hate.
> For all affections haue their change,
> And fancie onely loues to range. ♦

Moore (1916, p. 93) remarks that Shakespeare frequently uses songs "to incite
characters to or against action. Bassanio's choice of the leaden casket is directed by
the song of Fancy." Baskervill (1923, p. 94) : The lyric is so worded as to suggest
every principle that should guide the lover to his judgement. As a general definition
of fancy, it furnishes a warning against the judgement by appearances. As a conventional definition of the transitory love of the senses, it warns against a false ideal
of love. Finally, in its passing reference to the love of the heart, in contrast to that
of the eye, it suggests the nature of spiritual love, by the tenets of which Bassanio
is guided in making his choice. ♦ Noble (1923, p. 45) : [The song is used] to confer
distinction on Bassanio's approach to the caskets and as a means to allow him time
to consider his choice. . . . The tenour of the song is very obvious, the hint is very
plain to beware of that which is pleasing to the sight, for it has no substance and at
best its superficial glory is transient, for, when it ceases to be present to the view,
it is forgotten and its power to attract no longer exists. Such evidently was the line
of thought it suggested to Bassanio . . . for, almost without waiting for the last
strains of the song to fade away, he observes very abruptly,

> So may the outward shows be least themselves;
> The world is still deceiv'd with ornament.

A comment clearly enough inspired by the song. ♦

F[ox-] S[trangways] (1923, p. 472) : Is not the point [of the song] made obvious
by the rhymes? The audience at any rate are not in doubt, for they have already
heard [II.vii.65–73] Morocco taunted by all imaginable rhymes to "gold," and

Arragon hissed [II.ix.63–72] with all the sibilants that "*silver*" suggests. But now Bassanio is partly let into their secret, since he hears, with them, "bred, head, nourishèd" and "fed," and the refrain "Reply, reply," which may mean, among other things, "find a rhyme to these"; and then, lest he should still be in doubt the initial consonant, the "bell" rings fancy's "knell." Would not this, in that age of anagrams and acrostics, be enough for any lover, but certainly for one who has such spontaneous fancies at the sight of "fair Portia's counterfeit" as Bassanio has? ◆ A. K. Gray (1927, pp. 458 f.) : This song is an Echo Song. . . . The chorus here repeats in dying echoes the last word of the soloist, first at the end of the first stanza, after the soloist's injunction "Reply, reply!", and then at the end of the second stanza. Finally, I think . . . the chorus (probably three or four voices), plus the soloist, split into two sections, each taking a different stanza and both chanting together, until the song dies away on a double echo. . . .

> Soloist. Tell me where is Fancy brED,
>   Or in the heart or in the HEAD,
>   How begot, how nourishED?
>   Reply! reply!

> Chorus (dying away).   NourishED—rishED—shED—ED . . .

> Soloist. It is engendred in the eyes,
>   With gazing fED; . . . and Fancy dies
>   In the cradle where it lies.
>   Let us all ring Fancy's knELL
>   I'll *begin* it—Ding, Dong, BELL.

> Chorus (dying away). Ding-Dong-BELL-Dong-BELL-BELL-ELL.

Then the chorus divides in two, each section taking a different stanza, till the song closes on the double echo,

> Ding-dong-BELL——NourishED
>   —dong-BELL——rishED
>   —BELL——shED
>   —ELL——ED . . .

The song, dying away thus on the sound LED, Bassanio takes the hint. ◆ Granville-Barker (1947, I, 339 f.) takes sharp exception to the theory that the riddle of the caskets is revealed by vowel sounds in the song : Shakespeare was surely of a simpler mind than this—his audiences, too. And he had some slight sense of the fitness of things. Would he—how *could* he—wind up this innocent fairy tale with such a slim trick? Besides, how was it to be worked; how is an audience to be let into the secret? . . . Where, oh, where indeed, are such dramatic fancies bred? Not in any head that will think out the effect of their realization. ◆ [The notion that Shakespeare and his audience were of simpler mind than to notice such word-play seems to me without foundation in fact. On the contrary, Elizabethans appear to have been more expert at word-play than their modern descendants, for how else is it possible to account for the puns, patter, and quibbles for which Shakespeare was content to lose a world and consider it well lost? It is worth noting, further, that it is the low comedy scenes in his plays, scenes presumably directed to the unsophisticated groundlings, which are most rife with puns and verbal tricks. Finally, since the audience has already witnessed the wrong choices of Morocco and Arragon, it was already "let into the secret."] Empson (1947, pp. 43 f.) : Portia is far too virtuous to attempt to evade her father's devastating scheme; she fully approves of it ('If you do love me, you will find me out' [III.ii.41]); and yet, while Bassanio is choosing, she arranges that there should be a song continually rhyming with 'lead,' and ending in a conceit about coffins. The audience is not really meant to think that she is telling him the answer, but it is not posed as a moral problem, and seems a natural enough thing to do; she might quite well do it in the belief that he would not hear; the song is explaining to *them* the point about the lead casket, may be taken to represent the fact that Bassanio understands it, heightens the tension by repeating the problem in another form, and adds to their sense of fitness in the third man being the lucky one. ◆ New Arden (ind. ed. 1955) argues against the idea that the song was intended to hint at the right choice : There are strong reasons against [this notion]. Portia has said that she will not direct Bassanio . . . she believes the lottery will find the right husband . . . the S.D. . . . says Bassanio comments "*to himself*"; and . . . it would belittle Bassanio and Portia and cheapen the themes of the play. . . . The song can prepare the audience for Bassanio's sentiments without appearing to influence him at all. ◆ Long (1955, p. 107) : In most folk tales in which the "task" motif appears, the hero is assigned a series of tasks which he must perform before he may win riches or a beautiful princess. Usually the tasks number three—the third time is the charm— and usually the hero is enabled to perform his tasks by the aid of some helper, supernatural or otherwise. . . . Bassanio is the third suitor in the play. . . . [When] Bassanio must choose . . . we look for the helping device. In his predicament the song seems to supply the necessary aid. ◆ Seng (1958, *NQ*, pp. 192 f.) : Shakespeare certainly knew enough about music to write [a riddle] song if he chose to. The likelihood that he has done so [here] is rendered almost a certainty by the fact that he played on the same device suggested by Fox-Strangways and Gray in a quibbling verse in *Love's Labor's Lost* which was written about the same time. . . . Holofernes tells Nathaniel that he will "something affect the letter, for it argues facility." And he proceeds to astonish his friend by playing games with the same sound that gives the secret away to Bassanio. . . .

> The preyful princess pierc'd and prick'd a pretty
>   pleasing pricket;
> Some say a sore; but not a sore till now made sore
>   with shooting.
> The dogs did yell: put el to sore, then sorel jumps
>   from thicket,
> Or pricket sore, or else sorel. The people fall
>   a-hooting.
> If sore be sore, then L to sore makes fifty sores
>   one sorel.
> Of one sore I an hundred make by adding but one
>   more L. [IV.ii.58–63]

. . . It is because [Bassanio] hears the music that he realizes,

> So may the outward shows be least themselves;
> The world is still deceived with ornament.

The song repudiates material appearances; it rings "Fancy's knell" and enables Bassanio to choose reality. ◆ J. R. Brown (1959, p. 235) calls attention to the wording of the stage direction in the first quarto : This surely implies that Bassanio pays attention only to the caskets; there seems to be no other reason for the wording. And [the song enables Shakespeare to] avoid a recital of the inscriptions on the caskets which the audience has already heard twice. . . . Seng and others would argue that Bassanio's words on the conclusion of the song . . . are his reaction to the song; but the stage direction shows that they are rather the necessary continuation of his own "comments on the caskets." Moreover . . . he debates his choice for another thirty-four lines which would be a very odd waste of time if he believed that the song had given him the secret. ◆ [Brown's argument is plausible only to the student who reads the play in the Q₁ text; an audience witnessing this episode would be ignorant of the stage direction and would gather a wholly different impression. The audience sees Bassanio standing over the caskets and hears the song warning against judgement by appearances. They can have no inkling of Bassanio's thoughts other than, perhaps, to surmise that he is reading the inscriptions and reflecting on the possibilities of choice. Even from such reflections they would probably be distracted by the song. Thus they would probably regard his words at the conclusion of the song as commentary on it, and not as "the necessary continuation of his own 'comments on the caskets'." They would take the "thirty-four lines" to be his moralistic commentary on the song's warnings against superficial appearances, and as his attempt to rationally justify the hint it has given him.]

Sternfeld (1963, pp. 105 f.) : The song . . . has both a descriptive and a dramatic function. It does not charm Bassanio but conveys the happy fairyland of love and comedy. . . . The "touches of sweet harmony" in the household of Belmont are in vivid contrast to the mercenary wrangles of Shylock's surroundings, so wholly devoid of music.

TEXTUAL COMMENTARY

1. **Tell . . . bred**] Halliwell (ed. 1853-1865) cites a poem by Joseph Beaumont (1615–1699), "Whiteness, or Chastity" (ed. Grosart, 1880, II, 241), which he believes is a parody of this song. That poem begins,

> Tell me, where doth Whiteness grow ?
> Not on Beds of *Scythian* Snow;
> Nor on Alabaster Hills.

But the vague resemblance between Beaumont's poem and Shakespeare's song is probably merely coincidental, a result of the conventional rhetoric and meter which they share. Rushton (1873, p. 304) calls attention to a passage in John Lyly's *Euphues and his England*, 1580 (ed. Bond, 1902, II, 74) :

For as by Basill the Scorpion is *engendred*, and by meanes of the same hearb destroyed: so loue which by time & *fancie is bred* in an idle *head*, is by time and fancie banished from the *heart*: or as the Salamander which being a long space *nourished* in the fire, at the last quencheth it, so affection hauing taken hold of the fancie, and liuing as it were in the minde of the louer, in tract of tyme altereth and chaungeth the heate, and turneth it to chilnesse. [Italics are Rushton's.] ◆

Ford (1900, p. 5) cites a parallel to the first stanza from Thomas Lodge's *Rosalynde. Euphues golden legacie*, 1590 (sigs. C₂–C₂ᵛ) :

she accounted loue a toy, and fancie a momentary passion, that as it was taken in with a gaze, might be shaken off with a winke, and therfore feared not to dally in the flame. ◆

[He notes that Shakespeare's indebtedness to Lodge's *Rosalynde* in *As You Like It* is well known.]

fancie] Malone (ed. 1790) **:** Here, as in many other places, signifies *love*. ◆ Arden (ind. ed. 1927) **:** In *Twelfth Night*, I.i.14, and *Much Ado*, III.ii.31, "fancy" is "love," but it is sometimes used, as here, of a less deep and abiding affection. . . . So [Robert] Greene, [*Morando. The*] *Tritameron* [1584, sig. B₄]: "fancie is *Vox aequiuoca*, which either may be taken for honest loue, or fonde affection, for fancie oftimes commeth of wealth or beautie, but perfect loue euer springeth from vertue and honestie." ◆ Hill (1951, p. 162) **:** Fancy is identified throughout [the song] as an infant, which is born, and can die. One reason for this identification is that fancy is simply the first stage of something. A second obvious reason is that in European literature, love itself is identified with the infant Cupid. A third reason for the identification has been overlooked by scholars; though the fact is well-known. In Elizabethan English one meaning of the word "baby" is "image reflected in the pupil of the eye." The meaning occurs in the fairly common phrase "looking babies" said of lovers at gaze. From this general background there emerges then, one of the basic symbolic units of the poem, namely "baby." Curiously enough, man and woman, or lover and mistress, are nowhere mentioned in the poem overtly, any more than "image in the eye." However . . . if "baby" is taken as one of the basic units, it is reasonable to suppose that . . . [its presence] implies the presence of the man and woman who are the lovers, and the potential parents. ◆ [Hill's ingenious interpretation is supported by W. R.'s poem (p. 37, above) where "fancy" or "conceipt" is explicitly compared to a child in cradle. He might also have cited Shakespeare's *Timon*, I.ii.114 f.:

> Joy had the like conception in our eyes
> And at that instant like a babe sprung up.

The phrase "to look babies" is cited by W. G. Smith (1935, p. 528) as a common expression of the time.] ◆ New Arden (ind. ed. 1955) in a note on the word "engend'red" remarks : Portia and Bassanio are both aware that they have kindled each other's "fancy" . . . the song warns them that there must be a deeper love. ◆

3. **Replie, replie**] Capell ([1779–1783 ?], II, pt. 3, p. 64) : [These words show this song] to be a song in two parts, or by two Voices; follow'd by a chorus of divers assistant voices, which "*all*" [l. 10] indicates: it's matter is both pleasing and suitable, and, in one place, satirical; for the sentence, beginning—"*and fancy dies*" is expressive of love's changeableness, which has both its birth in the *eye* from one object, and its extinction or death from others. ◆ Noble (1923, p. 49) : Mr. W. J. Lawrence has suggested to me that . . . [this] is a refrain borne by "All" and I think his idea very feasible. . . . "All" taking up "Reply, reply" as a refrain would distinguish the query from the response as well as of course making more certain of Bassanio's attention being caught. Incidentally Mr. Lawrence's theory would strengthen the contention that the song is a solo and not a duet. ◆ Pattison (1948, p. 158) divides the song so as to give ll. 1–3 to a first singer, "Replie, replie" to a chorus, ll. 4–9 to a second singer, and the final line to a chorus.

4. **It . . . eye**] A proverbial notion; see Tilley (1926, p. 215) and (1950, L-501). It is also listed by W. G. Smith (1935, pp. 277, 281, and 489), and by C. G. Smith (1963, no. 186). Arden (ind. ed. 1927) notes that it occurs frequently in the works of Robert Greene, and cites *Mamillia* (1583), sigs. N3–N3v :

Loue commeth in at the eye not at the eares, by seeing natures workes not by hearing sugred wordes, and fancie is fedde by the fairnesse of the face not by the finenesse of the speech.

MUSIC

The original tune for the song is not known. The earliest extant music for it was composed by Dr. Thomas Arne in 1741, as a solo to be sung in *Twelfth Night*. Arne's setting omits the last four lines. A number of later settings are given by *A List* (1884, p. 28).

DRAMATIC FUNCTION

Were the original music for this song to be discovered it would probably reveal much about the function of the song in the play. It would, in any event, demonstrate whether or not the song revealed the secret of the caskets. Lacking the original music there is only the curious typographical arrangement of the words on which to base hypotheses about the rendition of the song. It seems to me that this arrangement—not changed in the First Folio version—may preserve a simpler method of performance than any suggested by previous editors.

Gray has suggested that this is an "Echo Song". While such songs are not unusual in the musical literature of the Renaissance, they rather belong with the madrigals, airs, and complex part-songs which were the recreation of the educated classes, and not with the carols, catches, and ballads of the common people. One of the simplest part-song forms of the period was the solo with a continuous burden. It was a type of vocal music well within the scope of the most primitive musical talent, requiring only the ability to remember a short melodic phrase and a few words of (usually nonsense) lyrics. According to Chappell ([1855–1859], I, 222),

> The burden of a song, in the old acceptation of the word, was the base, foot, or under-song. It was sung throughout, and not merely at the end of the verse.

If the final line of this song, assigned to "All" by the speech-prefix in Q_1, is considered a burden and not a refrain, the song could be performed as a solo with a continuous counterpoint chorus in such a way as to produce the same effect that Gray proposes with his "Echo" arrangement. "Ding, dong, bell" was a common song burden in Elizabethan times, and it is explicitly named as the burden to "Full fathom five" in *The Tempest*.

3+v.s.

2 Henry IV

10

TEXT: Quarto (1600), issue of E-gathering with four leaves, sig. D₃
(II.iv.36–38).
TYPOGRAPHY: Roman face prose.

When Arthur firſt in court empty the iourdan and
was a worthy King: how now Miſtris Doll?

GENERAL COMMENTARY

Capell ([1779–1783 ?], I, part i, p. 174) **:** Words of a miserable song, intitl'd "*Sir Lancelot du Lake:*" the song opens with them. ♦ Halliwell (ed. 1853–1865) **:** The stage-direction before these words in ed. 1600 is simply, "Enter sir John," but *singinge* is added in nearly contemporary writing in one copy of that edition. ♦ [This is the Huntington Library's copy (No. 69,317) of STC 22,288. It appears to be a very early prompt-copy, having manuscript insertions in a number of places. In addition to the s.d., the punctuation of the song is corrected by commas added after the words *court* and *iourdan*. The First Folio version separates the song from the spoken words, as do all the modern editors.] ♦ Arden (ind. ed. 1923) remarks that a stanza of this ballad is repeated by the fool in *Lear*, but has apparently confused the original ballad with an eclectic song in Thomas Heywood's *The Rape of Lvcrece* (1608, sig. C₁ᵛ),

> When *Tarquin* first in Court began,
> And was approued King:
> Some men for sodden ioy gan weepe,
> And I for sorrow sing.

The song in Heywood is a conflation of fragments from two ballads, "Sir Launcelot du Lake" and "John Careless." The latter is the source of the fool's song in *Lear*. Seng (1962, pp. 34 f.) **:** Shakespeare's audience, undoubtedly knowing the ballad, would have appreciated the ironies of this song. . . . As a jolting broadside ballad it is a good index to the old knight's taste in verse and music; beyond this, the substance of the song is wholly inappropriate to Sir John, for it celebrates the antique world of romance and chivalry, a world of knights and ladies far more

44

honorable than Falstaff and his dinner companions. . . . The kind of chivalry the song is about is a kind that died in England with John of Gaunt, Richard, and Hotspur. ¶ Not only is the substance of the song totally inappropriate to Falstaff, but it is also set in shocking contrast to the interpolated order to the servant: "Empty the jordan." The command echoes Falstaff's earlier concern with his diseases [I.ii.1–6, 272–278].

MUSIC

Two distinct melodies survive for the tune called "Flying Fame," the tune to which "Launcelot du Lake" was, according to broadside copies of the ballad, to be sung. The first melody—sometimes also known as "Chevy Chace"—is given by Chappell ([1855–1859], I, 199) and Wooldridge (1893, I, 91; reprinted 1961). In his *English Airs* (1840, II, i) Chappell gives a slightly different version of the same tune. The second tune called "Flying Fame" Chappell says he got from Rimbault, who claimed to have taken it from manuscript notations in a copy of Robert Hole's *Parthenia Inviolata, or Mayden-Musicke for the Virginalls and Bass-Viol* ([1614?]). This copy, a unique exemplar, is in the Music Division of the New York Public Library, but the fly-leaf which contained the tune Rimbault copied is now missing. Rimbault's tune is given by Chappell ([1855–1859], I, 272) and Wooldridge (1893, I, 92; reprinted 1961).

Unfortunately, the rubric "to the tune of" in broadside ballads is not for us a reliable index of the precise melody intended by the ballad-writer or ballad-printer. Tunes took their names from the ballads to which they were currently being sung; hence a popular tune might have a succession of names, all designating a single tune. On the other hand, a single ballad might be sung to two or more tunes; once it had given its name to those tunes a name would mask more than one melody. This free interrelationship of ballads, names, and tunes is further aggravated by the fact that most broadsides shared the common ballad-meter; the result was that any ballad could, theoretically, be sung to the tune of any other ballad of similar metrical structure. It is not surprising, then, that some surviving ballads bear merely the bland rubric "To any pleasant tune." And the above confusion is further confounded when the modern scholar discovers that popular tunes are notoriously vulnerable to change through usage, and that he must reckon with multiple versions of what was once a single melody.

Because of this interlocking directorate of ballad names and tunes, it is at least possible that the melody for Falstaff's ballad may survive in one of three additional tunes. It has already been noted that one of the tunes called "Flying Fame" was sometimes known as "Chevy Chace." But the "Ballad of Chevy Chace" is also associated with the tunes titled "Pescod Time" and "The Children in the Wood." There is a similar connection between "Flying Fame" and the anonymous tune proposed for song 50, below. These additional tunes may be found in Chappell ([1855–1859], I, 198, 201), Wooldridge (1893, I, 86–90, 92), and in Sternfeld (1963, p. 176; 1964, *Songs*, p. 22). See also C. Simpson (1966, pp. 97, 104, 368).

SOURCE

The fragment of song that Falstaff sings is from a broadside ballad entitled "The Noble Acts newly found, of *Arthur* of the Table Round." Its general character is sufficiently indicated by its first four stanzas:

> When *Arthur* first in Court began,
>   and was approued King:
> By force of Armes great Victories won,
>   and conquest home did bring:
>
> Then into *Brittaine* straight he came,
>   where fiftie good and able
> Knights then repaired vnto him
>   which were of the Round-table.
>
> And many Justes and Turnaments,
>   before him there were brest: [prest]
> Wherein both Knights did then excell,
>   and far surmount the rest:
>
> But one Sir *Lancelot du Lake*,
>   who was approoued well:
> He in his fight [fight ?] and deeds of Armes
>   all other did excell.

There is additional discussion of this ballad and its popularity in Lawlis (1956, pp. 130–134) and in Seng (1962, pp. 34 f. and notes).

DRAMATIC FUNCTION

Falstaff's small fragment of song has more than a merely episodic function; along with the other fragments of song in *2 Henry IV* it relates to major and minor themes of the play as a whole. But this song is especially connected with the central problem of the play, the "rejection of Falstaff" at the end. To facilitate this painful amputation—which had to come if Prince Hal was to "redeem the time" and become an ideal monarch—Shakespeare seems to have deliberately degraded the character of Falstaff in *2 Henry IV*. The comic old knight has been made not the cause of wit in other men, but the butt of their rudest jokes. The Falstaff of *2 Henry IV* is old, dishonest, and diseased. Age has given him an old man's vices, avarice and garrulity; it has left him with a young man's disease (*lues venereus*) and impotence. His concern with his health in *2 Henry IV* begins with his first entrance on the stage and is echoed throughout the play; and at its end he is swept from the scene along with Mistress Quickly and Doll Tearsheet who are haled off by the beadles.

11–12

TEXT: Quarto (1600), issue of E-gathering with four leaves, sig. K₂
(V.iii.18–23, 35–39).
TYPOGRAPHY: Roman face prose.

[11]

A firra quoth a, we fhall do nothing but eate and
make good cheere and praife God for the merry yeere, when
flefh is cheape and females dear, and lufty laddes roame here
and there fo merely, and euer among so merily.

[12]

Be merry, be mery, my wife has all, for women are
fhrowes both fhort and tall, tis merry in hal when beards wags
all, and welcome mery fhrouetide, be mery, be mery.

GENERAL COMMENTARY

Patterson (1916, pp. 444 f.) : The Christmas carol ... judging from printed
collections of medieval poetry, seems to have flourished most vigorously on English
soil. Here it developed a form peculiar to itself consisting usually of from four to
eight stanzas of three to four lines, rhyming often aaaa and furnished with a
chorus or burden of one or more lines, rhyming BB. Often the refrain was simply
the exhortation, "Be merry, be merry!" ◆ [From MS. Corpus Christi College
Cambridge 233, fol. 95ᵛ, he quotes the carol-burden

> Be merye, be merye
> J pray yu euery chon

and remarks that the carols in *2 Henry IV* are "genuine enough to have issued
directly from a medieval manuscript." For the meaning and origin of the term
carol, see Robbins (1959, pp. 559–582; and 1961, *passim*); also R. L. Greene (1935)and
E. K. Chambers (1947, pp. 66–121). Although the vast majority of extant carols are
religious songs for Christmas, there are numerous carols which celebrate other
feasts of the Church, or which are secular in nature.]

Seng (1962, pp. 37 f.) : Silence's first two songs are Shrovetide carols, once used
to celebrate the three days of feasting and revelry that preceded the onset of Lent.
Silence, too, has evidently heard "the chimes at midnight," and probably many a
carol as well in the long years of his life. "I have been merry twice and once ere
now" (V.ii.42), he tells Falstaff. Senile and drunken at the board he probably feels

that any party is a feast, and any feast a time for Shrovetide carols. . . . The songs are more appropriate than he knows. They celebrate a present feasting and revelry before a long lean Lent which is to come when King Henry V rejects Falstaff and his friends. The first song, hailing the glut of meat in the Lenten markets and regretting the scarcity of (suddenly Lenten-penitential) females, is probably further intended to remind an audience of Shallow's earlier boasts about his youthful amours in days long past. . . . The second song is a little more advanced in time; it eschews female company for a recreational night away from shrewish wives, a night of drinking with other greybeards.

TEXTUAL COMMENTARY

1. **A sirra . . . shall**] Spoken lines are mixed with the words of this song in the quarto text. Malone (ed. 1790) was the first editor to separate these words from the words of the song. Meter and rhymes indicate that Silence sings a single iambic tetrameter quatrain of the carol (do . . . cheere, and . . . yeere, when . . . dear, and . . . there) and the burden (so . . . merily).

1–3. **do . . . laddes**] The progression of the song from eating and drinking to females and lusty lads is traditional as well as inevitable; it has its roots in Bible and proverb: "The people sat down to eat and to drink, and rose up to play" (*Exod.* 32:6, *1 Cor.* 10:7), and the Renaissance English version of *post vinum Venus* cited by Tilley (1950, C-211) and W. G. Smith (1935, p. 594), "Without Ceres and Bacchus, Venus grows cold."

5–7. **Be . . . mery**] Again a quatrain, but with a trimeter fourth line. The quatrain (Be . . . all, for . . . tall, tis . . . all, and . . . ſhrouetide) rhyming *aaax* is frequent in carols. The last four words may be a burden or a rudimentary form of it. Flügel (1889–1903, pp. 176 f., 231 f., 241 f., 260 f.) reprints five similar burdens from early manuscripts.

5. **wife has**] Steevens (ed. 1793) and Reed (ed. 1813) unnecessarily emend to *wife's as*.

6. **shrowes**] This spelling of the word is common in Shakespeare (see *The Taming of the Shrew* IV.i.213 f., V.ii.28 f., 188 f.) and, according to Kökeritz (1953, p. 211), probably reflects its contemporary pronunciation.

tis . . . all] Arden (ind. ed. 1923) : The allusion is to the wagging of beards in lively conversation (cf. *Coriolanus* II.i.[95–97, "When you speak best unto the purpose, it is not worth the wagging of your beards"]) or in dancing (cf. Peele, *Edward I* [1593, sig. H₄ᵛ] . . . "set these Lords and Ladies to dancing, so shall you fulfil the olde English prouerbe, tis merrie in Hall when beardes wag all." ◆ [The proverb occurs as early as the fourteenth century in the Middle English romance, "Life of Alexander," in the Bodleian Library's MS. Laud 622,

> Swithe mury hit is in halle,
> When the burdes wawen alle,

and frequently thereafter in Renaissance English literature. See Tilley (1950, H-55) and W. G. Smith (1935, p. 238).]

MUSIC

The original music for Silence's two carols is unknown. The tunes given by Caulfield (n.d., II, 103–106) may be "traditional," but Caulfield is not to be trusted when he fails to cite his sources.

DRAMATIC FUNCTION

The irresponsible merrymaking in Justice Shallow's orchard in Gloucestershire contrasts ironically with the serious and responsible events that have been taking place in the London of the new King Henry V. Silence, senile and drunken, babbles the words and tunes of carols he has known from earlier days, unaware that those days are gone forever. Falstaff indulges the old man's reminiscences and patronizes his songs, all the while unaware that he himself has also been bypassed by time.

13–15

TEXT: Quarto (1600), issue of E-gathering with four leaves, sigs.
K₂–K₂v (V.iii.48–50, 56 f., 77–79).
TYPOGRAPHY: Roman face prose.

[13]

A cup of wine thats briske and fine, and drinke vnto
the leman mine, and a mery heart liues long a.

[14]

Fill the cuppe, and let it come, ile pledge you a mile
too th [*sic*] bottome.

[15]

Do me right, and dub me Knight, ſamingo.

GENERAL COMMENTARY

Douce (1839, p. 293) cites a passage from Thomas Young's *Englands Bane: or, The Description of Drunkenesse* (1617, sigs. B₃–B₃v) as a commentary on these fragments of song :

> Their father the Diuell will suffer no dissentions amongst them, vntill they have executed his wil in the deepest degree of drinking, and made their sacrifice vnto him, & most commonly that is done vpon their knees being bare. The prophanenes whereof is most lamentable and detestable, being duely considered by a Christian, to thinke that that member of the body which is appointed for the seruice of God, is too often abused with the adoration of a Harlot, or a base Drunkard, as I my selfe haue seen (and to my griefe of conscience) may now say haue in presence, yea and amongst others been an actor in the businesse, when vpon our knees, after healthes to many priuate Punkes, a Health haue beene drunke to all the Whoores in the world.

TEXTUAL COMMENTARY

2. **leman**] The term originally meant simply a lover or a sweetheart, but in late Middle English the word degenerated and came to mean an unlawful lover or paramour.

a mery ... long a] A proverbial expression. Cf. Tilley (1950, H-320a) and song 58, below.

5. **Do me right**] Malone (ed. 1790) quoting Steevens **:** To *do a man right* and to *do him reason* were formerly the usual expressions in pledging healths. He who drank a bumper, expected a bumper should be drunk to his toast. So in B. Jonson's [*Epicoene, or The*] *Silent Woman* [ed. Herford, 1925–1952, V, 226] ... Captain Otter says ... "Ha' you *done me* right, gentlemen?" [To the note from Steevens, Malone adds:] It was the custom ... to drink ... sometimes a less palatable potion on *their knees*, to the health of their mistresses. He who performed this exploit was dubbed a *knight* for the evening. So in [*A*] *Yorkshire Tragedy* [1608, sigs. A₃–A₃ᵛ]:

> *Sam.* Why then follow me, Ile teach you the finest humor to be drunk in, I learned it at London last week.
> *Am:* I faith lets heare it, lets heare it.
> *Sam-* The brauest humor, twold do a man good to bee drunck in't, they call it knighting in London, when they drink vpon their knees.
> *Am.* Faith that's excellent.
> [*Sam.*] Come follow me, Ile giue you all the degrees ont in order. ◆

[The expression "do me right" may have been commonplace. Walker (1934) finds the expression in Lodge's and Greene's *A Looking Glasse for London and England* (1594), in Chapman's *Al Fooles* (1605), and in Massinger's *The Great Dvke of Florence* (1636). It occurs as well in Thomas Randolph's manuscript play *The Drinking Academy* and in Marston's *Antonio and Mellida* (1602).

MUSIC

The original tunes of the first two fragments of song are not known. Caulfield (n.d., II, 103–106) gives late settings for all three snatches of song. The original music for 15 was composed by Orlando de Lassus and was probably first published in 1570 by the French printers Le Roy and Ballard. There are a number of versions of the song. See Sternfeld (1958, pp. 105–116), who summarizes the critical and bibliographical history of the original song, and gives the words and music of five of the versions. Cutts (1956, *SQ*, pp. 389–392) gives a version of the words and music of the song for four voices, taking the treble voice from the National Library of Scotland MS. 5.2.14, fol. 25ᵛ, and the altus, tenor, and bassus from the Bodleian MS. (see below), fols. 17–19.

THE SOURCE

There are (or were) three manuscript versions of the words for 15. In the Bodleian Library is "Songs of 3, 4, and 5 parts, English and Latten. Composed by severall Authors, Newly collected and finished and sowne together in the yeres 1655 and 1656." This manuscript has the altus, tenor, and bassus parts of what is really a four-part song. The text was published by Brougham ([1918], pp. 279 f.). Another manuscript which has since disappeared was once in the possession of James Walter Brown. It was described as being by "Thomas Smith Jan:8:An:1637," and was said to contain a slightly different version of the song with only the altus and bassus parts. (See J. W. Brown, 1921, pp. 285–296; 1920, pp. 572–579.) The third manuscript is in the National Library of Scotland, Adv. MS. 5.2.14. It is described by Cutts in *SQ* (1956, pp. 385–392). The text which follows is from his transcription:

> Monser myngo for quaifing does passe
> ane cup cress can or glasse
> in seller never was,
> his fellow found
> to drink profound,
> by task and turne so round
> to quaife corās so sound
> and that beir so fresh a braine
> (fresh a braine)
> sains staint or staine
> or foyll requyll or quarrell
> bot to the beir & barrell
> q^k he wirks to wine his name,
> (q^k he wirks to wine his name,)
> & stout does stand
> in Bacchus band
> wt pott in hand
> to purchase fame,
> q^k he calls wt cup and can
> come try my couradge man to man,
> and let him ó‚quer me that can,
> & spair not
> I cair not,
> whose hands can have the pott
> no fear falls to my lott.
> god bacchus doe me right
> and doub me Knight
> doe mingoe

This version of the words is obviously in the northern dialect, but it does not differ substantially from the version in the Bodleian MS., or from the text published by Brown.

DRAMATIC FUNCTION

Aside from their appropriateness to the immediate occasion, the eating and drinking in Shallow's orchard, the additional function of the three scraps of song seems clear. They are the kinds of song that might be appropriate to lusty young gallants in a London tavern, but they provide an ironically incongruous background for the old men sitting about the table in this scene. By these fragments of song the old men's meretricious remembrance of things past is put into sharp contrast with the realities of desire that has outlived the performance. While they drink, revel, and make plans for the future, that future has already, for them, been made vain.

16

TEXT: Quarto (1600), issue of E-gathering with four leaves, sig. K₃
(V.iii.107).
TYPOGRAPHY: Roman face prose.

And Robin Hood, Scarlet, and Iohn.

GENERAL COMMENTARY

Seng (1962, p. 39) : The songs in *2 Henry IV* end exactly as they had begun, with
a fragment of a ballad that refers to the ancient days of the past. In his typically
ranting fashion Pistol rushes in to announce that Prince Hal has succeeded to the
throne: "I speak of Africa and golden joys." To which Falstaff replies in kind:

> O base Assyrian knight, what is thy news?
> Let King Cophetua know the truth thereof. (V.iii.105 f.)

The antique reference is enough to set Silence off again . . . [and his song] like the
first one sung by Falstaff in the play evokes a world of the past, a world concerned
with a kind of honor and *gentilesse* that the fat old knight and his cronies in East-
cheap and Gloucestershire are far from sharing.

MUSIC

If the source of Silence's fragment is the ballad "Robin Hood and the Jolly
Pinder of Wakefield," the tune may be the one given by Chappell ([1855–1859],
II, 394). But see the discussion of the source, below.

SOURCE

In *Merry Wives* (I.i.177) Falstaff alludes to this same ballad, "What say you,
Scarlet and John?" The source of Silence's song fragment is probably "Robin
Hood and the Jolly Pinder of Wakefield." The earliest text of this ballad, an incomplete version which does not include the line quoted by Silence, is in the Percy
Folio MS. (B. M. Add. MS. 27,879, fol. 6), the missing parts of which can be supplied
from printed broadside copies in other collections. Child (1882–1898, V, 129–132)
gives a critical text with collations of variants in other early editions. Original
broadside copies of the ballad are in the Bagford, Pepys, Crawford, Roxburghe,
and Wood collections, and it was reprinted in the early *Robin Hood's Garland* (n.d.,
sigs. B₁–B₁ᵛ).

The broadside copy in the Pepys collection (II, 100) contains not only this ballad,
but also the one from which Falstaff sings a snatch earlier in the play. The associa-

tion of these two ballads both in *2 Henry IV* and in the Pepys broadside may be more than coincidental. It seems likely that the Pepys copy is a direct descendant of a broadside which may have been in Shakespeare's possession, and thus his direct source for the two fragments of song. A modern reprint of "The Jolly Pinder of Wakefield" other than Child's is in *RB* (1871–1899, IX, 531 f.).

The original ballad has forty-eight stanzas. The partial text that follows is quoted from the Pepys copy, and runs from the beginning of the ballad to the line sung by Silence:

> The Jolly Pinder of Wakefield;
> with Robin Hood, Scarlet, and John.
>
> In Wakefield there lives a jolly Pinder,
>   in VVakefield all on a Green,
>   in VVakefield all on a Green;
>
> There is neither Knight nor Squire, said the Pinder;
>   nor Baron that is so bold,
>   nor Baron that is so bold;
>
> Dare make a trespass to the town of VVakefield,
>   but his Pledge goes to the Pinfold, &c.
>
> All this beheard three witty young Men,
>   'Twas *Robin Hood*, Scarlet, and *John*, &c.

It is impossible to be certain about the precise source of Silence's song because the line he sings is almost a formula in Robin Hood ballads. In stanza 37 of "Robin Hood and the Tanner" (Child, 1882–1898, V, 139) it occurs again with a slight change:

> And ever hereafter, as long as I live,
>   We three will be all one;
> The wood shall ring, and the old wife sing,
>   Of Robin Hood, Arthur, and John.

"A new Ballad of *Robin Hood*, *William Scadlock*, and *Little John*" (Pepys, II, 120), begins:

> Now *Robin Hood*, *Will Scadlock*, and little *John*,
>   are walking over the plain,
> With a good fat buck which William Scadlock
>   with his strong bow had slain.

The line is also alluded to in Beaumont and Fletcher's *Phylaster*, 1620 (ed. Waller 1905–1912, I, 138):

> Your Robin-hoods, scarlets and Johns, tie
>   your affections
> In darkness to your shops.

DRAMATIC FUNCTION

This song, like the others which Silence sings, is prompted by a tag of speech preceding it. All of his songs help to establish an atmosphere of rowdiness and irresponsibility which reaches its apogee in Falstaff's cry on hearing of the ascendancy to the rule by Prince Hal, "the laws of England are at my commandment." The songs lead to and heighten the comic climax of the play and ultimately aggravate the downfall of Falstaff when he is rejected by King Henry V. They are comparable in their effect to the toping staves of Iago in *Othello*, which create a similar atmosphere, lead to the downfall of Cassio, and finally to the tragic catastrophe. In *2 Henry IV* the main catastrophe is Falstaff's; however cruel it may seem to modern sensibilities, it was certainly intended to be comic. It is not gallows humor, but the cynical comedy of the fabliau.

Much Ado About Nothing

17

TEXT: Quarto (1600), sigs. D$_1$–D$_1$^{v} (II.iii.64–76).
TYPOGRAPHY: Indented verse, roman face; s.d., *The Song*.

Sigh no more ladies, ſigh no more,
Men were deceiuers euer,
One foote in ſea, and one on ſhore,
To one thing conſtant neuer,
Then ſigh not ſo, but let them go,   5
And be you blith and bonnie,
Conuerting all your ſoundes of woe,
Into hey nony nony.

Sing no more ditties, ſing no moe,
Of dumps ſo dull and heauy,   10
The fraud of men was euer ſo,
Since ſummer firſt was leauy,
Then ſigh not ſo, &c.

GENERAL COMMENTARY

Moore (1916, p. 99) cites Benedick's remark at the conclusion of the song
(II.iii.83–85) as evidence that it serves to foreshadow the jealousy of Claudio.
Noble (1923, pp. 64–66) compares this song to "Love's but a frailty of the mind"
in Congreve's *Way of the World*, 1700 (ed. Bateson, 1930, p. 343), and finds Shakespeare's the superior in dramatic craftsmanship : The singer is made to participate
in the action. Every character is in sight of the audience—there is Benedick vainly
imagining himself concealed and awaiting the baiting, which the spectators know
he is about to receive; there are Don Pedro, Claudio, and Old Leonato, in whose
confidence the audience is included, all holding their sides with laughter, and
finally there is Balthazar singing, if the phrase can be allowed, with his tongue in
his cheek. The humour of the song is simple and every device is resorted to in

order to emphasize its thrust. ✦ New Cambridge (ind. ed. 1923) **:** Its theme leads up to the talk concerning Beatrice, and it was evidently intended to put Benedick into a receptive frame of mind, which it does. ✦ Arden (ind. ed. 1924) **:** Balthasar's song is more suggestive to the audience than to the actors on the stage. No one of them has, as yet, any notion of the conspiracy against Hero, but we have heard Don John's compact with Borachio and know that "the fraud of men" is soon to give cause for sighing to still another lady.... This song is one more example of Shakespeare's skill ... in adapting his incidental lyrics to the atmosphere of the play in which they occur. Balthasar does not sound too solemn a note of warning. ✦ Long (1955, p. 125) **:** The song apparently serves no dramatic function other than to reflect the light and humorous spirit of the scene in which it is placed. Its significance, as far as Shakespeare's dramatic technique is concerned, lies in the fact that it marks the first time that Shakespeare clearly assigns a complete song to an adult actor, rather than to a professional musician or singing boy, and that the actor who sings the song portrays the role of a nobleman and not that of a commoner or page. ✦ Auden (1957, p. 39) **:** We, of course, know that Benedict is not as heart-whole as he is trying to pretend. Beatrice and Benedict resist each other because, being both proud and intelligent, they do not wish to be helpless slaves of emotion; or, worse, to become what they have often observed in others, the victims of an imaginary passion. Yet whatever he may say against music, Benedict does not go away, but stays and listens. ¶ Claudio, for his part, wishes to hear music because he is in a dreamy, love-sick state, and one can guess that his *petit roman* as he listens will be of himself as the ever-faithful swain, so that he will not notice that the mood and words of the song are in complete contrast to his day-dream. For the song is actually about the irresponsibility of men and the folly of women taking them seriously, and recommends as an antidote good-humour and common sense. If one imagines these sentiments being an expression of a character, the only character they suit is Beatrice.... I do not think it too far-fetched to imagine that the song arouses in Benedict's mind an image of Beatrice, the tenderness of which alarms him. ✦ Sternfeld (1963, p. 106) **:** Balthazar ... is in a superior category to the attendant in Portia's household [who sings "Tell me where is fancy bred?" in *Merchant*]. He serves the Prince of Aragon and has courted Margaret, one of the gentlewomen attending Hero. [Hence], his protestations, in accordance with aristocratic prejudice, that "there's not a note of mine that's worth the noting."

TEXTUAL COMMENTARY

2. **Men ... euer**] A proverbial notion that lover's vows are not to be trusted. See Tilley (1950, L-570).

3. **in sea**] Omission of the definite article after prepositions is fairly common in Shakespeare. See Abbott (1884, p. 65).

8. **hey nony nony**] White (ed. 1883) **:** For the meaning of *nonny* decorum requires me to refer the reader to the definition of *fossa*, in Florio's *World of Words*, 1598. ✦ [The definition there given is "A ditch, a dike, a grave, a pit, a trench." White is evidently thinking of a meaning *nonny* came to have as a result of some-

times being used, as *NED* notes, "to cover indelicate allusions." It is so used in *Choyce Drollery: Songs & Sonnets* (1656, p. 67):

> But gone she is the blithest Lasse
>   That ever trod on Plain.
> What ever hath betided her,
>   Blame not the Shepherd Swain.
> For why, she was her own foe,
>   And gave her selfe the overthrowe
> By being too franke of her hy nonny nonny no.

Though these words probably have a bawdy meaning in their other occurrences in Shakespeare (*Lear*, III.iv.103, and *Hamlet*, IV.v.165), in this song they are surely nothing but an innocent and meaningless burden.]

   9. **moe**] A perfectly acceptable variant form of the word "more," needed here for rhyme.

   10. **dumps**] Naylor (1931, p. 23) : The dumpe (from Swedish dialect, *dumpa*, to dance awkwardly) was a slow, mournful dance. ◆ [He cites *Lucrece*, 1594 (*Poems*, 1938, p. 207, l. 1127), "Distres likes dumps when time is kept with teares," and might also have cited *Romeo* (IV.v.128 f.),

> When griping grief the heart doth wound,
> And doleful dumps the mind oppress.

But for a discussion of this term and its meanings see J. Ward (1951, pp. 111–121).]

   12. **leauy**] An acceptable form of the word, used again by Shakespeare in *Macbeth* (V.vi.1).

MUSIC

   The original music for this song is apparently unknown. Bontoux (1936, p. 331) mentions "L'adaptation musicale faite par J. Wilson, du vivant même de l'auteur, et dont nous trouvons une mention dans les directions théâtrales de l'époque," but adds that this setting is now lost. She does not cite the sources of her information about this putative setting, yet it is possible to infer them from a petrifact stage direction in the First Folio and from J. Payne Collier's comments upon it. About thirty lines preceding the song in the first folio version of *Much Ado* there occurs the stage direction,

Enter Prince, Leonato, Claudio, and Iacke Wilson.

The name "Iacke Wilson" is almost certainly a typesetter's preservation of a stage direction in a prompt-copy of *Much Ado* from which the first folio version was set. It is very likely the name of an actor-singer who took the part of Balthasar in some performance of the play. The first extensive notice of this curious stage direction was made by Collier (1841, p. 153) when he quoted Alleyn's diary entry for 22 October 1620:

This daye was our weding daye, and ther dind with us Mr Knight, Mr Maund, and his wife. Mr Mylyor, Mr Jeffes, and 2 frendes with them, a precher and his frend, Mr Wilson the singer, with others.

In connection with this entry Collier remarks, "It seems highly probable that this . . . was no other than 'Jacke Wilson,' who personated Bathazar [*sic*] in 'Much ado about Nothing,' and whose name is inserted in the first folio of Shakespeare instead of that of the character he represented."

Four years later Collier (1845, p. 33) took further notice of Wilson:

Hitherto it does not seem to have been known, that John Wilson was not merely a singer, but a composer, and in all probability the composer of "Sigh no more, ladies, sigh no more," as sung by him in the character of Balthazar.

This statement was mere fancy on Collier's part; there is no evidence at all that any John Wilson ever composed or even "set" music for "Sigh no more, ladies." Collier's imaginative leap was, no doubt, prompted by the fact that he knew of a seventeenth-century manuscript of "Take, O, take those lips away" from *Measure for Measure*, "with Wilson's name at the end of it, as the author of the music." A year later Rimbault (1846, pp. 4 f.) identified this song as being the composition of "Doctor John Wilson, Professor of Musick, in the University of Oxford." Rimbault's identification of the "composer" was certainly eased by the fact that the manuscript to which Collier referred was then in Rimbault's possession. It is now in the New York Public Library (MS. Drexel 4041). "Take, O, take" appears on fol. 32 of that manuscript; it does *not* have "Wilson's name at the end of it, as the author of the music," but merely the initials "J. W." The same song, however, does bear the name of John Wilson in B. M. Add. MS. 11,608 (fol. 56), Bodleian MS. Mus. b. 1 (fol. 19ᵛ), and in two early printed song-books (see Music, song 45). It is possible that the actor-singer "Iacke Wilson" was the same man who later became the famous composer and Professor of Music at Oxford, but there is not enough evidence for a certain identification, and the name is, after all, a common one. Further information on this question, in addition to the articles already cited, is to be found in Seccome (1922), W. M. Evans (1941, pp. 114 f.), Arkwright (1954), Duckles (1954, *JAMS*), Cutts (1955), Seng (1955, pp. 150–166), Cutts (1959, *NQ*; and *Musique*, pp. xlii–xlvi, 114, and 172).

If the "ghost" raised by Bontoux is ignored, the earliest known setting for "Sigh no more, ladies" is to be found in a seventeenth-century manuscript first described by Heseltine (1926, p. 116), who called attention to a set of part-books in the library of Christ Church College, Oxford. This manuscript, he notes,

contains several songs by [Thomas] Ford in what appears to be an arrangement for two tenors and a bass. Amongst them is the only known setting, by any contemporary of Shakespeare, of "Sigh no more, ladies." The text as given in the manuscript is not identical with Shakespeare's, but the tune fits Shakespeare's words, and may have been composed for them in a different and more satisfactory form than that in which it appears in the manuscript.

When he wrote this Heseltine (1925 [pp. 6–8]) had already published Ford's song with the words from Shakespeare underlaid. In fitting Shakespeare's words to the

Ford music Heseltine was compelled to double the first line of each verse and to make considerable use of repetition in the refrains. At the end of his arrangement Heseltine ([p. 9]) gives the words of Ford's song as they appear in Christ Church MS. 736–738:

> Sigh no more, ladies, sigh no more;
> Sighs may ease but not heal the sore.
>   Men were deceivers ever;
> One foot in sea and one on shore,
>   In one thing constant never.
>   Then sigh not so,
>   But let them go,
>   And be you blithe and bonny,
> Converting all your sounds of woe
>   Into Hey no nonny.
>
> Change your grief to a pleasing smile,
> Love as you do when you beguile.
>   Make your bright stars glance their beams.
> Your charming voice use as a wile.
>   Sweetly chanting love's false dreams.
>   So they shall sigh
>   And you live free,
>   And smile at mad men's folly.
> Daring assume inconstancy
>   That doth make you jolly.
>
> If this way take not as you would,
> Bear yourselves then as ladies should;
>   Cupid is a powerful god.
> Love truly and you men may mould
>   With a beck or with a nod.
>   Then constant be,
>   Conceal your scorn,
>   And freely tell them on it;
> But to lament and grieve and mourn,
>   No, no, fie upon it!

Extremely little is known about Thomas Ford. According to Fellowes (1954) he may have been born around 1580 and he died in 1648. He appears to have specialized in ayres for solo voice with lute accompaniment or unaccompanied for four voices. He is recorded as having been a musician in the service of Henry, Prince of Wales, and later of Charles I. Too little is known about him to speculate on his connection, if any, with Shakespeare. If Fellowes' conjecture about the date of his birth is reasonably correct, he might have been old enough to have composed the original music for Shakespeare's song; the likelier supposition, however, would be that Ford's song in the Christ Church College manuscript is his later reworking of the original song or a wholly independent composition except for the borrowed words.

Probably less reliable, from a scholarly point of view, is the transcription of Ford's music set to Shakespeare's words by Harold Eustace Key, printed by Gibbon (1930, p. 117), and reprinted by Long (1955, pp. 132 f.). Gibbon erroneously assigns the song to *As You Like It*; Long fails to mention that the lyrics in the Ford manuscript differ substantially from the lyrics in Shakespeare's play.

DRAMATIC FUNCTION

Among the commentators, the Arden editor and Auden seem to be most nearly right in assessing this song's dramatic function. It certainly does foreshadow the near tragedy about to be enacted, and with its romantic resignation it provides an excellent comic foil for Benedick's sophomoric cynicism:

> Now divine air! Now is his [Claudio's] soul ravish'd. Is it not strange that sheep's guts should hale souls out of men's bodies? Well, a horn for my money, when all's done. (II.iii.60–63)

The "hilarity" that Noble finds in this episode, the "light and humorous spirit" which Long finds in the scene, would probably escape an audience which has already heard, as Arden remarks, "Don John's compact with Borachio."

Though the comic conspiracy of Don Pedro, Claudio, and Leonato, aimed at causing Benedick to fall in love with Beatrice, is comedy of a very high order, the tenor of the song has little to do with this. Rather it is counsel to ladies to take their loving and lovers less seriously, to be as hedonistically carefree in their affections as men are reputed to be.

18

TEXT: Quarto (1600), sig. I₁ᵛ; (V.ii.26–29).
TYPOGRAPHY: Roman face prose.

The God of loue that fits
aboue, and knowes mee, and knowes me, how pittifull I de-
ferue.

TEXTUAL COMMENTARY

2–3. **how ... deserue**] Kittredge (ind. ed. 1941) paraphrases : "How much I
deserve pity (for my unrequited affection)"; but Benedick interprets it in the
sense of "How slight my deserts are" and protests that, though he may be without
merit as a singer, he is the greatest lover on record.

MUSIC

The tune to "The Gods of love" is contained in the Francis Willoughby Lute
Book, fols. 88ᵛ–89, in the University of Nottingham Library. J. Ward (1957, p. 164)
remarks that "the tune took only one of its names from Elderton's famous ballad;
it was also known as 'Turkeyloney,' a dance tune famous in its own right; and ...
as 'My lord Essex measures.' The same music, differently arranged, is called
'Pavane d'Anvers' in Susanne van Soldt's late 16th-century keyboard manuscript;
'Cascarda Chiara Stella' in Fabritio Caroso's *Il Ballarino* of 1581; and, most interesting of all, 'Gentil madonna del mio cor patrona' in Azzaiuolo's *Primo Libro de
Villote alla Padoana* (Venice, 1557), 'Gentil madonna' in Antonio Rotta's first book
of *Intabolatura de Lauto* (Venice, 1546), and 'Gentil mia donna' in British Museum
MSS., Royal Appendix 5962, fol. 17." Ward gives (*ibid.*, p. 164) a modern transcription of the tune from the Nottingham manuscript where it is titled "goddes of
love."

Attention had already been called to this tune a few years earlier by Dart
(1954, pp. 97 f.) who reported (p. 95) that it was also contained in Trinity College
Dublin MS. D.3.30 (Thomas Dallis's Lute Book), p. 323. But Dart, apparently
mistaking the orthography of the title in the Nottingham manuscript, called the
tune "the goddess of love," thereby obscuring the connection between the tune
and Elderton's famous ballad (which has only recently been recovered; see Source,
below).

J. Ward (1954, pp. 25 f.) gives a modern transcription of "Turkeyloney" from
MS. D.3.30, where this piece and a number of others for the virginal are sewn in
with the Dallis lute pieces. He also gives (*ibid.*, pp. 52 f.) a transcription of "Turkeyloney" from Trinity College Dublin MS. D.1.21 (William Ballet's Lute Book),
No. 91; and (*ibid.*, p. 53) a transcription of "Pavane d'Anvers" from B. M. Add.

MS. 29,485 (Susanne van Soldt's manuscript), fols. 17-17ᵛ. Of these three titles
Ward (*ibid.*, p. 52) says that "Turkeyloney" "seems the most appropriate since
this was one of the most popular of all Elizabethan dances and probably dates
from *ca.* 1570." He also remarks that Dolmetsch (1949, p. 101) has conjectured that
"Turkeyloney" is a corruption of the Italian *tordiglione*. A version of the tune is
also to be found in Chappell ([1855-1859], I, 96). C. Simpson (1966, pp. 261 f.) also
reproduces the music from the Ballet Lute Book.

SOURCE

The original of Benedick's song, known heretofore only in the Shakespearean
fragment and through parodies and moralizations, was discovered in 1958 by
James M. Osborn and his research assistant, Roger Lonsdale, in a manuscript in
Mr. Osborn's collection (see Osborn, 1958).

The discovery of this lost ballad confirms what Rollins (1920, *SP*, pp. 203 f.) long
ago inferred about it from the fragment quoted in Shakespeare and from the
moralizations and allusions in other sixteenth- and early seventeenth-century
literature. The author of the ballad was the famous actor and ballad-writer
William Elderton. His "Gods of Love" was apparently immensely popular, since
it was moralized, parodied, imitated, and alluded to frequently by writers in
Shakespeare's time. According to Rollins, the ballad appeared in 1562 and soon
equaled in popularity the author's earlier "Pangs of Love." Rollins points out that
"the authorship of 'The Gods' is well established ... [by] an extant ballad by
William Birch entitled 'The complaint of a sinner, vexed with paine[. . .] After
W[illiam]. E[lderton]. moralized'. . . . Elderton's rivals eagerly took advantage of
his success. When the ballad had been in the streets only a few days, the printer
Griffith licensed 'the answere to the iiij^th ballett made to the godes of loue';
another printer got out 'The Joy of Virginity, to the Gods of Love'; and Alexander
Lacy secured a license for 'The Gods of Love' (the first actual mention of Elderton's
own ballad in the Registers) in 1567-68, preparatory to reprinting it."

Related ballads were entered in the Registers for 1562-1563, and 1564-1565.
William Birch's moralization, STC 3076, is reprinted as No. 7 in Collmann (1912,
pp. 19-21), and there is an anonymous moralization in Clement Robinson's *A
Handefull of pleasant delites*, 1584 (ed. Rollins, 1924, pp. 42 f.). Allusions to Elderton's
ballad are to be found in George Turberville's "To his Ladie" in his *Epitaphes,
Epigrams, Songs, and Sonets* (1567, sigs. C₁ᵛ-C₂), in Thomas Heywood's *The Fayre
Mayde of the Exchange* (1607, sig. E₁), and in a song in *Bacchus Bountie*, 1593 (reprinted
in *The Harleian Miscellany*, 1808-1813, II, 309).

The text of the ballad which follows is from Osborn's manuscript, "The Braye
Lute Book," fols. 55ᵛ-56:

> The gods off loue ʸᵗ ſytts a boue
> & knowe me & knowe me
> howe ſorroffull I do ſerue
> Graunt my requeſt yᵗ at the leaſt
> ſhe ſhowe me ſhe ſhowe me
> ſomme pytty whan I deſerue/

that every brawle may turne to blys
   to Joy w^t all that Joyffull ys
      do thys my dere & bynde me
ffor ever & ever yor owne
   And as yow here doe ffynd me
      ſo let yor love be ſhowne/
ffor till I here this vnytye
   I langwyſhe in extremytye/

As yett I have a ſolle to ſave
   vpryghtly/vpryghtly/
      thoe trubled w^t dyſpare
I cannot ffynd/to ſett my mynde
   ſo lyghtlye ſo ſlyghtly
      as dye beffore yow be there

But ſyns I muſt nedes yow provoke
   come ſlake the thurſt ſtād by y^e ſtrok
that whan my hart ys taynted
   the ſorrofful ſyghts [*or* ſyghs] may tell
yowe myght have bene aquaynted
   w^t one that loved yow well
none have I tolde the jeﷺ dye
   that none but yow can remedye

Thoſe curſyd eyes that weare the ſpiyes
   to ffynd ye to ffynd ye/
      are blubbered now w^t teares
And eake the head that ffancy lead
   to mynde ye to mynde ye
      ys ffraght w^t deadly ffeares
and every parte ffrome topp to towe
   compellyth the hart to blede ffor woe
      alas lett pytty move yowe
ſome remedy ſone to ſend me
   & knowynge howe well to love yowe
      yor ſelffe vvocheſaffe to lende me/
I wyll nott boſt the vyctory
   but yelde me to yor curteſye

I reade of olde what hath bene tolde
   ffull truly / ffull truly
      off ladys longe agoe
whoſe pyttyffull harts have playd y^{er} parts
   as dewly as dewly
      as ever good wyll colde ſhewe

And yowe therffore that knowe my caſe
  reffuſe me not but grant me grace
    that I may ſay & holde me
to one tryūphe & truthe
  Even as yt hath bene tolde me
    ſo my godd lady dothe
ſo ſhall yow wynn the vyctory
  w^t honor ffor yor curteſye/

w^t curteſy nowe ſo bende ſo bowe
  to ſpeed me to ſpeed me
    as anſweryth my deſyre
As I wylbe yf ever I ſee
  yow nede me ye nede me
    as redy whan yow requyre
Unworthy thoe to come ſo nye
  that paſſynge ſhowe that ffedes myne eye
yet ſhall I dye w^t owt ytt
  yff pytty be not in yow
    butt ſure I do not dowt yt
nor any thynge yow can doe
to whome I doe com̄ytt & ſhall
  my ſelffe to worke yor wyll w^t all/
    ffinis

A completely modernized version of this text has been published by Osborn (1958, p. 11) in the London *Times*.

DRAMATIC FUNCTION

The popularity of Elderton's ballad insures that Shakespeare's audience would have recognized the incongruity of this song on Benedick's lips. Earlier Benedick had sophomorically despised the music that "ravish'd" the souls of others; now the hidden scoffer who thought he was free from the infection of love is forced to eat his own words. He is now both lover and singer, and almost "Benedick, the married man."

19

TEXT: Quarto (1600), sig. I₂ᵛ (V.iii.12–21).
TYPOGRAPHY: Indented verse, roman face; s.d., *Song*.

> Pardon goddeſſe of the night,
> Thoſe that ſlew thy virgin knight,
> For the which with ſongs of woe,
> Round about her tombe they goe:
> Midnight aſſiſt our mone, help vs to ſigh & grone.   5
> Heauily heauily.
> Graues yawne and yeeld your dead,
> Till death be vttered,
> Heauily heauily.

GENERAL COMMENTARY

Moore (1916, p. 87) : A surprisingly large number of the songs [in Shakespeare's plays] serve for what might be called pagan ritual, a fact which is conspicuous because Christian ritual is absent.... This class may be said to include ... the songs which occur in special ceremonies. ... That fairies and witches should sing was a convention sufficiently established; but the frequent occurrence of masque or other musical ceremonial in the middle and later plays is less easily explained. No doubt it is due, in part, to the taste of the masque-loving age.... These passages must have been effective on the stage, however excrescent they may seem to a modern reader, as ... where Don Pedro and Claudio, with attendants, enter the church at night, bearing torches, to honor the memory of Hero, whom they consider slain by slander. ♦ Noble (1923, pp. 66 f.) : The spectators are aware of the fact that Claudio is under a delusion as to Hero's death and accordingly there is something of comedy in the scene, hence it would not be decent that the hymn should be addressed to the popular Deity. Consequently it is addressed to Artemis, the Goddess of the Night, and Protectress of virgins, although the characters are all presumed to be professing Christians. Such an address by such people at once lends an air of insincerity to the whole—an insincerity not altogether inappropriate when we consider the unreal seriousness with which the very young Claudio takes himself—for it is obvious no such Deity is worshipped either by the musicians or by Claudio, so it is not likely that, on an occasion so pregnant with grief, the disconsolate lover would indulge is such a flight of poetical fancy. The Law, while not so strict, in respect of invocations of the Deity, as it afterwards became in James I's reign, sufficiently safeguarded religious susceptibilities by reason of the improbability of the Licenser of Plays permitting anything which appeared to him to savour of blasphemy. ♦ Long (1955, pp. 130–134) : This song appears to serve two distinct dramatic purposes: it provides an effective instance of dramatic irony, and . . . erases the effects on the audience of the tragic elements within the play. . . . ¶ The dramatic irony of this episode and its song arises from its relationship to the serenade to Hero for which the Prince requested Balthasar to obtain musicians [II.iii.87–91]. The proposed serenade has been considered an unresolved thread in the play's action, since the serenade is never performed. But, upon examination, it appears to be an anticipation of the passage now under consideration. ¶ . . . In stating the terms of the penance, Leonato expressly states that the visit to Hero's tomb should occur that same night. The result is that the dirge is sung at the time originally chosen by the Prince for his serenade to Hero. ¶ The irony thus created is obvious. Instead of a merry serenade under Hero's window in honor of a happily wedded Claudio and Hero, we witness a mournful ritual performed, not under Hero's marriage chamber, but before her tomb. . . . [It seems almost certain] that Shakespeare had this piece of dramatic irony in mind when he wrote the short sepulcher scene. . . . [Also, the song] has the effect of calming the tragic passions aroused in the audience by Hero's dishonor and simulated death. . . . The dirge provides a ritualistic exorcism which drives away the last traces of the somber shadow that temporarily obscures the comic spirit of the play.

TEXTUAL COMMENTARY

2. **virgin knight**] Johnson (ed. 1765) : *Knight*, in its original signification, means *Follower* or *Pupil*, and in this sense may be feminine. Helena, in *All's Well* [I.iii.119 f.] . . . uses knight in the same signification ["Dian no queen of virgins, that would suffer her poor knight surpris'd without rescue."] ◆ Malone (ed. 1790) quotes a note from Steevens, "Virgin *knight* is virgin hero. In the times of chivalry, a *virgin knight* was one who had as yet atchieved no adventure. Hero had as yet atchieved no matrimonial one." Malone comments : I do not believe any allusion was intended to . . . "matrimonial adventure." *Diana's knight* or *Virgin knight*, was the common poetical appelation of virgins, in Shakespeare's time. . . . In Spenser's *Faery Queene* [ed. Greenlaw, 1932–1949, III, 176]:

> Soone as that virgin knight he saw in place,
> His wicked bookes in hast he ouerthrew. ◆

Steevens (ed. 1793) denies the relevance of this quotation; he remarks that it refers to the woman Britomart, who is both a virgin and in knightly habiliments. [*NED*, citing this line from Shakespeare's song, seems to apply *virgin* in its ordinary sense to Hero; *knight*, then, may be taken metaphorically, applying to Hero as a follower of Diana. But Malone's interpretation of a technical sense seems to be supported by a usage in Beaumont and Fletcher's *Wit at Several Weapons* (*Comedies and Tragedies*, 1647; ed. Waller, 1905–1912, IX, 104):

> I am a Maiden-Knight, and cannot looke
> Upon a naked weapon with any modesty,
> Else 'twould go hard with me.

The term as applied to Hero probably refers to her merely as a follower of Diana.

6, 9. Heauily, heauily] Collier (ed. 1878) : This was the burden of an old ballad, as we find in a tract called "Laugh, and lie down," printed in 1605. [Sig. C_1, "This poore man . . . fell to sing the song of *Oken Leaues* began to wither: to the tune of Heauilie, heauilie."] All the folios corrupt it to "Heavenly, heavenly," and have thus puzzled some modern editors. ✦

7-8. Graues . . . vttered] Halliwell (ed. 1853–1865) : The slayers of the virgin knight are performing a solemn requiem on the body of Hero, and they invoke Midnight and the shades of the dead to assist, until *her* death be *uttered*, that is, proclaimed, published, or commemorated. ✦ Yale (ind. ed. 1917) : The meaning here is . . . that the graves are to yawn and yield their dead until death is scattered abroad among the world of men. ✦ Arden (ind. ed. 1924) : *Uttered* [can be understood] . . . to mean expelled or ousted, and so, overcome. According to this interpretation, the dead, I suppose, are to escape from their prisons until death shall finally be vanquished. . . . [Other editors believe] . . . *uttered* means commemorated, published or proclaimed. On the face of it this seems a better interpretation, for it is nearer the more usual meaning of the word; also . . . it better brings out the parallelism of the lines. But it makes a curious invocation. Does Claudio want the dead, as well as midnight, to assist him to sigh and groan? And how are we to interpret the word *death*,—as applying to death in general . . . or only to the death of Hero? Hardly the former; Claudio would have no wish to commemorate the grim abstraction. If the latter (Boas paraphrases, "till the death-dirge be sung"), it is . . . a good deal to expect the dead to arise from their graves simply to assist at the all too brief obsequies of Hero. . . . Delius makes *death* the object of *till*. He interprets: "Till death comes to us, let the words 'heavily, heavily' be uttered"; an ingenious reading, but one which necessitates a harshness of construction unparalleled in Shakespeare's songs. On the whole, though not entirely satisfactory . . . [the second reading] seems to give the best interpretation. ✦ Kittredge (ind. ed. 1941) : Release your dead that they may join with us in our mourning until her death has been lamented to the full. ✦ G. W. Knight (1953, p. 93) calls attention to the "suggestion of resurrection at the close of the song," noting that "indeed, Hero is restored."

MUSIC

The original music (perhaps it was a tune called "Heavily, heavily," the same as for the ballad noted by Collier, above) is not known. The earliest known setting for Shakespeare's song is probably the one by Arne for solo soprano. It is reprinted in Caulfield (n.d., II, 128). There is no indication in the stage directions or text of the quarto whether the song is to be performed by a soloist or by a chorus. Long (1955, p. 134) suggests that since Balthasar was to have sung the unperformed serenade, he may be the singer here. On the other hand, Leonato (V.i.289–294) seems to order Claudio and Pedro to sing the dirge. Yet, when the song is called for in V.iii, it is Claudio who orders the performance, "Now, music, sound, and sing your solemn hymn"; the phrasing of this order hardly suggests that he is one of the singers. Perhaps as in *Two Gentlemen* (IV.ii) a consort of viols is brought onto the stage to furnish accompaniment for Balthasar or a group of professional singers.

DRAMATIC FUNCTION

Noble is undoubtedly right in seeing in the pagan overtones of the song an unwillingness on the part of the author to run afoul of the licenser by representing genuinely religious rituals on the stage. The entire episode should be compared with the funeral obsequies over Fidele in *Cymbeline* (IV.ii.258 ff.), the speeches of Hymen and the nuptial song in *As You Like It* (V.iv), and the masque of Ceres, Iris, and Juno in *The Tempest* (IV.i). By using such devices Shakespeare could have the best of two worlds by avoiding the displeasure of the censor and at the same time employing the dramatic spectacle that religious ritual provides.

The extravagance and insincerity of the song, to which Moore and Noble call attention, can by explained by comparing this scene with the one in *Romeo and Juliet* (IV.v.15 ff.), and the elaborately artificial grief over Juliet's supposed death. In both instances the audience knows the heroines are not dead; under such circumstances a display of naturalistic, rather than conventional grief might have an awkward effect upon the feelings of the spectators of the play. Moreover the masque-like ceremonials and rituals that Shakespeare included in his plays probably involved more stagecraft and colorful pageantry than the bare text that comes down to us indicates. Elaborate spectacle seems to have been a much more important feature of Renaissance play-acting than it is of modern.

While it hardly seems that a scene in which a funeral dirge is the central element could drive away "the somber shadow that temporarily obscures the comic spirit of the play," as Long contends, it certainly helps in part to assuage the outraged feelings of the audience who have seen Hero unjustly and brutally slandered; and Claudio's and Pedro's compunction and formal act of repentance also dispose the audience for accepting the ultimate reconciliation of Claudio and Hero. Finally, as Knight points out, the song does foreshadow a "resurrection."

As You Like It

20

TEXT: Folio (1623), sig. Q₆ᵛ (II.v.1-8, 40-47, 52-59).
TYPOGRAPHY: Indented verse, italic face; s.d., *Song*.

Vnder the greene wood tree,
    who loues to lye with mee,
And tnrne his merrie Note,
    vnto the ſweet Birds throte:
Come hither, come hither, come hither: 5
    Heere ſhall he ſee no enemie,
But Winter and rough Weather.

     .   .   .

Who doth ambition ſhunne,
    and loues to liue i' th Sunne:
Seeking the food he eates,   10
    and pleas'd with what he gets:
Come hither, come hither, come hither,
    Heere ſhall he ſee. &c.

     .   .   .

If it do come to paſſe, that any man turne Aſſe:
Leauing his wealth and eaſe,   15
A ſtubborne will to pleaſe,
Ducdame, ducdame, ducdame:
Heere ſhall he ſee, groſſe fooles as he,
And if he will come to me.

GENERAL COMMENTARY

Halliwell (ed. 1853–1865) : Songs of the greenwood tree are of high antiquity in
England, and were probably suggested by some medieval ballad or poem of a

romantic character, such, for example, as the early metrical tale of Robin Hood preserved in MS. Cantab. Ff. v. 48 [fol. 128ᵛ] which commences as follows:

> In somer when the shawes be sheyne
>   And leves be large and long
> hit is fulle mery in feyre foreste
>   To here the foulys song
> To se the dere draw to the dale
>   And leffe the hilles hee
> And shadow hem in the leves grene
>   Under the grene woode tre

A very curious and early song of the greenwood tree is preserved in MS. Bibl. Reg. Append. 58 [fols. 55ᵛ–56ᵛ], in the British Museum, a musical MS. written about the year 1500, the notes being accompanied with the following words:

> My lytell fole ys gon to play
> sche wyll tary no longer with me
> he how frisca joly
> vnder the grynd wood tre
>   he how frisca joly
>   vnder the grenewood tre
>   he how frisca joly
>
> My lytell fole ys full of pley
> & prety sports can well asay
> both try & fett in her Aray
> frisca joly vnder the grenewood tre
> frisca joly vnder the grene wood tre
>   My lytell fole ys vt supra

There was, in Shakespeare's time, a song alluded to in *Ane compendius Buik. of Godly and Spirituall Sangis* [Edinburgh, 1600, sigs. N₃–N₄, which contain a moralization of this song, with the burden, "Hay trix, trym go tryx vnder the grene woid trie"] . . . which may possibly also have been in the poet's recollection; but the superiority of the beautiful lines in [Shakespeare's] text will be apparent from the following specimen . . . here taken from Deloney's *Second Part of the Gentle Craft* [1639, sig. F₄]:

> The Primrose in the greene Forrest,
>   the Violets they be gay:
> The double Dazies and the rest,
>   that trimly decks the way,
> Doth move the spirits with brave delights,
>   whose beauties Darlings be:
> With hey tricksie, trim goe tricksie,
>   under the greene wood tree. ✦

[There is further information on "Greenwood Songs" in Flügel (1889–1903, XII, 272), and Rollins (1919, *MLN*, 348 f.); there are other examples of the genre in

B. M. Addit. MS. 31,922 (fols. 43ᵛ-44, 45ᵛ-46), in Ravenscroft's *Pammelia* (1609, sig. B₁), and a burlesque in D'Urfey's *Songs Compleat* (IV, 1719, 122 f.).]

Long (1955, pp. 142 f.) **:** Amien's song expresses the sentiments of the majority of the noblemen-foresters. He invites the listener to participate in the joys of a sylvan existence where the only enemies to be met are winter and rough weather. The underlying theme of the play is thus restated. Jaques disagrees with the popular belief and expresses his cynical opinon in the last stanza of the song. ¶ The setting of the scene is also localized by the song. The greenwood tree mentioned therein may or may not have had a material representation on the stage, but a tree of some sort is a part of the setting. . . . Possibly the song was designed to aid the imagination of the spectator in creating a setting that had no substantial existence at all. ◆

Auden (1957, p. 40) **:** Of Jaques we have been told that he is a man . . . at odds with the world, ever prompt to strike a discordant note, a man, in fact, with no music in his soul. Yet, when we actually meet him, we find him listening with pleasure to a merry song. . . . The first two stanzas of the song are in praise of the pastoral life, an echo of the sentiments expressed earlier by the Duke. . . . The refrain is the summons, *Come Hither*, which we know is being answered. But the characters are not gathering here because they wish to, but because they are all exiles and refugees. In praising the Simple Life, the Duke is a bit of a humbug, since he was compelled by force to take it. ¶ Jaques' extemporary verse which he speaks, not sings, satirizes the mood of the song. . . . At the end of the play, however, Jaques is the only character who chooses to leave his wealth and ease— it is the critic of the pastoral sentiment who remains in the cave. But he does not do this his stubborn will to please, for the hint is given that he will go further and embrace the religious life. In neoplatonic terms he is the most musical of them all for he is the only one whom the carnal music of this world cannot satisfy, because he desires to hear the unheard music of the spheres. ◆

Seng (1958, *Encounter*, p. 68), asserts that there is no evidence that Jaques' parody is not sung **:** In the original text the words of the parody are assigned to Amiens. This may be a typographical error since the folio gives Amiens two speech-headings in a row. But it is not necessarily a mistake since Jaques says to Amiens, "I'll give you a verse to this note that I made yesterday in despite of my invention." To which Amiens replies, "And I'll sing it." It is entirely possible that Jaques then hands the lyrics of the parody to Amiens who obligingly sings them. Additional evidence that the parody is sung, not recited, is the fact that it is set in italics like the first two stanzas of the song which were certainly sung. ◆

Sternfeld (1963, p. 56) **:** The dialogue [ll. 9–32 following the song] lays emphasis on the etiquette to be observed by noblemen in contrast to the behaviour of professional musicians. The noble Amiens protests that his voice is ragged, that he sings only at the request of Jaques, but not to please himself. . . . But the two singing boys who perform "It was a lover and his lass" gloat over their professional status: they deliberately poke fun at the courteous disclaimers prescribed by Castiglione and Elyot. ◆ [Shakespeare, too, may be poking fun at courtiers who feel the need to slavishly follow the dictates of the courtesy books. Yet elsewhere Sternfeld applies the same rules of etiquette quite seriously in his critical interpretations of Shakespearean songs. See songs 35, 36, and 43. A less rigid view would probably hold that, even as now, there was a wide discrepancy in Shakespeare's day between the rules of conduct prescribed by the books of etiquette and the acceptance and practice of those rules by members of his society.]

TEXTUAL COMMENTARY

3. **tnrne**] The editors of the second folio (1632) corrected the turned "u". Most of the eighteenth-century editors followed Pope (ed. 1728) in emending the word to *tune*. Present-day editors follow the 1632 reading.

3–4. **tnrne ... throte**] Kittredge (ind. ed. 1939) : Adapt his pleasant tune to the modulation of the bird's song. Singer quotes Hall [*Virgidemiarum ... The three last Bookes. Of byting satyres*, 1597–1598, sig. G₅ᵛ], *Satires*, VI, 1 ... "Whiles thred-bare Martiall turnes his merry note." ♦

5, 12. **hither**] Kittredge (ind. ed. 1939) : Pronounced *hether*. ♦ [A judgement confirmed by Kökeritz, 1953, p. 212. See also V.iv.119 (sig. S₁ᵛ in the 1623 folio) where this word is spelled "hether" to rhyme with "together."]

9. **liue ... Sunne**] Capell ([1779–1783 ?], I, part 1, 58) : [The reading of some editors (*viz.*, Rowe, Pope, Theobald, Warburton, Johnson, and Hanmer), "to lye i' the sun,"] ... is a phrase importing absolute idleness, the idleness of a motley; but "*live i' the sun,*" which is Shakespeare's phrase, imports only—a living in freedom; a flying from courts and cities, the haunts of "*ambition,*" to enjoy the free blessings of heaven in such a place as the singer himself was retir'd to. ♦

14–19. **If ... me**] Moore (1916, p. 90) : The cynical strain in Jaques is nowhere better shown than in his parody of Amiens' song of sylvan contentment. ... Not infrequently the revelation of character [in Shakespeare's plays] is of this sort: the speaker shows his own nature by his comment on the song of another. ♦ Noble (1923, pp. 72 f.) : [This song] ... serves to make us acquainted personally with Jaques, of whom we have heard previously. In this scene, Jaques is the champion of realism just as eventually his contrary spirit leads him to become a convert to romanticism on the restoration of his friends' fortunes. Amiens sings of the joy of the careless existence, where one lies under the tree and emulates the notes of the birds with nothing to annoy, except the inclemency of the season. ... Then Jaques turns round and parodies the whole theme of the song.

17. **Ducdame**] Capell ([1779–1783 ?], I, part 1, pp. 58 f.) : The words—"*Come hither, come hither, come hither,*" are latinized by the composer ... and the Latin words crouded together into a strange single word, of three syllables, purely to set his hearer a staring; whom he bamboozles still further, by telling him—"'*Tis a Greek invocation.*" ♦ Halliwell (ed. 1853–1865) : The notes of the commentators on this word are by no means satisfactory. ... The mere fact of the word being a trisyllable shows at once the inconsistency of attempting to establish a connection with the old country song, commencing,—"*Dame, what makes your ducks to die ?,*" on which White and Farmer have so elaborately written. ... Hanmer's conjecture of *duc ad me* ... is forced and unnecessary, but perhaps not so improbable as to suppose Jaques was using some country call of a woman to her ducks. ... There is ... a passage in an uncollated MS. of *Piers Ploughman*, in the Bodleian

Library, which goes far to prove that Ducdamé is the burden of an old song [MS. Rawl. Poet. 137, fol. 6]. . . .

> Thanne sete ther some,
> And *sunge* at the ale,
> And helpen to erye that half akre
> With Dusadam-me-me.

The Shakespearean word may also be intended by the contraction, *Dmee!dmee! dmee!* in Armin's *Nest of Ninnies*. ◆ [Halliwell is citing Collier (1842, p. 32) for this expression which does read "Dmee" in the Collier reprint. But Collier misread his source, confusing the blackletter capital *O* with capital *D*. In Robert Armin's *A Nest of Ninnies*, 1608, sig. D₄ᵛ, the expression actually reads, "O mee, O mee, O mee."] A. A. (1859, p. 284) **:** Is it not literally as written *duc dà me*, "lead him from me?" Amiens has been describing the generous soul "Who does ambition shun," &c., and welcomes him with a "come hither, come hither." Jaques is describing the opposite character who thinks "a stubborn will to please," and goes on with his parody, "keep him from me," instead of "come hither." *Da* is the Italian preposition "from," answering to the Latin *a, ab, abs*. ◆ Tregeagle (1878, p. 55) **:** It seems not improbable that this word may be intended to represent the twang of a guitar. ◆ Lean (1878, p. 278) suggests that the word is Jaques' invention, a play on Amiens's name to poke fun at him **:** To Jaques' ear . . . it must have been a cynical enjoyment to hear the object of his chaff calling himself into a fools' circle—"Ductàmi"—Ami being the abbreviation which stands at the head of those passages in the play spoken by Amiens, as well as French for friend. ◆ *New Variorum* (ind. ed. 1890) quotes other learned guesses **:** "This phrase . . . resolves itself into the Gaelic *duthaich* (the *t* silent before the aspirate, pronounced *duhaic*), signifying a country, an estate, a territory, a piece of land; *da* or *do* signifying to, and *mi*, me—*i.e.*, this territory or ground is to me, or belongs to me; it is my land or estate." "It [is] . . . good honest Welsh, as nearly as the Saxon tongue could frame it. Its exact Cambrian equivalent is *Dewch da mi*, 'Come with (or to) me.'" ◆ Lee (ed. [1910–1914]) **:** In all probability a nonsensical parody of the conventional burden of an unidentified popular song. . . . Attempts have been made to connect "ducdame" with like sounding words in Latin, Italian, French, Gaelic, Welsh, Greek, and Romany. ◆ New Cambridge (ind. ed. 1926) **:** The word is one of those textual cruxes in Shakespeare to which great attention has been given. . . . The probable if not certain solution has now however been known for some years though it has not as yet, we believe, been set forth completely in print. The word is in short a corruption or mishearing of the Romani *dukrǎ mē*, which became *dukdǎ me* by the not infrequent change of *r* to *d*, these letters being closely connected in pronunciation in Romani. The expression, which means "I foretell, I tell fortunes or prophesy," fits the context perfectly. As the call of the Gipsy fortune-teller at fairs or public gatherings, it is a "Greek (=sharper's) invocation to call fools into a circle." . . . The interpretation also renders the reference to "the first-born of Egypt" [II.v.63] intelligible. . . . The point of Jaques' skit upon Amiens' song is now obvious: the members of the banished court are so many amateur Gipsies, forced to lead this uncomfortable life by the "stubborn will" of the Duke, who as the elder brother is "the first-born of Egypt." ◆ Allen (1934, p. 126) **:** I submit that "Ducdame" . . . is England's "leading lady," Queen Elizabeth; that the "circle" is her Court, and the fools within it her courtiers. ♦ Hotson (1952, pp. 125 f.) : As C. M. Ingleby correctly pointed out, *Ducdame* or *Duc' da mè* is the Italian for "Duke by myself" or "Duke-without-a-dukedom." To this elucidation we may add the reminder that "Duke" (*Duc* and *Duco* in French and Italian) was a contemporary English name for the great horn-owl or eagle-owl. This *gran duc*, according to Cotgrave [1611, sig. 2 F₁], "is bigger then a Goose, and keepes alwayes in forrests and desert places." It looks very much as though Jaques . . . is . . . taunting the absent Duke Senior, the foolish "Duke-by-myself". . . . Jaques rubs in his satire further by explaining *Ducdame* as "a Greek (i.e., sly, crafty) invocation to call fools into a circle." And as a parting shot, he says he will "rail against all the first-born of Egypt." The *first-born* is of course the exiled "ass," Duke-Senior-without-a-dukedom, who has craftily charmed these grossly foolish friends of his into sharing the miserable gypsy (Egyptian) existence of his exile. ♦

19. **to me**] Steevens (ed. 1793) "improves" Shakespeare by emending this phrase to *to Ami*.

MUSIC

The original music for this song has not been discovered. Chappell (1840, I, 62) has suggested that the song called "The Countryman's Delight" in D'Urfey's *Pills to Purge Melancholy* "appears to be the original" and he gives (II, 33) a somewhat modified version of it. Chappell's only evidence for his assertion seems to have been that the last line of every stanza in the D'Urfey tune is "Under the greenwood tree." But "Greenwood Songs" were so common in the sixteenth and seventeenth centuries, and this refrain so commonplace in them, that his evidence is no evidence at all. Moreover, the words of Shakespeare's song do not fit the D'Urfey tune.

Gibbon (1930, p. 56) sets Shakespeare's words to a "Greenwood" tune from Playford's *The English Dancing Master* (1651), a tune which "may date back to Elizabeth's day." He says that Shakespeare's words "exactly fit this traditional tune" if l. 5 is repeated. Long (1955, p. 144) reprints Gibbon's setting, which has no value other than to provide an early tune for Shakespeare's song.

There is a setting composed by Arne around 1740, given by Caulfield (n.d., II, 133). While this includes only the words of the first stanza, there is no reason to suppose that Arne did not intend his music for the second stanza as well as the parody. All three stanzas match metrically and could be sung to the same tune. The first would be a solo by Amiens, the second would be sung in chorus (a stage direction preceding it reads, "All together here"), and the parody could be a solo either by Amiens or Jaques. Although it is possible that Jaques simply recited the words he composed, the typographical and textual evidence of the Folio version suggests that the editors regarded the parody as being sung, probably by Amiens.

DRAMATIC FUNCTION

The Arcadian existence of Duke Senior and his men in the forest of Arden, living "like the old Robin Hood of England" and fleeting time "carelessly as they did in

4 + v.s.

the golden world," had already been prefigured by Shakespeare as early as 1595 when he wrote *Two Gentlemen*. Late in that play (IV.i) Valentine and Speed join company with a group of gentlemen outlaws, and live with them in a forest near Milan. A second motif of *As You Like It*, the romance of young lovers in a forest, had also been treated earlier in *Midsummer Night's Dream*. To these two dimensions of setting and romance Shakespeare now added a third: an elaborate use of song. *As You Like It* is virtually a "musical comedy" and sets a precedent for its three great successors, *Twelfth Night*, *A Winter's Tale*, and *The Tempest*.

The remark by Noble (1923, p. 72) that the songs in this play have as their function the "conveying [of] colour of scene and sense of atmosphere" to make good the lack of scenery, accurately describes the uses to which "Under the greenwood tree" and its companion song two scenes later, "Blow, blow, thou winter wind," are put. It is also worth noting that these two songs bear a relationship to each other similar to that of the two epilogue songs in *Love's Labor's Lost*: in both plays the companion songs find value in the seasons' extremes.

21

TEXT: Folio (1623), sig. R₁ᵛ (II.vii.174–190).
TYPOGRAPHY: Indented verse, italic face; s.d., *Song*.

Blow, blow, thou winter winde,
Thou art not ſo vnkinde, as mans ingratitude
Thy tooth is not ſo keene, becauſe thou art not ſeene,
    although thy breath be rude.
Heigh ho, ſing heigh ho, vnto the greene holly,   5
Moſt frendſhip, is fayning; moſt Louing, meere folly:
    The heigh ho, the holly,
    This Life is moſt iolly.
Freize, freize, thou bitter skie that doſt not bight ſo nigh
    as benefitts forgot: 10
Though thou the waters warpe, thy ſting is not ſo ſharpe,
    as freind remembred not.
        Heigh ho, ſing, &c.

GENERAL COMMENTARY

Halliwell (ed. 1853–1865) : Songs of the holly were current long before the time of Shakespeare. It was the emblem of mirth. Thus a song in MS. Harl. 5396 of the fifteenth century, commences,—

> Holy and hys mery men they dawnsyn
>   and they syng;
> Ivy and hur maydenys they wepyn
>   and they wryng. ◆

Patterson (1916, p. 443) : Lyrics in praise of the holly, emblem of winter's festivities and Christmas revels, were unusually popular in England during the last centuries of the Middle Ages. Most often the celebration took the form of a contest between holly and ivy, in which "sorry ivy" came off the worse. ◆ [Examples of such holly-ivy songs can be found in Robbins (1952, pp. 45–47).]
Noble (1923, p. 73) : [This song] ... affords an opportunity for the Duke to be informed of Orlando's circumstances without the spectators being wearied by the repetition of that which is already familiar to them. The theme of the song is a variant of *Under the greenwood tree*, only its misanthropic vein is more pronounced. Winter, with all its harshness, is more tolerable than the ingratitude and insincerity of man. ◆ Long (1955, pp. 147 f.) : In this song we again find a statement of the principal theme of the play. It is also no coincidence that the song, with its comments on man's ingratitude, should be sung immediately after Orlando carries

Adam onto the stage, both having suffered extremely from man's ingratitude and feigned friendship. . . . The song may also have served to cover the removal of the banquet from the stage. . . . The lyric of the song, in its appropriateness, suggests that it was written especially for the play. The mixture of cynicism and jollity set forth by the lyric does not find a general expression in English song until it appears in the cavalier lyrics. ✦ Auden (1957, pp. 40 f.) : The Duke, confronted with someone who has suffered an injustice similar to his own, drops his pro-pastoral humbug, and admits that, for him, exile to the forest of Arden is a suffering. ¶ The song . . . is about suffering, but about the one kind of suffering which none of those present has had to endure, ingratitude from a friend. The behaviour of their brothers to the Duke and Orlando has been bad, but it cannot be called ingratitude, since neither Duke Frederick nor Oliver ever feigned friendship with them. ¶ The effect of the song upon them, therefore, is a cheering one. Life may be hard, Injustice may seem to triumph in the world, the future may be dark and uncertain, but personal loyalty and generosity exist and make such evils bearable.

TEXTUAL COMMENTARY

1. **Blow ... winde**] Halliwell (ed. 1853–1865) : Perhaps the remote original of this song may be found in one written about . . . 1300, preserved in MS. Harl. 2253 [fol. 72ᵛ; reprinted by C. Brown (1932, pp. 148–150)], and beginning,—

> Blow, northerne wynd,
> Sent thou me my suetyng;
> Blow, northern wynd.—Blou, blou, blou! ✦

2. **Thou ... vnkinde**] Malone (ed. 1790) : That is, thy action is not so contrary to thy *kind*, or to human nature, as the ingratitude of man. ✦

3. **Thy ... seene**] Warburton (ed. 1747) : This song is designed to suit the Duke's exiled condition, who had been ruined by *ungrateful flatterers*. Now the *winter wind*, the song says, is to be preferr'd to *man's ingratitude*. But why ? *Because it is not* SEEN. But this was not only an aggravation of the injury, as it was done in secret, *not seen*, but was the very circumstance that made the keeness of the ingratitude of his faithless courtiers. Without doubt, Shakespeare wrote the line thus,

Because thou art not SHEEN,

i.e., smiling, shining, like an ungrateful court-servant, who flatters while he wounds, which was a very good reason for giving the *winter wind* the preference. ✦ Johnson (ed. 1765) : I question whether the original line is not lost, and this substituted merely to fill up the measures and the rhyme. Yet even out of this line, by strong agitation, may sense be elicited, and sense not unsuitable to the occasion. *Thou winter wind*, says the Duke, *thy rudeness gives the less pain*, as thou art not seen, as thou art an enemy that dost not brave us with thy presence, and whose unkindness is therefore not aggravated by insult. ✦

6. **Most ... folly**] The line is based on two proverbial notions; see C. G. Smith (1963, Nos. 110, 126) and Tilley (1950, F–41, F–437). The word *meere* has the sense of complete, entire; see Abbott (1884, pp. 26 f.).

9. **that**] The relative pronoun after a noun used vocatively is normal usage in Shakespeare. See Abbott (1884, p. 178).

11. **warpe**] Hudson (ed. 1880–1881) : In the Poet's time the verb *warp* was sometimes used for *weave*,—a sense now retained only in the substantive. . . . In Hickes' *Thesaurus* is found a Saxon proverb, "Winter shall *warp water*." ♦ [Steevens (ed. 1793) first cited Hickes (1705, I, 221) in this connection, but the example does not apply. The "proverb" is from the Exeter Book "Maxims" (ed. Krapp, 1936, p. 159), and reads,

> winter sceal geweorpan. weder eft cuman.

"Geweorpan" is intransitive and does not govern "weder," and "weder" can hardly be translated as "water." The proverb means, "Winter must change, [warm] weather come again." Hudson continues :] And Propertius [*Elegies*, IV.iii.48] has a line containing the same figure: "Africus in glaciem frigore nectit aquas." ["The African (that is, southwest) wind knits the waters into ice with cold."] The appropriateness of the figure may be seen in the fine network appearance which water assumes in the first stages of crystallization.

MUSIC

The original music for the song is not known. The earliest recorded setting, by Arne about 1740, is printed in Caulfield (n.d., II, 138). Arne's setting for the song is incomplete since it does not include the refrain. Linley (1816, II, 8) has made up for this omission by composing music for the refrain and including it with Arne's setting. Long (1955, p. 149) has set the words to "Gathering Peascods" from Playford's *The English Dancing Master* (1651), as transcribed by Chappell ([1855–1859], I, 258), and composed a tune of his own for the refrain.

DRAMATIC FUNCTION

It has been frequently pointed out that the words of the song are a substantial repetition of the philosophy expressed by Duke Senior earlier in the play (II.i.3–11):

> Are not these woods
> More free from peril than the envious court?
> Here feel we but the penalty of Adam,
> The seasons' difference; as, the icy fang
> And churlish chiding of the winter's wind,
> Which, when it bites and blows upon my body
> Even till I shrink with cold, I smile, and say
> 'This is no flattery; these are counsellors
> That feelingly persuade me what I am.'

Of these lines Kittredge (ind. ed. 1939) remarks : The Duke means that he and his companions have returned to a state of nature; but not, of course, to a state of nature as it was before the fall of man. They suffer none of the penalties of civilization, but they are not exempted from the buffeting of the weather and the other pains to which mankind became subject on the expulsion from Eden. His point is that these natural results of the sin of Adam are much more endurable than the artificial dangers and annoyances of court life. ◆

Noble (1923, p. 76) calls attention to the "boisterous winter of Amiens' songs" which later gives way to "the bright and cheery Spring" of "It was a lover and his lass." There is no question of a literal transition from winter to spring in this play, such as occurs, for example, in *A Winter's Tale*, since all the natural imagery in *As You Like It* implies that the forest of Arden is in the full bloom of a temperate season throughout the action. The winter mentioned in the refrain of "Under the greenwood tree" and throughout this song is a remembered winter, and has a double symbolic function. It represents, on the one hand, all the evils that blight man's world, and particularly the moral or social evils of civilization. Spring, correspondingly, symbolizes what is good in man's world, the pure joy of living and, particularly, the social virtues. Thus a winter of hardship, fraud, and ingratitude gives way in the course of the play to a spring of love, repentance, and reconciliation. At the same time the winter-spring symbolism reminds the audience that there is another, more real world outside the forest of Arden, a world from which the Duke and his followers are only temporarily aliens. An Arcadian spring must also yield in turn to a winter of practical life.

Noble is undoubtedly correct in seeing as the technical function of the song the avoidance of needless repetition of Orlando's circumstances, matter already known to the audience.

22

TEXT: Folio (1623), sig. R₅ᵛ (IV.ii.10–19).
TYPOGRAPHY: Indented verse, italic face; s.d., *Muſicke, Song.*

What ſhall he haue that kild the Deare?
His Leather skin, and hornes to weare:
Then ſing him home, the reſt ſhall beare this burthen;
Take thou no ſcorne to weare the horne,
It was a creſt ere thou waſt borne,   5
Thy fathers father wore it,
And thy father bore it,
The horne, the horne, the luſty horne,
Is not a thing to laugh to ſcorne.

GENERAL COMMENTARY

Malone (ed. 1790) : Shakespeare seems to have formed this song on a hint afforded by the novel which furnished him with the plot of his play [Lodge's *Rosalynde. Euphues golden legacie*, 1590, sig. H₃ᵛ]:

What newes Forrester? hast thou wounded some deere, and lost him in the fall? Care not man for so small a losse, thy fees was but the skinne, the shoulder, and the hornes: tis hunters lucke to ayme faire and misse: and a woodmans fortune to strike and yet goe without the game. ◆

Noble (1923, pp. 74 f.) : [The scene in which this song occurs] is evidently intended to cover up the break of two hours agreed upon in the previous scene [IV.i.181] between Rosalind and Orlando—a device rendered superfluous by the modern drop curtain. I can see no sound reason why scenes 1 to 3 should not proceed as one uninterrupted scene. . . . If [this play] were more generally regarded as a pictorial representation of sylvan life in its various phases, then the idea of making this hunting party a connecting link between two incidents would be better appreciated. ◆ New Cambridge (ind. ed. 1926) : This short scene is full of difficulty for an editor. First of all, what exactly is supposed to be happening? It is clear, we think, that Jaques has just encountered a party of lords returning from a deer-hunt, ending in a kill. They are elated with their success, and Jaques, delighting as ever to foster human folly, eggs them on. . . . There shall be a procession in which the deer-slayer shall be borne in triumph . . . to the Duke's presence: it will be fitting also that he wear the deer's horns and skin, as the insignia of victory. In all this, we do not doubt, Shakespeare had in mind folk-customs connected with the hunt and going back to the days of pre-Christian sacrifice which are now lost in oblivion. ◆ [The New Cambridge editors' conjecture is supported by E. K. Chambers (1903,

I, 166) who traces the custom back to primitive times : Naturally the worshippers at a festival would dance in their festival costume; that is to say, in the garb of leaves and flowers worn for the sake of the beneficent influence of the indwelling divinity, or in the hides and horns of sacrificial animals which served a similar purpose. . . . A good example of the beast-dance is furnished by the "horn-dance" at Abbots Bromley in Staffordshire. . . . In this six of the performers wear sets of horns. These are preserved from year to year in the church, and according to local tradition the dance used at one time to take place in the churchyard on a Sunday. [Chambers also notes (I, 258) how extensive such customs were among primitive peoples:] In Italy, in Gaul, in southern Germany, apparently also in Spain and in England, men decked themselves for riot in the heads and skins of cattle and the beasts of the chase, blackened themselves or bedaubed themselves with filth, or wore masks fit to terrify the demons themselves. ◆ New Cambridge continues :] . . . Moreover, if we may judge from the horned Falstaff in *M.W.W.* [V.v] and the hunting scene in Munday's *Death of Robert, Earl of Huntington* [1601, sig. B₂ᵛ] which introduces 'Frier *Tuck* carrying a Stags head, dauncing', stags' heads were for some reason popular on the stage at this time. In any event it is obvious that the decking of the victor in the victim's horns and hide, the hoisting of him upon the shoulders of his fellows and the bearing him 'home' to the Duke with boisterous song and triumph formed the staple of this scene, in which action is far more important than dialogue, and which with its riotous character and traditional appeal would be very popular with an Elizabethan audience.

TEXTUAL COMMENTARY

1–2. **What . . . weare**] That some sort of hunting custom is referred to here, having to do with apportioning parts of the kill, seems beyond question. There is a similar reference in Robert Greene's *Mamillia* (1583, sig. H₄), "Shall euery man get his fee of the Deare, and I get nothing but the hornes?" Frankis (1958, pp. 65–68) gives additional evidence of the existence of the custom in citing a number of poetic texts where dying deer make last testaments disposing of parts of their bodies to the hunters who brought them down. He calls attention especially to "The testament of the bucke" in MS. Rawlinson C. 813 (ed. Padelford, 1908, pp. 350–352). In Shakespeare he cites the remark of Falstaff in *Merry Wives* (V.v.27–30):

> Divide me like a brib'd buck, each a haunch. I will keep my sides to myself, my shoulders for the fellow of this walk, and my horns I bequeath your husbands.

And the remark of Jaques quoted by a lord in *As You Like It* (II.i.47 f.),

> "Poor deer," quoth he, "thou mak'st a testament
> As worldlings do. . . ."

He remarks that Shakespeare seems to make use of this "testament of the deer" theme in the Foresters' Song.

3. **Then . . . burthen**] Editors from the eighteenth century to the present time have been completely unable to agree about this line. The textual problem involved was set up by Theobald (ed. 1740) : This is no admirable Instance of the Sagacity of

our preceding Editors, to say Nothing worse. One should expect, when they were
Poets [Rowe, and especially Pope who had made Theobald the "hero" of the
Dunciad in 1728], they would at least have taken care of the *Rhymes*, and not foisted
in what has Nothing to answer it. Now, where is the Rhyme to, *the rest shall bear
this Burthen*? Or, to ask another Question, where is the Sense of it? Does the Poet
mean, that He, that kill'd the Deer, shall be sung home, and the Rest shall bear
the Deer on their Backs? This is laying a Burthen on the Poet, that We must help
him to throw off. In short, the Mystery of the Whole is, that a Marginal Note is
wisely thrust into the Text: the Song being design'd to be sung by a single Voice,
and the Stanza's to close with a Burthen to be sung by the whole Company. ◆
[Since Theobald's irascible note in 1740 the modern editors have coped with this
difficult line as follows. Following Theobald, Warburton (ed. 1747), Johnson
(ed. 1765), and Hanmer (ed. 1770–1771), have edited the text,

> *Then sing him home;—take thou no scorn*
> *To wear the horn, the horn, the horn*

with *the reſt . . . burthen* as a stage direction opposite ll. 4–6.
 Capell (ed. [1767–1768]) prints *Then . . . home* in black-letter, and discards *the
reſt . . . burthen* completely.
 Malone (ed. 1790), Steevens (ed. 1793), Reed (ed. 1813), and Boswell (Variorum,
ed. 1821), have,

> *Then sing him home:*
> *Take thou no scorn to wear the horn*

with *the reſt . . . burthen* as a stage direction opposite ll. 4 and 5.
 Dyce (ed. 1875–1876) and Collier (ed. 1878) regard l. 3 as a stage direction for
ll. 4–9, but White (ed. 1883) assigns it only to ll. 4–5.
 Oxford (ed. [1892]), Arden (ind. ed. 1920), Kittredge (ed. 1936), and Neilson
(ed. 1942) retain the first half of l. 3 as part of the song, and make *the reſt . . .
burthen* a stage direction for ll. 4–9.]
 Variorum (ed. 1821) notes that l. 3 is omitted from Hilton's musical setting of the
song, and concludes that the line must have been "spoken by one of the persons as
a direction to the rest to commence the chorus." But Halliwell (ed. 1853–1865) cites
Knight as observing that Hilton's song is a round which required a single couplet
for each of the four voices. The New Cambridge editors (ind. ed. 1926) preserve the
folio text, but ingeniously rearrange the third line:

> What shall he have that killed the deer?
> His leather skin and horns to wear.
> Then sing him home—the rest shall bear
> This burthen.

They maintain that ll. 4–9 are "this burthen" to be taken up by the chorus. Noble
(1930, "A Song," p. 478) disputes their view at some length, arguing that the song
is a solo except for the words "Then sing him home," which are rendered in
chorus. He bases his argument for the most part on the technical meaning of the
word "burthen," pointing out that the word is not a synonym for "chorus."

4*

J. D. Wilson (1930, p. 514) defends the arrangement of the song in the New
Cambridge text on the grounds that it carefully preserves the Folio version.
Brennecke (1952, pp. 347–351) proposes that *the reſt . . . burthen* is an interpolated
stage direction, and that "Then sing him home" is an interjected line of dialogue,
meant to be spoken. The arrangement he suggests is as follows : A forester would
sing out the first couplet of the lyric. Another would interrupt by crying out
"Then sing him home!", which would mean two things. First, "Let our chorus
carry the singer to the completion of the song"; second, "Let us carry this hunter
into the presence of the Duke." Such double meaning is by no means uncharacter-
istic Shakespearean technique. Following the direction, "The rest shall bear this
burthen," lines 4 and 5 would then be sung by a chorus of foresters, introducing
the "horn" jest; and the next two lines by a forester alone; the concluding couplet
by the chorus, emphasizing the horn once more (and possibly with a repeat as the
procession moves off the stage). ◆ Seng (1959, pp. 248 f.) : It seems highly unlikely
that the third line belongs with the song, but there is no reason why the entire line
cannot be regarded as an interjected line of dialogue. There is strong internal
evidence in the play itself for such an interpretation. . . . ¶ Jaques, always ready for
a bitter joke, meets a party of foresters returning from a successful hunt. "Which,"
he asks, "is he that killed the deer ?" When the successful hunter identifies himself,
Jaques suggests that the deerslayer be borne back to the Duke in triumph on the
shoulders of his fellows. But there is an ironic edge to the honors that Jaques is so
eager to confer: the horns of the deer are to be placed on the head of the hunter
"for a branch of victory". The "branch", of course, is the age-old symbol of the
cuckold. The jest would never escape an Elizabethan audience, and it does not
escape the assembled foresters. "Have you no song, Forester, for this purpose ?"
asks Jaques. Yes, there is a song. A forester sings out the first couplet, then Jaques,
spreading over the whole group the jest he had started, cries out to the foresters:
"Then sing him home, the rest shall beare this burthen", thus serving the purposes
of the episode, the play, and the playwright perfectly by planting horns on the
heads of everyone present. ¶ Musically speaking, "this burthen" which the rest
shall bear may be the lines of the song which follow; but in the double meaning . . .
it is the horns themselves, man's inheritance by gift of nature and a fallible wife. ◆
[The *double entendre* seems to have been a traditional feature of "forester" poems.
Stevens (1961, p. 222) remarks: "Among the balets of Henry VIII's MS." (B. M.
Add. MS. 31,922) "are . . . some 'forester' poems. They belong, apparently, to the
same world as the rest of the courtly poems of the manuscript. But their tone is
hardly up to drawing-room expectations. The erotic undercurrent can hardly be
missed." He reprints two of these poems (pp. 400 f., 408 f.), and adds in a note that
"Forester-songs with an erotic double-meaning are a feature also of German
literature of this period."]

   3. **burthen**] According to Chappell ([1855–1859], I, 222 f.), "The burden of a song,
in the old acceptation of the word, was the base, foot, or under-song. It was sung
throughout and not merely at the end of a verse." But the word appears also to
have been used very loosely to refer to a chorus or a refrain. The pun which exists
here is not unique. *Burthen* is almost the exclusive spelling in the Folio for either
sense of the term, and Shakespeare makes the same pun in *Two Gentlemen* (I.ii.85)
and in *Taming of the Shrew* (I.ii.68). There is a striking parallel to the lines in Shake-

speare's song in John Trussell's *The First Rape of Faire Hellen* (ed. Shaaber, 1957, p. 439):

> Diuers there are vnknowne, that in like case,
>   doe beare the burthen of a Cuckold skorne:
> Yet if that none do them in words disgrace,
>   they neuer feare the wearing of the horne.

The word *burthen* here has obviously only the sense of *onus*.

4. **weare the horne**] Be a cuckold. No scholar has yet answered the problem raised by Coleridge in his comment on this song (ed. Raysor, 1930, I, 105) : I question whether there exists a parallel instance of a phrase that, like this of 'horns', for cuckoldism, is universal in all languages, yet for which no one has yet discovered even a plausible origin. ♦ [Brand (1900, pp. 407–422) collects pages of curious information, folklore, and conjecture on the subject, but arrives at no decision as to the origins of the notion. A modern and brief account of the most plausible theories is to be found in Lucas (1927, IV, 205–207)].

5. **It . . . crest**] Kittredge (ind. ed. 1939) : Cf. Valerio's oration on the horn at the end of Chapman's *Al Fooles* [1605; ed. Parrott, 1910–1914, II, 160] . . . especially "What worthier Crest can you beare then the Horne?" ♦

9. **laugh to scorne**] Ultimately a biblical expression. See Nehemiah 2:19 and Matthew 9:24.

MUSIC

The earliest known music for this song is a round for four voices published in John Hilton's *Catch that Catch can, or A Choice Collection of Catches, Rovnds, & Canons for 3 or 4 Voyces*, 1652. This music was reprinted by John Playford as a round for three voices in *Catch that Catch can: Or the Musical Companion* (1667, sig. H₂ᵛ ; sig. F₄ᵛ). The British Museum's copy of Hilton's 1652 book—press mark C.40.m.9(3) —has seriously deteriorated and only a few fragments remain, but the melody in the Playford songbooks is the same.

A facsimile of Hilton's round from Playford's 1673 edition is to be found in Elson (1901, p. 224). The most reliable modern edition is in Metcalfe (n.d., p. 19). Gibbon (1930, p. 111) takes his version from Metcalfe, and Long (1955, p. 151) reprints Gibbon with a few changes. The arrangements given by Kimmins (1928, pp. 60 f.) and Kines (1964, p. 48) are without scholarly merit.

If the music published by Hilton in 1652 is the original melody of the song, it is certainly not his own composition; he was born in 1599, the year in which the play probably was first produced (E. K. Chambers, 1930, I, 270, 402 f.). But as his 1652 songbook records in its title, the catches, rounds, and canons included were "Collected and Published" by him, and were not necessarily his own compositions. They may have been, in part, the work of the earlier John Hilton who contributed a madrigal to *The Triumphes of Oriana* (1601, sig. B₃ᵛ). The omission of the third line in the later Hilton's setting or arrangement of the tune does not prove that it was not the original music. As Halliwell, following Knight, noted in 1856, a round for four voices required such a change. It seems likely that the Hilton round may preserve the original melody of the foresters' song.

DRAMATIC FUNCTION

As Shakespeare had earlier in the play paraphrased "Blow, blow thou winter wind" in a speech put into the mouth of Duke Senior (II.i.3–11), so also he put into Touchstone's mouth a prose paraphrase of the cynical wisdom of the foresters' song (III.iii.49–58):

> Here we have no temple but the wood, no assembly but horn-beasts. But what though? Courage! As horns are odious, they are necessary. It is said, "Many a man knows no end of his goods." Right! Many a man has good horns and knows no end of them. Well, that is the dowry of his wife; 'tis none of his own getting. Horns? Even so. Poor men alone? No, no! the noblest deer hath them as huge as the rascal.

What the song and Touchstone's speech both convey is that the cuckold need take no scorn for his embarrassing situation. Cuckoldry is the world's second oldest profession. Horns are a familial crest that goes back to antiquity. Father and grandfather were "horn mad" in their time, and the rest of mankind, should they now dare to laugh the cuckold to scorn, shall in their own time "bear this burthen."

The same playful cynicism that runs through the two earlier songs in the play makes itself felt also in this one. The song of the foresters seems to imply that the world of men is a practical, not an Arcadian, world, and that life finds out its own moral limits. The foresters, like Touchstone, are philosophical about the perils that lie in wait for married men. But is there any other refuge than philosophy? That horns bring with them a certain amount of odium no one will deny; but they are "necessary," that is to say, inevitable.

What the song seems to show is that the Arcadian detachment of the courtier-huntsmen has given them a tolerant perspective on their former lives. They have been given an insight into human failings that might have made them misanthropists, like Jaques, but instead they have come to an awareness of human fallibility, and that awareness is softened and mellowed by an abounding sense of good humor.

23

TEXT: Folio (1623), sig. S₁ (V.iii.17–34).
TYPOGRAPHY: Indented verse, italic and roman face; s.d., *Song*.

It was a Louer, and his laſſe,
  With a hey, and a ho, and a hey nonino,
That o're the greene corne feild did paſſe,
  In the ſpring time, the onely pretty rang time.
When Birds do ſing, hey ding a ding, ding.   5
Sweet Louers loue the ſpring,
And therefore take the preſent time,
With a hey, & a ho, and a hey nonino,
For loue is crowned with the prime.
  In ſpring time, &c.   10

Betweene the acres of the Rie,
With a hey, and a ho, & a hey nonino:
Theſe prettie Country folks would lie.
  In ſpring time, &c.

This Carroll they began that houre,   15
With a hey and a ho, & a hey nonino:
How that a life was but a Flower,
  In ſpring time, &c.

GENERAL COMMENTARY

Herford (ed. 1899) : This song seems to have become immediately popular. It was embodied within a few months, at latest, of the appearance of the play in Thomas Morley's *First Booke of Ayres* (1600). It is doubtless Shakespeare's own, being apparently suggested, however, by the song sung by Lodge's Corydon [*Rosalynde. Euphues golden legacie*, 1590, sigs. R₄ᵛ–S₁] at the wedding feast—a less dainty but not unskillful handling of the same motive. Here is . . . the first stanza:

  A blyth and bonny country lasse,
    heigh ho the bonny lasse
  Sate weeping on the tender grasse,
    and weeping said, will none come woo me ?
  A smicker boy, a lyther swaine,
  That in his love was wanton faine,
    with smiling looks came straight unto her. ◆

Noble (1923, p. 76) **:** The scene, wherein the song is contained, was evidently added—it has no bearing whatever on the development of the action, unless we assume that it was designed that, by means of the song, lapse of time should be indicated, that the season had now changed from the boisterous Winter of Amiens' songs to the bright and cheery Spring of the Pages'. It is, however, more probable that the episode was especially devised to meet the growing taste for song and possibly to counter the attractions of the Children at Blackfriars, where there were the best trained choristers the metropolis possessed . . . yet it is no less clear that Shakespeare did not allow the feature to go to waste, but caused it to serve the same dramatic end, as did the other songs in the comedy, namely to act as scenery. ✦ [Noble (1933, p. 24) takes an even severer view of this song contending that the song was put into the play after the publication of Morley's *First Booke of Ayres* in 1600. He remarks **:** The whole scene in which the song occurs appears to have been specially devised. It has nothing to do with the evolution of the action; it is a waste of time and is a diversion and nothing more. ✦] Long (1955, pp. 152 f.) follows Herford in comparing this song to the one in Lodge's *Rosalynde* **:** The styles of the two songs are similar, but Shakespeare places his song before the wedding and introduces a hymeneal song in the courtly masque tradition after the weddings have been performed. We may also judge that [Shakespeare's song] had a comparatively elaborate musical setting, since two pages (probably skilled singing boys) are introduced for the purpose of singing it. Thus, while Lodge ends his story by shifting from the euphuistic songs to a traditional song style, Shakespeare, at the same point in the story, shifts from the rustic, as represented by the earlier songs in the play, to the more ornate and "artificial" songs which conclude the play. Our imaginations are removed from the fairy-tale existence led by the Duke and his party . . . to a setting more akin to the life actually led by gentlefolk in Elizabeth's England. ✦ [The original setting was probably Morley's (see Music, below) and does not seem especially "elaborate." Moreover, it is as difficult to see "artificiality" in this song as it is to see "rusticity" in the three earlier songs in the play.] Sternfeld (1963, p. 56) **:** The two singing boys . . . gloat over their professional status: they deliberately poke fun at the courteous disclaimers prescribed by Castiglione and Elyot and proceed to give the song:

> Shall we clap into it roundly, without hawking or spitting or saying we are hoarse, which are the only prologues to a bad voice ? ✦

[But see rebuttal to his commentary on song 20, above.]

2. **With . . . nonino**] A nonsense refrain, a variation on the "Hey nonny nonny" refrain, or burden, common in songs of the time. B. M. Addit. MS. 31,922 (fol. 36) has a short lyric of four lines made up solely of variations on this phrase. It is reprinted by Flügel (1889–1903, XII, 236).

3. **corne feild**] Wheat field.

4. **the onely . . . time**] The obvious printing error is variously emended by the modern editors. Pope-Hanmer have *the pretty ſpring time*; Malone-Variorum change *rang* to *rank*; Cambridge-Neilson give what is now the accepted reading, changing *rang* to *ring*.

7–10. **And therefore . . . time, &c.**] Johnson (ed. 1765) was the first editor to move these lines to the end of the song. Fellowes (1933, p. 9) explains the Folio error as follows : The position in the Folio of what is numbered as the fourth verse in Morley's version can be readily explained by the suggestion that only two verses were sung in the Play. To have sung all four with their repetitions would have unduly delayed the action. And if two verses only were to be sung, the last would best follow the first. ◆

9. **prime**] Spring; see *Two Gentlemen* (I.i.47–49).

11. **Betweene . . . Rie**] Lee (ed. [1910–1914]) : The reference seems to be to balks or banks of unploughed turf which, in the common-field system of agriculture prevailing in Elizabethan England, divided the acre strips of land from one another. ◆

15. **Carroll**] The word originally meant a ring dance with a song; but see commentary on songs 11–12, above.

How . . . flower] See Psalm 103:15: "As for man, his days are as grass: as a flower of the field, so he flourisheth."

MUSIC

What is probably the original music for this song is contained in Thomas Morley's *The First Booke of Ayres. Or Little Short Songs, to Sing and Play to the Lvte*, 1600 (sigs. B$_4$v–C$_1$), an imperfect unique copy in the Folger Shakespeare Library. There is a 1639 manuscript version with slight differences in the words in the National Library of Scotland Adv. MS. 5.2.14, fol. 18. The music in both versions is substantially the same, and there are only minor differences among the words in the *First Booke of Ayres*, the manuscript, and the Shakespearean text.

Brennecke (1939, pp. 139–146) reviews the existing evidence about the relationship between the words and music of this song, and the possible acquaintance of Shakespeare and Morley with each other, and concludes that the song was a collaborative effort on the part of the two men. He suggests that the finished song, words by Shakespeare and music by Morley, was almost simultaneously offered to the public through performance in Shakespeare's new play and publication in Morley's new book. Moore (1939, pp. 149–151) argues against Brennecke's theory of collaboration, quoting Fellowes' opinion that the words of the song are probably older than either Shakespeare or Morley, and that Morley composed music for them to make a song which was later adopted by Shakespeare—or someone else— for use in *As You Like It*. Fellowes is further quoted as believing that the text in the Folio is a corruption of the text in Morley's book. For a fuller discussion of the putative Shakespeare–Morley relationship see Shakespeare and Morley, song 25, below.

Facsimiles of the song in Morley's book are given by SQ (1951, II, 280) and by Long (1955, p. 154). There is a facsimile of the Adv. MS. version in Halliwell (ed. 1853–1865, VI, 249). A scholarly modern edition of the printed song is given by Dart (1958, pp. 26–28, 29–31). Fellowes' edition (1932, pp. 26–31) is also based on the 1600 printed copy; he gives an exact transcription of the vocal part and the lute accompaniment (plus a copy of the lute tablature), but omits the bass viol part. He also provides a concert arrangement of the song. In addition, there are a number of popular editions of the tune, usually in modern arrangements: Wooldridge

(1893; reprinted 1961, I, 114 f.), Bridge (n.d., pp. 7–16), E. Edwards (1903, No. 2), Vincent (1906, p. 24), Naylor ([1912], pp. 48–50), Potter (1915, pp. 16 f.), Kimmins (1928, pp. 54 f.), Hardy (1909, pp. 99–101; 1930, p. 33), Gibbon (1930, p. 112), Bontoux (1936, p. 313), Greenberg (1956, pp. 204–206), H. A. Chambers (1957, pp. 16 f.), and Kines (1964, pp. 46 f.).

There has apparently never been a scholarly transcription of the 1639 manuscript version, but the copies by Chappell ([1855–1859], I, 205) and Elson (1901, pp. 192 f.) are supposedly based on this version.

DRAMATIC FUNCTION

Noble is probably right in seeing this song as without a mechanical function in the play. As far as plot, action, and characters are concerned, the song is completely extraneous. But this lack of a technical dramatic function does not prevent it from being the loveliest of Shakespeare's songs. The nearest equivalent to it in his plays is the "language of flowers" scene (IV.iv) in *Winter's Tale* and as a lyrical canticle to the joys of spring and young love it is matched, if at all, only by Thomas Nashe's "Spring, the sweete spring" in *Summers last will and Testament* (1600, sigs. B₃–B₃ᵛ; ed. McKerrow, 1910, III, 238 f.).

If the song lacks function on the levels of plot development and dramatic situation, it transcends those mechanic uses to serve the play on the higher level of poetry. All the songs in *As You Like It* are intimately related to the moral atmosphere of the scenes in which they occur. There is a pattern of development running through the songs which parallels the pattern of developing moral action in the play as a whole.

The play opens with two crimes against justice: Duke Frederick, having usurped the rule, banishes his brother, the rightful Duke Senior. Oliver, having oppressed his brother, Orlando, deprives him of his inheritance and even seeks to take his life. The victims of this double tyranny take refuge in the forest of Arden, and both are embittered by the treatment they have received. That bitterness is reflected in the misanthropic attitudes of the first three songs in the play. Yet apparently as time passes in the forest the memory of their wrongs is effaced by the detached joys of an Arcadian existence. Far from the haunts of men they

> Find tongues in trees, books in the running brooks,
> Sermons in stones, and good in everything.

The "catastrophe" of this comedy is the four nuptials which bring it to a close; but more important than the denouement of the plot is the resolution of the play in which the wrongdoers repent and are forgiven by those whom they have wronged. The play turns not on crime and punishment, but on crime, forgiveness, and absolution. It is this resolution—the repenting, forgiving, absolving—that "It was a lover and his lass" heralds. The pages' song is intended to announce rebirth and spring in the moral order of this play's little universe.

24

TEXT: Folio (1623), sig. S₁ᵛ (V.iv.147–152).
TYPOGRAPHY: Indented verse, italic face; s.d., *Song*.

Wedding is great Iunos crowne,
O bleſſed bond of boord and bed:
'Tis Hymen peoples euerie towne,
High wedlock then be honored:
  Honor, high honor and renowne
  To Hymen, God of euerie Towne.

GENERAL COMMENTARY

Capell ([1779–1783 ?], I, part 1, p. 69) **:** The following masque-like eclarcissement, which is wholly of the Poet's invention, may pass for another small mark of the time of this play's writing; for precisely in those years . . . the foolery of masques was predominant; and the torrent of fashion bore down Shakespeare, in this play and *The Tempest*, and a little in *Timon* and *Cymbeline*. ◆ New Variorum (ind. ed. 1890) cites White and then Rolfe **:** "Both the thought and the form of the thought in this 'Song' seem to me as unlike Shakespeare's as they could well be, and no less unworthy of his genius. . . . I think it is not improbable that the whole of Hymen's part is from another pen than his." [And Rolfe writes,] "We are inclined to agree with White; and it may be noted also that lines 127–149 [that is, the entire masque episode] make an awkward break in the dialogue, which would run along very naturally without them." ◆ Moore (1916, p. 87) **:** A surprisingly large number of the songs [in Shakespeare's plays] serve for what might be called pagan ritual, a fact which is especially conspicuous because Christian ritual is absent. . . . No doubt it is due, in part, to the taste of the masque-loving age, and . . . to the passion which King James and his queen entertained for musical pageantry. ◆ Kittredge (ed. 1936) **:** The speeches of Hymen and the nuptial song . . . have often been regarded as un-Shakespearean—that is, as not good enough for Shakespeare, and therefore, in all probability, an insertion by some dramatic journeyman. But Hymen is no interloper. An actual marriage could not be brought upon the stage; some kind of symbolism was needed; Hymen makes an appropriate master of ceremonies, and his speeches are every bit as good as they need be. In real life, no one expects formalities to soar. ◆ Long (1955, p. 160) **:** The dramatic functions performed by the "Still Musicke" and the wedlock hymn are several. To begin with, this portion of the scene is a wedding ceremony to which the music lends solemnity. Furthermore, the wedding is graced by the presence of a god whose deity is marked by the music accompanying his entrance upon the stage. The song, in addition to its ritualistic use, serves the more prosaic purpose of dramatic economy, for it replaces what would have been a difficult explanation for Hymen's presence in the play.

TEXTUAL COMMENTARY

1. **Wedding . . . crowne**] By her marriage to Jupiter, Juno became queen of the Olympian deities. She was primarily the goddess of women, and in the old Roman religion her festival, the *Matronalia*, was kept on March 1. She is frequently associated with Hymen in connection with marriage festivities. Cf. Ovid, *Metamorphoses* (ed. Miller, 1951, I, 601 ff., VI, 428).

3. **'Tis . . . towne**] Steevens (ed. 1793) cites Johnson's comparison with some lines from Catullus (ed. Cornish, 1912, pp. 72 f.) :

> quae tuis careat sacris
> non queat dare praesides
> terra finibus: at queat
> te volente. ✦

["The land which would lack your [Hymen's] rites would not be able to provide protectors for its borders, but would, if you were willing."]

3. **Hymen**] Or Hymenaeus, was the god of marriage and his appearance and favor at a wedding were supposed to insure happy marriage. Cf. Ovid, *Metamorphoses* (ed. Miller, 1951, IV, 758 f., VI, 428 f.).

MUSIC

The original music for the song is not known. The earliest known music for these words was composed around 1740 by Thomas Chilcot, and is included in his *Twelve English Songs* ([1750 ?], p. 31).

DRAMATIC FUNCTION

However excrescent this masque episode may seem to modern taste, there is strong textual evidence that it is authentically Shakespearean. Hymen's first speech (V.iv.114–118),

> Then there is mirth in heaven
> When earthly things made even
>   Atone together.
> Good Duke, receive thy daughter;
> Hymen from heaven brought her,

echoes Rosalind's own speech (lines 18–25) earlier in this scene:

I have promis'd to make all this matter even.
Keep your word, O Duke, to give your daughter;
Keep yours, Orlando, to receive his daughter;
Keep your word, Phebe, that you'll marry me,
Or else, refusing me, to wed this shepherd;
Keep your word, Silvius, that you'll marry her
If she refuse me; and from hence I go,
To make these doubts all even.

Hymen's second speech (ll. 137–142) stylistically parallels these admonitions of Rosalind. The classical deities referred to in this scene are frequently mentioned elsewhere in Shakespeare. Hymen six times, Juno eighteen times. All in all, the masque was probably good theater, and a colorful way of binding up four marriage knots.

Some editors have regarded Hymen's first speech as a song, and it has, in fact, been set to music by both Arne and Bishop (see *A List*, 1884, p. 8). But this is clearly a mistaken notion, for the Folio text is a good one and all the songs are plainly marked. The stage direction heading this first speech reads,

Enter Hymen, Rofalind, and Celia.
Still Muficke.

What is called for is quiet music playing in the background as Hymen speaks. It is also possible, if Hymen descended by machine from above, that the music was used to cover the noise of the mechanism. That his first speech is printed in italics is of no moment, since most of the other verses in the play are also.

Twelfth Night

25

TEXT: Folio (1623), sig. Y₅ (II.iii.40–45, 48–53).
TYPOGRAPHY: Indented verse, italic face; s.d., *Clowne ſings*.

O Miſtris mine where are you roming?
O ſtay and heare, your true loues coming,
That can ſing both high and low.
Trip no further prettie ſweeting.
Iourneys end in louers meeting,   5
Euery wiſe mans ſonne doth know.

   .   .   .

What is loue, tis not heereafter,
Preſent mirth, hath preſent laughter:
What's to come, is ſtill vnſure.
In delay there lies no plentie,   10
Then come kiſſe me ſweet and twentie:
Youths a ſtuffe will not endure.

GENERAL COMMENTARY

Capell ([1779–1783?], II, part 4, p. 145) **:** The Clown's "*Song*" should be a new composition, and not borrow'd as are the scraps that come after it; but excepting that it breaths better sense than those old ballads, it has all the cast of them, and is doubtless an imitation. ♦ Moore (1916, p. 85) **:** [This song] serves for characterization more than for convivial humor. There is something pathetically human about the gross old knight and his withered dupe, sitting in the drunken gravity of midnight to hear the clown sing of the fresh love of youth.... ♦ Noble (1923, p. 82) **:** The song serves as a prelude to a 'good evening', the kind of diversion formerly known to undergraduates as a 'binge'. The song leads to a catch, and from that to snatches of ballads, and generally to so noisy and riotous a time that Malvolio is constrained to intervene, and the resentment bred by this interference ... gives birth to the conspiracy against him. The most captious critic cannot cavil at the skill with which the whole scene is contrived—the episode is a development of the song. ♦ Long (1955, p. 168) : In marked contrast to the music which pleases the melancholy Duke [I.i.1–7], the next episode . . . presents a gay love song, a catch, and snatches of other convivial songs. . . . Such a rousing portrayal of "the good life" must needs have included songs. . . . The increasing noisiness of the party is marked by the types of songs mangled by the tipplers. ♦ Auden (1957, pp. 41 f.) : Taken by themselves, the songs in this play are among the most beautiful Shakespeare wrote. . . . But in the contexts in which Shakespeare places them, they sound shocking. . . . ¶ True love certainly does not plead its cause by telling the beloved that love is transitory; and no young man, trying to seduce a girl, would mention her age. He takes her youth and his own for granted. Taken seriously, these lines are the voice of elderly lust, afraid of its own death. Shakespeare forces this awareness on our consciousness by making the audience to the song a couple of seedy old drunks. ♦ Hollander (1959, pp. 232 f.) : When Toby and Andrew cry out for a love song, Feste obliges them, not with the raucous and bawdy thing that one would expect, but instead, with a direct appeal to their actual hostess, Olivia. This is all the more remarkable in that it is made on behalf of everyone in the play. "O Mistress Mine" undercuts the Duke's overwhelming but ineffectual mouthings, Viola's effective but necessarily misdirected charming, and, of course, Aguecheek's absolute incompetence as a suitor. The argument is couched in purely naturalistic terms: "This feast will have to end, and so will all of our lives. You are not getting younger ('sweet and twenty' is the contemporaneous equivalent of 'sweet and thirty', at least). Give up this inconstant roaming; your little game had better end in your marriage, anyway." The true love "That can sing both high and low" is Viola-Sebastian, the master-mistress of Orsino's and Olivia's passion.

TEXTUAL COMMENTARY

7–12. **What . . . endure**] Noble (1923, p. 81) : That the song . . . is by Shakespeare cannot reasonably be doubted, for not only is its style Shakespearean, but also the suggestion of proverb, contained in the second stanza, is characteristic of his authorship. In that stanza, with its succinct insistence on present joys and the uncertainty of those deferred, together with the twofold meaning of 'Youth's a stuff will not endure', is outlined the very spirit of the comedy, and altogether the stanza is too apt to have been written otherwise than expressly for the play. ♦

9. **still**] Constantly, always. See Abbott (1884, p. 51).

10. **In . . . plentie**] Warburton (ed. 1747) : This is a proverbial saying corrupted; and should read thus,

In DECAY *there lies no plenty.*

A reproof of avarice, which stores up perishable fruits till they *decay*. To these fruits the Poet, humorously, compares youth or virginity; which, he says, is a *stuff will not endure*. ♦ Steevens (ed. 1793) : No man will ever be worth much, who delays the advantages offered by the present hour, in hopes that the future will offer more. So in . . . Richard III [IV.iii.53]: "Delay leads impotent and snail-pac'd beggary." ◆ [The line is probably related to the proverb "Delay in love is dangerous"; see Tilley (1950, D-196).]

11. **sweet and twentie**] Capell ([1779–1783 ?], II, part 4, p. 145) **:** Then give me a kiss, sweet, give me twenty kisses. ◆ Halliwell (ed. 1853–1865) **:** Twenty times sweet. So, in *The Merry Wives of Windsor* [II.i.202 f.], "Good even and twenty," twenty times good even. . . . It may be worth observation that *twain-ty* occurs in the Devonshire dialect as a term of endearment to little children, possibly in the sense of, double sweet. ◆ Arden (ind. ed. 1929) **:** I have always felt convinced that to interpret "sweet and twenty" otherwise than as a term of endearment is to destroy the charm of this exquisite song. . . . We need only glance at the lines before and after . . . and the full meaning and the only possible meaning of the words . . . will surely force itself upon us.

MUSIC

Music for a sixteenth-century tune called "O Mistress mine" survives in three early versions. The earliest is Thomas Morley's *The First Booke of Consort Lessons* (1599, 1611), an instrumental arrangement for treble lute, pandora, cittern, bass viol, flute, and treble viol. The entire score has not survived, the treble lute and bass viol parts of both editions having been lost. The tune is carried in the treble viol part which survives in the 1611 edition at the Royal College of Music. A second version of the tune is contained in a set of six variations by William Byrd in the Fitzwilliam Virginal Book (ca. 1619); and the third is the melody to Thomas Campion's song, "Long have mine eyes gazed with delight," in John Gamble's Commonplace Book (New York Public Library MS. Drexel 4257, No. 118).

Whether Shakespeare's song was originally sung to this basic tune is a matter of considerable controversy, and it appears that the controversy will not be settled to the satisfaction of all the musical and literary scholars who have engaged themselves in it until new evidence is discovered (see Shakespeare and Morley, below).

There are scholarly modern editions of both the Morley and Byrd versions of the music. Beck (1959, pp. 148 f.) reprints the *Consort Lessons* "O Mistresse mine," and Byrd's setting and variations are given by Fuller-Maitland (1899, I, 258) and Fellowes (1950, pp. 41–44). Duckles (1954, *RN*, p. 99) prints the tune as set to Campion's words.

There have been numerous attempts to fit Shakespeare's words to either the Morley or Byrd tunes. Beck (1953, p. 20) sets Shakespeare's words to the Morley tune, and Chappell ([1855–1859], I, 209) does the same for the Byrd tune. Other settings of Shakespeare's words to this melody can be found in Bridge (n.d., pp. 1–3; 1923, pp. 77 f.), Elson (1901, pp. 209 f.), Vincent (1906, pp. 22 f.), Kimmins (1928, pp. 44–47), Hardy (1909, pp. 50–52; 1930, pp. 68 f.), Bontoux (1936, pp. 337 f.), and Kines (1964, p. 9).

Morley's *Consort Lessons* was published in 1599, and according to its preface (sig. A₂) was "Newly set forth at the coast & charges of a Gentle-man, for his priuate pleasure, and for diuers others his frendes which delight in Musicke." It thus appears to antedate Shakespeare's play by at least a year. If "Newly set forth" means that Morley was simply publishing a collection of old tunes in his own new arrangements, the melody in his book may have existed a great many years before Shakespeare's play was written. Similar evidence suggests that the tune arranged by Byrd may have been much older than its appearance in the early seventeenth-century Fitzwilliam Virginal Book would indicate. Both Naylor (1905, pp. 13 f.) and Reese (1954, p. 851) note that the tunes in this collection in large part derive from the sixteenth century. Finally, when the tune does appear as a song with a complete set of words in the Gamble Commonplace Book, the lyrics are from a poem by Campion. As Duckles (1954, *RN*, p. 100) points out, the Campion poem as it appears here has a tenuous connection with the standard name for the tune in the first line of the fifth stanza,

> Then, mistress mine, take this farewell.

There might be some temptation to regard this as the "original" setting were it not for the fact that the Campion lyrics appeared even earlier in Philip Rosseter's *A Booke of Ayres* (1601) set to an entirely different melody. This song is reprinted by Fellowes (1922, pp. 35–38). The version here lacks the last two stanzas of the Gamble song.

All these facts suggest that the tune called "O Mistress mine" had an independent existence antedating its appearance in Morley's *Consort Lessons* and in the manuscript musical collections. It appears to have been a popular melody that was reworked by various composers as they saw fit. If Morley arranged it for a consort, Byrd as a set of variations for the virginal, and some anonymous song-maker fitted a Campion poem to it, Shakespeare, too, may have adapted it for his poem (if it is his), "O Mistress mine, where are you roaming?"

It should be noted, however, that songs beginning "O Mistress mine" are far from uncommon in early English literature. In *The First Booke of Ayres. Or Little Short Songs, to Sing and Play to the Lvte* (1600, sigs. C_2–C_2^v), Morley has words and music for a song beginning, "Mistress mine, well may you fare"; this song could quite conceivably be sung just as well to the tune in his *Consort Lessons* as to the one to which it is set. And there is a lyric from the fifteenth century (reprinted by Robbins, 1952, pp. 133 f.) which begins, "O Maistres myn, till yow I me commend." In a period of conventional love-poems, songs beginning with an address to the poet's mistress must have been legion. One of these may have first given the tune its title; indeed, it may even have been the one that Shakespeare borrowed for use in his play if the words of "O Mistress mine, where are you roaming" are not his own.

SHAKESPEARE AND MORLEY

Since about the middle of the nineteenth century there has been a general tendency on the part of Shakespeare critics to regard the "O Mistress mine" tune as the original melody of the song in Shakespeare's play. Almost as often, the composition of this tune has been attributed to Thomas Morley because, as Chappell notes ([1855–1859], I, 209), it was included in both the 1599 and 1611 editions of the famous composer's *Consort Lessons*. Its later appearance in the Fitzwilliam Virginal Book as a set of variations by Byrd was apparently regarded by these critics as derived from the Morley "original." Morley's claim to the tune, and its use as the melody for Shakespeare's song, seemed to be further substantiated by the fact that Morley had indeed set to music another Shakespeare song, "It was a lover and his lass." Since this song appeared in his *The First Booke of Ayres. Or Little Short Songs, to Sing and Play to the Lvte* (1600) there seemed no substantial reason to deny either the originality of his composition or that the words by Shakespeare were intended to go with the music to which he had set them. Whatever doubts might be raised about Shakespeare's "O mistress mine, where are you roaming?" and the independently published tune "O Mistress mine," there were no such questions about the other song. But since about 1926 critics have been seriously divided over what relationship, if any, existed between Shakespeare and Morley, and their controversy has largely centered on the song in *Twelfth Night*.

Heseltine (1926, pp. 120 f.) denied all connection between Morley's *Consort Lessons* tune and Shakespeare's song : There is no authority whatever for associating Shakespeare's poem with this tune; the words do not even fit the music, which is metrically of a quite different construction. The tune looks as though it belonged to a five-line stanza with a rhyme-scheme *a-a-b-b-a*, the last three lines being repeated. The words may have been those of a popular song which Shakespeare adapted and made use of as a starting-point for a flight of his own fancy—or, as is far more probable, Shakespeare may have had nothing to do with the matter, and the similarity of title in tune and lyric is mere coincidence. ◆ Brennecke (1939, pp. 139–149) took a categorically opposite view, and even attempted to demonstrate the hypothesis that Shakespeare and Morley collaborated in the production of the songs for *As You Like It* and *Twelfth Night*. Concerning "It was a lover and his lass" Brennecke remarks (p. 145) : The conclusion seems inevitable that the song was a joint composition . . . poem by Shakespeare and music by Morley, worked out in conference between the two and then immediately and almost simultaneously exposed in the play and in the book of airs. The probabilities amount almost to a certainty that (1) Shakespeare and Morley were acquainted, (2) Shakespeare composed his lyric late in the spring of 1600, (3) Morley had access to it, with Shakespeare's permission, early in the summer, (4) Morley composed music for it as one of the items in the collection on which he was working, (5) Shakespeare, pleased with the music, and by way of fair exchange for the use of his words, had it produced at the first performance of his comedy. [Brennecke goes on (p. 149) to explain the "collaboration" on "O Mistress mine" with the hypothesis that in this instance the music came first:] To summarize the matter in a few words, Shakespeare had heard a popular tune, "O mistress mine," probably in the arrangement devised by his musical friend and co-worker. Having in mind the opening words, the general melodic lilt and the musical atmosphere of the song, he proceeded to compose the lyric we know, giving free rein to his fancy as he did when working on his literary sources. Whereupon Morley very conceivably again entered the picture as a musical journeyman, made the necessary small alterations in his notation [to make the tune fit Shakespeare's words], and the piece was ready for the stage. ◆

Moore (1939, pp. 149–152) attempts to refute Brennecke's hypotheses by citing a number of musical authorities, among them Heseltine, Dent, Scholes, and

Fellowes. He remarks that "I have been unable to find any recent authority who does not seem to hold that Morley's music had originally no relationship with Shakespeare's 'O mistress mine'." He further notes that both Dent and Fellowes cast suspicion on Shakespeare's authorship of "It was a lover and his lass." He concludes : I cannot find, either in the songs themselves or in the considered judgment of competent musicologists, any evidence whatever to show that Shakespeare and Morley collaborated. ◆

Gordon (1947, pp. 121–125) also disputes Brennecke's contentions : In actual fact there is not the slightest evidence that Morley wrote any song for use in a Shakespearean play and no ground for assuming that he had more than a casual acquaintance with the poet. . . . Why Morley rather than Byrd is proposed as the composer is hard to explain. It is just as likely that Byrd composed the air as that Morley did, and perhaps more likely that neither did. . . . All the pulling and hauling in the world will not make the structural divisions of the song correspond with those of the music. The tune in Morley's *Consort Lessons* is not the tune to Shakespeare's "O mistress mine." [As for the song in *As You Like It*, he notes that the music is certainly by Morley and is obviously set for the Shakespeare song, but adds:] It is not provable . . . that the music was written at Shakespeare's request, or . . . with his knowledge, or . . . intended for use in 'As You Like It,' or was ever sung on the Shakespearean stage. . . . All we know of the Shakespeare–Morley relationship is the simple fact that Morley used a Shakespeare lyric for one of his ayres. Everything else is myth. ◆ Dart (1948, p. 8) remarks "There is little reason to ascribe the tune of 'O Mistress Mine' to Morley though the arrangement [in the *Consort Lessons*] is very probably his."

Long (1950, pp. 17–22) repeats the general conjectures of Bridge (1923, pp. 19, 21), later elaborated by Brennecke, "that Shakespeare and Morley . . . were associated in a professional capacity if not personal friends," and apparently accepts the view that there was some collaborative effort between the two men for the songs in *As You Like It* and *Twelfth Night*. He finds further evidence of such an association in Shakespeare's possible use of the instructions about the gamut, or Elizabethan musical scale, from Morley's *A Plaine and Easie Introduction to Practicall Musicke* (1597) in *Taming of the Shrew*. But Marder (1950, pp. 501–503) denies that Shakespeare's knowledge of the gamut would have come from Morley's book, pointing out that there are many other sources—including his education—from which Shakespeare would have derived such musical knowledge; and Moore (1950, p. 504) flatly denies the assumption that Shakespeare and Morley may have collaborated on the two songs, adding that "no competent musical authority in the last generation has held any such view."

Beck (1953, pp. 19–23) passes over the collaboration controversy, choosing instead "to re-examine the problem of the relation between text and music" for the song from *Twelfth Night*. He reviews the question of whether the music in Morley's *Consort Lessons* and in the Fitzwilliam Virginal Book was ever meant to go together with the words of the song in Shakespeare's play. He takes note of the fact that a number of scholars have declared the tune and the words incompatible because fitting them together is structurally awkward. He goes on, however, to analyze the structural members of the Morley and Byrd versions of the tune, and of the Shakespeare verses, and concludes that "a happy marriage of the two is perfectly possible if not inevitable. . . . The key to the situation is the discovery of the scheme for underlaying the text, which makes the union plausible and natural." He gives (p. 20) his own solution of the problem, the Morley tune with the Shakespeare words underlaid. He closes his essay by remarking that "whether or not Thomas Morley was the composer or arranger of 'O Mistresse mine' or the song was known before he picked it up, there can be little doubt that the tune as published in his *Consort Lessons* is the one meant to go with the verses in Shakespeare's play. In any case it will be interesting to see what those scholars, who have ruled out completely the possibility of some collaboration between the composer and playwright, make of these findings." Long (1954, pp. 15 f.) disagrees with Beck : I cannot see that any new evidence has been presented that would be decisive. . . . In regard to the matching of Morley's tune and Shakespeare's lyrics, the problem is still unsolved, as it must remain until additional documentary evidence appears. . . . The way [Beck] . . . matches the tune and the text is ingenious and probable, but, while the union does not involve any modification of the tune, it does involve the repetition of the first two lines of the text. While this may not be a 'distortion', it is an alteration of the text published in the Folio of 1623. ◆

[The case for collaboration between Shakespeare and Morley set forth by Bridge, Brennecke, and Long depends on extremely tenuous evidence, and unless Long's "additional documentary evidence" is forthcoming must be regarded as nearly pure conjecture. Beck's successful fitting of the Shakespeare words to Morley's version of the tune makes available to producers of the play a contemporary tune for the song, even if it is not demonstrably the original one. But Duckles' discovery (1954, pp. 98–100) of the same tune set to a Campion poem—a poem that appears elsewhere with a wholly different tune—suggests that the tune called "O Mistress mine" was a popular tune, in the public domain long before Morley, or Byrd, or the composer who set it to the Campion poem took it up for their own purposes. Finally, the fact that Shakespeare's words can, by careful underlaying, be set to either the Morley or the Byrd versions of the tune, suggests that they may have originally been set to some popular version of the same tune, now lost, a tune to which they fitted perfectly.]

DRAMATIC FUNCTION

This song, like the snatches sung by Silence in *2 Henry IV*, creates an atmosphere of festivity, and also, unlike his songs, serves as sheer musical entertainment. Moore's view of the comic overtones is especially perceptive, and echoes a passage in Castiglione that must have been familiar to Renaissance gentlemen who modeled their conduct on *The Courtier*. Ancient knights and aged courtiers ought to eschew the activities that are more appropriate to youth, for, Castiglione remarks (tr. Hoby, 1561, sigs. M_4v-N_1), songs of love

> conteine in them woordes of loue, and in olde men loue is a thing to bee iested at: although otherwhile he seemeth amonge other miracles of his to take delite in spite of yeres to set a fier frosen herts.

26–29

TEXT: Folio (1623), sig. Y₅ (II.iii.67, 81 f., 84, 91).
TYPOGRAPHY: Italic face prose; s.d., *Catch sung.*

[26]

Hold thy peace, thou Knaue [. . . .]
     [Hold thy peace, and I prithee hold thy peace
     Thou knave,
     Hold thy peace thou knave,
     Thou knave.]

[27]

Three merry men be wee.

[28]

There dwelt a man in Babylon, Lady, Lady.

[29]

O the twelfe day of December.

GENERAL COMMENTARY

Hudson (ed. 1880–1881) : With Sir Toby as wine goes in music comes out, and fresh songs keep bubbling up in his memory as he waxes mellower. A similar thing occurs in *2 Henry IV*, where Master Silence grows merry and musical amidst his cups. ♦ Elson (1901, p. 215) : The absolute fidelity to nature of this entire scene is remarkable; it is the half-drunken man, exactly as one may find him to-day, whose readiest vent of high spirits is in song; nothing can stop him, nothing check his torrent of fragmentary harmony. ♦ Naylor (1931, pp. 86 f.) : At Sir Toby's suggestion, they . . . sing a catch, or, in his own words, "draw *three* souls out of *one* weaver," an allusion to the *three* vocal parts which are evolved from the *one* melody of the catch, as well as a sly reference to "weavers" singing catches. . . . It is not a good catch, but sounds humorous if done smartly, and perhaps its very roughness suits the circumstances. Next, after Maria's entrance, Toby either quotes the titles, or sings odd lines of four old songs . . . and when Malvolio comes in, furious with the noise they are making in the middle of the night, he applies precisely those epithets to their proceedings that our histories lead us to expect—e.g., "gabbling like *tinkers*," "*alehouse*," squeaking out your "*coziers'* catches" ("*cozier*" is "cobbler"). ◆ Long (1955, p. 172) : After the ending of Feste's love song, the party grows more boisterous; the three, well into their drink, decide to sing a merrier type of song. . . . The musical quality of their performance was not high, to judge from Maria's description of it as "catterwalling."

TEXTUAL COMMENTARY

1. **Hold . . . Knaue**] The line is not sung here but simply identifies the catch which is sung five lines later in the Folio when it is called for by a stage direction. The complete words of the catch, given in brackets, are a modern transcription of the words in Thomas Ravenscroft's *Deuteromelia* (1609, sig. C₄).

2. **Three . . . wee**] Part of what may be the source for this fragment of song is preserved in Peele's *Old Wiues Tale* (1595, sig. A₃ᵛ):

> Three merrie men, and three merrie men,
> And three merrie men be wee.
> I in the wood, and thou on the ground,
> And Iacke sleepes in the tree.

Whatever the original song was, it seems to have been extremely popular because it is referred to many times in seventeenth-century drama (see Dekker and Webster's *West-Ward Hoe*, 1607, sig. H₄ᵛ; Lodowick Barrey's *Ram-Alley: Or Merrie-Trickes*, 1611, sig. C₃; and the manuscript play, *The Welsh Embassador*, ca. 1623 (ed. Littledale, 1921, p. 64). Imitations and parodies of the refrain were frequent until after the Restoration (see the ballad, "Robin Hood and the Tanner," in Child, 1882–1898, V, 139, stanza 36; Fletcher's *The Bloody Brother*, 1639, sigs. G₁ᵛ–G₂; *An Antidote against Melancholy: Made up in Pills*, 1661, sig. K₃; Playford's *Catch that Catch can: or the Musical Companion*, 1667, sig. G₂; 1673, sig. E₄ᵛ; and his *Musick's Delight on the Cithren*, 1666, sig. G₇ᵛ). Tilley (1950, M-590) records it as proverbial.

3. **There . . . Lady**] The source is probably from one of the numerous versions of the broadside ballad, "The Constancy of Susanna," which was based on Daniel 13, the story of Susanna and the Elders. A broadside ballad, "the godly and constant wyse [wyfe ?] Susanna," was entered in the Stationers' Registers for Thomas Colwell in 1562/3, and subsequent entries for what seem to have been other ballad versions of the story were made in 1592, 1624, and 1675 (see Rollins, 1924, *SP*, nos. 991, 2528, 2563, and 379). These few entries must not be supposed to cover all the ballads on the subject which were circulated in the years following Colwell's registration of his. According to Rollins (1919, *PMLA*, p. 305) : A ballad that made a hit was re-issued over and over again. Printers who owned the copyright of a street song like . . . "The Constancy of Susanna" might well boast of having made a good bargain; for such favorites were reprinted for almost three hundred years, successive publishers revising the spelling, recasting the verses (or ordering a ballad-writer to make them over), and coolly altering the dates so that the ballad-singer might go forth and swear conscientiously to his audience that the ballads were "absolute new." ◆

Surviving copies of the ballad of Susanna exist in a number of collections, notably Pepys (I, 33, 496), Douce (I, 30), and RB (I, 60 f.). A modern reprint of this last is in *RB* (1871–1899, I, 190–193).

4. **O . . . December**] Kittredge (ind. ed. 1941) suggests that this line is taken from the old ballad of "Musleboorrowe ffeild" in the Percy Folio MS. (B. M. Add. MS. 27,879, fols. 25ᵛ-26; reprinted by Child, 1882–1898, VI, 378). The ballad begins,

> On the tenth day of December,
> And the fourth yeere of *King* Edwards raigne,
> Att Musleboorowe, as I remember,
> Two goodly hosts there mett on a plaine.

Friedman (1953, p. 74) notes that a version somewhat closer to Toby's quotation is preserved in *Choyce Drollery: Songs & Sonnets* (1656, p. 78). It begins,

> On the twelfth day of *December*,
> In the fourth year of King *Edwards* reign.

According to Child (1882–1898, VI, 378) the Battle of Musselburgh Field was actually fought on 10 September 1547 when 18,000 Englishmen invaded Scotland and defeated, with much slaughter, an opposing force of 30,000 Scotsmen.

MUSIC

[26]

The original music for the catch "Hold thy peace" was long thought to be that preserved in Thomas Ravenscroft's *Deuteromelia* (1609, sig. C₄). It has been frequently reprinted: Hawkins (1776, II, 378), Metcalfe ([1864], p. 17), Elson (1901, p. 211), Vincent (1906, p. xxix), Heseltine (1928, p. 29), Hardy (1930, p. 69), Naylor (1931, p. 192), and Long (1955, p. 173). A more elaborate version of the same catch from the 1612 David Melvill manuscript is reprinted by Bantock (1916, pp. 153 f.).

On the other hand Vlasto (1954, pp. 223, 228, and 231) calls attention to another tune for the round in King's College, Cambridge, MS. K C 1, no. 32 in that collection, which dates from 1580 or earlier. It is possibly this tune to which the song in *Twelfth Night* was sung.

[27]

According to Chappell ([1855–1859], I, 216) the original music for "Three merry men" is from "a MS. common-place book, in the handwriting of John Playford," and agrees with the earliest known occurrence of the words in Peele's *Old Wiues Tale*. Chappell reprints this tune as does Naylor (1931, p. 182) and Long (1955, p. 174). But the music given by Chappell (1840, II, 99) and by Elson (1901, p. 214) is totally different, and seems to have been the tune to a number of Robin Hood ballads, one of which imitates the refrain of the song in Peele (see commentary on l.2, song 27).

[28]

The tune to which the Susanna ballad was sung is uncertain. Naylor (n.d., p. 21) remarks that "There is some evidence that the *Ballad of Constant Susanna* was sung to a corrupt version of the tune called 'Greensleeves.' It does not fit particularly well, but that was no final reason in the old days for not using a tune." He does not give his evidence for assigning this tune to the ballad, but in *Shakespeare and Music* (1931, pp. 182 f.) he sets the words of the ballad to a "correct" version of the "Greensleeves" tune which he says "fits the words quite well." Long (1955, p. 174) and Kines (1964, p. 13) take their versions from Naylor. But C. Simpson (1966, pp. 410–412) calls attention to a number of sixteenth-century ballads modeled on William Elderton's famous "The panges of Loue and louers f[i]ttes," which begins, "Was not good Kyng Salamon/Rauished in sondry wyse." All these ballads share a common metrical pattern, a pattern which is interrupted by the distinctive refrain "Lady Lady" and "most dere Lady," and probably also shared the tune "King Solomon" to which the Elderton ballad gave the name. The ballad of Susanna belongs to this group, and the words of the song in Shakespeare can be easily fitted to the tune which Simpson (p. 412) gives.

[29]

The original tune of the ballad of "Musleboorrowe ffeild" is not known.

DRAMATIC FUNCTION

The various snatches sung by Sir Toby Belch have as their function nothing more than the creation of an atmosphere of tipsy revelry during the midnight hours. Most of their humor is lost on a modern audience, unfamiliar with the original tunes and ballads from which the lines are taken. Two of the songs in Sir Toby's repertory seem to have been extremely popular. Shakespeare's audience, knowing—and probably able to sing—the originals of his songs, must have derived considerable pleasure from sheer recognition as the drunken knight bawled out line after line with greater and greater gusto.

30

TEXT: Folio (1623), sig. Y₅ (II.iii.110–121).
TYPOGRAPHY: Mixed verse and prose, italic and roman face.

To. Farewell deere heart, ſince I muſt needs be gone.
Mar. Nay good Sir *Toby.*
Clo. His eyes do ſhew his dayes are almoſt done.
Mal. Is't euen ſo?
To. But I will neuer dye.   5
Clo. Sir *Toby* there you lye.
Mal. This is much credit to you.
To. Shall I bid him go.
Clo. What and if you do?
To. Shall I bid him go, and ſpare not?   10
Clo. O no, no, no, no, you dare not.

GENERAL COMMENTARY

Elson (1901, p. 216) **:** There now follows a musical scene which is *sui generis*; an entire song is woven by Shakespeare into the action. Sir Toby's bewildered mind is ready to catch any passing impression, provided it lead to music, on which at the moment his thoughts are most intent. As Malvolio comes to the words, "She is very willing to bid you farewell" [II.iii.109], he is at once reminded of a song by Robert Jones, a famous lutenist and composer for that instrument and for the voice. ◆ Arden (ind. ed. 1929) **:** On this ballad Percy remarks, "*Corydon's Farewell to Phyllis* is an attempt to paint a lover's irresolution, but so poorly executed, that it would not have been admitted into this collection, if it had not been quoted in *Twelfth Night.* . . ." According to Halliwell-Phillipps, "This ballad first appeared in the [*First*] *Booke of* [*Songes and*] *Ayres*, composed by Robert Jones, 1600. Jones does not profess to be the author of the words of this song . . . but there is every reason to believe that the ditty referred to in *Twelfth Night* was first published in this work, a collection of new, not of old songs. ◆ Naylor (1931, p. 70) **:** "Farewell dear heart," is an interesting case of a newly published song being inserted in a new play. Robert Jones set it for the lute with four voices in 1600. The date of *Twelfth Night* is 1601. ◆ Long (1955, p. 173) **:** After first insulting the musicianship of Sir Toby, Malvolio gives him a choice of giving up his roistering or of quitting the house. To this, Sir Toby, stung by the slur on his musical ability and by Malvolio's effrontery, shapes his retort in a mock-sad vein, using a popular ayre by Robert Jones for his reply. The clown, delighted by the device, picks up the words of the song. The two sing a slightly altered version of the song to its conclusion. . . . ◆ Cutts (1957, p. 17) suggests that Shakespeare adapted parts of the first two stanzas of Jones's song to create the single jocose stanza sung by Toby and the clown. He adds that in telescoping the first half of the first stanza with the second half of the second stanza, Shakespeare evidently intended the whole new stanza to be sung to Jones's tune for a single stanza.

TEXTUAL COMMENTARY

3. **eyes ... done**] The clown evidently refers to the effects of drinking on Sir Toby's eyes.

11. **no, no, no, no**] Some modern editors drop one of these *no*'s to justify the metrics of the line, but the words in Jones's *First Booke of Songes and Ayres* read exactly as they do in Shakespeare. An allusion to this song appears in *A Poetical Rhapsodie*, 1602 (ed. Rollins, 1931, I, 110): "Say, shall shee goe? Oh no, no, no, no, no."

MUSIC

The original song from which Sir Toby and the clown sing a part is contained in Robert Jones's *The First Booke of Songes and Ayres* (1600, sigs. D$_4$v–E$_1$). There is a manuscript copy of the song dating from about 1639 in the National Library of Scotland, Adv. MS. 5.2.14 (fol. 8), and a text of the words alone in Richard Johnson's *The Golden Garland of Princely pleasures and delicate Delights* (1620, sigs. F$_5$–F$_5$v).

The best modern edition of the song in Jones's book is probably the one given by Dart (n.d., pp. 24 f.). There are other editions in J. S. Smith (1812, II, 204 f.), Rimbault (1850, p. 52), Naylor (n.d., pp. 23 f.), and Fellowes (1925, pp. 24 f.). Popular settings of the Jones tune to Shakespeare's words are given by Elson (1901, pp. 216–218), Vincent (1906, pp. 1 f.), Naylor (n.d., p. 22; 1931, p. 183, a partial setting), Gibbon (1930, p. 115), Long (1955, p. 175), Cutts (1957, p. 24), and Kines (1964, pp. 16 f.).

Heseltine (1926, p. 68) notes that "the popularity of the song is attested by the appearance in the composer's fourth book [*A Mvsicall Dreame. Or the fovrth Booke of Ayres*, 1609, sig. E$_2$v], nine years later, of a song identical in metre and very similar in melody, 'Farewell, fond youth, if thou hadst not been blind'."

THE SOURCE

The text which follows is from Jones's songbook. The lyrics given in the Adv. MS. and in Johnson's *Golden Garland* substantially agree with it.

> Farewel dear loue since thou wilt needs be gon,
> mine eies do shew my life is almost done,
>   nay I will neuer die,
>   so long as I can spie,
>   there be many mo
>   though that she do go
> there be many mo I feare not,
> why then let her goe I care not.

2

Farewell, farewell, since this I finde is true,
I will not spend more time in wooing you:
    But I will seeke elswhere,
    If I may find her there,
    Shall I bid her goe,
    What and if I doe?
Shall I bid her go and spare not,
Oh no no no no I dare not.

3

Ten thousand times farewell, yet stay a while,
Sweet kisse me once, sweet kisses time beguile:
    I haue no power to moue,
    How now, am I in loue
    Wilt thou needs be gone?
    Go then, all is one,
Wilt thou needs be gone? oh hie thee,
Nay, stay and doe no more denie mee.

4

Once more farewell, I see loth to depart,
Bids oft adew to her that holdes my hart:
    But seeing I must loose,
    Thy loue which I did chuse:
    Go thy waies for me,
    Since it may not be,
Go thy waies for me, but whither?
Go, oh but where I may come thither.

5

What shall I doe? my loue is now departed,
Shee is as faire as shee is cruell harted:
    Shee would not be intreated,
    With praiers oft repeated:
    If shee come no more,
    Shall I die therefore,
If shee come no more, what care I?
Faith, let her go, or come, or tarry.

DRAMATIC FUNCTION

The original song has to do with a lover who is unable to depart since he cannot accept the fact that he has been rejected by his mistress. The words of the song

5+v.s.

show his vaccilations as he is torn between his pride and his longings for the lady who will no longer have him. Knowing that this parting is to be his last, he would linger out its moments as long as possible.

When Malvolio's words, "bid you farewell," call the song to Sir Toby's mind, he sings out the first line and is immediately taken up by Feste, who perceives in the words of the song an ironic application to his and Sir Toby's present altercation with the steward. Feste and Sir Toby proceed to sing appropriate lines at each other as Malvolio's indignation steadily mounts. Humorless, and no more addicted to frivolous love songs than he is to cakes and ale, Malvolio probably perceives that he is the butt of their song without being aware of the comic implications of the lines they sing.

31

TEXT: Folio (1623), sig. Y₅ᵛ (II.iv.52–67).
TYPOGRAPHY: Indented verse, italic face; s.d., *The Song*.

> *Come away, come away death,*
> *And in ſad cypreſſe let me be laide.*
> *Fye away, fie away breath,*
> *I am ſlaine by a faire cruell maide:*
> > *My ſhrowd of white, ſtuck all with Ew, O prepare it.*   5
> > *My part of death no one ſo true did ſhare it.*

> *Not a flower, not a flower ſweete*
> *On my blacke coffin, let there be ſtrewne:*
> *Not a friend, not a friend greet*
> *My poore corpes, where my bones ſhall be throwne:*   10
> > *A thouſand thouſand ſighes to ſaue, lay me ô where*
> > *Sad true louer neuer find my graue, to weepe there.*

GENERAL COMMENTARY

New Variorum (ind. ed. 1901) quotes Staunton : "On comparing the Duke's description [II.iv.2–7, 43–49] of that 'antique song' he heard last night, with this ballad, the difference is so striking, as to beget suspicion that the latter was an interpolation, and not the original song intended by the poet. It appears, indeed, to have been the privilege of the singer formerly, whenever the business of the scene required a song, to introduce one of his own choice; hence we frequently find in our old dramas, instead of the words of a ballad, merely a stage direction, 'A Song', or 'He sings'." ◆ [While it is true that the original texts sometimes fail to designate what song is to be sung, that is no reason for concluding that the song in such a place was left to the discretion of the singer. When acting companies printed their plays—or allowed them to be printed—they were furnishing the public with reading and not acting versions. Such publication was intended to wring the last ounce of profit out of a play which had exhausted its commercial usefulness on the stage, or to correct (and compete with) a pirated version published earlier. The "acting versions" of the plays were the manuscript or printed prompt copies which a theatrical company would have jealously guarded. It may be presumed that these texts were more complete and specific than the "reading texts" which have come down to us.] New Variorum also quotes Innes : "Nevertheless, a song of the woeful fate of a swain who dies of love may very fitly be described as 'dallying with the innocence of love,' especially by the Duke, who would rather like to believe that he is dying of love himself." ◆ Noble (1923, pp. 83 f.) : The context of the song is not without interest—limits are imposed on the kind of air to be set to the words; we are told that it must avoid "light airs and recollected terms".... In the second place it must be such that

> The spinsters and the knitters in the sun,
> And the free maids that weave their thread with bones,
> Do use to chant it. [II.iv.45–47]

Clearly a folk idiom is indicated, and a rhythm that is too insistent or regular must be avoided.... While it is agreed that it was the original intention that Viola should sing here, yet it is submitted that the song she sang was other than the one now standing and allotted to Feste. Leaving aside the debatable resemblance of the present song to the Duke's description of it, for Viola, even though disguised as a youth, to sing it were a dramatic impropriety, which Shakespeare was not in the habit of committing. The song, which had been chanted by the spinsters and free maids, might have been appropriate, but not this one. In any case, the scene has been so much altered, and there is now so much matter specially contextual to the song as rendered by Feste, that it is quite impossible ... to attempt to restore the original. ◆ Garvin (1936, pp. 326–328) disagrees with Noble's contention that this was not the song originally intended. She suggests that Orsino's description of the song (II.iv.3–7, 43–49) "fits the Old French *chansons de toile*." She discusses the characteristic qualities of such songs and concludes that Shakespeare's song might have been intended to "show Viola's role in the play as that of the devoted and passionate handmaiden of the man she loves, performing even extravagant services for him with amazing tolerance" even as did the heroines of the Old French songs for the men they loved. She observes that if Shakespeare knew the traditional content and character of the *chansons de toile*, he may have intended with his song to suggest to his audience the traditional genre and, along with the comments made by Orsino on the song, to "point and define the whole play. Viola, the patient lover; the Duke, capricious and inconsiderate; Olivia, the conventional, imperious, courtly mistress."

Moore (1916, p. 89) : The melancholy Duke Orsino moves to melancholy music. At the opening of the play he is listening to a mournful air, and in the next act he calls for a despairing song of love. ◆ Noble (1923, p. 83) : Orsino is an exotic in search of a sensation, he is the Renaissance counterpart of the aesthete so mercilessly satirized by Gilbert, and his love affair and his affectation for music, so exquisitely conveyed in the first scene [I.i.1–15], are much on the same level.... [And now] he affects not even to remember who sang to him the night before.... Perhaps the most delightful feature of [this song] ... is its humorously playful pity for the Duke's sad love grief; no one takes the poor nobleman's passion at a high value, and Feste hints that a beneficial medicine for such constancy might be found in employment. ◆ Davies (1939, p. 69) : It would be stupid to overlook the effect of the song ... in establishing an atmosphere of romantic melancholy, and this is a fact which can only be appreciated by watching the play in performance. The air, first played and later sung by Feste, hangs over the scene and colours it through and through with its peculiar sweet sadness and its implications of unrequited love. It would not be ridiculous to suppose that the song was introduced to help Viola in her delivery of some of her loveliest lines. ◆ Auden (1957, p. 42) :

Outside the pastures of Eden, no true lover talks of being slain by a fair, cruel maid, or weeps over his own grave. In real life, such reflections are the day-dreams of self-love, which is never faithful to others. ¶ . . . Shakespeare has so placed the song as to make it seem an expression of the Duke's real character. Beside him sits the disguised Viola, for whom the Duke is not a playful fancy, but a serious passion. It would be painful enough for her if the man she loved really loved another, but it is much worse to be made to see that he only loves himself, and it is this insight which at this point Viola has to endure. ◆ Hollander (1959, pp. 223 f.) : Feste's other songs differ radically from "O Mistress Mine." He sings for the Duke a languorous ayre, similar to so many that one finds in the songbooks. It is aimed at Orsino in the very extravagance of its complaint. It is his own song, really, if we imagine him suddenly dying of love, being just as ceremoniously elaborate in his funeral instructions as he has been in his suit of Olivia. ◆ [Elsewhere (1961, p. 157) the same author writes :] The song . . . is a highly extravagant, almost parodic version of the theme of death from unrequited love. Its rather stilted diction and uneasy prosody are no doubt intended to suggest a song from an old miscellany. "Come away" is a banal beginning, appearing at the start of four song texts in Canon Fellowes' collection. We may also presume that the setting employed was rather more archaic than that of the well-polished lute accompaniments of the turn of the century. ◆ Sternfeld (1963, p. 117) : Duke Orsino, after listening to a full rendition of two stanzas, fulfils his social obligation of recompensing the singer but shows no sign of having been soothed. The melancholy god [II.iv.75 f.], far from protecting him . . . still pursues him. Orsino dismisses Feste and the attendants, and returns to his objective, never to be achieved in the play:

> Once more Cesario
> Get thee to yond same sovereign cruelty.

Admittedly, the song has a subsidiary function, in that it is not addressed solely to the Duke but affects the audience as well. The element of 'mood music' in a comedy whose first line is

> If music be the food of love, play on . . .

is not to be discounted. But a careful study convinces one that the songs in Shakespeare are primarily addressed to the protagonists on the stage and that this function was understood by the audience. The playwright does not endeavour to condition his audience by music . . . [as in] the modern theatre or cinema.

TEXTUAL COMMENTARY

1. **Come . . . away**] Sternfeld (1963, p. 89) finds a similarity between the repetitions at the beginning of this song and those at the end of 44 : Of either song it might be said that

> it is silly sooth,
> And dallies with the innocence of love,

[*Twelfth Night*, II.iv.47 f.] for both the Duke ... and Mariana ... pamper themselves with these magic songs. ◆ [*NED* citing this example explains, "Come on your way toward me, and do not linger."]

2. **fad cypreſſ**] Malone (ed. 1790) : In the books of our author's age the thin transparent lawn called *cyprus*, which was formerly used for scarfs and hatbands at funerals ... was, I believe, constantly spelt *cypress*. So, in the *Winter's Tale* [Folio (1623, sig. 2B₃)],

Cypreſſe blacke as ere was Crow.

... The meaning here [may be] "Let me be laid in a shroud made of *cyprus*, not in a coffin made of cypress wood." But in a subsequent line of this song the shroud, we find, is *white*. There was indeed white cyprus as well as *black*; but the epithet *sad* is inconsistent with white, and therefore I suppose the wood to have been here meant. ◆ Steevens (ed. 1793) : In a shroud of *cypress* or *cyprus*. ... There was both black and white *cyprus*, as there is still black and white *crape*; and ancient shrouds were always made of the latter. ◆ Arden (ind. ed. 1929) : As the shroud is mentioned three lines further on, this is probably not black crape but a coffin of dark cypress wood, the "black coffin" [of line 8]. ◆

3. **Fye ... away**] All the modern editors adopt the emendation of Rowe (ed. 1709), "Fly away, fly away"; but Hotson (1954, pp. 143 f.) insists that the Folio reading is correct : Shakespeare's original expresses grief's paradox with extreme and powerful contrast. Ugly death is lovely, dear life hateful. It is "Come, sweet death!" and "Get thee gone, loathsome life!" [There is a] passion of self-loathing in "Fie, away" as in Hamlet's "Fie upon't! Foh!" [II.ii.616]. ... For passion, the feeble "Fly away, fly away" substitutes prettiness, waters down the cry into a fond fanciful adieu, a sentimental leave-taking of life. ◆ [Hotson forgets, however, that a sentimental song was precisely what Orsino requested. Yet in Thomas Ravenscroft's *Melismata* (1611, sig. C₂) occurs a song titled "The Mistris to the Courtier" which begins with a line that may support the Folio reading: "Fie away, fie away, fie, fie, fie."]

5. **Ew**] A tree of the genus *Taxus*, especially the common yew of Europe and Asia, *Taxus baccata*. It is often planted in and around church-yards, and so has come to be associated with death and mourning.

6. **My ... it**] Arden (ind. ed. 1929) : The Cowden Clarkes render it, "No one so true as I did ever take part in death's tragedy." As [another] paraphrase, I should venture ... "No one died for love so true to love as I." ◆

7-8. **Not ... ſtrewne**] Granville-Barker (1947, I, 127, note) : The distribution of ... herbs and flowers was an ordinary funeral custom. Carew Hazlitt ... [1870, II, 175], quotes Misson: "when the Funeral Procession is ready to set out 'they nail up the Coffin, and a Servant presents the Company with sprigs of Rosemary: everyone takes a Sprig and carries it in his hand till the Body is put into the Grave, at which time they all throw in their Sprigs after it.'" ◆

8. **ſtrewne**] Pronounced *strown*, to rhyme with *throwne* in l. 10. Cf. Kökeritz (1953, p. 211) and the rhymes *shrew-shew* and *Shrow-so* in the First Folio's *Taming of the Shrew* (sigs. T₃ᵛ and V₁).

9. **not ... throwne**] Let no mourning friends attend my burial in the church-yard.

MUSIC

The original music for this song is unknown. The earliest of the modern settings, by Arne, is in *The Shakespeare Vocal Album* (1864, p. 90).

THE SINGER

The question as to whether Feste or Viola (Cesario) sang this song in the "original" version of the play is apparently first raised at length by Eduard and Otto Devrient in their German edition of Shakespeare's plays (1873–1876, I, 183–188). They note that when Viola assumes her disguise as Cesario she says to the sea-captain (I.ii.55–58):

> I'll serve this Duke,
> Thou shalt present me as a eunuch to him;
> It may be worth thy pains. For I can sing
> And speak to him in many sorts of music.

They point out further that when the Duke calls for "That old and antique song we heard last night" (II.iv.3) he clearly seems to expect Cesario to sing it. That Feste should have to be sent for to render the song they regard as the result of a *Theatercalamität* and a hasty reworking of the scene for some performance of the play in which the actor who played Cesario was incapable of singing. The make-shift substitution of Feste, they feel, somehow became petrified in the First Folio text. Less than two years later Fleay (1875, p. 299) called attention to the same two passages as evidence that "Viola was evidently intended to be the singer." In the following year (1876, p. 228) he raised the same question again, and also pointed out that Curio's response to the Duke's call for a song at the beginning of II.iv is in prose. He regards such prose passages as being usually evidence of later additions to the "original" drama.

Noble (1923, p. 80) **:** That it was not the original intention to assign all the singing to Feste is evident from the fact that Viola was to be presented to the Duke . . . as a eunuch who could "sing and speak to him in many sorts of music." Further it is patent that to Viola was to be appointed that "old and antique song" . . . where by an obvious device Feste is substituted. . . . If all were known, it is not improbable that in this change is contained an interesting piece of theatrical history. From *Hamlet* and *Othello* we know that Shakespeare's company had from about 1601 until 1604 a leading boy capable of playing upon the lute and of singing ballads of the plaintive kind alluded to by Orsino. Probably on the occasion of a revival [of *Twelfth Night*] there was no boy available capable both of taking such a part as Viola's and of singing. ♦

E.K. Chambers (1930, I, 406) takes no cognizance of a possible Feste-Viola sub-stitution and rejects Fleay's theory that the play was composed at two different times; he finds Fleay's evidence for the theory, "that the songs were originally given to Viola," insufficient. But New Cambridge (ind. ed. 1930, pp. 91 f.), while not supporting Fleay about two periods of composition for the play, does espouse

the theory that Feste has been substituted as the singer of this song in place of
Viola : Of this substitution there can be no reasonable doubt.... First, as Fleay
notes, we have a request (in verse) that Cesario should sing the song, followed by
Curio's strange answer (in prose) that the singer is not present and the, to my
mind, still stranger or at least lamer, explanation (also in prose) of how Olivia's
fool comes to be in Orsino's house. Furthermore, as Fleay adds, the Duke "afterwards points out the special character of the song (ll. 43–48) to Cesario, who had
also heard it, and who had been just asked to sing it." Both adaptation and substitution are palpable. ◆ [Yet the substitution which the New Cambridge editor
finds "palpable" in II.iv has elsewhere in the play, he admits, been carefully
prepared for, since he continues (pp. 93 f.) :] the change, though a little clumsily
effected in the scene in question, is cleverly led up to in I.v. where at the Fool's
first entrance he is accused of truancy, so that the audience may be prepared to
find him ... in other houses than Olivia's. Moreover, seeing that Feste's presence
in the Duke's palace is referred to at III.i.37–41, and again at the opening of V.i.
when Orsino and the Fool encounter, it is clear that the substitution in II.iv. was
not just an isolated change in the cast for the sake of a single song, but involved
changes affecting several scenes at least. Again, the striking thing about Feste ... is
that he is a singing Fool, and something of a musician as well ... [for] he is com-
missioned to carry out some kind of musical performance, perhaps accompanied
by dancing, at the beginning of Act III. ... Is it not a fair inference from all this
that the text of *Twelfth Night*, as we have it, has been revised ... to give scope for a
Clown with a voice? ... Noble thinks the revision took place between 1603 and
1606, but new clowns did not join Shakespeare's company every year, and since
William Kemp left the Chamberlain's Men in c. 1599 it is difficult to escape the
conclusion that the singing Fool in question was Robert Armin, Kemp's successor
at the Globe. ◆

Greg (1955, p. 297) also accepts the theory of a substitution of Feste for Viola as
the singer of this song, and points to the putative revisions which made this
substitution possible as evidence that the First Folio text is derived from a prompt
copy of the play. Long (1955, pp. 176 f.) also agrees that there has been a substitution of singers and a revision of II.iv. He suggests a reconstruction of the "original"
scene. According to his view, ll. 1–7 are spoken by the Duke and followed by the
song (ll. 52–67) rendered by Viola; ll. 8–14 are dropped, as being a makeshift to
enable Feste to come for the song; ll. 15–42 are "original," and follow Viola's
singing as commentary on her song by Viola and the Duke; ll. 43–51 and 68–82 are
also part of the revision, and the "original scene" resumes at the second half of
l. 82. According to Long such an arrangement would not interrupt the action of
the play in the least.

Plausible as the arguments for substitution and revision are, they do not prove
the case; for the fact remains that II.iv. reads perfectly well as it stands in the present
folio text. Moreover, the evidence offered to support a theory of substitution-
revision can be explained in other ways as well. First of all, Viola's remark to the
sea-captain, "I can sing," may be nothing more than her excuse to the Duke to
explain the discrepancy between her male attire and her high voice. That the boy-
actor playing the role had an unchanged voice is indicated again by the Duke's
remark (I.iv.32 f.),

> thy small pipe
> Is as the maiden's organ, shrill and sound.

Arguing the case for a substitution-revision, the New Cambridge editor points out that the revising is crude in II.iv, but hastens to add that elsewhere it has been very carefully done, and that the plausibility of Feste as the singer has been very carefully worked out. But if such care *has* been exercised, why did the reviser fail to do the easiest and most necessary thing of all, namely to excise Viola's remarks at I.ii.56–59? The simple elimination of these four lines would have perfectly concealed the "substitution" and would have been more easily accomplished than the "revisions" that have been painfully worked out in other places.

Secondly, the whole question of actor-singers in Shakespeare's company is largely conjectural since we do not possess enough historical evidence to come to any certain judgements. The little we do know about them reveals almost nothing about whether they had changed or unchanged voices. Presumably the boy who played Ophelia and Desdemona (if, indeed, he was the same person) had a voice "not crack'd within the ring," and could play upon a lute. But whether he ever played the part of Viola and sang songs in some other version of *Twelfth Night* is pure guesswork.

That Viola does not sing "Come away, come away death" when the Duke calls for a song is not necessarily surprising. Viola-Cesario is his page; why should he not command him to procure music? Again, when the Duke asks for "that old and antique song we heard last night," he seems to suggest (unless he is using the royal *we*) that Cesario was an auditor, not a performer on that earlier occasion.

DRAMATIC FUNCTION

The song which Feste sings is both fitting to him as a singer and to the Duke as a hearer. As a plaint of a man forsaken by his mistress it establishes the same atmosphere and characterizes the Duke in the same way as the music and speech that opens the play. Like Mariana in *Measure for Measure*, the Duke desires to please his woe by feeding it with love-sick songs. In the process he reveals himself not as a mature and forceful nobleman, but as an infatuated lover as greensick as any Troilus or Romeo.

32

TEXT: Folio (1623), sig. Z₄ (IV.ii.78–85).
TYPOGRAPHY: Mixed verse and prose, italic and roman face.

Clo. Hey Robin, iolly Robin, tell me how thy Lady does.
Mal. Foole.
Clo. My Lady is vnkind, *perdie*.
Mal. Foole.   5
Clo. Alas why is ſhe ſo?
Mal. Foole, I ſay.
Clo. She loues another.

GENERAL COMMENTARY

Baskervill (1929, p. 87) : Probably dialogue songs were often presented by one singer with skillful impersonation. In singing ... "A Robyn Joly Robyn" ... the actor who played the part of Feste ... may have attempted two voices as he had just done in the incident in which he impersonated the parson. ✦

Halliwell (ed. 1853–1865) : The air to which it was sung is to be found in the Cithern Schoole by Anthony Holborne, 1597. In the Musicall Dreame, composed by Robert Jones ... 1609, is a ballad of Robin Hood, part of the burden of which is,—"Hey, jolly Robin." In an old MS. at Edinburgh is a series of fragments worked into a medley, amongst which is the following,—"Jolly Robin, Goe to the green-wood, to thy lemman." ✦ [Halliwell was unaware of the existence of the source of this song. The music to which he refers, in Holborne's *The Cittharn Schoole* (sig. D₂), has no connection with this song, but may be the tune for a fragment of song by Ophelia in *Hamlet*. See song 38.] Arden (ind. ed. 1929) : These words form the first two lines of a song ... found in a MS. volume dating from the early part of the sixteenth century. ... Naylor [1931, p. 184] gives the old music for the song, which he thinks to be of the same period as "Farewell, dear heart." ✦

Sternfeld (1963, p. 113) believes that the role of Feste was played by Robert Armin; he notes that the opening lines of the song contain a variant of Armin's Christian name, and that Davies of Hereford used the same nickname in addressing a poem to Armin in 1610. But these facts are not evidence, and it is even difficult to see how they are relevant.

MUSIC

The original music for this song, composed by William Cornyshe (ca. 1465–ca. 1523), is in B. M. Add. MS. 31,922 (fols. 53ᵛ–54). There are scholarly editions of the song by Reese (1954, p. 770) and Stevens (1962, pp. 38 f.), as well as editions by Naylor (n.d., pp. 25–27), Gibbon (1930, p. 35, from Naylor), and Greenberg (1961, pp. 84–87). Naylor (n.d., p. 25; 1931, p. 184) gives an arrangement of the tune to Shakespeare's words, and this is reprinted by Long (1955, p. 179). The fragment given by Kines (1964, p. 12) has no relation to the Cornyshe tune, and is useless.

SOURCE

The words for this song were probably composed by Sir Thomas Wyatt and are to be found in B. M. MS. Egerton 2711 (fol. 37ᵛ). What purports to be an "exact transcript" of this manuscript by G. F. Nott, the early editor of the poems of Wyatt and Surrey, is B. M. Add. MS. 28,636 (fol. 34). Nott (1815–1816, II, 188 f.) gives a modernized version of the poem. Flügel (1889–1903, XII, 272) is an inaccurate copy of Nott's "exact transcript" which is itself not entirely correct. Nott's errors are perhaps due more to the careless hand in the Egerton MS. than to editorial carelessness.

The Egerton MS. contains a number of poems believed to be written in Wyatt's autograph. Though this poem is not among them, it does have the name "Wyat" inscribed in the upper left-hand margin, so ascription of the words to him may be regarded as fairly authoritative, the manuscript having apparently passed through his own hands. Flügel cites the signature "Cornysh" at the end of the music manuscript (B. M. Add. MS. 31,922, fol. 54) as evidence that Cornyshe is the author of the poem; but his name there very likely indicates nothing more than the fact that he composed or set the music to Wyatt's poem. Wyatt and Cornyshe were in Henry VIII's court at the same time and almost certainly knew each other. It would not be surprising if he had set to music some of Wyatt's lyrics even as he had set the verses of another contemporary of both, the poet John Skelton. Stevens (1961, p. 111) also casts some slight doubts on Wyatt's authorship of the words : There is nothing specifically in Wyatt's manner here; and the opening lines certainly reflect an older tradition (Wyatt nowhere uses the word 'leman').... [While] it is not impossible that he wrote the trifle which Cornish set ... another explanation which fits the facts is that Wyatt's poem is a later handling and amplification of a popular song already known at court. It was possibly sung to the original tune, which Cornish's version may incorporate. ✦ [But Stevens bases his judgement chiefly on the music manuscript which contains only the first two stanzas of the words. His supposition would seem to be that for this "older song" Wyatt composed three additional stanzas, preserved along with the first two in the Egerton MS. Without further evidence his conclusion can be regarded only as an hypothesis.]

There is another fragmentary version of the poem in B. M. Add. MS. 17,492 (fol. 22ᵛ), seven lines in length, followed by a complete version of the poem with an additional stanza (fols. 24–24ᵛ). The text which follows is from the Egerton manuscript.

> A Robyn
> Joly Robyn
> tell me how thy leman doeth
> and thou shall knowe of myn
> My lady is vnkynd pde   5
> alack whi is she so
> she loveth an othr better then me
> and yet she will say no
>
>   Responce
> I fynde no suche doublenes   10
> I fynde women true
> my lady loveth me dowtles
> and will chaunge for no newe
>
>   le plaintif
> Thou art happy while that doeth last   15
> but I say as I fynde
> that womens love is but a blast
> and torneth lik the wynde
>
>   Responce
> Suche folkes shall take no harme by love   20
> that can abide their torn
> But I alas can no way prove
> in love but lake & morn
>
>   le Plaintif
> But if thou wilt avoyde thy harme   25
> lerne this lessen of me
> at othr fieres thy selfe to warme
> and let them warme with the

Both Nott and Flügel recognized that the last two stanzas are obviously inappropriate to their headings; they corrected this confusion by leaving the headings as they were and by inverting the stanzas. But the scribe's error in the Egerton MS. was not that he inverted the last two stanzas, but that he omitted a stanza from the middle of the poem, a stanza which can be supplied from Add. 17,492:

> Yf that be trew yett as thov sayst
> that women turn theⁱr hart
> then spek better of them thov mayst
> In hop to han thy partt

If this stanza is inserted immediately after the "Responce" of l. 19, the order of the stanzas in the Egerton MS. may be allowed to stand, with the stanza beginning at

l. 20 headed "le Plaintif" and the one beginning at l. 25 headed "Responce." The explanation that the copyist dropped a stanza and then confused the remaining stanza headings is more plausible than the theory that he reversed two of the stanzas. MS. 17,492 does not include any stanza headings; the Egerton MS. does not include enough, for it is obvious that the first four lines of the poem belong to "Responce," l. 5 to "le Plaintif," l. 6 to "Responce," and ll. 7–8 again to "le Plaintif."

DRAMATIC FUNCTION

Even as he and Sir Toby had used a previous dialogue song to bait Malvolio, so now Feste uses Sir Thomas Wyatt's song of the forsaken lover to gull the steward, who is also, in some sense, a forsaken lover—of the Lady Olivia. Bound and confined in darkness according to the standard Elizabethan therapy for the mad or possessed, Malvolio can hardly appreciate the comedy of the song: he is the lover, Olivia the "lady," and the "other" she loves is Viola disguised in male habiliments.

33

TEXT: Folio (1623), sig. Z₄ (IV.ii.130–141).
TYPOGRAPHY: Indented verse, roman face.

I am gone fir, and anon fir,
  Ile be with you againe:
In a trice, like to the old vice,
  your neede to fuftaine.
Who with dagger of lath, in his rage and his wrath   5
  cries ah ha, to the diuell:
Like a mad lad, paire thy nayles dad,
  Adieu good man diuell.

GENERAL COMMENTARY

Noble (1923, p. 84) : The interest of the song lies entirely in its illustration of Shakespeare's dramatic craftsmanship, and helps to bear out Irving's remark that no actor could ever complain that Shakespeare had sent him tamely off the stage. Imagine to yourself a stage projecting out into the orchestra and without a drop scene, and try to devise an effective method of ending the situation, and you will then the better appreciate the genius of this song as covering the Clown's exit. Feste is enabled to withdraw gradually and with mock ceremony and to disappear on the final insult 'devil', hurled derisively at the much-wronged Malvolio. ◆ Hollander (1959, p. 234) : Feste's bit of handy-dandy . . . is a rough-and-tumble sort of thing, intended to suggest in its measures a scrap from a Morality, plainly invoking Malvolio . . . as a devil in hell. ◆ Sternfeld (1963, p. 113) : The 'old Vice' (buffoon) of the earlier Tudor stage was the predecessor of the Elizabethan fool, and the Vice twitting the devil was a thinly veiled form of the Elizabethan jester mocking the Puritan—a musical jester goading an anti-musical puritan.

TEXTUAL COMMENTARY

1. **anon**] Straightway, at once. See *NED*.
3. **trice**] Immediately. The word has no connection with *thrice* (e.g., "in three seconds"), but is a late Middle English word of obscure origin, related to Middle Dutch *trisen* and Dutch *trijsen*, "to hoist, to pull." From the verb is derived the substantive which, according to *NED*, first occurs in 1440 in the expression "at a trice," meaning "at a single pluck or pull"; hence, "immediately."
  old vice] Johnson (ed. 1765) : Was the fool of the old moralities. Some traces of this character are still preserved in puppet-shows, and by country-mummers. ◆

Halliwell (ed. 1853–1865) quotes Nares as remarking that the Vice in old plays "was grotesquely dressed in a cap with ass's ears, a long coat, and a dagger of lath. One of his chief employments was to make sport with the devil, leaping on his back and belabouring him with his dagger, till he made him roar. The devil, however, always carried him off in the end. The moral was, that sin, which has the courage to make very merry with the devil, and is allowed by him to take very great liberties, must finally become his prey." Arden (ind. ed. 1929) : The Vice . . . was often furnished with a dagger of lath, with which he . . . tried to cut [the devil's] talons (Cf. "pare thy nails"). The fool of Shakespeare's plays was a descendant of the Vice, and a more modern descendant is the harlequin. ✦

7. **paire . . . nayles**] Malone (ed. 1790) : The reason why the Vice exhorts the Devil to pare his nails, is, because the Devil was supposed from choice to keep his nails always unpared, and therefore to pare them was an affront. So in Camden's *Remaines [of a Greater Worke, Concerning Britaine*, 1614, sig. D_1^v]:

> I will follow mine owne minde and mine old trade,
> Who shall let me? the diuels nailes are vnparde. ✦

[Behind the unwillingness of the devil in the moralities to pare his own nails may lie a primitive folk-superstition. In *The Comedy of Errors* (IV.iii.72 f.) occur the lines,

> Some devils ask but the parings of one's nail,
> A rush, a hair, a drop of blood, a pin,

which suggest that the devil was believed to want such things, perhaps with a view to gaining some power thereby over the individual from whom they were taken. Hence the devil, in turn, would avoid paring his own nails lest the parings fall into the hands of an adversary. Such beliefs concerning *excrementa* are common among primitive peoples; see Bourke (1891, pp. 346 f.). It should also be remembered, however, that long talons are appropriate to the devil, since he uses them to torture his infernal victims.]

8. **good . . . diuell**] Malone (ed. 1790) quotes Johnson's conjecture : "This last line has neither rhime nor meaning. I cannot but suspect that the fool translates Malvolio's name, and says: *Adieu, goodman mean-evil.*" Malone replies : The last two lines of this song have, I think, been misunderstood. They are not addressed in the *first* instance to Malvolio, but are quoted by the clown, as the words, *ah, ah!* are, as the usual address in the old Moralities to the Devil. ✦ Kittredge (ind. ed. 1941) : Goodman, A title appropriate for a person below the rank of gentleman. It was an insult to the devil, for [*Lear* (III.iv.148)] "the prince of darkness is a gentleman."

MUSIC

The original setting of this song—if it is a song and not merely a rhyme—is unknown. But the text is set off and indented in the Folio, and assigned to Feste who sings elsewhere in the play, and so is likely to be a song. Caulfield (n.d., I, 153) gives musical notation for an incorrect version of the first two lines, but does not indicate the source for his music.

DRAMATIC FUNCTION

A standard belief of the times was that madness might be occasioned by diabolic possession. Hence Feste gulls Malvolio by pretending to be a Vice from a morality play, and mockingly addresses the devil who has taken possession of "mad" Malvolio. It is Feste's final gibe at the steward, and at the end of the song he departs to fetch "light and paper and ink" so Malvolio can pen a note to his mistress; in doing so he is only implementing the earlier wish of Sir Toby (IV.ii.72–77),

I would we were well rid of this knavery. If he may be conveniently deliver'd, I would he were; for I am now so far in offence with my niece that I cannot pursue with any safety this sport to the upshot.

34

TEXT: Folio (1623), sig. Z₆ (V.i.398–417).
TYPOGRAPHY: Indented verse, italic face; s.d., *Clowne ſings*.

When that I was and a little tine boy,
  with hey, ho, the winde and the raine:
A fooliſh thing was but a toy,
  for the raine it raineth euery day.

But when I came to mans eſtate,   5
  with hey ho, &c.
Gainſt Knaues and Theeues men ſhut their gate,
  for the raine, &c.

But when I came alas to wiue,
  with hey ho, &c.   10
By ſwaggering could I neuer thriue,
  for the raine, &c.

But when I came vnto my beds,
  with hey ho, &c.
With toſpottes ſtill had drunken heades,   15
  for the raine, &c.

A great while ago the world begon,
  hey ho, &c.
But that's all one, our Play is done,
  and wee'l ſtriue to pleaſe you euery day.

GENERAL COMMENTARY

Warburton (ed. 1747) : This wretched stuff not *Shakespeare's*, but the Players! ◆
Capell ([1779–1783 ?], II, part 4, p. 153) : Either this song was one then in vogue
which . . . the Clown (Mr. Kemp, perhaps) might be found famous for singing; or
else, the composition of the Clown, and so lug'd into the play without rime or
reason; or if indeed Shakespeare's writing,—of which it has small appearance,—a
thing idly drop'd from him upon some other occasion, and recommended by the
air it was set to: for to the play it has no relation. . . . Whoso wishes to strike a few

sparks of reason from it, must ... turn decypherer; as thus: The pursuits of the speaker, and his disappointments in some of them, in four stages of life, are severally describ'd in as many stanza's. ... Infancy; the follies of which were consider'd as follies and not regarded,—"A foolish thing was but a toy:" his Youth inclin'd him to knavery, and to be a little light-finger'd; but in this he had but sorry success, for—"*gainst knaves and theives men shut their gate:*" ... Manhood; when, thinking to rule the wife he then took by big-talking and "*swaggering,*" he throve ill. ... Age, (wickedly express'd by—"*when I came unto my beds,*") drove him to be a companion with "*toss-pots.*" ... The concluding stanza is a meer badinage. ◆ Steevens (ed. 1793) : Though we are well convinced that Shakespeare has written slight ballads for the sake of discriminating characters more strongly, or for other necessary purposes, in the course of his mixed dramas, it is scarce credible, that after he had cleared his stage, he should exhibit his Clown afresh, and with so poor a recommendation as this song, which is utterly unconnected with the subject of the preceding comedy. I do not therefore hesitate to call the nonsensical ditty before us, some buffoon actor's composition, which was accidentally tacked to the Prompter's copy of *Twelfth Night*, having been casually subjoined to it for a diversion, or at the call, of the lowest order of spectators. ◆ C. Knight (ed. [1838–1843]) : We hold [this song] to be the most philosophical Clown's song upon record; and a treatise might be written upon its wisdom. It is the history of a life, from the condition of "a little tiny boy," through "man's estate," to decaying age—"when I came unto my bed;" and the conclusion is, that what is true of the individual is true of the species, and what was of yesterday was of generations long past away,—for "A great while ago the world begun." ◆ Staunton (ed. 1858–1860) : It is to be regretted, perhaps, that this 'nonsensical ditty' ... has not been long since degraded to the footnotes. It was evidently one of those jigs, with which it was the rude custom of the Clown to gratify the groundlings upon the conclusion of the play. These absurd compositions, intended only as a vehicle for buffoonery, were usually improvisations of the singer. ◆ Weiss (1876, pp. 204 f.) : When the play is over, the Duke plighted to his page, Olivia rightly married to the wrong man, and the whole romantic ravel of sentiment begins to be attached to the serious conditions of life, Feste is left alone upon the stage. Then he sings a song which conveys to us his feeling of the world's impartiality; all things proceed according to law; nobody is humoured; people must abide the consequences of their actions, "for the rain it raineth every day." A "little tiny boy" may have his toy; but a man must guard against knavery and thieving; marriage itself cannot be sweetened by swaggering; whoso drinks with "toss-pots" will get a "drunken head"; it is a very old world and began so long ago that no change in its habits can be looked for. The grave insinuation of this song is touched with the vague, soft bloom of the play. As the noises of the land come over the sea well-tempered to the ears of islanders, so the world's fierce, implacable roar reaches us in the song, sifted through an air that hangs full of the Duke's dreams, of Viola's pensive love, of the hours which music flattered. The note is hardly more presageful than the cricket's stir in the late silence of a summer. How gracious has Shakespeare been to mankind in this play! He could not do otherwise than leave Feste all alone to pronounce its benediction; for his heart was a nest of songs whence they rose to whistle with the air of wisdom. ◆ Collier (ed. 1878) : It seems to us a brief and humorous epitome of the life of a rogue, such as it has been from the beginning of the world. ◆ White (ed. 1883) : This clown was a singing clown; a functioner on S.'s stage whose position was as clearly defined as that of the singing chambermaid is on our own. This song was one of those with which he was in the habit of amusing the groundlings. It is none of S.'s. ◆ Bradley (1916, p. 169) : Those critics who see in Feste's song only an illustration of the bad custom by which sometimes ... the clown remained, or appeared on the stage only to talk nonsense or to sing some old 'trash' ... may conceivably be right in perceiving no difference between the first four stanzas and the last, but they cannot possibly be right in failing to perceive how appropriate the song is to the singer, and how in the line

> But that's all one, our play is done,

he repeats an expression used a minute before in his last speech [(V.i.379 f.) "I was one, sir, in this interlude—one Sir Topas, sir; but that's all one."]. ◆ MacSweeney (1918, p. 40) agrees with Staunton that this song is "one of those jigs. . . ." He argues that Quince's ballet, referred to by Bottom in *Midsummer Night's Dream* (V.i.360 f.) may have been just such a jig to conclude their play. He adds : 'Twelfth Night' might therefore end with the Clown singing while the players, in whole or in part, dance to the music of his final song. ◆ Noble (1923, p. 85) : Appropriately enough, Feste winds up this high-spirited comedy with an Epilogue in the form of a song round a popular refrain, which in all probability the groundlings would take up. . . . Every one, whose life is at all worth living, has capacity for nonsense in its proper season, and where could it be more timely than at the end of *Twelfth Night*, for the wise nonsense contained in this ditty serves as a commentary on the events of the play, and is a fitting corollary to the first song, *O mistress mine*? ◆ L. B. Wright (1927, p. 263) : The epilogue song by Feste ... is thoroughly extraneous; it merely serves as a comic afterpiece by the clown and has no relation to the play itself. Some of the other clown songs in the play are only slenderly functional, if at all. ◆ Arden (ind. ed. 1929) : Before we criticize too closely the language of Shakespeare's clowns ... we shall do well to remember a remark of Coleridge: "Shakespeare has evinced the power which above all other men he possessed, that of introducing the profoundest sentiments of wisdom where they would be least expected, yet where they are most truly natural." ... It is too easy to describe these stanzas as "wretched stuff" ... as a "nonsensical ditty" ... as "scarcely worth correction"; ... below the surface nonsense of the inimitable Feste we have often looked down into the profoundest depths of knowledge and wisdom; and it is just possible that we may expect to do the same here. ... May we not have before us, in whatever humble guise, the philosophy of human life—the life at least of the average Elizabethan dramatist, the average sinner—nay, what is the difference, the average man. One stanza, and we have left behind us forever the innocence of childhood; the rest of the ditty will conduct us through the less happy stages of adult human life, where guilt reaps its own reward. ... Indeed, I think that while there may be something in this song "to gratify the groundlings," there is also something that may claim the authorship of Shakespeare; it is just his manner—to remind us that we must return to realities, that life is a serious business, and that "it is not good to stay too long in the Theater" (Bacon, *Advance-*

ment of Learning, II.iv.5 [1605, sig. 2E₃ᵛ]). Finally, it may be some earlier effort of the writer; and yet more to the purpose, the text of the song is certainly corrupt, and does not fairly represent its author, whether Shakespeare or another. ♦ New Cambridge (ind. ed. 1930) : We can, of course, only speculate, but for my part I . . . [refuse] to believe that Shakespeare can have been personally responsible for the song as a whole, even if . . . Bradley be allowed his plea on behalf of the last stanza. . . . And if the first four verses are not Shakespeare's then the most likely author for them is [Robert] Armin . . . who was writing ballads as early as 1592, and having, I suggest, scored a theatrical hit with the Shakespearean. 'He that has and a little tiny wit' in *King Lear* [(III.ii.74–77)] hoped to repeat it with a variation of his own on the same theme. In other words, I believe that the song at the end of *Twelfth Night* may have been written after the production of *King Lear*, which took place, if we adopt the generally accepted date, in the year 1606. The alternative is to assume that Shakespeare was not only complacent enough to allow Armin to add the song to *Twelfth Night* in 1602, but himself admired it so much as to write a variant of it for *King Lear*. ♦ [This argument begs the question. The most plausible view would be that Shakespeare wrote both songs; and in any event it seems unlikely that the scrap of song in *Lear* is the sort that would be apt to stop a show or score a hit, even at the hands of so talented a comedian as Armin was reputed to be. Yet in his notes to the song proper, the Cambridge editor argues even more aggressively that Armin was the author of the song in *Twelfth Night* :] Feste's song seems a mere development, and a clumsy one [of the quatrain in *Lear*] which contains all the 'philosophy' which Knight, one of the few champions of the song among the older critics, professed to find in it. I suggest that it is Armin's composition—his *Nest of Ninnies* [(1608)] is full of doggerel. . . . Shakespeare may have countenanced the song, he may even . . . have contributed himself the last stanza (though the phrase 'that's all one' seems to have been a favourite of Armin's, and occurs in the preface of *A Nest of Ninnies*) but he could not have written the fourth stanza. ♦

[The phrase "that's all one" does not, in fact, occur in the passage referred to; the text from Armin (1608, sig. A₂) reads:

> If you should flie out like rancke riders, or rebell like the Irish, twere much because my presumption challenges better being in you. But since all is one, and one all, that's car'd for.

Moreover the expression, far from being limited to Armin, seems to have been commonplace. It occurs twice elsewhere in *Twelfth Night* (I.v.137, V.i.201), and frequently in other plays of Shakespeare (see *Two Gentlemen*, III.i.263; *Merry Wives*, I.i.30; *Midsummer Night's Dream*, I.ii.51; *1 Henry IV*, IV.ii.51 f.).

Noble (1930, p. 576) quotes the Reverend Henry Todd: "I regard the Clown's song as autobiographical. . . . He confesses that when he married he became victim of petticoat government . . . that, when he came to have a family, he was an habitual drunkard and the constant companion of drunkards. . . ." Kittredge (ind. ed. 1941) : Editors and critics have vied with each other in denouncing this delightful ditty as nonsensical and un-Shakespearean. Knight goes to the other extreme. . . . At all events, it is an appropriate ending for a merry play, and I can see no earthly reason for suspecting that it was not Shakespeare's own. ♦

Ing (1951, p. 224) **:** *When that I was* is principally interesting for its simple 'popular' form, with the second and fourth lines of a quatrain as refrain, and the use of very loose syntax in the other lines to ensure perfect conformity to the tune pattern. The triplet hurry of unstressed syllables suggests an almost nursery-rime movement to make the syllables fit. ♦ Hotson (1954, pp. 167–172) **:** For lack of understanding of its drift, this song has naively been received as a tale in rime but little reason. . . . But is Feste the man to waste his wit in nonsense? He knows precisely what to provide as a fitting farewell to wassail and saturnalian excess. . . . ¶ Must we really be reminded that ribaldry was the proper and age-old function of the Fool? Shakespeare's colleague Robert Armin played not only Feste but Lear's Fool as well. Knavish, licentious speech is common to both roles. . . . Historically, the Fool and indecency cannot be parted. To make up for his mental shortcomings, Nature was commonly believed to have endowed the Fool with an excess of virility, symbolized by his *bauble*. . . . *Thing* in its 'bauble' sense is the key word . . . in the first stanza of Feste's song. In the Fool's childish state as a little tiny boy, a *foolish thing* was no more than a harmless trifle. Far otherwise, however, when he was grown 'fit for breed'—a lecherous knave and thief of love, on the prowl after other men's wives. . . . Feste has already given us his exquisite love songs; now we are to be sent away with 'a song of good life'. What he trolls out is a Drunkard's Progress . . . a moral and musical reminder that the wassailing of the Twelfth Night saturnalia had better not be followed as a way of life. ¶ . . . In the second stanza . . . the lecherous knave finds that his goatish vice renders him an outcast, shut out in the rain. In the third stanza, unable to mend his ways . . . he makes a shiftless, beggarly, wrangling marriage. Lion-drunk, he dings the pots about, swaggers with his own shadow, and his screeching wife drives him forth— out in the rain. ¶ The final phase exhibits him in the torpor . . . of the swine-drunk. . . . *Beds* is inevitably plural: the various spots where he happened to fall. . . . ¶ Again, out in the rain. . . . With a sorrowful hey-ho, the wind and the rain, and the implied early death they bring with them, form the inevitable burden . . . and for the drunken fool without the wit to come in out of the rain, it is all but ended. What of it? *But that's all one.* . . . Then turning smoothly into Robin Armin the player, Feste is out of his moral and into an Epilogue, to beg a gracious *plaudite* of the hearers. ♦ Hollander (1959, pp. 236 f.) **:** [Feste's] final song is a summation of the play in many ways at once . . . a kind of quick rehearsal of the Ages of Man. In youth, "A foolish thing was but a toy": the fool's bauble, emblematic of both his *membrum virile* and his trickery, is a trivial fancy. But in "man's estate" the bauble represents a threat of knavery and thievery to respectable society, who shuts its owner out of doors. The "swaggering" and incessant drunkenness of the following strophes bring Man into prime and dotage, respectively. Lechery, trickery, dissembling and drunkenness, inevitable and desperate in mundane existence, however, are just those activities which, mingled together in a world of feasting, serve to purge man of the desire for them. The wind and the rain accompany him throughout his life, keeping him indoors with "dreams and imaginations" as a boy, pounding and drenching him unmercifully, when he is locked out of doors, remaining eternal and inevitable throughout his pride in desiring to perpetuate himself. The wind and the rain are the most desperate of elements, that pound the walls and batter the roof of the warm house that shuts them out, while, inside it, the revels are in progress. Only after the party is ended can man face them without desperation.

TEXTUAL COMMENTARY

1. **tine**] Arden (ind. ed. 1929) **:** Was originally a noun, meaning a large vat; hence the phrase "a little tine," to denote a smaller vessel. The word occurs four times in Shakespeare [here, and *2 Henry IV* (V.i.29, iii.60 f.), and *Lear* (III.ii.74)] . . . and is always preceded by "little." ♦

2. **with . . . raine**] New Cambridge (ind. ed. 1930) notes the connection between the song in *Lear* (song 51) and this one, "the common refrain being a palpable reference to a wet season." But there is no reason to suppose that there is a topical reference to climate in the refrain. It appears to have been a common one in songs of the time, a fact which is evidenced by a passage in *Laugh and Lie Downe: Or, The Worldes Folly* (1605, sig. B₄):

> These passages who hath paste, and is come vnto the ende of his pilgrimage, let him sing with me in this purgatorie: *Oh the winde, the weather, and the rain.*

4. **for . . . day**] W. G. Smith (1935, p. 94) gives this notion as proverbial.

9–11. **wiue . . . thriue**] A proverbial rhyme; see W. G. Smith (1935, pp. 108, 235) and Tilley (1950, T-264).

13–15. **But . . . heades**] Noble (1930, "Feste's Song," p. 576) quotes the Reverend Todd: "'Beds' implies 'offspring' and is to be distinguished from the marriage bed with which it has been frequently confused by commentators." Kittredge (ind. ed. 1941) **:** If this stanza is taken as continuous in sense with the preceding stanza, the meaning may well be: 'I was such a swaggering reveller that I could never prosper, but whenever I went to bed I always had a drunken head, like other toss-pots'. . . . The plurals, *beds* and *heads*, seem to signify the different occasions on which he went to bed drunk. . . . Another possible interpretation of . . . bed is 'when I arrived at the bedtime of life'; . . . See . . . Overbury [*A Wife Now The Widdow* . . . (1614, sig. H₃)]: "It is bed-time with a man at threescore & ten." ♦ Hotson (1947, p. 351) **:** This puzzling passage . . . is obviously concerned with heavy drinking. Some light may possibly be thrown on it by a line from *Les propos des bienyvres* (Rabelais, *Garg.* I.v.): "Par ma fy, ma commère, je ne peuz entrer en bette." In the Flammarion edition (Paris, 1917 [actually n.d., but published in 1906]), ii. 291a., *bette* is glossed "boisson, action de boire." Urquhart's translation [1653, *Master Francis Rabelais, translated into English by Sir Thomas Urquhart of Cromarty and Peter Anthony Motteux* (1904, I, 24)], "By my figgins, godmother, I cannot as yet enter into the humour of being merry, nor drink so currently as I would," shows that he firmly grasped the sense of *entrer en bette*. But there exists an earlier version by Shakespeare's contemporary, John Eliot, embedded in his *Ortho-epia Gallica*, 1593. . . . The line runs "By my fe Gossip I cannot enter into my bets." Eliot must have assumed that the gallicism "bets" for "drinking" was currently understood among Englishmen. Feste's "came unto my beds" is very close. . . . And if he *did* mean "When I took to drinking reg'lar," his consequence, "With tosspots still had drunken heads," follows as an unforced conclusion.

[Hotson seems since to have changed his mind; see general commentary (1954, pp. 167–172) by him, above.] ♦ J. D. Wilson (1947, p. 379) takes issue with Hotson's reading, and maintains that the real difficulty is neither the sense of "But when I came unto my beds," which (he says) follows naturally enough on "But when I came alas to wive"; nor the plural "beds," which can be explained as a forced rhyme for "heads." The real crux, according to Wilson, is the line "With toss-pots still had drunken heads." He remarks : A. W. Pollard proposed to read it "We . . . heads," and I feel pretty sure he was right. Since "with" is the first word of the line above, the misprint would be easy, more especially if the *e* of "we" was written blind so that the word looked like "wt." In any case, the "toss-pots" can hardly be anybody but Master and Mistress Feste, or the "drunken heads" be other than theirs. . . . Not great poetry, but doggerel good enough for Robert Armin. ♦ [Cotgrave (1611, sig. K₂ᵛ) gives:

> Bettes. *Beets, &c, (as before in* Bette*;) also, tipling, sipping, bowsing, quaffing; and hence;* Entrer en bettes. *To grow merrie, or mellow in drinking; or to fall a chattering, as gossips do when they haue drunke hard, together.*

But the most likely interpretation of "came unto my beds" would still take the final word in its English sense.]

17. **begon**] An old form of the past tense, surviving from the old past plural *begun*; see *NED.*

MUSIC

The earliest surviving music for this song is a "traditional" tune surviving in a number of closely related versions. Its earliest published appearance is in Vernon (n.d. [1772], p. 3), and it is possible that it may have been composed by Vernon. Linley (1816, I, 34 f.) gives the tune and attributes it to a man called Fielding, possibly the theatrical composer Henry Fielding (1707–1754). He is followed in this respect by Chappell (1840, I, 109; II, 65), but in his *Popular Music* Chappell ([1855–1859], I, 225) reproduces the tune as having "no other authority than theatrical tradition." Sternfeld (1963, pp. 189–191, and 1964, *Songs*, pp. 22–25) gives transcriptions of both the Vernon and the Chappell versions of the tune.

This tune, or slight variants of it, can also be found in Elson (1901, pp. 321 f.), Vincent (1906, pp. 67 f.), Hardy (1930, II, 72), Bontoux (1936, pp. 359 f.), Long (1955, p. 182), H. A. Chambers (1957, pp. 57 f.), and Kines (1964, p. 18).

DRAMATIC FUNCTION

There seems to be no reason for denying the authenticity of the song. With the exception of the word "toss-pots," a nonce word in Shakespeare, the diction of the song is not at all unusual. Critics who deny Shakespeare's authorship of the song might be embarrassed should the authorship of all the broadside ballads become known, for it is likely that the youthful Shakespeare spun out ballads for popular consumption along with Elderton, Deloney, and the rest of the "pot poets."

It is entirely proper that so tuneful a play as *Twelfth Night* should end with a song, just as its predecessor had ended with two of them. Although it was customary for a jig to end the performances of plays in the public theaters, this song does not fit into the category (see Baskervill, 1929, for a description of the form that genre took).

The indecent meanings that Hotson—and Hollander after him—find in the text depend on an egregious twisting of meaning that linguistic specialists would be unlikely to support. The license regularly accorded fools certainly allowed indecency, but did not guarantee it. Short of more forthright evidence, Hotson's interpretations remain only conjectures.

The analyses provided by Weiss and White may be florid and extravagant, yet both of them probably speak more truly of the song than its many detractors. In its logical development—from boyhood, to youth, to maturity, to middle age—the song does trace, as Hollander and others note, an "Ages of Man." It is also a call back to reality from the revels and romanticism of the play. Whatever else it may be would best be left to viewers of the play. No one who has ever heard it sung to Vernon's music would wish it omitted.

Hamlet

35

TEXT: Second Quarto (1604), sig. K₄ (IV.v.23–26, 29–32, 35, 37–39).
TYPOGRAPHY: Unindented verse, roman face; s.d., *ſhee ſings* and *Song*.

How ſhould I your true loue know from another one,
By his cockle hat and ſtaffe, and his Sendall ſhoone.

     .   .

He is dead & gone Lady, he is dead and gone,
At his head a graſgreene turph, at his heeles a ſtone.

     .   .

White his ſhrowd as the mountaine ſnow.   5

     .   .

Larded all with ſweet flowers,
Which beweept to the ground did not go
With true loue ſhowers.

GENERAL COMMENTARY

Malone (ed. 1790) quotes Sir Joshua Reynolds : There is no part of this play, in its representation on the stage, more pathetick than this scene; which, I suppose, proceeds from the utter insensibility Ophelia has to her own misfortunes. ◆ Bradley (1904, pp. 60 f.) : In [the latter part] . . . of a tragedy Shakespeare often appeals to an emotion different from any of those excited in the first half of the play, and so provides novelty and generally also relief. As a rule this new emotion is pathetic; and the pathos is not terrible or lacerating, but, even if painful, is accompanied by the sense of beauty and by the outflow of admiration or affection, which come with an inexpressible sweetness after the tension of the crisis. . . . So it is with . . . the introduction of Ophelia in her madness . . . where the effect, though intensely pathetic, is beautiful and moving, rather than harrowing. ◆ Davies (1939, pp. 119 f.) : The boy who played Ophelia would be a trained singer. . . . The stage direction for her entrance in the First Quarto reads: ' *Enter Ofelia playing on her lute*

and her haire downe singing'; the flowing hair was a conventional Elizabethan sign
of madness, and the presence of the lute means that Ophelia, like any Court lady,
is a musician and will play and sing like one. . . . Sometimes the songs are crooned
or sung in a small and pathetic voice in order to accentuate the pitifulness of the
situation. Pathetic the scene is, but it is also terrible, and this aspect of it can only
be brought out by an intelligent actress who can sing. ◆ McCullen (1952, p. 193) :
[Ophelia's] songs increase the perturbations of friends who become more and more
alarmed because of the disorder and danger in her behavior. As for Ophelia herself, her singing increases the tragic impression of her isolation in madness.
Harping on thwarted love and death, chief causes of her madness, she sings songs
that increase the impression that hardly anyone can escape the intrigues, the
passions, and the madness of Elsinore. The chaos of her mind, which has sloughed
off the modesty formerly prominent in her behavior, increases impressions that
tragic developments have already moved beyond the possibility of control, and
the fact that her singing arouses Laertes to destructive action motivated by blind
passion further intensifies the tragic gloom. ◆ Auden (1957, p. 42) : It is generally
desirable that a character who breaks into impromptu song should not have a
good voice. No producer, for example, would seek to engage Madame Callas for
the part of Ophelia, because the beauty of her voice would distract the audience's
attention from the real dramatic point which is that Ophelia's songs are to the
highest degree *not* called-for. We are meant to be horrified both by what she sings
and by the fact that she sings at all. The other characters are affected but not in the
way people are affected by music. The King is terrified, Laertes so outraged that he
becomes willing to use dirty means to avenge his sister. ◆ [It should not be overlooked, however, that the ability to read and sing music competently, and to play
upon the lute or some other instrument, was among the ordinary accomplishments expected of a Renaissance lady. Furthermore, the music given to Ophelia
in this play and to Desdemona in *Othello* suggests that Shakespeare's troupe had at
this time a skilled singing boy who could carry off these roles.] Nosworthy (1958,
p. 63) : The portrayal of madness must always have imposed a strain on the boy-
actors, and the standard pattern of rhetorical lunacy deriving from *The Spanish
Tragedy* and the Senecan tradition can hardly have seemed attractive to Shakespeare at this stage of his career. Ophelia's "snatches of old tunes" may therefore
constitute a resolution of difficulties by evasion. ◆ [The evidence of the stage
direction in the "bad" first quarto, cited by Davies, is probably decisive as to how
the song was rendered on Shakespeare's stage. A pirater might have come away
from a performance in the Globe Theater and proceeded to garble lines and con-
fuse speech assignments, but he is hardly likely to have forgotten what he *saw* on
the stage.] Vyvyan (1959, p. 50) : [As Ophelia enters] she is out of her mind, and
singing. The song is not really about her father; it has all to do with the betrayal
and death of true love—of herself and Hamlet's self. ◆

Sternfeld (1963, pp. 54 f.) : Desdemona . . . sings an old song in the privacy of
her bed-chamber with only her maid as an involuntary audience. . . . But Ophelia
sings one ditty after another before the Court of Denmark. Such behaviour was
strange, indeed, and contrary to all sense of propriety for an Elizabethan gentle-
woman—or man, for that matter. ¶ Thomas Morley's affable remarks [in *A
Plaine and Easie Introduction to Practicall Musicke* (1597)] implying that "the art of

singing was cultivated with equal zeal and discernment in every grade of social rank" have long since been dismissed as without proper foundation. These comments are at variance with contemporary writings on etiquette which governed the behaviour of nobility and gentry. . . . [Castiglione condemns] the frequent and unsolicited performance of music by members of the aristocracy . . . with a reminder that, were such activity to be pursued, class distinctions between a nobleman and his music-performing servants would be broken down. . . . To ensure the proper attitude in ladies as well as gentlemen, Castiglione [advises]: "when she cometh to dance, or to show any kind of music, she ought to be brought to it with suffering herself somewhat to be prayed, and with a certain bashfulness. . . ." ◆

[Sternfeld presses his argument from the courtesy books more than this episode really allows. In the first place, on neither of the occasions when Ophelia sings is she actually giving a public recital. She sings her first two songs before Gertrude and Horatio, her last three before Gertrude, Horatio, Claudius, and Laertes—a group of auditors who can be referred to as "the Court of Denmark" only in a very limited sense. It would be a puristic "courtier" indeed who would find impropriety in her singing before this intimate group. Had Ophelia, instead, rendered her songs before the full Court of Denmark in I.ii., or during the play-within-the-play scene (III.ii.), she would deserve the strictures that might be laid on her conduct by Castiglione and the other courtesy-book writers.

In the second place, Sternfeld's argument depends on the unproved assumption that Castiglione and the writers who derived from him were the exclusive arbiters of taste for Shakespeare and his contemporaries, that the rules of personal conduct set down in *The Covrtyer* and similar books were the acknowledged norm of practical English behavior. At the least such an assumption overlooks the ordinary cultural lag that exists in every society between the theory and practice of etiquette. Finally, it should be noted that Morley's "affable remarks" were intended to sell his book; they were obviously aimed at his unskilled contemporaries who felt that a performing knowledge of music was the path to social advancement. For a concise description of the various—and often conflicting—attitudes toward music in sixteenth- and seventeenth-century England, see Woodfill (1953, pp. 201–239). Also see Preface, above.]

Seng (1964, *DUJ*, pp. 78 f.) **:** The surface irony detected by most of the commentators—that the ballad relates to the death of Polonius—is not wrong; it simply does not go far enough. The song does, after all, tell of a loved one who has unexpectedly died and who has been buried without loving rites. . . . [But] the next level of interpretation ought to relate Ophelia's song more closely to its context. Ophelia's appearance on her entrance confirms what the audience has already heard about her, that she is mentally deranged. . . . Her first question is, "Where is the beauteous Majesty of Denmark?" We can echo with Granville-Barker, "Aye, indeed, where is she?" Certainly not in the wretched and haggard Queen confronting the mad girl. In timid words that betray her apprehension Gertrude responds, "How now, Ophelia?" Her nondescript question receives its only answer in [ll. 1–2 of] the song. It is easy to imagine the Queen's guilty start, her sudden dread of what the crazed girl may say. We sense it in her appalled question: "Alas, sweet lady, what imports this song?" . . . [It] clearly imports, among other things, that Gertrude once had a true-love whom she failed to distinguish from "another one." ... [But] "He is dead and gone, lady." "Nay, but Ophelia—" the Queen interrupts, only to be told ... that the true-love was one "Which bewept to the grave did not go With true-love showers." That obviously interpolated negative chides Gertrude for her inadequate mourning for King Hamlet, and perhaps for worse offences as well. ✦

[As though deliberately establishing the atmosphere for these ironic reverberations, Shakespeare has Gertrude stress her own sense of guilt in the lines immediately preceding her exchange of words with the mad girl. In an aside to the audience the Queen says (IV.v.17–20):

> To my sick soul (as sin's true nature is)
> Each toy seems prologue to some great amiss.
> So full of artless jealousy is guilt
> It spills itself in fearing to be spilt.]

TEXTUAL COMMENTARY

2. **By ... shoone**] Warburton (ed. 1747) : This is the description of a pilgrim. While this kind of devotion was in fashion, love-intrigues were carried under that mask. Hence the old ballads and novels made pilgrimages the subjects of their plots. The cockle-shell was one of the essential badges of this vocation: for the chief places of devotion being beyond the sea, or on the coasts, the pilgrims were accustomed to put cockle-shells upon their hats to denote the intention or performance of their devotion. ✦ Arden (ind. ed. 1928) : [A cockle-hat was] a hat with a scallop-shell stuck in it, the sign of a pilgrim having been at the shrine of St. James Compostella. ✦ [The origins of the cockle-shell symbol go back earlier than any of the editors suggests. The shell is a sign of spiritual regeneration by grace since in the early Church it was used to pour the waters of Baptism. As such a symbol it was incorporated into church architecture and into medieval paintings. As a pilgrim's badge it symbolized the repentance for sin and spiritual regeneration which were the objects of pilgrimages.] Vyvyan (1959, p. 141) : This has nothing to do with Polonius. In reality [Ophelia] is singing about her own true love, of whose identity no one is in doubt. He is to set out on a pilgrimage of expiation ... to cross the sea ... to obtain forgiveness. It might well be that the sea is the waters of death; and beyond them, perhaps, is a holier shrine. And so I take this to be Shakespeare's valediction to a pilgrim soul. ✦

shoone] The archaic plural for *shoes*; *Sendall ſhoone* are sandals.

4. **At ... stone**] Some sort of primitive burial custom is involved, perhaps one to keep the ghost from walking. So in Keats's "Isabella, or the Pot of Basil" (ll. 298 f.),

> Red whortle berries droop above my head
> And a large flint-stone weighs upon my feet.

See also Wells (1950, p. 143), who gives a ballad (No. 69) from the Child collection which refers to the same custom.

5. **White ... shrowd**] The customary color of shrouds at the time; cf. *Twelfth Night* (II.iv.56), "My shroud of white, stuck all with yew."

6. **Larded**] Covered, lined, or strewn with. See *NED*. This burial custom is also referred to by Gertrude at Ophelia's funeral (V.i.266–269), and in *Twelfth Night* (II.iv.60 f.).

7. **not**] Kittredge (ind. ed. 1939) : All the quartos and Folios have 'not.' We are to regard it as Ophelia's insertion in the verse. She suddenly remembers that the words of the song do not quite agree with the facts of her father's burial, which was hasty and without the usual ceremonies. ◆ [If the lost source of Ophelia's song were to be discovered, it would probably reveal that Shakespeare made a number of other changes as well in adapting the popular ballad to his purposes. Surviving analogues suggest that the "true-love" of the original ballad was a woman, not a man. Hence to fit the song to Ophelia, Shakespeare would also have had to change some pronouns around. In doing so he would be making the same sort of adaptations in the words of the song that we know he made a little later when he changed the words of Desdemona's "Willow Song" to make it dramatically appropriate to her situation.]

MUSIC

What may be the original music for Ophelia's first song survives in two related melodies, one a "traditional" tune deriving from the Drury Lane Theatre in the eighteenth century, the other a popular tune called "Walsingham" that goes back at least to the sixteenth century. The tune usually heard on the stage today is some version or other of the "traditional tune" copied down early in the nineteenth century by William Linley or Samuel Arnold from the dictation of actresses who had played the role of Ophelia at the Drury Lane in the eighteenth century.

Numerous modern printings of this traditional melody are available: Linley (1816, II, 50), C. Knight (ed. 1838–1843, *Tragedies*, I, 151 f.), Chappell (1840, II, 20; [1855–1859], I, 236), Caulfield (n.d., II, 83–85), Gibbon (1930, p. 106), Naylor (1931, p. 189), Bontoux (1936, p. 346), Sternfeld (1963, p. 62), and Kines (1964, p. 32). Closely related to this tune is one from the *Beggar's Opera* (1728) called "You'll think ere many days ensue," reprinted by Chappell (1840, II, 19), Elson (1901, p. 236), and Sternfeld (1963, p. 62).

The "authenticity" of this melody as the original tune for Ophelia's song depends from a tenuous chain of evidence, indeed. According to Chappell ([1855–1859], I, 236),

> The late W. Linley (an accomplished amateur, and brother of the highly-gifted Mrs. Sheridan) collected and published "the wild and pathetic melodies of Ophelia, as he remembered them to have been exquisitely sung by Mrs. Forster, when she was Miss Field, and belonged to Drury Lane Theatre;"and he says "the impression remained too strong on his mind to make him doubt the correctness of the airs, agreeably to her delivery of them." Dr. Arnold also noted them down from the singing of Mrs. Jordan, and Mr. Ayrton has followed that version in his Annotations to Knight's *Pictorial Edition of Shakespeare*.

Both Dorothea Jordan and Mrs. Forster played the role of Ophelia at the Drury Lane late in the eighteenth century; it is reasonable to suppose that the music they sang would have come from scores in the theater-library (destroyed along with the theater in the fire of 1812). Furthermore, as Sternfeld (1963, p. 60) remarks, "Knight drew largely on the knowledge of Samuel Arnold (1740–1802), who shared the honours of conducting at the Drury Lane Theatre with the older Linley and Linley's son William (1771–1835)." Thus there seems little question that the melodies they copied down would have been authentic Drury Lane tunes for the songs of Ophelia.

To suppose, however, that those tunes could have originated in Shakespeare's Globe Theater requires uncritical acceptance of the following hypotheses: that Shakespeare was the natural father of Sir William D'Avenant, that the "son" possessed the musical scores from the Globe, that he passed them on to his protégé Thomas Betterton, and that Betterton brought them to the Drury Lane. Some sort of case can be made out for each step in the argument—even for the antique scandal on which the whole is founded—but taken in its entirety the argument is too tangential to be credited.

Naylor (1931, p. 190) asserts what is probably the fact about the "traditional melody" for Ophelia's song, that it is a "badly damaged version" of the ancient tune called "Walsingham," an extremely popular tune in Shakespeare's day, and one which survives in a number of musical collections contemporary with the dramatist. "Walsingham" is contained in the Fitzwilliam Virginal Book with settings by John Bull and William Byrd (ed. Fuller-Maitland, 1894–1899, I, 1–18, and 267–273); Byrd's variations are given by Fellowes (1950, pp. 24–30) and Bull's by Dart (1963, pp. 46–59). The basic tune is to be found in Chappell ([1855–1859], I, 123), Wooldridge (1893; reprinted 1961, I, 69), and Naylor (1931, p. 190). Sternfeld (1963, p. 61) gives the Bull tune fitted to words from the Percy Folio MS., and (1964, *Music and Letters*, p. 111; 1964, *Songs*, p. 10) the tune from William Barley's *A new Booke of Tabliture* (1596) in the harmonization by Francis Cutting with Shakespeare's words underlaid. He also gives (1964, *Songs*, p. 8) the tune as harmonized by Byrd with both the words from Shakespeare and from Huntington Library MS. HM 198 fitted to it. See also C. Simpson (1966, p. 471).

Other early occurrences of the "Walsingham tune" and modern transcriptions: Lady Nevell's Virginal Book (ed. Andrews, 1926, pp. 173–180), Cambridge University Library MSS. Dd. 5.20 (ed. Dart, 1955, p. 200) and Dd. 2.11 (fols. 96^v–97), the John Weld Lute Book (fols. 9^v–10), Will. Forster's Virginal Book in the B. M. Royal Library (fol. 39^v), B. M. Add. MS. 30,486 (fol. 2), Anthony Holborne's *The Cittharn Schoole*, 1597 (sig. C$_3$^{v}), and Cutting's version (ed. Lumsden, 1954, pp. 45–47). These numerous early versions of the melody, either under the title "Walsingham" or "Have with you to Walsingham," clearly mark it as a tune of enormous popularity.

Naylor's contention that the "traditional" Drury Lane tune for Ophelia's song is a corruption of the older tune, "Walsingham," is further strengthened by the fact that "Frauncis new Iigge, betweene Frauncis a Gentleman, and Richard a Farmer" (Rollins, 1922, pp. 2–10), a ballad that has verbal parallels with Ophelia's song, is also in part "To the tune of Walsingham." Hence if the "traditional" melody does represent a survival of the music heard on Shakespeare's stage, the original tune was more likely preserved by imitations and parodies of "Walsingham songs" than by the dubious "tradition" leading back through the Drury Lane Theatre and Betterton and D'Avenant to Shakespeare and the Globe play-house.

ANALOGUES

Although the source of Ophelia's first song has not survived, there exists an interesting analogue to it in "As ye came from the holy land of Walsingham," a ballad which has been handed down in three manuscripts and one printed version. The text which follows, perhaps a reworking of the lost source on which Shake-speare drew, is from the Percy Folio MS. (B. M. Add. MS. 27,879, fols. 251–251ᵛ; ed. Hales, 1867–1868, III, 471 f.). Slightly different versions of the same ballad are in Bodleian MS. Rawlinson Poetry 85 (fol. 123; ed. Latham, 1951, pp. 22 f.), and Hunt-ington Library MS. HM 198 (ed. Bennett, 1941, pp. 473 f.). The printed version is in Thomas Deloney's *The Garland of Good-Will*, 1678 (sig. G₅ᵛ). Sternfeld (1964, *Music and Letters*, pp. 111–113) reprints the Huntington version in modern orthography, with collations of variants in the other three texts.

> As yee came fr: the Holye
>
> AS: yee came ffrom the holy Land
> of walsingham
> mett you not wth my true loue
> by the way as you Came
> how shold I know yor true loue
> that haue mett many a one
> as I came ffrom the holy Land
> that haue come that haue gone
>
> Shee is neither white nor browne
> but as the heauens ffaire
> there is none hathe their fforme diuine
> on the earth or the ayre
> such a one did I meete good Sir:
> with an angellike fface
> who like a nimph like a quene did appeare
> in her gate in her grace
>
> Shee hath left me heere alone
> all alone as vnknowne
> who sometime loued me as her liffe
> & called me her owne
> what is the cause shee hath left thee alone
> & a new way doth take
> that sometime did loue thee as her selfe
> & her ioy did thee make

I haue loued her all my youth
but now am old as you see
loue liketh not the ffalling ffruite
nor the whithered tree
for loue is like a carlesse child
& fforgets promise past
he is blind he is deaffe when he list
& infaith neuer ffast

his desire is ffickle ffond
& a trustles ioye
he is won with a world of dispayre
& lost with a toye
such is the [*lacuna in MS.*] kind
Or the word loue abused
vnder which many childish desires
& conceipts are excused

Butloue is a durabler ffyre
in the mind euer Burninge
euer sicke neuer dead neuer cold
ffrom itt selfe neuer turninge   ffinis

The reprint of the Deloney version in Mann (1912, pp. 365 ff.) purports to be from the 1631 edition of *The Garland* in the Bodleian Library, but the Bodleian's unique copy of that book is imperfect, lacking all of signature G which probably contained the Walsingham ballad, so the source of Mann's text is uncertain. It was probably the 1678 edition where the poem appears in the G gathering, the source of the reprint by Dixon (1851, pp. 111 f.).

The authorship of the ballad is disputed. Since it is subscribed "Sr W. R:" in the Rawlinson manuscript, editors of Ralegh's works usually claim it for him (see Latham, 1951, p. 121). Deloney's claim to it is based on nothing more than the likelihood that the poem may have appeared in the 1631 edition of *The Garland of Good-Will*. But Deloney died in 1600, and, in any event, neither ballad-writers nor ballad-printers were above appropriating the wares of others. As between the two men, attribution to Ralegh should be regarded as the more probable.

Another analogue of the lost original also turns up in the Percy Folio MS. (fols. 258–258ᵛ); ed. Hales, 1867–1868, III, 526–528). It begins:

Gentle: heardsman tell to me
of curtesy I thee pray
vnto the towne of walsingham
which is the right and ready way

vnto the towne of walsingam
the way is hard ffor to be gon
& verry crooked are those pathes
ffor you to ffind out all alone

weere the miles doubled 3^{ise}
   & the way neuer soe ill
itt were not enough for mine offence
   it is soe greuious & soe ill

In the remainder of the ballad the pilgrim explains that she is a woman in man's disguise; she tells how she treated her faithful lover with such haughtiness and disdain that he went away and died as a result of her cruel treatment. Now, she says, she is going on a pilgrimage of repentance, and seeks only to die as he did.

A parody of the lost ballad in the Percy Folio MS. (fol. 47; ed. Hales, 1867–1868, I, 253 f.) is further evidence of its popularity:

Came you not from Newcastle
   came yee not there away
met yee notmy true loue
   ryding on a bony bay
why shold not I loue my loue
   why shold not my loue loue me
why shold not I loue my loue
   gallant hound sedelee

And I haue Land att Newcastle
   will buy both hose & shoone
and I haue Land att Durham
   will feitch my hart to boone
and why shold not I loue my loue
   why shold not my loue loue me
why shold not I loue my loue
   gallant hound sedelee./
              ffins.

At least two broadside ballads belong to the "Walsingham" genre. "The contented Couckould" (ed. Rollins, 1929–1932, II, 24) begins,

Seest thou not my true Loue,
   seest not my Louer go downe,
And seest thou not my true louer then
   com thorough *New-Castle Towne.*

And metest thou not my true Loue
   by the way as you came
How should I know your true Loue,
   that haue met many a one,
She is neyther whit nor black
   but as the heauens faire
Her lookes are very beautifull,
   none may with her compare.
She hath falsied her word
   and left me heere alone.

6+v.s.

The other broadside is "Attowel's Jigg" (ed. Rollins, 1922, p. 2):

> As I went to Walsingham,
>   to the shrine with speed,
> Met I with a iolly Palmer,
>   in a Pilgrims weede.

The popularity of the lost ballad is also indicated by imitations and parodies preserved in early seventeenth-century drama. In Beaumont and Fletcher's *The Knight of the Burning Pestle*, 1613 (sig. E$_3$v; ed. Waller, 1905–1912, VI, 192), Old Merrythought who is a veritable fountain of popular songs of the time carols out,

> As you came from Walsingham, from that holy land,
>   there met you not with my tru-loue by the way
> as you came.

The song is burlesqued in Daubridgecourt Belchier's *Hans Beer-Pot His Invisible Comedie*, 1618 (sig. B$_3$),

> As I went to Walsingham
> To that holy Land,
> Met I with an olde balde Mare,
> By the way as I came,

and there is a clear allusion in William Rowley's *A Match at Midnight*, 1633 (sig. B$_4$),

> Did her not see her true Loves,
> As her came from London,
> Oh, if her saw not her fine prave Loves,
> *Randall* is quite undone.

From the text in Shakespeare, and from the variety of imitative material which has survived, it is possible to make some reasonable conjectures about the lost source of Ophelia's song. It was evidently written in ballad-meter like the fragments in *Hamlet* and most of the parodies and imitations. Since it employs the dialogue device of question and answer, it may have been a jig. It is even possible to infer the narrative pattern: A deserted lover meets on the roadway a pilgrim returning from the shrine of Our Lady of Walsingham. The lover's mistress has also gone on a pilgrimage to Walsingham, but has failed to return. The lover inquires of the stranger he has met whether she has been seen on the way. Asked how she can be recognized, he attempts to describe her. This opening, the encounter and the inquiry, seems to be the common mark of "Walsingham songs."

It is a fascinating beginning for a story which is capable of a number of endings, depending on the taste and temperament of the writer. In the Ralegh version, the old lover deserted by his (apparently) young mistress, takes melancholy refuge from his sorrows by philosophizing on old age and the nature of true love. In "The contented Couckould" the lover also philosophizes in melancholy vein, but ultimately proves that he is made of sterner stuff by resolving, at the conclusion of the first part, to pursue and recover his lady. This feat he accomplishes in a sequel when he sails to Gravesend, finds his wife with another man, but successfully brings her, repentant, home.

These two denouements can be taken to represent the literary and the broadside developments of the lost folk-ballad. Ophelia's song differs from both in being much closer to its source. Moreover, for his own dramatic purposes, Shakespeare has apparently reversed the roles of the lovers: in his song it is the mistress who awaits in longing the return of her pilgrim-lover. From a wayfarer she learns that he has been stayed forever on his pilgrimage by death. This simple note of tragedy is almost a motif of the folk ballad. If this hypothetical reconstruction of the lost ballad is correct, then Ophelia's song is, *au fond*, far more meaningful than most critics have suspected; it has, indeed, an organic relationship to the action of the play.

DRAMATIC FUNCTION

Coleridge alone, among commentators on this song, seems to have divined the memories that may underlie it in Ophelia's deranged mind. In his lectures on Shakespeare (ed. Raysor, 1930, I, 33 f.) he called attention to the conjunction in her songs of

two thoughts that had never subsisted in disjunction, the love for Hamlet and her filial love, and the guileless floating on the surface of her pure imagination of the cautions so lately expressed and the fears not too delicately avowed by her father and brother concerning the danger to which her honor lay exposed.

The last the audience has seen of Ophelia before she enters deranged, singing and playing on a lute, is the time when she sat beside Hamlet, a naive auditor of the play-within-the-play. Prior to this occasion she has known herself to be in love with Hamlet and has thought that Hamlet loved her. Laertes' cautions on the perils of such a relationship she had accepted with charming good humor, her father's strictures with loving and dutiful obedience. She must have known as well as either of them that Lord Hamlet was a prince out of her star, yet she was willing to bide her time patiently, waiting his formal proposals. She had good reason to expect them. The remarks made by Gertrude at her funeral,

> I hop'd thou shouldst have been my Hamlet's wife;
> I thought thy bride-bed to have deck'd, sweet maid,
> And not have strew'd thy grave   (V.ii.267–269),

cannot have been unique on this occasion. And long before her death Polonius himself admitted that his own earlier judgement of Hamlet's "tenders of affection" might have been in error.

But the events which have transpired between the time of her appearance at the court play and her entrance "with her haire downe singing" have undone her world. Her father has been killed—by her mad lover as she believes—and hastily interred. Her brother is abroad at school in a foreign land. Hamlet has been hustled out of Denmark and been put aboard ship for England. The distraught girl could hardly turn to King Claudius, and the "beauteous Majesty of Denmark," Gertrude, has apparently been avoiding her. For Ophelia, as for Hamlet, Denmark has become a prison, and she is all alone at Elsinore. It is the realization of this fact, coming on top of all the earlier horrors, that destroys her sanity.

In the light of such a background the "true-love" of the ballad is now seen to be Hamlet. He has gone across the seas on a mysterious voyage whose import is unknown to her. Yet the song that she sings fancifully explains to her the mystery of his disappearance, illuminates in her deranged mind the few paltry facts she possesses. Hamlet has left Elsinore to make a pilgrimage to Walsingham—he has reason enough to do penance—and he can be recognized on the road by the habiliments of the pilgrim. To her, so much, at least, must seem plausible. But the old song has its own inexorable logic, and the romantic fiction of its tragic story becomes the only reality Ophelia knows: "He is dead and gone, Lady." For an audience viewing this scene, irony is added to the pathos. The nightmare delusion which assails the poor girl's mind is, in fact, the very reality which Claudius had intended.

Ophelia's song begins with an imaginary wayfarer's echo of her simple query about her missing lover; it ends with the equally simple statement about his burial in a foreign land. Hamlet has been laid to earth by strangers, and without the tribute of Ophelia's true-love tears. Such a burial is a foreshadowing of her own barren rites a few scenes later in the unconsecrated plot of Elsinore churchyard.

36

TEXT: Second Quarto (1604), sig. K₄ᵛ (IV.v.48–55, 58–66).
TYPOGRAPHY: Indented and unindented verse, roman face; s.d., *Song*.

To morrow is S. Valentines day,
All in the morning betime,
And I a mayde at your window
To be your Valentine.
Then vp he rofe, and dond his clofe, and dupt the chamber
    doore,   5
Let in the maide, that out a maide, neuer departed more.

.   .   .

By gis and by Saint Charitie
  alack and fie for fhame,
Young men will doo't if they come too't
  by Cock they are too blame.   10
Quoth fhe, Before you tumbled me, you promifd me to wed,
(He anfwers.) So would I a done by yonder funne
       And thou hadft not come to my bed.

GENERAL COMMENTARY

Halliwell (ed. 1853–1865) : This song alludes to the custom of the first girl seen by a man on the morning of this day being considered his Valentine or true-love. . . . The custom of the different sexes choosing themselves mates on St. Valentine's Day, February 14, the names being selected either by lots, or methods of divination, is of great antiquity in England. ◆
Bradley (1904, p. 165) : There are critics who . . . still shake their heads over Ophelia's song. . . . Probably they are incurable, but they may be asked to consider that Shakespeare makes Desdemona, 'as chaste as ice, as pure as snow,' sing [*Othello*, IV.iii.57] an old song containing the line,
      If I court moe women, you'll couch with moe men. ◆
Moore (1916, pp. 91 f.) : The ballad snatches in the mouth of Ophelia, weirdly contrasting with the secluded innocence of her life, indicate clearly the joint causes of her derangement. The objectionable ballads, doubtless childhood recollections of a nurse's songs, are discordant echoes of Hamlet's defection. ◆ Kittredge (ind. ed. 1939) : In her madness Ophelia sings a song that she has heard in childhood. Her nurse . . . may well have been as free-spoken as Juliet's. Everybody knows what happens in the way of indecorous speech when delirium stirs up the dregs of memory and puts an end to reticence. ◆ Davies (1939, p. 120) : The coarseness

of the second song is ... characteristic of madness. ... Many people reveal an astonishing knowledge of obscene language and of songs when their wits leave them. If this song is sung loudly and shamelessly the effect is shocking to the audience, and the interjection of "He answers" into the second verse increases this effect as it stresses the brutality of the song. ♦ Granville-Barker (1947, I, 120 f.) : [Ophelia's] poor mind travels to a perverted mirroring of the tragedy of her love for Hamlet. ... Wiseacre warnings against that manner of undoing [that is, going to a man's chamber] could not save her from this one [madness]. The merry bit of bawdry which follows ... may remind her listeners (and us) that it was with such humor Hamlet so brutally bespattered her as they sat watching the play. Here is its echo now upon her pitiably innocent lips. ♦ McCullen (1952, p. 191) : One of the major functions of songs by mad figures in tragedies is comic relief. For instance, whereas thoughtful spectators find in Ophelia's songs only a heightening of tragic emotions, those who respond primarily to the spectacle or suggestion of a particular moment are likely to be amused at much of her singing, because her songs of love have a tinge of the forbidden. The deeper significance of her singing escapes anyone who fails to relate it to the tragic problems of the entire play. ♦ Patrick (1953, pp. 139–144) reviews the question of whether or not Ophelia was unchaste. Against her innocence he cites evidence from *Hamlet*, from analogous plays and alleged sources, and from the traditional legend. In conclusion he suggests that Shakespeare deliberately left the moral character of Ophelia ambiguous in order to provide the interest that complexity and multi-possible answers give to a play. Sternfeld (1963, pp. 64 f.) : The true Elizabethan heroine would regard with the utmost disdain such uncontrolled behaviour [as Ophelia's playing and singing]. Marlowe's Helen, Kyd's Bel Imperia, Webster's Vittoria, Fletcher's Evadne are proud creatures. They do not entertain with song, but they command their servants to do so. Nor do they arouse our sympathy in the way we might feel compassion for a small child or a bird. Gertrude may err, suffer and even squirm, but she remains a queen, and she most certainly would fall out of character were she to sing. ... But it is precisely Ophelia's characterization as a helpless and power-less creature that makes her so poignantly pathetic, and this condition is empha-sized by her singing. ... In her distraught state she reverts to the songs a nurse may have taught her; not the aristocratic ayre, but crude songs of the common folk. ♦ Seng (1964, *DUJ*, pp. 80–83) : One comes to feel that Ophelia chooses her audiences carefully. She sings her first song to Gertrude and Horatio, to the mother and the closest friend of her beloved Hamlet. Her second song follows immediately on the entrance of King Claudius. It is an apt commentary on the sensuality of his character; it may even cast a glance at the nature of his relations with Gertrude, as if to say that older men, too, "will do't if they come to't". ... [But] its chief reference certainly is to the real and supposed relationships between Hamlet and Ophelia. ... While its bawdry seems to echo ... Hamlet's treatment of the girl in the Nunnery Scene and in the moments just preceding the Mousetrap Play, those critics who point out these connections and then go on their way have called our attention to only the smallest part of the story which underlies the song. ... The Valentine's song which Ophelia sings may have been learnt in childhood (if adult characters in plays have had childhoods); but that she is finally moved to re-member and in her madness sing it—the seeds for such behaviour were first planted by Laertes and Polonius. For the song expresses precisely the disaster they warned her against. ♦

Baskervill (1921, pp. 565–614) believes Ophelia's song may belong to a group of English lyrics which surround the ancient folk custom by which a young lover was permitted to visit and spend the night with his betrothed before marriage. He proposes three types of songs as being related to this custom. There are "Open the door (or window)" songs, which have to do with the lover's arrival at the girl's house, and his pleas to be allowed to enter; "Go from my window" songs, which are the girl's conventional protests; and, finally, the aubades of various kinds which warn the lover away in the early morning hours, or deplore the need for his departure. Various examples of these songs are given by Chappell (1840, I, 63; [1855–1859], I, 60–62, 140–142). Rollins (1924, *SP*, no. 2120) has suggested that the original of Ophelia's song may have been the ballad registered with the Company of Stationers on May 16, 1591, titled "A pleasaunt songe of Twoo stamering lovers which plainely doth vnto your sighte bewraye their pleasaunt meetinge on Sainct Valentines daie."

TEXTUAL COMMENTARY

1. **S. Valentines day**] The custom appears to have risen in consequence of a popular notion that it was on this day that birds chose their mates. So in *Midsummer Night's Dream* (IV.i.142 f.),

> Saint Valentine is past.
> Begin these woodbirds but to couple now?

According to Thurston (1926–1938, II, 216), there is nothing in the life of St. Valentine to justify the tradition, nor does it seem to be traceable to an early Christianization of the pagan rites in honor of Februata Juno.

5. **dupt**] Did up; opened.

7. **By gis**] Johnson (ed. 1765) : I rather imagine it should read, By Cis,—that is, By St. Cecily. ♦ [Actually it is a minced oath for "By Jesus." See *NED*.]

Saint Charitie] Not a saint's name; the expression means "By holy charity," and was a common oath of the time. So in *The Troublesome Raigne of John, King of England* (1591, sig. E₄ᵛ),

> Frier   *Benedicamus Domini*, was euer such an iniurie.
> Sweete S. *Withold* of thy lenitie, defend vs from
>   extremetie,
> And heare vs for S. Charitie, oppressed with austeritie,

where St. Withold's name is italicized, but not the common noun "charity."

9. **doo't**] The verb *do* has a specifically indecent sense in Shakespeare's day; *NED* gives a 1601 occurrence as euphemistic for "to copulate." Shakespeare frequently plays on the *double entendre*; cf. *2 Henry IV*, II.i.44.

10. **By Cock**] Like *By gis*, above, a minced oath: "By God."

MUSIC

Even as for [35] a traditional tune for this song survives from the Drury Lane Theatre. It has no more claim than the other to authenticity. It first appears as a Shakespeare tune in Linley (1816, II, 51), who transcribed it from the singing of the actress Mrs. Forster (Miss Field), who had played the role of Ophelia at the Drury Lane in 1785 (see Genest, 1832, VI, 379). It was reprinted by C. Knight (ed. [1838–1843], *Tragedies*, I, 152 f.) in his *Pictorial Edition* of Shakespeare, and has since appeared in numerous collections: Chappell (1840, II, 20; [1855–1859], I, 227), Caulfield (n.d., II, 86), Naylor ([1912], p. 38), Gibbon (1930, p. 107), Naylor (1931, p. 190), Bontoux (1936, p. 347), Sternfeld (1963, p. 64; 1964, *Songs*, pp. 10 f.), and Kines (1964, p. 33). Bontoux says the tune is "remontant probablement au XVe siècle," but she gives no source for her information.

According to Chappell ([1855–1859], I, 144 f.) it is a very common tune, occurring in several of the ballad operas and circulating in somewhat variant versions under the titles "Who list to lead a soldier's life" and "Lord Thomas and Fair Ellinor." In D'Urfey's *Songs Compleat* (1719–1720, IV, 43 f.) it is given as the tune to some lyrics from Thomas Heywood's *The Rape of Lvcrece* (1608). While it is possible that the tune may go back to the time of Shakespeare, there is still no evidence that this music might have been heard on his stage.

In an appendix to Wooldridge (1893; reprinted 1961), Kidson (p. 60) gives one stanza and some music for a song called "My Valentine." The lyrics he gives seem to be a late corruption of Ophelia's song. Kidson notes that the words "are found on ballad sheets":

> O! it happened to be one Valentine Day,
>   One morning so early betime,
> That a pretty, pretty maid came to my bedside,
>   And she wanted to make me her valentine.

DRAMATIC FUNCTION

Ophelia may have learned her song from a "free-spoken" nursemaid—or from almost anyone else in that free-spoken age; but the critics who are so concerned to salvage her innocence tend frequently to forget that it was not Hamlet alone who sullied it. Ophelia's father and brother have had their share in the spoliation of her mind's purity and her childlike trust. The cynicism of Laertes' remark (I.iii.5–10),

> For Hamlet, and the trifling of his favour,
> Hold it a fashion, and a toy in blood;
> A violet in the youth of primy nature,
> Forward, not permanent—sweet, not lasting;
> The perfume and the suppliance of a minute;
> No more,

must have come as a shock to her gentle nature which believed men were what they seemed to be. Nor is Laertes content with a mere generalized admonition in his efforts to school her in lack of trust. He goes on to express in the plainest terms his suspicions about Hamlet's intentions, suspicions which, as far as Ophelia is concerned, nothing in Hamlet's conduct to her thus far would ever have occasioned (I.iii.29–32):

> Then weigh what loss your honour may sustain
> If with too credent ear you list his songs,
> Or lose your heart, or your chaste treasure open
> To his unmast'red importunity.

Her brother's little lecture Ophelia charmingly turns aside, but he has sown doubts in her mind which Polonius' cruder tactics and language exploit to the full. The very abruptness and impatience with which her father catechizes her is an accusation of guilt where no guilt has been (I.iii.95–98):

> I must tell you
> You do not understand yourself so clearly
> As it behooves my daughter and your honour.
> What is between you? Give me up the truth.

Between Hamlet and Ophelia have been only "tenders of his affection," as she submissively responds. But her words only warm her father to the subject at hand (I.iii.101–103):

> Affection? Pooh! You speak like a green girl,
> Unsifted in such perilous circumstance.
> Do you believe his tenders, as you call them?

His remarks bear the same implications as his son's: no one is to be trusted or taken at face value. Ophelia's confused reply, "I do not know, my lord, what I should think," is clear evidence that the habit of mistrust, so ingrained in her father and brother, is something new to her. For, indeed, she had believed Hamlet; and, as it turns out, though tragically and too late, her trust was not misplaced. Yet father and son are concerned to throw a lurid light across the relationship. Polonius' bitter joke, "Tender yourself more dearly, Or ... you'll tender me a fool" (*i.e.*, "Behave yourself more carefully or you will (1) make a fool of me (2) bring a bastard grandchild to me") is not lost on Ophelia. Its slander on her honor and on her love for Hamlet stirs her to rebellious protest: "My lord, he hath importun'd me with love In honourable fashion." Polonius, however, is not one to brook rebellion in a green slip of a girl. "Ay, fashion you may call it. Go to, go to!" Ophelia makes one further effort to keep her vision of the world undefiled. She cannot believe that she could have been so mistaken in Hamlet, nor Hamlet so base in his protestations of love. Her appeal is to religion, for Hamlet "hath given countenance to his speech, my lord, With almost all the holy vows of heaven." But Polonius is not to be shaken from his own unlovely view of man and the world. Those "holy vows of heaven" are mere "springes to catch woodcocks." Years of politicking at court have taught him better than to believe in men's words, no matter how buttressed with religious oaths, and he rides roughshod over her trustful nature. He orders her to "be scanter" henceforth of her maiden presence,

6*

to set her entreatments at a higher rate than "a command to parley"; as for those "holy vows," (I.iii.127–131),

> they are brokers,
> Not of that dye which their investments show,
> But mere implorators of unholy suits,
> Breathing like sanctified and pious bawds,
> The better to beguile.

The very diction in which he couches his warning is a slander.

It may be argued that Laertes and Polonius are merely exercising the prudent judgement of men of the world, men who know something of Renaissance courts and courtiers; and only the briefest acquaintance with the social history of Elizabeth I's court suggests that even in that stronghold of Diana a father would need be wary about his daughter. Yet those critics who would urge that Polonius is merely prudent here will be hard put to defend him a few scenes later when he tells Claudius that he will "loose" his daughter to Hamlet for purposes of entrapment; and how is Polonius to be defended at all for the role of *agent provocateur* that he suggests Reynaldo take with Laertes' friends about the son's sexual morals?

The fact of the case seems to be that Polonius is only too willing to sacrifice morals to political expediency; and it is his spying, sneaking, and eavesdropping that finally brings about his own death. The interview with Ophelia may have begun as a rash and frightened father's attempt to warn his daughter about the ways of the world, but it ends as a groundless slander. Even during the interview there is no question in an audience's mind that the relations between Hamlet and Ophelia have been other than honest. Any niggling doubts about the matter are surely resolved by Gertrude's remark at Ophelia's grave, "I hop'd thou shouldst have been my Hamlet's wife," and Hamlet's equally open declaration (V.i.292–294),

> I lov'd Ophelia. Forty thousand brothers
> Could not (with all their quantity of love)
> Make up my sum.

This is not the language of trifling, beguilement, or seduction.

The relative importance of these successive interviews of Ophelia to the rest of the play can be gauged by the fact that Shakespeare gives almost the entire scene (I.iii) to them. The distorted vision of the world that Polonius and Laertes impress on Ophelia in this episode is clearly the beginning of her tragedy. That vision is reinforced by Hamlet's later "brutal" treatment of her, but his actions are motivated by the sense that she has already betrayed him. Thus the heroine of the song is far from being the Ophelia that Hamlet knew; rather she is the Ophelia that Polonius and Laertes, without real cause, had feared their daughter and sister might become.

37–39

TEXT: Second Quarto (1604), sig. L₂ (IV.v.164, 166, 187, 190–199).
TYPOGRAPHY: Unindented verse, roman face; s.d., *Song*.

[37]

They bore him bare-faſte on the Beere,
And in his graue rain'd many a teare [. . . .]

[38]

For bonny ſweet Robin is all my ioy.

[39]

And wil a not come againe,
And wil a not come againe,   5
No, no, he is dead, goe to thy death bed,
He neuer will come againe.
His beard was as white as ſnow,
Flaxen was his pole,
He is gone, he is gone, and we caſt away mone,   10
God a mercy on his ſoule [. . . .]

GENERAL COMMENTARY

Moore (1916, pp. 96 f.) : At times . . . [Shakespeare uses songs] to heighten the
emotion of a special situation, as well as to incite to action, as in Ophelia's ravings.
[He instances the effects of the mad songs on Laertes, who reacts to them by saying
(IV.v.168 f.),

> Hadst thou thy wits and didst persuade revenge,
> It could not move thus.]

. . . And when Claudius suggests that Laertes kill Hamlet, by fair fight or by poison,
the young man is ready for either means of revenge. ◆ Granville-Barker (1947,
I, 125–127) : There is every difference between this and our recent sight of [Ophelia],
between that phantom of a happy girl singing to her lute and this subdued, silent
figure. She has been to the garden to gather herbs and flowers—halfway, so to
speak, to the meadow where she is soon to meet her death. And now she begins a
solemn sort of mimicry of the funeral her father was denied. She chants [ll. 1 f.]
and bends over the bier, which only she can see. . . . She ceremoniously scatters
her rosemary and rue, and distributes it and the flowers to her fellow-mourners.

Then the poor brain loses hold for a moment even of its own fantasy, and she carols out . . . [l. 3], but recollects, and chants for a second psalm [ll. 4–11]. . . . She cannot quite make out, I think, why they are not ready to follow with her to the grave. But if they will not go, she must. So she bids them a solemn "God be wi' ye!" and departs, head bowed, hands folded, as quietly as she came; and the rough crowd at the door stand silent to let her pass. ♦ Vyvyan (1959, pp. 51 f.) ; The mad Ophelia now returns for her last scene: "There's rosemary, that's for remembrance. Pray, love, remember." There is no trace of bitterness in her, hers is pure love to the end. . . . [He quotes ll. 4–7.] It is not for the loss of a father, but of a lover, that love dies. So she prays for mercy upon every soul, and wanders away to drown. ♦ [Vyvyan fails to note that l. 8 could scarcely refer to Hamlet, yet it is surely part of the same song.] Seng (1964, *DUJ*, p. 83) ; Ophelia leaves the stage after her Valentine's song. She returns to sing again only after Laertes, brought from Paris by the news of his father's sudden death, joins Gertrude and Claudius on the stage. It is a small and appropriate group of auditors for her final songs. With Ophelia's entrance all that remains of the little family is brought together for the final time; it is only now, in two of her three fragments of song, that Ophelia's thoughts are seen to be focussed exclusively on her father. ♦ [See also general commentary for songs 35 and 36, above.]

TEXTUAL COMMENTARY

1–2. **They . . . teare**] All the folios have between these lines the burthen *Hey non nony, nony, hey nony*. This line does not appear in Q_2, nor is there any evidence that the pirate-auditor responsible for Q_1 knew it to be part of the song. The tendency of many of the modern editors to follow the folio reading can probably be attributed to the theatrical effect—the shock value—this line achieves when it is included in the song. Thus Sternfeld (1963, p. 57) points out that "the nonsense syllables . . . relate more logically to lads, lasses and springtime than to lamentation and tears." Furthermore, it should be noted that this burthen was frequently used in bawdy lyrics of Shakespeare's day to cover obvious obscenities. It is so used in Ravenscroft's *Melismata. Mvsicall Phansies* (1611, sig. E_3v):

> He that will an Ale-house keepe must haue three things
> in store,
> a Chamber and a feather Bed, a Chimney and a
> hey no-ny no-ny hay no-ny no-ny, hey
> nony no, hey nony no, hey nony no.

And a song in *Choyce Drollery: Songs & Sonnets* (1656, p. 67) uses the refrain similarly:

> But gone she is the blithest Lasse
> That ever trod on Plain.
> What ever hath betided her,
> Blame not the Shepherd Swain.
> For why, she was her own foe,
> And gave her selfe the overthrowe
> By being too franke of her hy nonny nonny no.

See *NED* "nonny." See also the song "Downe: sate the shepard" in the Percy
Folio MS. (ed. Hales, 1867, pp. 57 f.).

Malone (ed. 1790) compares these lines with Chaucer's "Knight's Tale," ll. 2877 f.:

> He leyde hym, bare the visage, on the beere;
> Therwith he weep that pitee was to heere.

3. **For . . . ioy**] Chappell (1871–1880, I, 181) notes that if the lyrics of this song are
ever recovered they will probably be found to begin with the line, "Now Robin is
to the greenwood gone," and end with the refrain, "For bonny sweet Robin is all
my joy," because "the tune exists in manuscripts, sometimes under one name and
sometimes under the other." Rollins (1924, *SP*, no. 2642) suggests that "A newe
medley beginning 'Robin is to the grene gone' 'As I went to Walsingham',"
entered in the Stationers' Registers by Simon Stafford on September 3, 1604, may
have been Stafford's attempt to capitalize on the success of these songs in *Hamlet*.
(For the connection of the tune called "Walsingham" with *Hamlet* see song 35,
above.) Morris (1958, pp. 601–603) **:** [This song] serves the same function as the
more directly intended Valentine song. . . . The significance of "For bonny sweet
Robin is all my joy" lies in the important clue that the line gives in establishing the
chief reason for Ophelia's insanity. There can be little doubt that a partial cause is
the death of her father . . . but the major cause must be laid to her loss of Hamlet,
which she refers to in this line in terms of the loss of the delights of physical love. ¶
. . . I believe it can be shown that the name *Robin* was, in the sixteenth century, one
of the cant terms for the male sex organ . . . [as] in Gascoigne's "The Lullabie of a
Lover" [ed. Cunliffe, 1907–1910, I, 44]:

> Eke Lullaby my loving boye,
> My little Robyn take thy rest,
> Since age is colde, and nothing coye,
> Keep close thy coyne, for so is best:
> With Lulla[b]y be thou content,
> With Lullaby thy lustes relente,
> Lette others pay which hath mo pence,
> Thou art to pore for such expence.

. . . Proof that Shakespeare knew the name as a lewd tag may be found possibly in
2 Henry IV . . . [when] Falstaff and Shallow reminisce about their youth and profli-
gacy and especially about their encounters with the 'bona roba' Jane Nightwork. . . . Shallow asks if Jane Nightwork 'holds her owne,' and Falstaff answers
that she grows old:

> *Shal.* Nay, she must be old; she cannot choose
> but be old; certain she's old; and had Robin Nightwork
> by old Nightwork before I came to Clement's Inn.
> [III.ii.220–223]

¶ Some additional proof of the phallic associations of *Robin* can be found . . . in
popular nomenclature for at least one of the plants of the time. The flower, rather
significantly, is mentioned by Gertrude in her report of Ophelia's death: long

purples [IV.vii.171]. All writers on the flowers in Shakespeare identify long purples with *orchis mascula* or with *arum maculatum*. They resemble closely our Jack-in-the-Pulpit, which gives a good idea of the plant's physical characteristics. Among the common names of the *arum maculatum* is *Wake-robyn*. That this meaning is vulgar seems to be corroborated by the list of other names for the plant in [Henry] Lyte's [*A Niewe Herball, or Historie of Plantes*, 1578, sigs. 2D$_5$v–2D$_6$]: Priestespyntill, Cockowpintell, and Cockowpynt. ◆

[Similar corroboration might be gained from van Wijk (1911, I, 922) who, among more than one hundred popular names in English for *Orchis mascula* gives the following: bloody butchers, butcher's fingers, cock-flowers, cuckoo-flower, cuckoo-pint, dead men's fingers, Johnny-cocks, long purples, and priest's pintle. But the fact remains that the sixteenth-century botanical identity of "long purples" is not known. The herbals of Shakespeare's day do not list this popular name; works like van Wijk's apparently draw their information from later plant-lore; as a result modern scholars have had to guess at the plant Shakespeare intended by "long purples" and "dead men's fingers."

One or the other of two quite different flowers seems likely. Ellacombe (1878, p. 114) insists that the word refers to "the common purple Orchises of the woods and meadows (Orchis morio, O. mascula, O. maculata, and Gymadenia conopsea)." Singleton (1922, pp. 209 f.) confuses her botany and her orthography when she identifies the long purple with the *Arum masculatam* or *Orchis mascula*, and remarks that it "is related to our woodland Jack-in-the-Pulpit," and gives as popular names for it the names that the herbalists give to *Arum maculatum* but not to the *Orchis*, which is from a wholly different family. Rohde (1935, p. 13) notes that long purples "have never been satisfactorily identified," but suggests the *Arum maculatum* as a likely candidate. Since John Gerarde in *The Herball or Generall Historie of Plantes* (1597, sigs. 2V$_6$–2V$_7$; ed. Woodward, 1928, pp. 193 f.) concurs with Lyte about the "grosser names" given to *A. maculatum*, Rohde's suggestion has genuine merit. Furthermore, the description and illustration in Sowerby (1914, p. 135; fig. 1348) fulfills the phallic requirements and digital euphemism in a way that no flower of the family *Orchidaceae* does.

Other discussions of the botanical identity of "long purples" are to be found in Beisly (1864, pp. 160 f.), Grindon (1883, p. 129), Bloom (1903, pp. 33 f.), and Savage (1923, pp. 46–49). There are excellent colored illustrations of the relevant flowers in Martin (1965, plates 81 and 88).

Additional support for Morris's interpretation of the word is offered by a Shakespearean proper name. Tailors are continually ridiculed in Renaissance literature for lacking manliness; so the tailor in *Midsummer Night's Dream* is called Robin Starveling, and is assigned to play the role of Thisby's mother in the rustics' play.

Morris, concluding his argument, suggests that the etymological derivation of *Robin* as a phallic term may be from the French *robinet*, "faucet" or "spigot." In illustration of the "attributes and grosser pranks of Robin Goodfellow" he refers the reader to the title-page of *Robin Good-fellow, his Mad Prankes and Merry Iests* (1628), where the puck is pictured as a satyr with erect phallus in the middle of a ring of dancing men and women. The picture is reproduced in Ramsbottom (1953, facing p. 135).]

Le Comte (1960, p. 480) **:** Before embracing a salacious interpretation ... and

putting Ophelia as nicknamer in the literary company of Mellors the game-
keeper ... Morris ought to have mentioned, if only to dismiss, the topical allusion
theory which associates Hamlet with the ill-fated Earl of Essex and Ophelia with
Robert Devereux' neglected and mournful wife. . . . Morris omits a point in favor
of his theory, namely Hamlet's accusation to Ophelia, "You nickname God's
creatures" (III.i.148) . . . which Dover Wilson annotates as follows: "Ham. seems
to allude to indecent names given to fruit and vegetables; Dowden cites [*Romeo*
(II.i.35 f.)] 'that kind of fruit As maids call medlars when they laugh alone'." ◆
Sternfeld (1963, p. 58) : "Bonny Robin" songs deal with lovers, unfaithfulness and
extra-marital affairs, as [in Robert Jones's *A Mvsicall Dreame. Or the fovrth Booke of
Ayres*, 1609 (sig. L₁ᵛ)]

> Loue passions must not be withstood,
> Loue euerywhere will find vs,
> I liude in field and towne, and so did he,
> I got me to the woods, loue followed me.
> He[y, iolly ro]bin. ◆

Seng (1964, *DUJ*, pp. 83 f.) : Between ... two funeral dirges Ophelia once more
alludes in song to the circumstances of her relationship with Hamlet. For her
brother, who was not present to hear her Valentine's song, she now has another,
very similar in its implications. . . . Much of the relevance that this little fragment
may have had for Shakespeare's audience is lost on us, since the ballad from which
the line comes has apparently not survived. Yet . . . a great deal may be inferred.
It is very likely that the source of Ophelia's lyric was a Robin Hood ballad. By
Shakespeare's time these stories had already long undergone epic degeneration,
and the name Maid Marian had become a by-word for promiscuity. Hence if
Ophelia in this song is picturing herself as Marian to Hamlet's Robin Hood, she is
merely envisioning once again the nightmare world of her Valentine's song. ◆

4-11. **And ... soule**] Seng (1964, *DUJ*, p. 83) : It is a dirge for an old man, white
of beard and with the flaxen hair of the very aged. If these mock funeral rites
mean anything at all, it is that they remind the audience that the same political
expediency which shaped Polonius' life and procured his death followed him even
to his grave. It was political expediency that dictated his unseemly burial, that
denied him the state obsequies due to a counsellor of his rank. ◆

6. **goe ... bed**] The shift in subject and uneven metrics of this clause make it
sound like Ophelia's interpolation or change in her source. In context "gone to his
bed" or something like it would sound better. Perhaps the interpolation, if it is
one, is meant to foreshadow her suicide as she sings to herself.

7-10. **He ... mone**] Malone (ed. 1790) : [These lines] and several circumstances
in the character of Ophelia, seem to have been ridiculed in *Eastward Hoe* ... by
Ben Jonson, Chapman, and Marston . . . [1605, sig. D₄]:

> *His head as white as mylke,*
> *All flaxen was his haire:*
> *But now he is dead,*
> *And laid in his Bedd,*
> *And neuer will come againe.*

MUSIC

Ophelia's first fragment of song is usually sung on the stage to one or the other of two traditional tunes. Arranged for the melody called "Walsingham" it is to be found in Chappell (1840, II, 20), Caulfield (n.d., II, 87), Bontoux (1936, p. 348), and Sternfeld (1964, *Songs*, p. 11). At other times it has been set to the traditional tune for song 39, editions of which are listed below.

What appears to be the original tune for "Bonny Sweet Robin" survives in numerous early manuscripts and printed music books. It was obviously a very popular melody, circulating under various titles such as "Bonny Sweet Robin," "Robin is to the Greenwood Gone," or, simply, "Robin." Sternfeld (1963, pp. 76 f.) has recorded thirty extant examples in early manuscripts and books. There are doubtless other versions of the tune still undiscovered. Of these thirty versions all but one are for instrumental performance; the single example that does come down to us with words does not include the line sung by Ophelia. That the melody which survives in so many instrumental versions began, however, as a popular song, there can be no question. The variety of names by which it is called attests this fact, as does the existence of other ballads meant to be sung to this tune. Thus it is given as the tune to "A Dolefull adewe to the last Erle of Darby" and to "A Courtly New Ballad of the Princely Wooing of the fair maid of London, by King Edward" (Rollins, 1924, *SP*, nos. 617, 2642); and even the jailer's daughter in *Two Noble Kinsmen* (1634, sig. I₃) "can sing the Broome, and Bony Robin."

Scholarly editions of some of the early instrumental arrangements are given by Fuller-Maitland (1894–1899, I, 66 f.; II, 77–81), and Dart (1955, p. 195; 1963, pp. 6 f.). Copies of the tune, derived from these arrangements, are to be found in Chappell (1840, II, 110; [1855–1859], I, 234), Wooldridge (1893; reprinted 1961, I, 153), Naylor (1931, p. 191), Bontoux (1936, p. 348), and Sternfeld (1963, pp. 72–75; 1964, *Songs*, p. 13). The tune is also given by C. Simpson (1966, p. 60).

Since none of the thirty extant versions of the tune has the words of Ophelia's snatch underlaid, there is some question as to what part of the famous melody should be used for them. The fragment Ophelia sings seems to be a refrain from the original song, and it can be fitted to either the opening or the closing strains of the tune. Her words have been set to the closing strain in Wooldridge (1891; reprinted 1961, I, 153), Naylor (1931, p. 191), and Sternfeld (1963, p. 70; 1964, *Songs*, p. 11); to the opening strain in Chappell (1840, II, 110), Elson (1901, p. 242), and Sternfeld (1963, p. 70). The setting given by Caulfield (n.d., II, 87) is spurious; he has arbitrarily set the words to the traditional tune for 36.

The tune for song 39 derives from a melody "traditional" at the Drury Lane Theatre (see commentary on Music for song 35, above). It exists in numerous copies: Linley (1816, II, 52), C. Knight (ed. [1838–1843], *Tragedies*, I, 153 f.), Chappell (1840, II, 20 f.; [1855–1859], I, 237), Caulfield (n.d., II, 88 f.), Elson (1901, pp. 237 f.), Naylor (n.d., pp. 38, 40; 1931, p. 191), Gibbon (1930, p. 107), Bontoux (1936, p. 349), and Sternfeld (1963, p. 69; 1964, *Songs*, p. 14). It has been pointed out by Chappell ([1855–1859], I, 237) that the tune seems to be a version of one called "The Merry Milkmaids" which appeared in Playford's *The English Dancing Master* (1651). Sternfeld (1963, pp. 68 f.) prints both tunes on facing pages for comparison.

The fact that both songs 37 and 39 are dirges, and that some music historians assign them the same tune, might suggest that they are fragments of the identical original song. Close examination of the metrics and the rhyme schemes, however, supports the view that these are independent fragments from separate sources.

DRAMATIC FUNCTION

All three of these songs can be seen to be intimately related to the tragic fortunes of the family of Polonius. Two are dirges for the dead father, while the ballad-fragment reminds the audience of the love between Ophelia and Hamlet, and of Polonius' and Laertes' fears and warnings concerning that love. Rash and distraught, Laertes wholly fails to comprehend his own measure of responsibility for the events that have befallen. Yet a close examination of this episode seems to show that Shakespeare has taken pains to make the irony clear.

Laertes storms onto the stage midway in IV.v. filled only with thoughts of avenging his father's death. As yet he knows nothing of his sister's madness. Claudius promises the angry youth the revenge he seeks, and at the same time absolves himself from any guilt or complicity in Polonius' death. It is at this point that Ophelia enters. Stunned with horror, Laertes looks at the crazed girl. Almost as if anticipating her language of flowers a few moments later he cries out, "O rose of May," and then,

> is't possible a young maid's wits
> Should be as mortal as an old man's life? (ll. 159 f.)

Immediately after her first dirge he reverts—now with renewed purpose—to thoughts of revenge:

> Hadst thou thy wits, and didst persuade revenge,
> It could not move thus.

Ophelia's only reply to her brother is to assign him a part—the refrain—in a ballad she will sing of a "false steward that stole his master's daughter." Her words mean nothing to Laertes; he fails to recall that it was just such false lovers that he had once warned her against. He is heedless of every thought except revenge: "This nothing's more than matter," he says, meaning that the nonsense she speaks, a symptom of her madness, is more than a material cause to prompt his vengeance. There is appalling irony in Ophelia's next words:

> There's rosemary, that's for remembrance. Pray
> you, love, remember. And there is pansies,
> that's for thoughts. (ll. 175–177)

But this, too, falls on a wooden understanding.

Some months earlier Laertes had told Ophelia to regard Hamlet's attentions as

> a fashion, and a toy in blood;
> A violet in the youth of primy nature. (I.iii.5–7)

Now she pays him back in verbal kind:

> I would give you some violets, but they
> wither'd all when my father died. (ll. 184 f.)

And then, finally, as if in summary of all the earlier hints and allusions, the wild and incredible song: "For bonny sweet Robin is all my joy." That she should sing such a song in the midst of her imaginative funeral rites for her father, and in the actual presence of her brother, is Shakespeare's final bitter irony. She "speaks things in doubt, That carry but half sense," says an anonymous "Gentleman" at the beginning of IV.v. Ophelia's "half sense," however, carries just about as much poignancy as an audience can bear.

40

TEXT: Second Quarto (1604), sigs. M₂–M₃ (V.i.69–72, 79–82, 102–105, 129).
TYPOGRAPHY: Indented verse, roman face; s.d., *Song*.

In youth when I did loue did loue,
    Me thought it was very ſweet
To contract ô the time for a my behoue,
    O me thought there a was nothing a meet.

　　　　·　　　　·　　　　·

But age with his ſtealing ſteppes   5
    hath clawed me in his clutch,
And hath ſhipped me into the land,
    as if I had neuer been ſuch.

　　　　·　　　　·　　　　·

A pickax and a ſpade a ſpade,
    for and a ſhrowding ſheet,   10
O a pit of Clay for to be made
    for ſuch a gueſt is meet.

　　　　·　　　　·　　　　·

[. . .] or a pit of clay for to be made.

GENERAL COMMENTARY

Granville-Barker (1947, I, 135 f.) notes that the stage direction for Hamlet's entry occurs eight lines earlier in the Folio than it does in Q₂. He remarks that this is a dramatically significant difference since it gives Hamlet an opportunity to hear the opening verses of the song: From the tenor of the letters to Horatio and the King do we not expect a Hamlet returning primed to prompt vengeance—for his own attempted murder also now? It is one more in the series of such surprises that he should quietly glide back into the action, and stand there so indifferent and detached. He is spiritually far off too. For it is Ophelia's grave that is digging, and the Clown's song is a counterpart to hers . . . and the allusive pattern is completed by Hamlet's fastidious comment [V.i.73 f.]:

> Has this fellow no feeling of his business,
>   that he sings at grave-making?

Had he no feeling either, who could turn his back obliviously upon the havoc he had made? It is he that is digging his grave. ◆ Sternfeld (1963, pp. 128 f.) maintains that the song is more than Ophelia's requiem : It is also a funeral oration for Yorick, harking back to Hamlet's youth and the persons and ideas whose memory he treasures. In this sad scene with its frivolous overtones the role of the clown is vital. . . . His riddles and jokes about grave-diggers and grave makers are relevant to the main theme, as is the song. The resemblance to a chorale prelude is not so much in its character as in its extensive dimensions—with the interspersed prose it occupies sixty lines. ◆

Steevens (ed. 1793) : Dr. Percy is of the opinion that the different corruptions in these stanzas, might have been "designed by the poet himself, the better to paint the character of an illiterate clown." ◆ Noble (1923, p. 120) : It is interesting to observe . . . the manner in which the sexton's perversion of his text makes the ballad have a more direct bearing on the task on which he is immediately engaged. He is down in the grave and he substitutes 'pit' for 'house', because pit is in his mind. Again, the naturalness of 'A pickaxe and a spade, a spade' ought to be noticed—the repetition of 'a spade' is due in the first place to his labours and in the next to his fading memory, which can only with difficulty recall the words of the ballad.

TEXTUAL COMMENTARY

3–4. ô, a] Variorum (ed. 1821) : All but the quartos omit these A's; which are no part of the song, but only the breath forced out by the strokes of the mattock. ◆ New Cambridge (ind. ed. 1934) : [W. G.] Clar[k]. is prob. right in explaining the 'a' in this line and the next as 'the drawling notes in which he sings'. ◆

5–8. But . . . such] Johnson (ed. 1765) : This stanza is evidently corrupted; for it wants what is found in the other two, an alternate rhyme. We may read thus, till something better shall occur:

> But age, with his stealing *sand*,
> Hath claw'd me in his clutch:
> And hath *shifted* me into *his* land,
> As though I had never been such. ◆

[Johnson is right in calling attention to a corruption, here, but it was probably quite deliberate. The clown has a bad memory for the lyrics of his song.]

5. age . . . steppes] A proverbial expression; see Tilley (1950, A-70).

13. or . . . made] All the folios and most of the modern editors complete this line by adding l. 12. Only Capell (ed. [1767–1768]) strictly follows Q2 and leaves the line incomplete.

MUSIC

A contemporary tune for "I loathe that I did love," the source of the grave-digger's song, is to be found in B. M. Add. MS. 4900 (fols. 62ᵛ–63), the voice part written in staff notation, the lute part in tablature. Sternfeld (1963, facing p. 152) gives facsimiles of both. There are scholarly modern editions of the manuscript song by Heseltine (1927–1931, IV, 10) and Sternfeld (1963, p. 154; 1964, *Songs*, p. 16). There are careful editions of the voice part alone in Pattison (1948, p. 167) and Sternfeld (1963, p. 155), and a less exact copy in Chappell ([1855–1859], I, 217, "Second Tune") with an "arranged" accompaniment. In his edition of the *Songs* (1964, p. 15) Sternfeld gives an adaptation of the manuscript tune to fit the words of the gravedigger's song. The tune alone is given by C. Simpson (1966, p. 340).

An entirely different tune, also supposed contemporary with Shakespeare's play, survives only in an 1814 copy by William Crotch, who found the tune written into the margin of one of Tottel's *Songs and Sonnettes* (1557) while assisting G. F. Nott in an edition of Wyatt and Surrey. That particular copy of Tottel's miscellany has since been lost. There are reprints of the tune copied by Crotch in Chappell ([1855–1859], I, 217, "First Tune"), Wooldridge (1893; reprinted 1961, I, 52), Elson (1901, pp. 303 f.), Gibbon (1930, p. 36), and Sternfeld (1963, pp. 152 f.; 1964, *Songs*, p. 14), who also carefully analyzes both tunes. The tune transcribed by Crotch is also given by C. Simpson (1966, p. 341).

Which of these two melodies, if either, was used by Shakespeare's gravedigger will probably never be known; but one of them must have attained a certain degree of popularity, since "The Louer complayneth of his Ladies vnconstancy" in *A gorgious Gallery, of gallant Inuentions*, 1578 (ed. Rollins, 1926, p. 35), is "to the Tune of I lothe that I did loue."

According to Chappell ([1855–1859], I, 200 f.), the traditional stage melody for this song is one titled "The Children in the Wood." The use of this tune for the gravedigger's song has no authority; perhaps like the spurious gravedigger's song in Thomas D'Urfey's *Songs Compleat* (1719, V, 92 f.), it is the importation of some eighteenth-century stage manager.

SOURCE

The gravedigger's song is a garbled and fragmentary version of a poem by Thomas Lord Vaux titled, "The aged louer renounceth loue." It was first printed in Richard Tottel's *Songs and Sonettes*, 1557 (ed. Rollins, 1928–1929, I, 165 f.), but also exists in a number of early manuscript copies: MS. Ashmole 48 (ed. T. Wright, 1860, pp. 34–36), MS. Harleian 1703 (fols. 100–100ᵛ), B. M. Add. MSS. 38,599 (fols. 134ᵛ–135), 4900 (fol. 62; first stanza, only), and 26,737 (fol. 107ᵛ), which is a mis-arranged and incomplete version of the poem. The text which follows is from the Rollins edition of Tottel.

The aged louer renounceth
loue.

I Lothe that I did loue,
   In youth that I thought swete:
As time requires for my behoue
Me thinkes they are not mete,

My lustes they do me leaue,   5
My fansies all be fledde:
And tract of time begins to weaue,
Gray heares vpon my hedde.

For age with stelyng steppes,
Hath clawed me with his cowche: 10
And lusty life away she leapes,
As there had bene none such.

My muse dothe not delight
Me as she did before:
My hand and pen are not in plight,   15
As they haue bene of yore.

For reason me denies,
This youthly idle rime:
And day by day to me she cryes,
Leaue of these toyes in time.   20

The wrincles in my brow,
The furrowes in my face:
Say limpyng age will hedge him now,
Where youth must geue him place.

The harbinger of death,   25
To me I see him ride:
The cough, the colde, the gaspyng breath,
Dothe bid me to prouide.

A pikaxe and a spade,
And eke a shrowdyng shete,   30
A house of claye for to be made,
For such a gest most mete.

Me thinkes I heare the clarke,
That knols the careful knell:
And bids me leaue my wofull warke,   35
Er nature me compell.

My kepers knit the knot,
That youth did laugh to scorne:
Of me that clene shalbe forgot,
As I had not ben borne,   40

Thus must I youth geue vp,
Whose badge I long did weare:
To them I yelde the wanton cup
That better may it beare.

Loe here the bared scull,   45
By whose balde signe I know:
That stoupyng age away shall pull,
Which youthfull yeres did sowe.

For beauty with her bande
These croked cares hath wrought: 50
And shipped me into the lande,
From whence I first was brought.

And ye that bide behinde,
Haue ye none other trust:
As ye of claye were cast by kinde,   55
So shall ye waste to dust.

DRAMATIC FUNCTION

It is either a failing memory or an ill acquaintance with the original song—
perhaps a little of both—which accounts for the gravedigger's mangling of his text.
From the very outset he confuses the metrical pattern (in the original it is 3–3–4–3,
a perfectly respectable meter), and attempts to impose on it instead a common
ballad meter (4–3–4–3) that may have been more familiar to him. Once off stride,
he never recaptures the original with any accuracy; when he cannot remember
what follows the lines or stanzas he sings, he fills in with fragments from other
parts of the song.

He begins his song by borrowing "In youth" from the second line of his source,
but bridges the gap which that borrowing leaves by repeating the "Me thinkes"
of Vaux's fourth line as the "Me thought" of his own second and fourth lines. He
then drops a whole stanza of the original, only to resume with the first two lines
of the third quatrain in the original, and quotes with fair accuracy until he arrives
at "cowche," itself a misprint in Tottel's 1557 *Songs and Sonettes* (all the manuscripts and later editions give the correct reading, "crutch"), when he makes a not
so crude emendation of his own, "clutch." For the seventh line of his song he goes
to the fifty-first line of his source, leaving the first rhyme blind, but returns to the
proper stanza to complete his second quatrain with the correct rhyme, even if he
does garble the last line. He next omits four stanzas in the original to hit on a fifth
that is appropriate to his activities. This stanza he again throws into ballad meter
by repeating the final foot of the first line. In the second line he anticipates the last
one by beginning with "for," but corrects himself, and in the third he substitutes
the simpler and more direct "pit" for the metaphor "house."

The incongruity of the song with the task which prompts it—a grave being dug for Ophelia—is a reflection of the disordered moral universe of the whole play. The lives of all the characters seem to have been infected by Claudius' original crime. First to fall victim to the general moral sickness are those very institutions which were intended in their origins to confer dignity on important human occasions. King Hamlet himself has had no decent period of mourning, since

> The funeral bak'd meats
> Did coldly furnish forth the marriage tables

for the hasty wedding of Claudius and Gertrude. The courtship of Hamlet and Ophelia is next blasted. Polonius dies without dignity behind an arras, and with even less dignity is hastily interred in his grave. The drowned Ophelia receives but "maimed rites," and these only a few minutes after the gravedigger has been callously singing, and Hamlet bitterly jesting, over her grave.

The song and its setting—the grisly quibbles and speculations by the two clowns and by Hamlet and Horatio about death—dominate the scene. Three fourths of V.i. is given over to evoking the "metaphysical shudder." The song tells of love and death, youth and old age, and so echoes those earlier songs of Ophelia. The scene has its antecedents in the medieval Dance of Death, but also sounds the great seventeenth-century diapason that is heard in Donne's sermons and meditations, Browne's *Urn-Burial*, and in the sweeping peroration that closes Ralegh's fragmentary *History of the World*.

The Merry Wives of Windsor

41

TEXT: Folio (1623), sig. D₆ᵛ (III.i.17–21, 23–26, 29).
TYPOGRAPHY: Italic face prose.

To ſhallow Ruiers to whoſe
falls: melodious Birds ſings Madrigalls: There will we make
our Peds of Roſes: and a thouſand fragrant poſies. To ſhal-
low: [. . .]
Melodious birds ſing Madrigalls:——When as I ſat in Pa-
bilon: and a thouſand vagram Poſies. To shallow, &c.

To shallow Riuers, to whoſe fals:

GENERAL COMMENTARY

Moore (1916, p. 83) : At times the dramatist uses the song in by-play to secure the most humorous scenes, amusing not for buffoonery but for revelation of human nature. . . . Sir Hugh Evans, the Welsh parson, half dead with fear as he awaits his opponent at the duelling place, sings to keep up his courage, and gets Marlowe confused with the Psalter. ◆ Long (1961, p. 6) : The good parson, fearfully awaiting his duelling opponent, Dr. Caius, sings in a vain attempt to keep up his courage. In his confusion, instead of singing a pious psalm he sings lines from the amorous lyric.

TEXTUAL COMMENTARY

2. **Birds sings**] A common grammatical usage in the Folio. See Abbot (1884, pp. 235–237). The very same reading occurs in the version of the poem in *England's Helicon* (1600) (ed. Rollins, 1935, I, 184 f.).
5–6. **When . . . Pabilon**] Malone (ed. 1790) : This line is from the old version of the 137th Psalm [*The Whole Booke of Psalmes, collected into Englysh metre by T. Starnhold, I. Hopkins & others*, 1562]. The word *rivers* . . . may be supposed to have been brought to Sir Hugh's thoughts by the line of Marlowe's madrigal that he has just repeated; and in his fright he blends the sacred and prophane song together.

MUSIC

To ascertain what tune Parson Evans used for his strange blend of erotic and spiritual song is probably beyond the competence of any editor or music historian. Contemporary melodies exist for both of the songs from which he sings garbled fragments. According to Chappell ([1855–1859], I, 213) the music antiquarian Sir John Hawkins discovered the tune for "Come live with me and be my love" in a manuscript "as old as Shakespeare's time." The melody for the psalm-tune is even earlier, dating at least from Sternhold's and Hopkins' metrical edition of the psalms in 1562.

Which, if either, of these tunes was heard on Shakespeare's stage cannot be known; that both were used for the song seems unlikely. The comedy of the scene in which Parson Evans nervously awaits his duel with Dr. Caius depends more plausibly on his evident confusion of the lyrics than of the melodies. Since a parson would certainly know the psalm tune, this probably would have been the melody for the whole of his song. An audience that had sung the metrical psalm at church would surely have been amused to hear a parson singing an erotic love song to the same tune. The music for the Sternhold and Hopkins psalm can be uneasily fitted to the words of Parson Evans's song.

The original tune for "Come live with me" was extremely popular, being adopted (Lamson, 1936, no. 275) for at least six ballads. An instrumental version of the tune occurs in William Corkine's *The Second Booke of Ayres* (1612, sigs. G_4v–H_1), a transcript of which is given by C. Simpson (1966, p. 120). Other versions of the tune are given by Chappell (1840, II, 89; [1855–1859], I, 215), Elson (1901, p. 307), Naylor (n.d., p. 51; 1931, p. 182), Gibbon (1930, p. 154), Long (1961, p. 7), Kines (1964, p. 25), and C. Simpson (1966, p. 121).

There is a scholarly edition of the psalm-tune in Frost (1953, p. 189), and in C. Simpson (1966, p. 585). Another copy in Gibbon (1930, p. 41) is reprinted by Long (1961, p. 7).

SOURCES

The chief source of the song is a poem first published in *The Passionate Pilgrime. By W. Shakespeare* (1599, sigs. D_5–D_5v; ed. Rollins, 1938, p. 316), and then in *Englands Helicon* (1600, sigs. $2A_1v$–$2A_2$; ed. Rollins, 1935, pp. 184 f.), where it is correctly attributed to Christopher Marlowe. The poem also survives in a number of manuscript copies (see Rollins, 1935, II, 188). The version in Jaggard's *Passionate Pilgrime* is incomplete, lacking the fourth and sixth stanzas. The text below is from *Englands Helicon*.

The passionate Sheepheard to his loue.

Come liue with mee, and be my loue,
And we will all the pleasures proue,
That Vallies, groues, hills and fieldes,
Woods, or steepie mountaine yeeldes.

And wee will sit vpon the Rocks,
Seeing the Sheepheards feede theyr flocks,
By shallow Riuers to whose falls,
Melodious byrds sings Madrigalls.

And I will make thee beds of Roses,
And a thousand fragrant poesies,
A cap of flowers, and a kirtle,
Imbroydred all with leaues of Mirtle.

A gowne made of the finest wooll,
Which from our pretty Lambes we pull,
Fayre lined slippers for the cold:
With buckles of the purest gold.

A belt of straw, and Iuie buds,
With Corall clasps and Amber studs,
And if these pleasures may thee moue,
Come liue with mee, and be my loue.

The Sheepheards Swaines shall daunce & sing,
For thy delight each May-morning,
If these delights thy minde may moue;
Then liue with mee, and be my loue.

FINIS.   *Chr. Marlow.*

The lyrics of the metrical version of Psalm 137 in the Sternhold and Hopkins
hymnal, 1562 (sigs. 2A$_7$v–2A$_8$v) are:

Whenas we sat in Babylon, the riuers rounde about:
and in remembraunce of Sion the teares for grief burst out.
We hangd our harps & instruments, the willow trees vpon,
for in that place men for their vse, had planted many one.

Then they to whom we prisoners were,
    sayde to vs tauntingly:
Now let vs heare your Ebrue songes,
    and pleasant melody.
Alas (sayd we) who can once frame,
    his sorowfull hart to syng:
The prayses of our louing God,
    thus vnder a straunge kyng?

But yet if I Jerusalem,
    out of my hart let slyde:
Then let my fingers quyte forget,
    the warblyng harp to guyde.

And let my tong within my mouth,
    betyde for euer fast:
If that I ioy, before I see,
    thy full deliueraunce past.

Therefore (O Lorde) remember now,
    the cursed noyse and cry:
That Edoms sonnes againste vs made,
    when they razed our citie.
Remember Lorde theyr cruell wordes,
    when as with one accorde.
They cryed, on sack, and raze their wals,
    in despite of theyr Lorde.

Euen so shalt thou (O Babilon)
    at length to dust be brought:
And happy shall that man be calld,
    that our reuenge hath wrought.
Yea blessed shall that man be calld,
    that taketh thy children yonge:
To dash theyr bones against hard stones,
    whiche lye the streates amonge.

The popularity of Marlowe's poem is amply attested by the imitations which followed it and by the numerous references to it in the literature of the period. In *Englands Helicon* it is immediately followed by "The Nimphs reply to the Sheepheard," a poem sometimes attributed to Ralegh (cf. Rollins, 1935, II, 190). Both of these poems were quoted by Izaak Walton in *The Compleat Angler or the Contemplative Man's Recreation* (1653, sigs. F_1v-F_2v). The most famous imitation of them is probably John Donne's "The Baite" (ed. Grierson, 1912, I, 46 f.); and others are to be found in *Englands Helicon* (ed. Rollins, 1935, I, 186–188), in W. N.'s *Barley-breake, Or, A Warning for Wantons* (1607, sigs. C_3-C_3v), and Alexander Craig's *Amorose Songes* (1606, sigs. K_4-K_7v). Among numerous allusions to the poem are those by Marlowe himself in *The Rich Iew of Malta* (1633), and *Dido Queene of Carthage* (1594; ed. Brooke, 1910, pp. 289, 394, 429); in *Choice, Chance, and Change: Or, Conceites in their Colours* (1606, sig. B_2); and in Deloney's *The pleasant Historie of . . . Iacke of Newberie* (1626; ed. Mann, 1912, p. 49). The psalm-tune, of course, would have been even more familiar to Shakespeare's audience because of its use in church services.

DRAMATIC FUNCTION

Shakespeare had already used in *Twelfth Night* a comic situation similar to the one he employs here. In that play Viola, disguised as a youth, and Sir Andrew Aguecheek were egged on by Sir Toby and his friends to engage in a duel which neither of them really desired. The two would-not-be combatants were made to confront each other on the field of honor, each of them terror-stricken by false stories of the other's prowess. In *Merry Wives* Sir Hugh, the Welsh parson, is challenged to a sword duel by the French physician Dr. Caius, who mistakenly believes the Parson is seeking the affections of Mistress Anne Page. Sir Hugh has no desire to fight save insofar as he must seem to want the meeting to save his honor. Dr. Caius, on the other hand, has clearly challenged the wrong man; the opponent he should have challenged is Slender, the love-sick young man who stands about on the duelling field throughout the episode sighing, "O sweet Anne Page!" When the Frenchman and Welshman do meet on the field at Frogmore, they are restrained from swordplay by the host of the Garter Inn. They perceive that they have been gulled by the Englishmen, and depart as friends and allies, vowing to be revenged on the Host who has made a laughingstock of their affair of honor.

Sir Hugh, like Bottom in *Midsummer Night's Dream*, sings to show that he is not afraid. That a parson facing the perils of a duel should sing from the psalms of lamentation is appropriate enough; but this parson is so distracted with fear that he lapses, instead, into the profanest of love songs, a frankly Ovidian invitation to prove all the pleasures of Eros afield.

42

TEXT: Folio (1623), sig. E$_6$ (V.v.97–106).
TYPOGRAPHY: Indented verse, italic face; s.d., *The Song*.

Fie on ſinnefull phantaſie: Fie on Luſt, and Luxurie:
Luſt is but a bloudy fire, kindled with vnchaste deſire,
  Fed in heart whoſe flames aſpire,
  As thoughts do blow them higher and higher.
Pinch him (Fairies) mutually: Pinch him for his villanie.   5
  Pinch him, and burne him, and turne him about,
  Till Candles, & Star-light, & Moone-ſhine be out.

GENERAL COMMENTARY

Capell ([1779–1783?], II, part 3, p. 98) **:** Lilly, in his "Endymion," has a pinching by fairies, and a direction for singing while they pinch; but no song in his play's copy, which is of the year 1591: The action Shakespeare copy'd, undoubtedly; but let none imagine that Lilly's song was recover'd by him, and this it; for it speaks its author most plainly. ♦ Noble (1923, pp. 59 f.) **:** Like *You spotted snakes* . . . in *A Midsummer Night's Dream* [this] is a dance song. The song is punctuated by pinchings and burnings, meanwhile the children circle round [Falstaff] after the manner usual in juvenile games. The song in its setting bears close resemblance to the song round Corsites in Lyly's *Endimion* and the similarity is too great to be accidental. Clearly Shakespeare was inspired by the management of the song in his predecessor's comedy. ♦ Long (1961, p. 8) **:** In writing the scene, Shakespeare no doubt remembered earlier scenes from Lyly's play . . . and from the anonymous *The Maydes Metamorphosis* [1600] in which mortals are surrounded and pinched by dancing fairies. As these two plays had been performed a little earlier by choirboy companies . . . he may have discovered in this scene a chance to create humor at the expense of the singing boys who were enticing customers away from the playhouse of the Lord Chamberlain's Men. The introduction of singing boys into *The Merry Wives* would thus point up the resemblance between Shakespeare's scene and those of the choirboys. ♦ [The precise relationship between Shakespeare's song and the song in Lyly's play—or other songs of the type—is purely a matter of speculation. There was no song included in the 1591 quarto of *Endimion*, although there was a stage direction for one:

> The *Fayries daunce, and with a song pinch him, and hee falleth a sleepe: they kisse* Endimion, *and depart.*

Nor was there a song in the first quarto (1602) or second quarto (1619) versions of Shakespeare's play, though these also have stage directions calling for one:

Here they pinch him, and sing about him.

The first song of this sort to appear in print does not turn up in a play at all, but in Thomas Ravenscroft's *A Briefe Discovrse Of the true (but neglected) vse of Charact'ring the Degrees . . . in Music* (1614, sigs. C₁ᵛ–C₃):

> Dare you haunt our *hallowed greene*,
> none but *Fayries* heere are seene,
> > downe and sleepe,
> > Wake and weepe:
> pinch him *blacke*, and pinch him *blew*,
> that seekes to steale a louer true.
> When you come to hear vs *sing*,
> or to tread our *Fayrie ring*,
> pinch him *blacke* & pinch him *blew*,
> O thus our nayles shall handle you.
> thus our nayles shall handle you.]

Lawrence (1924, pp. 418–423), argues that this song was written by Ravenscroft for a hypothetical revival of Lyly's play in 1600 by the boy players of St. Paul's Cathedral. He notes that the fifth and sixth lines of this song could only refer to *Endimion*, but adds that if they were omitted the song would be equally suitable for Shakespeare's play.

The lyrics for Shakespeare's song first appear in the 1623 Folio, the lyrics for Lyly's song in *Endimion* in Edward Blount's edition of the play, *Sixe Covrt Comedies* (1632, sig. E₄). The words of the song in Blount's edition are as follows:

> PInch him, pinch him, blacke and blue,
> Sawcie mortalls must not view
> What the Queene of Stars is doing,
> Nor pry into our Fairy woing.
> > Pinch him blue.
> > And pinch him blacke.
> > Let him not lacke.
> Sharpe nailes to pinch him blue and red,
> Till sleepe has rock'd his addle head.
> For the trespasse hee hath done,
> Spots ore all his flesh shall runne.
> > Kisse *Endimion*, Kisse his eyes,
> > Then to our Midnight Heidegyes.

Wherever Blount got this song, it certainly fits the situation in *Endimion*.

It seems plausible that there is some kind of relationship between these three songs; they have curiously similar meters (with the exception of the last two lines of Shakespeare's song), and behind them may lie a common melody for which all three authors composed their own lyrics. Yet it is barely possible that they have no interrelationship at all, but simply go back (along with the lost song in *The Maydes Metamorphosis*, 1600) to folklore belief. Pinching was the usual form of torment that fairies were supposed to inflict on mortals. According to Sidgwick (1908, p. 134):

Such jocund and facetious spirits are said to sport themselves in the night by tumbling and fooling with servants and shepherds in country houses, pinching them black and blue.

References to this belief are frequent in literature of the time; thus it was fairy-pinchings that Caliban feared in *The Tempest* (I.ii.328 f., II.ii.4, V.i.276).

Noble (1923, p. 61) **:** The dance and song seem to be the natural and most effective means of achieving Falstaff's final discomfiture and humiliation, but that is not the sole office it has to fulfil. What better means could be devised whereby the little farce relative to Anne Page and her suitors could be effected than by the commotion necessarily attendant upon the baiting of Falstaff by pinching and burning him and by singing and dancing round him? ◆ G. W. Knight (1953, p. 103) **:** Here music and fairies succeed the rough and tumble of farce: and they are set against the earthy whale-like corpulence of Falstaff. . . . Essential earthiness and its tempestuous desires are punished first by a corresponding indignity . . . and next by fairies and music: these latter suggesting the antithesis of lust, uncleanness, and all earthiness of instinct. ◆ Long (1961, pp. 8 f.) **:** Another clear result of the music in the scene is its use to sustain sound during the pantomime which it accompanies. The concluding song provides the only intelligible sound at this point of the play; Falstaff is groaning and yelping with pain and fright while Dr. Caius steals away the wrong person and Fenton carries off Anne—both actions done as a dumb show. . . . As a final result we may note that the music underscores the climax of the play. We have earlier observed Shakespeare placing music at climactic points in his comedies. We thus find him following a practice which he had utilized frequently enough to be considered a pattern of dramatic technique.

TEXTUAL COMMENTARY

1. **Fie . . . Luxurie**] Collier (ed. 1878) cites a parallel to this line in Greene's *Groats-worth of witte* (1592, sig. C1v), in Lamilia's song:

> Fie fie on blind fancie,
> It hinders youths ioy:
> Faire virgins learne by me,
> To count loue a toy.

2. **bloudy fire**] Malone (ed. 1790) cites a parallel in *Tempest* (IV.i.52 f.) **:** A *bloody fire*, means *a fire in the blood*. . . .

> The strongest oaths are straw
> To the fire i' th' blood. ◆

7. **be out**] That is, extinguished; fairies and preternatural spirits are supposed to wander only during the night hours.

MUSIC

The original music for the song is not known. The only setting given by *A List* (1884, p. 33) is one doubtfully attributed to John Addison (1766–1844), dated about

1811, and reprinted by Caulfield (n.d., II, 100–102). Long (1961, p. 11) has set the words to an instrumental score called "The Fairie-round" in Anthony Holborne's *Pavans, Galliards, Almains, and other short Æirs . . .* (1599).

DRAMATIC FUNCTION

It would be hard to overestimate the importance of spectacle in Shakespeare's theater. Limited as the Elizabethan stage may have been in some respects, it was apparently exploited in other ways to satisfy audiences that craved pageantry and colorful ceremony. It was certainly a taste for spectacle among the wealthier classes and the nobility which prompted the development of the costly and luxurious masques to which Ben Jonson, Inigo Jones, and others were to give so much of their talents and energy. A similar love of the spectacular must have been present in the lower classes as well; there is no other explanation for the numerous masque-like elements in the plays of Shakespeare and his contemporaries. The song scene in this play is in reality a masque which has been integrated with the action of the plot.

It should be noted that the final punishment visited on Falstaff is an eminently comic one, and does not blunt with severity the edge of the comedy. The colorful pageantry—costumes, dancing, music and song, and candlelight on the darkened stage—would delight any audience.

There is no record of an Elizabethan performance of the play at Court; but there is the legend that Shakespeare wrote the play at the express command of Elizabeth who wished to see Falstaff in love. The legend may well be true. In a court performance there would be choirboys available to take the part of fairies.

43

TEXT: Quarto (1609), second issue with preface, sig. F₁ (III.i.125–136).
TYPOGRAPHY: Indented verse, italic face.

> *Loue, loue, nothing but loue, ſtill loue ſtill more:*
> *For o loues bow. Shoots Bucke and Doe.*
> *The ſhafts confound not that it wounds*
> *But ticles ſtill the ſore:*
> *Theſe louers cry, oh ho they dye,*   5
> *Yet that which ſeemes the wound to kill,*
> *Doth turne oh ho, to ha ha he,*
> *So dying loue liues ſtill,*
> *O ho a while, but ha ha ha,*
> *O ho grones out for ha ha ha----hey ho,*   10

GENERAL COMMENTARY

Noble (1923, p. 129) **:** Pandarus, the singer . . . is a senile voluptuary of the type of Dryden's Limberham and Otway's Sir Jolly Jumble. . . . [His song] is true to his character of encouraging physical love, and is appropriate to the emotional ecstasies of Paris and Helen, to whom he sings it. Thus we have the sort of song adopted by Shakespeare in *As You Like It*. Amiens sang of the rough weather, whose discomforts he and his companions were experiencing, and in the misanthropic vein to which he was addicted. Pandarus sang of physical love to two of its most abandoned devotees and in the thorough spirit of a pandar. . . . The song is a curious contrast to *O mistress mine*—both alike insist on present joys, but from different motives. One is from an eager would-be participant, the other is the temptation by a mere promoter of intrigue. One is the natural call of fresh youth, the other is the revolting depravity of wicked senility. The more Pandarus's song is examined, the more strongly does it impress itself as one of the very greatest dramatic song masterpieces in our language. ◆ Sternfeld (1952, pp. 131, 135) **:** The noble Pandarus, like Balthasar [in *Much Ado*] and Amiens, is a lord and therefore reluctant to give, in public, a performance usually assigned to professionals. He protests to Paris that he is not full of harmony and to Helen that his art is rude, and he dallies some seventy lines before obliging with his song. But this courtly, sophisticated, self-indulgent, lecherous song characterizes the ills with which the Trojan gentry is infested as surely as Amiens paints the outdoor life of the Forest of Arden.... Pandarus' air, then, is the music of a depraved Elizabethan gentry, just as the broken consort which he interrupts. ◆ Sternfeld (1963, pp. 136 f.) : Pandarus's public performance as vocalist and instrumentalist enhances the Italianate, luxuriant impropriety of this court scene. Moreover, the metrical complexity of the song is such that an accompaniment, though not obligatory, would aid the performance.... The prose dialogue which frames Pandarus's song stresses its decadence by the excessive repetitions of ... "fair" [and] "sweet".... When it is over ... another epithet conveys the sensuousness of the Trojan court [*viz.*, "hot"].... Thus, the excessively sweet music becomes a symbol of excessively hot love and, in general, of the depravity of the gentry. ◆ [Sternfeld is certainly correct in calling attention to the decadence of the song, a quality amply evidenced by the *double entendres* of its lyrics if by nothing else.]

TEXTUAL COMMENTARY

1. **still**] Always, continually.

3. **shafts confound**] Malone (ed. 1790) : To confound ... formerly meant to destroy. ◆ Reed (ed. 1813) quotes John Monck Mason : Pandarus means to say that "the shaft confounds," not because the wounds it gives are severe, but because "it tickles still the sore." To *confound* does not signify here to *destroy*, but to annoy or perplex; and *that it wounds* does not mean *which* it wounds, but *in* that it wounds, or because it wounds. ◆ [An unresolvable grammatical ambiguity in ll. 4 and 5 will permit either meaning. The Folio and all the modern editors correct *shafts confound* to *shaft confounds*.]

4. **sore**] Arden (ind. ed. 1922) : Probably here, as in *Love's Labour's Lost*, IV.ii.[58–63], there is a play on the word as meaning a buck of the fourth year. ◆ New Variorum (ind. ed. 1953) : Rann ... [1789] suggests that a pun is intended on "sorel," a buck in the third year. Deighton ... [1906] agrees, and cites *Love's Labor's Lost* ... "The preyful princess pierced ... a ... pricket; Some say a sore; but not a sore, till now made sore with shooting." [The New Variorum editor comments:] "Sore" and "sorrel" are both substantive uses of adjectives meaning reddish brown. "Sorrel" is a buck of the third year, "sore" one of the fourth. The terms are also applied to hawks. ◆ [A contemporary explanation of the terminology applied to deer of different ages is given in *The Retvrne From Pernassvs: Or The Scourge of Simony* (1606, sig. D₂ᵛ):

> It was my pleasure two dayes ago, to take
> a gallant leash of Grey-hounds, and into my fathers
> Parke I went, accompanied with two or three Noble
> men of my neere acquaintance, desiring to shew them
> some of the sport: I causd the Keeper to

> seuer the rascall Deere, from the Bucks of the
> first head: now sir, a Bucke the first yeare
> is a Fawne, the second yeare a pricket, the
> third yeare a Sorell, the fourth yeare a Soare,
> the fift a Buck of the first head, the sixt
> yeare a compleat Buck.

Thus a pun on *soare* and *sore*.]

6. **wound to kill**] *NED* gives as an obsolete meaning of *kill*, "to strike, or knock."
Or the sense of the phrase may merely be "a killing wound."

7. **ha ha he**] Reed (ed. 1813) : A passage in Massinger's *The Fatall Dowry* [1632,
sig. I₁] may prove the aptest comment on . . . this despicable ditty:

> *Musique and a Song, Beaumelle within—ha, ha, ha.*
> *Cha.* How's this? It is my Ladies laugh! most certaine
> When I first pleas'd her, in this merry language,
> She gaue me thanks. ◆

New Variorum (ind. ed. 1953) : Boyle . . . [1902, p. 35] cites Tourneur's *Atheist's
Tragedy* . . . [ed. Nicoll [1929], p. 203],

> *D'am.* Here's a sweete Comedie. T'begins with
> O Dolentis, and concludes with ha, ha, he.

[The New Variorum editor comments:] The Accidence of the authorized grammar
[*A Shorte Introdvction of Grammar*, 1566–1567, by William Lily and John Colet] says,
"An Interiection is a part of speach, which betokeneth a sudayne passion of the
minde, vnder an vnperfect voyce. Some are of . . . Laughing: as *Ha ha he*." Perhaps,
therefore, the same form "ha ha he" should appear in lines [9 and 10]. See *Much
Ado*, IV.i.20–21 . . . "How now! interiections? why then, some be of laughing, as
ha, ha, he." ◆

7–10. **Doth . . . hey ho**] Seng (1964, *MLJ*, p. 214) : The depraved grossness of the
song, the basic animal metaphor, the puns on *shaft, sore,* and *die* (not to mention
the indecent suggestivity of some of those words), are exactly what we would
expect from *un vieux lubrique*. No sophisticated reader of the play, aware of its
general tone and of the cynical depravity of many of its characters, could read the
lyrics of this song and remain unaware of the fact that they are "sick" in the way
that some modern jokes are sick. But it is the last few lines that are particularly
interesting because of their allusion to Lily's Grammar. Pandarus uses two interjections as vehicles to express the tenor of his thoughts about the essential nature
of physical love: it begins in pain and effort, but culminates in delicious and
luxurious abandonment. There is a world of Havelock Ellis compressed into the
last four lines of the song. But Shakespeare's use of such an innocent vehicle to
express such a lubricious tenor is also clear. By doing so he ironically poises the
sensibility of the innocent schoolboy against the sensibility of the aged lecher,
making the one the implicit foil of the other. ◆

8. **So dying**] An indecent pun, "in achieving sexual climax." So in *Antony and
Cleopatra* (I.ii.147–149):

I do think there is mettle in death, which commits some loving act upon her, she hath such a celerity in dying.

10. **grones**] Probably also in the obscene sense, as in *Hamlet* (III.ii.259 f.): "It would cost you a groaning to take off my edge."

hey ho] Noble (1923, p. 130) : The old man is fatigued with his effort, hence the sigh of weariness and relief when he has finished.

MUSIC

The original music for Pandarus' song is not known, and neither *A List* (1884) nor Roffe (1878) mentions any modern setting for it. Sternfeld (1963, p. 138) notes that it is "prosodically closer to a madrigal than to ballad poetry" and that its "bizarre pattern is well suited to the decadence it expresses." He gives (p. 140, and 1964, *Songs*, p. 19) the words to an adaptation of a contemporary melody called "The Good Shepherd's Sorrow."

DRAMATIC FUNCTION

Pandarus' reluctance to sing is a clear example of his awareness of the social convention that dictated that gentlemen and aristocrats should not be too forward in exhibiting their musical accomplishments in public. Yet while acceding to one social convention he flagrantly violates another. As Sir Thomas Hoby's *The Covrtyer of Covnt Baldessar Castilio* (1561, sigs. M_4v–N_1) would have informed him, the courtier

> shall knowe his age, for (to saie the trueth) it were no meete matter, but an yll sight to see a man of eny estimation being olde, horeheaded and toothlesse, full of wrinckles, with a lute in his armes playing vpon it singing in the middes of a company of women, although he coulde doe it reasonablye well. And that, because suche songes conteine in them woordes of loue, and in olde men loue is a thing to bee iested at. . . .
>
> And in case olde men wil sing to the lute, let them doe it secretly, and onely to ridde their mindes of those troublesome cares and greuous disquietinges that oure life is full of.

Noble properly compares this song with "O Mistress mine"; both are examples of a common genre, the "invitation to love," a poetic convention that goes back to classical times. But alike as they may be in form, the two songs are utterly different in tone. Feste sings a lyric of fresh young love to two drunken old men in the middle of a midnight binge. The incongruity of the song to its auditors is comic without ever being unhealthy. But Pandarus' song has neither joyous youth nor rollicking comedy to redeem it. The song is as depraved as the singer, as decadent as the circumstances that prompt it. It is preceded by prurient conversation about Pandarus' efforts to forward Troilus' suit for Cressida; it has an appropriate *coda* in the salacious discussion of the "generation of love" which follows it.

The song is also, as Noble remarks, a "masterpiece," though perhaps not in the sense in which he intended that word. The basic metaphor of the song compares the assaults and consummation of physical desire with the hunting of a deer. On another level the lyrics explore the sadistic-masochistic character of physical love-making in graphically naturalistic detail. The whole effect of the song is to describe a sensual love which culminates only in a permanently unsatisfied satiety.

All's Well That Ends Well

44

TEXT: Folio (1623), sig. V₃ (I.iii.74–83).
TYPOGRAPHY: Mixed verse and prose, italic and roman face.

Was this faire face the caufe, quoth fhe,
Why the Grecians facked *Troy*,
Fond done, done, fond was this King *Priams* ioy,
With that fhe fighed as fhe ftood, *bis*
And gaue this fentence then, among nine bad if one be   5
good, among nine bad if one be good, there's yet one
good in ten.

GENERAL COMMENTARY

Capell ([1779–1783 ?], I, part 1, pp. 6 f.) : [The clown sings] part of another old ballad, which the word "*Helen*" has brought into his mind. . . . "*Was this fair face*" &c. seem rather to have been spoken *of* Helen, than *by* Helen herself: neither have the words "*one*," and "*nine*," any reference to Paris, and nine of his brothers; but contain a reflection of the speaker herself . . . upon the general badness of women. . . . What the corruption was, that the singer is tax'd with, will be hard to say positively; only, that the proportion of bad to good was probably not set so high in the genuine fragment. ♦ Moore (1916, pp. 98 f.) : Not only is the song used to heighten the scene in which it occurs, but it may at the same time foreshadow what is to come. The clown's song . . . possibly serves this purpose; for Helena is the one good woman in ten. ♦

Long (1961, pp. 15 f.) notes from the New Cambridge (1955) editors that "this may be a part of an old ballad entitled 'The Lamentation of Hecuba and the Ladyes of Troy' whose text has been lost." The possible identification of the song with this lost ballad was earlier made by Rollins (1924, *SP*, no. 1464) from an entry in the Stationers' Registers to Edward White on 1 August 1586. Assuming the song's ballad-origin, Long attempts to regularize the lines in Shakespeare "to fit the simple tunes to which ballads were usually set."

TEXTUAL COMMENTARY

3. **Fond . . . ioy]** Warburton (ed. 1747) **:** This is a Stanza of an old ballad, out of which a word or two are dropt, equally necessary to make the sense and the alternate rhime. For it was not *Helen*, who was King *Priam's* joy, but Paris. The third line therefore should be read thus,

> Fond done, fond done, *for Paris, he.* ◆

Malone (ed. 1790) **:** In confirmation of Dr. Warburton's conjecture, Mr. Theobald has noted from Fletcher's *Maid in the Mill* [1647, sig. 4A₄] the following . . .

> And here fair *Paris* comes, the hopefull
> youth of Troy,
> Queen *Hecub's* darling-son, King *Priams*
> onely joy. ◆

5–7. **And . . . ten]** Warburton (ed. 1747) **:** This second stanza of the ballad is turned to a joke upon the women: a confession, that there was one good in ten. Whereon the Countess observed, that he corrupted the song; which shews the song said, *Nine good in ten.*

> *If one be bad amongst nine good,*
> *There's but one bad in ten.*

This relates to the ten sons of *Priam*, who all behaved themselves well but Paris.

MUSIC

No original music exists for this song—if it is a song. Elsewhere in the play the clown seems to *recite* his scurrilous rhymes. Linley (1816, II, 16) not finding any other music for this lyric composed a setting of his own.

DRAMATIC FUNCTION

Moore's suggestion that the song foreshadows Helena's role as the "one good woman" goes about as far as this bit of doggerel can be stretched. But perhaps these verses best characterize the clown. He is given to riddling rhymes and scurrilous speeches, and it is to be expected that an (almost) all-male audience would be amused by an antifeminine lyric. Such *dicta* have amused men in a literary fashion since the Wife of Bath's fourth and fifth marriages, but the antecedents of antifeminism have their roots in a far earlier age than that.

Measure for Measure

45

TEXT: Folio (1623), sig. G₂ (IV.i.1–6).
TYPOGRAPHY: Indented verse, italic face; s.d., *Song*.

Take, oh take thoſe lips away,
*   that ſo ſweetly were forſworne,*
And thoſe eyes: the breake of day
*   lights that doe miſlead the Morne;*
But my kiſſes bring againe, bring againe,   5
Seales of loue, but ſeal'd in vaine, ſeal'd in vaine.

GENERAL COMMENTARY

Noble (1923, pp. 88 f.) **:** [The purpose of this song] is to give colour effect to the desolate situation of the jilted Mariana on the occasion of her first presentation to the audience.... Thus, in part, it is ... [static, like the songs in Shakespeare's earlier plays,] but, at the same time, it also partakes of the character of the later songs in its use as scenery and in its greater relevancy to the dramatic matter in hand. We have previously heard ... of Mariana's sad love story and of the sordid motive which prevented the consummation of her nuptials, and accordingly, when we are introduced into her presence, a song is being sung to her, which voices the wail of a broken heart and whose design is suitably to please her woe by feeding it, for women curiously find comfort in nursing their sorrows. It breaks off suddenly on the approach of the Duke ... a fine dramatic point in itself. Although the song illustrates her 'continuance of her first affection', yet she thinks it meet to excuse herself for being found 'musical'—the song, thus woven into the body of the action and dialogue, provides the Duke with a suitable opening remark before entering on his main business. ♦ Auden (1957, p. 38) **:** Here ... we have an unhappy woman listening to a song. But Mariana ... is not trying to forget her unhappiness; she is indulging it. Being the deserted lady has become a role. The words of the song ... mirror her situation exactly, and her apology to the Duke when he surprises her, gives her away. ♦ Long (1961, pp. 20 f.): The dramatic function of the song seems to be aimed at an immediate characterization of Mariana upon her entry. The probability that she is an addition to Shakespeare's gallery of melancholics appears when we compare her remark about the music, it "pleas'd my woe," to Jaques' comment [*As You Like It*, II.v.12–14] that he could "sucke melancholy out of a song,/As a Weazel suckes egges:" and to Duke Orsino's craving for sad music [*Twelfth Night*, I.i.2–3], "Giue me excesse of it: that surfetting,/The appetite may sicken, and so dye." Thus, from the effect of the song and knowledge previously given us of Mariana's plight, our sympathies are instantly drawn to her.... The statements of Mariana and the Duke concerning the psychological effects of music are drawn from Renaissance musico-medical lore. She speaks of music as pleasing to her woe, that is, in her present state music increases her melancholy which, in turn, provides a type of pleasure. ◆ Sternfeld (1963, pp. 88 f.) : The dialogue which follows the boy's song ... shows that this song was intended to invoke the Ethos of music.... Mariana's purpose is "to make bad good" as the boy's song of deserted love consoles her.... But to give oneself up to this melancholy stanza with its emphasis on the doleful phrase "seal'd in vain" is also an act of self-indulgence and therefore likely to provoke good to harm. Seemingly Mariana realizes this. When the Duke enters the garden she prevents the boy from continuing, is impatient to be relieved of his embarrassing presence, and apologizes for having been discovered "so musical," that is, for having had recourse to the palliative of a melancholy song.... [Her] real need is not so much for music to relieve her dejected spirit as for advice based on the law of God, which the Duke ... offers her. ◆

Rowe (ed. 1709) argues that the existence of this song in *Measure for Measure* is "yet another Proof" of the authenticity of the Cotes-Benson edition of Shakespeare's *Poems* (1640), which includes this song with an additional stanza probably taken from Fletcher's *The Bloody Brother* (1639, sig. H$_4$v). Rowe quotes the additional stanza and continues : The reason why this Stanza was left out ... is this—it is plain that the second makes the Song to be from a Man to a Woman; whereas in the Play it is from a Woman to a Man. From *Mariana* to *Angelo*. For to have brought in *the Hills of Snow which his frozen Bosom bears*, had here been highly ridiculous. ◆ Warburton (ed. 1747) : This is part of a little sonnet of Shakespeare's own writing, consisting of two Stanzas, and so extremely sweet, that the reader won't be disappointed to have the other [which he then quotes]. ◆ Malone (ed. 1790) : This song is found entire in Shakespeare's *Poems*, printed in 1640; but that is a book of no authority: yet I believe that both of these stanzas were written by our author. ◆ New Cambridge (ind. ed. 1922) : The lines just quoted [from Fletcher] do not sound Shakespearean; but note [Mariana's words to the singer following the first stanza in Shakespeare] 'Break off thy song.' ◆ [The New Cambridge editors seem to imply that Mariana's remark indicates the existence of a second stanza to the song even at the time of Shakespeare's play.] Noble (1923, p. 89) : The fact that ... [a second stanza to this song] appeared in Fletcher's play ... has given rise to a discussion as to their authorship. R. G. White ... disposed of the whole question conclusively. 'The first', he pointed out, 'is animated purely by sentiment, the second, delicately beautiful as it is, is the expression of a man carried captive solely through his sense of beauty. The first breathes woman's wasted love; the second, man's disappointed passion. The first could not have been written by Fletcher; the second would not have been written by Shakespeare as a companion to the first.'

White's contention is so convincing as to preclude the necessity of dwelling upon the difference in lyrical style in the two verses. ♦ E. K. Chambers (1930, I, 455) : The song . . . is good enough for any one. If not Shakespeare's, one could fancy it Campion's. . . . But it recurs, with a less good second verse, more clearly within Fletcher's compass, in *The Bloody Brother*, which several experts . . . place before 1623. . . . A musical interpolation in a Jacobean revival is always possible. ♦ Cutts (1959, *Musique*, p. 172) follows other scholars in finding a considerable difference between the two stanzas. He proposes that the first stanza was written by Shakespeare for *Measure for Measure*, then appropriated by Fletcher, who added a stanza, for his own play. Sternfeld (1963, p. 90) concurs, referring to the second stanza as "poetically inferior."

Noble (1923, p. 90) : The source of both verses may be traced to "Ad Lydiam," one of four fragments ascribed to Cornelius Gallus, but generally considered to be forgeries. ♦ [See Source, below.]

TEXTUAL COMMENTARY

5–6. **But . . . vaine**] Capell (n.d. [1779–1783 ?], II, part 3, p. 51) : What the moderns could mean by their suppression of the final couplet's repeatings, cannot be conceiv'd; for . . . such repeatings may be made, with some art, to have the best effect possible. But Mr. Dowland, or whoever else had the setting of it, may perhaps have judg'd otherwise, and these repeatings have been omitted from the beginning: for so we find them in . . . Fletcher; who to this stanza, which he has borrow'd, has joined a second the most unlike it that can be, this breathing sweets that are natural, the other conceits for Hurlothrumbo or Mr. Bayes in his altitudes. ♦ [The repetitions are omitted also in all the early printed and manuscript versions of the song. See Music, below.]

6. **Seales of loue**] Barton (1929, p. 148) : Written instruments under seal . . . were so commonly used as symbols of love and kisses by poets of that day that the metaphor would have become trite, if Shakespeare had not made it immortal in such passages as [this].

MUSIC

The earliest known music for this song is usually attributed to John Wilson, the famous composer and Oxford Professor of Music. If there was a song included in the earliest production of the play, around 1604–1605, Wilson cannot have been the composer since he was born around 1595. But if it is supposed that the song was added to the original version for some later revival of the play prior to the printing of the Folio (1623), he may well have been the composer. He was apparently extremely precocious, having composed a number of songs for *The Maske of Flowers*, 1614, some of which he republished in his *Cheerfull Ayres*, 1660. Moreover, he is known to have been familiar with Shakespearean theatrical music: *Cheerfull Ayres* includes two of Robert Johnson's songs for *The Tempest*, and his own "Lawn as white as driven snow" for *Winter's Tale*. On the other hand, if Wilson did not compose the original music for "Take, o take those lips away," that song as it stands in his published works and in the manuscript copies may be his setting of the original theatrical air by another, and anonymous, composer. Finally, it is also possible that the extant song is a relic from Fletcher's play and wholly unrelated, except in the words of the first stanza, to Shakespeare. Or, indeed, the music may be utterly independent of the theater. It does not seem likely that these possibilities can be further narrowed.

Early printed versions of the song are to be found in John Playford's *Select Musicall Ayres and Dialogves* (1652, 1653; sig. G₂ᵛ in both editions); *Select Ayres and Dialogues* (1659, sig. B₁), *The Treasury of Musick* (1669, p. 1), and some later song-books. Manuscript versions of the words and music are in B. M. Add. MS. 11,608 (fol. 56), Bodleian MS. Music b. 1 (fol. 19ᵛ), Christ Church Oxford MS. 434 (fol. 1); and New York Public Library MSS. Drexel 4257 (no. 16), and 4041 (no. 44). Cutts (1959, *Musique*, p. 114) remarks that the song may also at one time have been included in B. M. Add. MS. 29,481 (fol. 19ᵛ), but adds that this version is no longer extant. The words alone appear in Folger Library MS. 452.4 (fol. 20), a common-place book dating from about 1640. All the above versions of the song basically agree with the two-stanza text which appears in Fletcher's *The Bloody Brother* (1639).

There are modern copies of most of the above settings. Cutts (1959, *Musique*, pp. 1, 85) gives the versions in MSS. Mus. b. 1 and Add. 11,608; Long (1961, pp. 22, 135) gives Drexel 4041 and a facsimile; Sternfeld (1963, p. 94) reproduces the song from *Select Musicall Ayres*, 1652, with an unfigured bass, and (pp. 95 f.; and 1964, *Songs*, p. 17) in a harmonized version. Less reliable versions are those by Bridge (n.d., p. 26) and Hardy (1930, pp. 2 f.) from the 1652 book; Gibbon (1930, p. 123) from the 1653 version; and Bontoux (1936, p. 334) from the 1659 songbook. Vincent (1906, p. 32) gives his own arrangement of the Wilson tune, and Elson (1901, pp. 167 f.) does not indicate the source of his transcription. Lindsey (1924, p. 351) erroneously asserts that the song is to be found in Wilson's *Cheerfull Ayres*, 1660. It is not; unfortunately his mistake has been reproduced by Cutts (1959, *Musique*, p. 115) and Long (1961, p. 22).

SOURCES

A remote source for the verses in Shakespeare and Fletcher may be a Latin poem that turns up in Renaissance collections. The text which follows is from the *Satyricon* of Petronius Arbiter, 1587 (sigs. h₁–h₁ᵛ):

> Lydia bella puella, candida,
> Quae bene superas lac & lilium,
> Albamque simul rosam rubidam,
> Aut expolitum ebur Indicum.
> Pande puella, pande capillulos
> Flauos, lucentes vt aurum nitidum.
> Pande puella collum candidum,
> Productum bene candidis humeris.
> Pande puella stellatos oculos,

Flexaque super nigra cilia.
Pande puella genas roseas,
Perfusas rubro purpurae Tyriae.
Porrige labra, labra corallina,
Da columbatim mitia basia:
Sugis amentis partem animi:
Cor mihi penetrant haec tua basia.
Quid mihi sugis viuum sanguinem?
Conde papillas, conde gemipomas,
Compresso lacte quae modo pullulant.
Sinus expansa profert cinnama:
Vndique surgunt ex te deliciae.
Conde papillas, quae me sauciant
Candore, & luxu niuei pectoris.
Saeua non cernis quod ego langueo?
Sic me destituis iam semimortuum?

[Beautiful Lydia, fair maiden, you surpass [in fairness] milk and lily, and even the white-red rose, or polished Indian ivory. Display, mistress, display your fine flaxen hair, luminous as glossy gold. Display, mistress, that white neck handsomely rising from your white shoulder. Display, mistress, those starry eyes with jet brows bent over them. Display, mistress, your rosy cheeks, suffused with red of Tyrian hue. Put forth your lips, your coral lips, and give me gentle dovelike kisses; you suck out part of my distracted mind. Those kisses of yours pierce me to the heart; why do you suck my living blood? Hide those breasts, conceal those twin fruits that spring even now with hidden milk. Your ample bodice gives off [odors of] cinnamon. From everywhere about you rise up sensual delights. Hide those breasts which wound me with the whiteness and splendor of your snowy bosom. Cruel one, can you not guess why I languish? Do you abandon me thus, already half-dead?]

A modern edition of the poem is to be found in Gaselee (1925, pp. 68 f.), and a bibliography in Walther (1959, p. 536).

The existence of the Latin poem suggests an hypothesis which would account for the various versions of the lyrics which have come down to us. If it is supposed that some author anterior to both Shakespeare and Fletcher wrote his own English poem in imitation of "Ad Lydiam"—his verses may even have been set to music as a song—Shakespeare might have borrowed part for use in *Measure for Measure*, omitting the second stanza as not appropriate to Mariana; further, he might have repeated the phrases in ll. 5 and 6 to make the words fit music he had in mind. Fletcher and Wilson, some years later, may have taken up both stanzas for use in *The Bloody Brother*, scoring a success with it in that play, a success which would account for all the manuscript and printed versions of the English song. These are all in closer verbal agreement with Fletcher's song than they are with Shakespeare's. It is worth noting that none of the early manuscript or printed versions of the song have the Shakespearean repetitions. Any arguments based on the qualitative merits of the two stanzas seem a waste of breath; they resolve themselves merely to subjective value-judgements.

The two stanzas below are the words of the song as they appear in *The Bloody Brother* (1639, sig. H$_4$v):

> Take, Oh take those lips away
> that so swetly were forsworne,
> And those eyes, like breake of day,
> lights that doe misleade the Morne,
> But my kisses being againe
> Seales of love, though seal'd in vaine.
>
> Hide, Oh hide those hils of Snow,
> which thy frozen blossome beares,
> On whose tops the Pincks that grow
> are of those that April weares.
> But first set my poore heart free,
> bound in those Ioy chaines by thee.

DRAMATIC FUNCTION

As the various commentators suggest, the song creates a mood of melancholy and characterizes Mariana for an audience who is seeing her for the first time, late in the play.

Long (1961, p. 19) suggests that Shakespeare may have borrowed the idea of introducing a song at this point from George Whetstone's *Promos and Cassandra* (1578), a play in which he notes the existence of "seven songs placed at intervals within the work." Whetstone probably is the most direct source of Shakespeare's play, but Kittredge (ed. 1936) points out that behind Whetstone's play is "the fifth novel in the eighth decade of the *Hecatommithi* of Giovanni Battista Giraldi (surnamed Cinthio or Cintio), first printed in 1565," and he notes also that the story was current in Europe in several different versions before Giraldi made use of it.

The occurrence of but a single song in Shakespeare's play suggests that its appearance here may be completely extraneous. Act IV of *Measure for Measure* could easily omit the first fifteen lines (including the song), and begin with the Duke's inquiry:

> I pray you tell me, hath anybody enquir'd for me here to-day? Much upon this time have I promis'd here to meet.

Hence it seems possible that the song may be a Jacobean interpolation into Shakespeare's text.

46

TEXT: First Quarto (1622), sig. E₄ (II.iii.71–75).
TYPOGRAPHY: Indented verse, italic face.

And let me the Cannikin clinke, clinke,
And let me the Cannikin clinke, clinke:
A Souldier's a man, a life's but a ſpan,
Why then let a ſouldier drinke.

GENERAL COMMENTARY

Moore (1916, p. 93) observes that Shakespeare frequently uses songs as incitements to action : Iago sings . . . to incite Cassio to become drunk before the brawl with Roderigo. [Moore also (p. 85) discerns a foreshadowing of peril in Shakespeare's use of drinking songs:] Only the drinking songs of Falstaff and Sir Toby are free from the powerful overtones of dramatic significance with which Shakespeare charged his music; the other Bacchic passages are prophetic of impending disaster. ♦ Noble (1923, p. 124) : [Iago] is versed in men's weaknesses, and knows, none better, how to play upon the strings of their feelings. Therefore when he seeks to subvert military order by luring Cassio, an officer on duty, on to a drinking bout, he has studied beforehand the most effective means to employ, and he decides upon song as the surest way of making abandoned gaiety most inviting. ♦ Arden (ind. ed. 1928) : Probably an old toping stave. The following extract is from *New Eng. Dict.*: "carruse and hold the cannikin klynclene." . . . Halliwell quotes from *The Knave in Graine, New Vampt,* 1640 [sig. G₃ᵛ]: "*Lod.* Clinke, boyes. *Toma.* Drinke, boyes. *Stult.* And let the Cannikin clinke boyes." ♦ Sternfeld (1963, pp. 144 f.) : That a song should function as wine's proverbial ally is to be expected, but the contrast with the drunken scene in *Antony and Cleopatra* [II.vii.] is worth noting. In the Roman play a "boy" is directed to sing a song on the galley of Pompey who "doth this day laugh away his fortune." But it is part of Iago's skill and cunning that he does not depend on an attendant. By himself performing and thereby precisely timing his own adult songs Iago becomes, not fortune's fool, but the master of his fate. (That he is not important or rich enough to command a boy-singer is by the way.) Moreover, by pretending to be full of song, as good-natured and kindly people were supposed to be, "honest" Iago disarms any suspicion Cassio may have harboured.

TEXTUAL COMMENTARY

2. **clinke, clinke:**] The Folio omits the second *clinke* and all the modern editors follow this reading. Johnson, Capell, Hanmer, and Malone, however, remove this word from the end of l. 2 only to add it to the end of l. 1, thereby making the first line read: "And let me the cannikin clink, clink, clink." Since the original drinking song is lost—if it ever existed outside Shakespeare's play—only the Folio or Q_1 readings have any authority.

3. **a life's . . . span**] New Arden (ind. ed. 1962) notes that this is from the Prayer-Book version of Ps. xxxix.6: "Thou hast made my days as it were a span long." The expression also occurs proverbially; see W. G. Smith (1935, p. 262) and Tilley (1950, L-251). In a slightly altered form it occurs in *As You Like It* (III.ii.137–140).

MUSIC

The original tune for this song is not known. Lamson (1936, p. 549) records "Let the cannikin clink, boys" as the tune to a ballad "Some say we shall be overthrown" in MS. Ashmole H. 23 (fol. 46), a fact which suggests either that Iago's song became popular enough to give its name to the tune to which it was sung or, more likely, that Shakespeare simply appropriated the song from the popular music of his time.

A List (1884, p. 49) cites a 1673 setting by Pelham Humfrey as the earliest known music for Iago's first song; but this citation is a typographical error. The entry belongs to a Willow Song by Humfrey. Caulfield (n.d., II, 66) gives what may be a "traditional" tune, but he is extremely unreliable as an editor; his omission of a composer's name is not necessarily evidence that the music he prints is old. Sternfeld (1963, p. 146; 1964, *Songs*, p. 1) has arranged the words to the tune "Joan Sanderson" from Playford's *Dancing Master*, 1686.

DRAMATIC FUNCTION

The actual stage-time of the drinking episode can hardly occupy more than a few minutes, yet an audience watching the play finds nothing incredible about the short time Cassio takes to get drunk. Had Shakespeare attempted to establish temporal verisimilitude in this episode, he would have had to delay the main action of the play unreasonably. Hence he used song to bridge the difficulty. The effect of the songs is not only to establish an atmosphere of drunken wassail, but to "stretch" stage-time and make Cassio's rapid drunkenness plausible. It is probably awareness of this time problem that caused the playwright to have Cassio hedge the difficulty by admitting (II.iii.40–45) that he is a poor drinker.

47

TEXT: First Quarto (1622), sig. E₄ (II.iii.92–99).
TYPOGRAPHY: Indented verse, italic and roman face.

King *Stephen* was a worthy peere,
His breeches coft him but a crowne,
He held 'em fixpence all too deere,
With that he cald the Taylor lowne,
He was a wight of high renowne,
And thou art but of low degree,
Tis pride that puls the Countrey downe,
Then take thine owd cloke about thee.

GENERAL COMMENTARY

Johnson (ed. 1765) : These stanzas are taken from an old song, which the reader will find recovered and preserved in a curious work lately printed. . . . ◆ [*Reliques*, 1765 (I, 172–175). A more accurate transcript of Percy's Folio MS., though still not an exact one, is to be found in Hales and Furnivall (1867–1868, II, 322–324). Percy's manuscript is now B. M. Add. MS. 27,879, and has the "old song" to which Johnson refers on fol. 143ᵛ.] Kilgour (1876, pp. 183 f.) : The song under the name of "Tak yer auld cloak about you" . . . still flourishes as a song to be sung on convivial occasions. . . . I am not aware that, as a song to be sung, it exists in England anywhere, or to any extent. Judging from the lines in *Othello*, the English version had been adapted to English history. On the other hand the Scotch version is adapted to Scotch history. The English version . . . in Shakespeare . . . seems to me to have a very modern aspect. . . . I have been . . . assuming that there was an English version of the entire song . . . I am not aware that there is any proof. . . . If the song was originally Scotch, does this throw any light upon the question whether Shakespeare was ever in Scotland ? . . . Of course Shakespeare might have heard the song sung by a Scotchman in London. ◆ J. W. E. (1876, pp. 249 f.) denies Kilgour's notion that this was a Scotch song, though he admits that it was a "Northern Song," popular in the north counties of England and southern counties of Scotland. He remarks that "almost all the distinctively Scottish songs appear to have perished during the fanaticism that waged war against those which were not 'godly'," and points out that the earliest Scottish version of this song is the one in the *Tea-Table Miscellany* which, he says, post-dates by many years the authentic English version in the Percy Folio MS. Chappell (1876, p. 250) : The earliest version now extant seems to be the one in Percy's Folio MS. . . . The earliest Scotch copy is of some seventy or eighty years' later date, in Ramsay's *Tea-Table Miscellany*; and there is further reason to think [this song is] of English origin, because its tune is English, being an alteration of . . . *Green Sleeves*. ◆ A. A. (1876, p. 358) : The song . . .

appears to be popular in Germany as in Scotland. J. Heinrich Voss gives a version of it (*Der Flausrock*), of which I send the first stanza:—

> Ein Regensturm mit Schnee und Schlossen
> Zog düster über Land und Meer,
> Dass traufengleich die Dächer gossen;
> Die Küh' im Felde brüllten sehr;
> Frau Käthe, die zwar niemals zanket,
> Sprach hastig: 'Geh' doch, lieber Mann,
> Geh' hin, eh' Blässchen uns erkranket,
> Und zieh' den alten Flausrock an!' ◆

[A rainstorm with snow and sleet swept gloomily over land and sea; along the gutters the roofs overflowed. The cows in the field loudly bellowed. Frau Kathe who never, to be sure, quarreled, said quickly, "Pray go, dear spouse; go out ere Bossy falls sick on us. And put your greatcoat on.] Arden (ind. ed. 1928) : This is the seventh verse of the song "Bell my Wiffe" in Percy Folio Ms. . . . There are eight verses, and each has the last line almost identical, which appears to have been the name of the tune. Chappell [1855–1859, II, 505, n.] says the tune is evidently formed out of "Green Sleeves" . . . and has little doubt that words and music are both of English origin. Chappell never willingly admits a tune to be either Scotch or Irish. The Percy Folio editors say, "The dialect in which it is written, and the general character of the piece . . . clearly imply a northern origin."

TEXTUAL COMMENTARY

1. **King Stephen**] Stephen of Blois, king of England (1135–1154). His popular reputation for niggardliness may have grown out of his historical disrepute as an imposer of heavy taxes and oppressor of the poor. The Peterborough Chronicle for the years 1137 and after gives an unflinching account of these aspects of his reign.

peere] A nobleman, equal in rank to other members of the aristocracy. The term is applied to King Stephen as the first peer among the barons of feudal England.

The traditional account of King Stephen and his breeches is alluded to by Trinculo in *The Tempest* (IV.i.222–224), when he applies the name to the drunken Stephano on beholding Prospero's garments: "O King Stephano! O peer! O worthy Stephano, look what a wardrobe here is for thee!"

2. **His breeches**] Steevens (ed. 1793) cites Greene's *Qvip for an Vpstart Courtier* (1592, sig. B₄ᵛ):

> I tell thee sawcy skipiack, it was a good and a blessed time here in England, when K. *Stephen* wore a pair of cloth breeches of a Noble a payre, and thought them passing costlye.

A similar reference is to be found in Thomas Dekker's *The Gvls Horne-booke* (1609, sig. B₃ᵛ): "His breeches were not so much worth as K. *Stephens*, that cost but a poore noble."

crowne] Probably not a very valuable coin in Shakespeare's day since Orlando (*As You Like It*, I.i.2 f.) describes his inheritance as "but poor a thousand crowns," and Adam (II.iii.38 f.) calls five hundred crowns "the thrifty hire" saved from a lifetime of work.

4. **lowne**] Arden (ind. 1928) : Lout, stupid fellow. Still in use provincially. This word and "auld" ["owd," l. 8], below, are decidedly Scotch. [New Arden (ind. ed. 1962) glosses the word "lout (variant of 'loon')," apparently following *NED*. Some editors emend the word to "clown," but the change seems unnecessary since Shakespeare uses the word again in *Pericles* (IV.vi.19), "lord and lown." The phrase was probably commonplace. Thomas Dekker, *The Gvls Horne-booke* (1609, sig. A₂), has: "any man, woman, or child, be he Lord, be he Lowne, be he Courtier, be he Carter, of the Innes a Court, or Innes of Citty."]

MUSIC

The traditional Scots melody for "Tak your auld cloak about ye," apparently a northern variant of the song from which Iago sings a single stanza, is to be found in a number of folk-song collections: Oswald ([1750–1760 ?], II, 29; [1760 ?], II, 29; [1770 ?], I, 65), Bremner (n.d., I, 14 f. in all editions), J. Johnson (n.d., III, 258 f.), Dale (n.d., I, 13), Ritson (1794, I, 219; 1869, I, 286–288), Stenhouse (1839, III, 258 f.; 1853, II, 258 f.), Thomson (n.d., IV, 4), R. Chambers (1862, p. 113; 1890, pp. 112–115), Alexander (1866, I, 12), Greig (n.d., II, 194 f.), and Elson (1901, pp. 202 f.). Sternfeld (1963, p. 148) reprints the music from Oswald; and (1963, p. 149; 1964, *Songs*, p. 1) gives the tune from Bremner with Shakespeare's words set to it.

Chappell ([1855–1859]) does not give the music for the tune but remarks in a note (II, 505) that it "is evidently formed out of *Green Sleeves*." The opening strains do have a strong resemblance to "Green Sleeves," but the tune as a whole should probably be regarded as independent. The music in Caulfield (n.d., II, 68) is not related in any way to the Scots tune called "Take your auld cloak about thee," but is rather a version of "Chevy Chase."

ANALOGUES

The original song, from which Iago sings a stanza, has apparently not survived; but there are two analogous versions, one in the Percy Folio MS. (B. M. Add. MS. 27,879, fol. 143ᵛ), the other in Ramsay (1793, I, 105–107), which purports to be a reprint of Ramsay's first (1724) edition. Since it is clear that neither song is the source for Iago's fragment of song, there seems little point in quoting more than the relevant stanzas from each of the analogues. The first quotation is from the Folio MS., and is followed by the Scots version:

> King Harry was a verry good K
>   I trow his hose cost but a Crowne
> he thought them 12 d. ouer to deere
>   therfore he called the taylor Clowne
> he was King & wore the Crowne
>   & thouse but of a low degree
> itts pride that putts this cumtrye downe
>   man put thye old Cloake about thee

> In days when our King Robert rang,
>   His trews they cost but ha'f a crown;
> He said, they were a groat o'er dear,
>   And call'd the taylor thief and loun.
> He was the king that wore the crown,
>   And thou'rt a man of laigh degree;
> 'Tis pride puts a' the country down,
>   Sae tak thy auld cloak about thee.

The song in Shakespeare seems to be distinctly from an English (or southern) version of this ballad, a version which has apparently not survived excepting the small fragment in *Othello*. The single possible northern form in that fragmentary version is the *owd* in l. 8, which may be nothing more than a misprint for *old*. The Folio reading of that word is *awl'd*, conceivably in the sense of "full of holes, or ragged." The orthography in the Percy Folio MS. is most unusual, but it seems to reflect only English forms. It is usually dated around the middle of the seventeenth century. Ramsay's version is extremely late and may, indeed, be a Scots rendering of an English poem. There is no reason to suppose, as Scotsmen do, that all ballads come from the North.

DRAMATIC FUNCTION

For the dramatic function of this song, see the remarks of Moore and Noble, and the general discussion of song 46, above.

48

TEXT: Folio (1623), sig. 2v₃ (IV.iii.41–57).
TYPOGRAPHY: Mixed verse and prose, italic and roman face.

Def. The poore Soule ſat ſinging, by a Sicamour tree.
Sing all a greene Willough:
Her hand on her boſome her head on her knee,
Sing Willough, Willough, Wtllough.
The freſh Streames ran by her, and murmur'd her moanes   5
Sing Willough, &c.
Her ſalt teares fell from her, and ſoftned the ſtones,
Sing Willough, &c.   (Lay by theſe)
Willough, Willough.   (Prythee high thee: he'le come anon)
Sing all a greene Willough muſt be my Garland.   10
Let no body blame him, his ſcorne I approue.
(Nay that's not next. Harke, who is't that knocks?
  Æmil. It's the wind.
  Def. I call'd my Loue falſe Loue: but what ſaid he then?
Sing Willough, &c.
If I court mo women, you'le couch with mo men.

GENERAL COMMENTARY

Johnson (ed. 1765) : This [passage] is perhaps the only insertion made in the
latter editions which has improved the play. The rest seem to have been added for
the sake of amplification or of ornament. When the imagination had subsided, and
the mind was no longer agitated by the horror of the action, it became at leisure to
look round for specious additions. This addition is natural. *Desdemona* can at first
hardly forbear to sing the song; she endeavours to change her train of thoughts,
but her imagination at last prevails, and she sings it. ◆ Bradley (1904, pp. 60 f.) :
In . . . [the latter part] of a tragedy Shakespeare often appeals to an emotion
different from any of those excited in the first half of the play, and so provides
novelty and generally also relief. As a rule this emotion is pathetic; and the pathos
is not terrible or lacerating, but, even if painful, is accompanied by the sense of
beauty and by the outflow of admiration or affection, which comes with an inexpressible sweetness after the tension of the crisis. . . . So . . . in *Othello* the passage
where pathos of *this* kind reaches its height is certainly that where Desdemona and
Emilia converse, and the willow-song is sung, on the eve of the catastrophe. ◆
Moore (1916, pp. 99 f.) : Perhaps the most familiar example . . . [of Shakespeare's
use of song to secure] lyric foreboding is the song of Desdemona . . . [which] is

beautifully echoed in the dying words of Emilia ... [that] confirm Othello's resolution to slay himself. ♦ Noble (1923, p. 125) : The singing of the ballad assists in making the misery of Desdemona almost unbearable to the spectator; it makes the scene quite vivid even for the reader sitting in his library. ♦ Davies (1939, p. 123) : Here, as in the case of Ophelia, Shakespeare uses the ability of the boy actor to sing in order to heighten the tragic effect. ... This similarity causes some speculation as to whether Ophelia and Desdemona were played by the same boy, for only two or three years elapse between the plays ... [but] the ability to sing would be the rule rather than the exception among boy actors. The air chosen is a particularly felicitous one, written in the minor, and with a refrain which rises for a moment into the major, only to sink again with a curious sweet melancholy. ♦ Granville-Barker (1947, II, 69) : Upon [Desdemona's] weariness fancies and memories play freely. Reminder of the wedding sheets (imaging—so she had meant them to—the end as the beginning of their wedded joy) begets the fancy to be shrouded in them some day. From that evolves the memory of her dead mother, and of the maid Barbara and *her* "wretched fortune," and the song which "expressed her fortune." ♦

Brennecke (1953, pp. 35–38) summarizes the changes Shakespeare made in the original ballad, and the additions he made to it : He invented Desdemona's mother's maid Barbara, whose lover went mad and who died while singing this song. He interrupted the song with ... simple and yet tense dramatic interjections. ... Entirely out of its context and rhyme, Shakespeare required Desdemona to sing [l. 11] ... lifting the idea from stanza 7 of the song, and recalling, with the audience, how the Moor had so brutally struck her in public that very afternoon. ... Finally, Shakespeare causes Desdemona, who only vaguely recalls the words "false love" from stanza 4, and "She was born to be false" from stanza 7 [of the original ballad], to improvise an entirely original couplet, both touching and grim in its implications. ♦ Sternfeld (1959, p. 159) : The climax of [Desdemona's] song has the most significant variation [from the original]. That the first line [of Desdemona's final couplet] is in effect the second line of the model is unimportant in comparison with the acid reproach of promiscuity that rankles in Desdemona and comes to the fore, destroying the lyric integrity of the original. At this point her version is less song than unwitting self-expression. How ironical and touching that the dying Emilia, in Act V, should return to the burden, 'willow, willow, willow'. The swan song, turned leitmotif, is the only quotation of its kind in Shakespeare where a fragment of song is repeated in the same play. Emilia's coda thus becomes an act of transfiguration. Desdemona's variation, on the other hand, depends for its effectiveness on the playgoer's knowledge of the model. ... ♦ Cutts (1959, *NQ*, pp. 251 f.) finds a correspondence between Desdemona's song of Barbary and her own situation : Desdemona in her extreme melancholy is subconsciously hinting that Othello has "prov'd mad" and that he has forsaken her. The song will not go from her head because the likeness of her own situation to Barbary's is too forceful. Like Barbary she must sing the song but before she does so she utters the line about Lodovico which is surely another parallel. In contrast to her lord ... Lodovico has behaved so gentlemanly. ♦ Sternfeld (1963, p. 54) : The pathos of Desdemona's song resides in her incomprehension of Othello's lack of faith in one he professed to love and who loved him. In her extreme misery she sings an old song in the privacy of her bed-chamber with only her maid as an involuntary audience.

TEXTUAL COMMENTARY

1. **singing**] This word varies in different copies of the First Folio. Sig. 2v₃ in the Devonshire copy reads *fining*. The ballad in B. M. Add. MS. 15,117 has *fighinge*, the reading of all the early quartos—except Q₃ (1655) which has the curious compromise *finghing*—and all the modern editors since Malone (ed. 1790).

Sicamour tree] Arden (ind. ed. 1928) **:** Our sycamore, or *Great Maple*, was introduced to Britain perhaps as early as the fourteenth century. . . . It was highly appreciated as a shade tree, and was the subject of both legend and poetry. . . . Folkard [1884, p. 586] says "In Sicily, it is known as the Tree of Patience, and is regarded as emblematic of a wife's infidelity and a husband's patience." ◆

2. **all . . . Willough**] These words are the title to a tune in two early music manuscripts. See Music, below.

4. **Wtllough**] An obvious misprint, corrected in Q₂ (1630) and all subsequent editions.

8. **Lay . . . these**] Desdemona interrupts her song to address these words to Emilia, handing her some jewels or articles of clothing.

9. **Prythee . . . anon**] Probably noticing that Emilia dawdles over her task, Desdemona interrupts the song again, for she is mindful of Othello's command (IV.iii.7–9),

> Get you to bed on th' instant. I will be return'd forthwith. Dispatch your attendant there. Look't be done.

10. **Garland**] Douce (1839, pp. 104 f.) **:** It was the custom for those who were *forsaken in love* to wear willow garlands. This tree might have been chosen as the symbol of sadness from . . . [verse 2] in psalm 137 . . . or else from a coincidence between the *weeping* willow and falling tears. Another reason has been assigned. [He quotes from Swan's *Specvlvm Mundi* (1635, sig. 2M₁ᵛ :]

> Vitex, or the *chaste tree* (. . . because, saith *Plinie*, certain matrons among the Athenians, desirous to live chaste, did lay the leaves of it in their beds under them) . . . groweth up much like a willow tree. . . .
>
> It is a singular medecine for such as would live chaste, in what sort soever it be taken, whether in powder, or decoction, or the leaves worn about the body. . . .
>
> *Willow* is of a much like nature; and therefore it is yet a custome, that he which is deprived of love, must wear a willow garland. ◆

Arden (ind. ed. 1928) cites Folkard (1884, p. 586) **:** "The willow seems from the remotest times to have been considered a funereal tree and an emblem of grief." ◆ [Folkard's entire discussion is of interest in connection with this symbol. It seems unlikely, however, that forsaken lovers in Shakespeare's day actually wore a willow garland; the term was probably a metaphor, only, at that time.]

11. **Let . . . approue**] Bradley (1904, p. 206) **:** When Desdemona spoke her last words [(V.ii.124) in answer to Emilia's "O, who hath done this deed ?"], "Nobody— I myself. Farewell," perhaps [this] line of the ballad . . . was still busy in her brain. ◆

12. **Nay . . . next**] Emotionally distraught, Desdemona confuses the order of the verses in the ballad she is singing. Compare Hamlet's correction of Polonius (II.ii.432), "Nay, that follows not."

16. **If . . . men**] Brennecke (1953, pp. 35–38) : In spoken utterance Desdemona would never spontaneously use so indecorous a word as 'couch.' Ironically enough, her very purity and delicacy contribute to her undoing. When Othello demands [IV.ii.38] "Swear thou art honest," she can only reply, "Heaven doth truly know it." . . . Thus communication between the two breaks down. Desdemona's inability to bring her husband to make a circumstantial accusation, which she might refute in clear, if in necessarily indelicate, terms, becomes increasingly apparent. . . . From here on he repeatedly calls her 'whore,' a word whose very sound and connotation she can repeat only with greatest loathing [IV.ii.161–164]:

> I cannot say 'whore.'
> It doth abhor me now I speak the word;
> To do the act that might th' addition earn
> Not the world's mass of vanity could make me.

But what she cannot say, she sings. The last couplet of her song tells us that she is inwardly and explicitly aware of the cause of Othello's passion. . . . Desdemona invents and sings it as if in a dream or a deep reverie, thereby revealing more of her subconscious awareness than any spoken words could indicate.

MUSIC

Two early tunes, either of which may preserve the original music for Desdemona's song, have survived. The first is contained in B. M. Add. MS. 15,117 (fol. 18) along with words and lute accompaniment in what appears to be a concert setting. There are facsimiles of the manuscript in Potter (1915, facing p. ix), Bridge (1923, p. 22), Heseltine (1926, p. 127), and Sternfeld (1963, facing p. 38). Scholarly transcriptions are given by Fellowes (n.d., II, 8 f.), Heseltine (1927, I, 19 f.), Pattison (1948, pp. 169 f.), and (with some inaccuracies) by Cutts (1959, *Musique*, pp. 1 f.). The versions given by Chappell ([1855–1859], I, 207 f.) and Wooldridge (1893; reprinted 1961, I, 106 f.) have modern harmonizations; those by Noble (1923, p. 152 [ed. Fellowes]) and Cutts (1957, pp. 21–23) give the manuscript music, but with Shakespeare's words underlaid. There are also a number of less reliable popular editions of the tune with either Shakespeare's words or the lyrics of the manuscript: Bridge (n.d., pp. 17–20), Elson (1901, pp. 291 f.), E. Edwards (1903, no. 1), Potter (1915, pp. 20 f.), Gibbon (1930, pp. 107 f.), Bontoux (1936, pp. 341–344), H. A. Chambers (1957, pp. 45 f.), and Kines (1964, p. 38). Sternfeld (1963, pp. 41–44; 1964, *Songs*, pp. 2–4) reproduces the manuscript music with both its own and Shakespeare's words underlaid. C. Simpson (1966, p. 789) gives a transcript of the 15,117 tune alone.

A second tune which also has some claim to being regarded as a possible original melody for Desdemona's song survives in two instrumental versions and (partly) in a related vocal piece. Under the title "All of grene willowe" it appears in Thomas Dallis's Lute Book (Trinity College, Dublin, MS. D.3.30, fols. 25–26) and, in a more ornamented version, in Folger Library MS. V.a.1.59 (*olim* 448.16; fol. 19). There is a facsimile of the Dallis MS. in Sternfeld (1963, facing p. 47), and facsimiles of the Folger MS. in Seng (1958, "Willow Song," p. 420) and Sternfeld (1963, facing p. 46). The related vocal piece was recently discovered by Professor John Ward when he matched a fragmentary Western Reserve University manuscript with a fragmentary Willow Song in the New York Public Library (Drexel 4183), and found a surprising amount of agreement between the Folger tune and that of the restored song. For a full account of the discovery see J. Ward (1966, 845–855).

It was long thought that Add. MS. 15,117 was the exclusive source for the music of Desdemona's ballad; but recently Sternfeld (1959, pp. 159 f.) proposed that her lyrics could equally well be fitted to the Dallis-Folger tune, and he has since published his arrangements (1963, pp. 45 f., 48 f.; 1964, *Songs*, pp. 6 f.). While he has also edited and arranged the British Museum song (see above), Sternfeld now appears to feel that the Dallis-Folger music has the more likely claim to being the "original" melody. He remarks (1963, pp. 34 f.):

> If we are correct in assuming that Desdemona sings on the spur of the moment an old song, unaccompanied, the dramatic context does not permit a lute accompaniment. It would not be feasible, either for Desdemona or for Emilia to manage a lute while Emilia undresses her mistress. The entire character of her recitation, the spontaneous way in which she breaks into her swansong, modifies and breaks it off, precludes forethought or an elaborate instrumental accompaniment where phrases in the lute complement phrases in the voice. The version in the manuscript is by a professional musician . . . and is of a complexity that qualifies it as a concert piece. . . . Its vocal part, on the other hand, would be suitable in the stage performance of the tragedy once it is adapted to Shakespeare's text.

The arrangement to the Dallis-Folger tune which Sternfeld proposes has much to recommend it. It is far less elaborate in its use of refrains than the 15,117 version, it has a simple and folk-like quality, and it survives in the same form as other popular tunes of Shakespeare's day: brief instrumental arrangements bearing short titles to designate the name of the tune. It is precisely in this form that such other famous tunes as "Walsingham" and "Bonny Sweet Robin" have come down to us. See Music, songs 35 and 38, above.

SOURCE AND ANALOGUES

There is no reason to suppose that the willow song in the British Museum manuscript (Add. MS. 15,117, fol. 18) was Shakespeare's direct source for Desdemona's song, but the verbal resemblance between the two songs is so close that the manuscript version can unquestionably be regarded as a surviving redaction of the original song which Shakespeare adapted for use in *Othello*. The text which follows is from the manuscript:

> The poore soule sate sighinge by a Sickamore tree,
> Singe willo, willo, willo
> with his hand in his bosom & his heade vpon his knee

o willo willo [willo] willo
O willo willo willo willo,
shalbe my gareland
Singe all a greene willo,
willo willo willo,
Aye me the greene willo must be my gareland

he sight in his singinge and made a greate moane,
singe &c
I am deade to all pleasure, my trewe loue he [*sic*] is gone,
&c
The mute bird sate by hym, was made tame by his moanes
&c
The trewe teares fell from hym would haue melted the stones,
singe &c

Com all you forsaken & mourne you with mee
who speakes of a false loue, mynes falser then shee.
singe &c
Let Loue no more boast her, in pallas nor bower
it budds but it blastethe, ere it be a flowere./
Singe &c

Thowe faire & more false, I dye with thy wounde
thowe hast lost the truest Louer that goes vpon the ground.
singe
Let nobody chyde her, her scornes I approue,
shee was borne to be false, and I to dye for loue/
Singe &c

Take this for my farewell and latest adewe,
write this on my Tombe, that in loue I was trewe.
Singe &c

According to Cutts (1957, p. 19), the MS. 15,117 version apparently intended the use of three refrains with every two lines of the song; such an arrangement fits the music in the manuscript perfectly. The three refrains, illustrated in the first stanza underlaying the music in the manuscript, are (l. 2) "Singe . . . willo," (ll. 4–6) "o willo . . . gareland," and (ll. 7–9) "Singe . . . gareland." The remaining lines of the song are scribbled in the bottom right-hand corner of the page across blank music staves, and their impatient contractions (" &c") are obviously intended to suggest that each successive two-line stanza be filled out with refrains exactly as the first stanza is.

In *Musique* (1959, p. 119) Cutts conjecturally reconstructs what he supposes Shakespeare's adaptation of the ballad to have been. The words in brackets represent his expansion of the abbreviations in the 1623 Folio:

The poore Soule sat singing, by a Sicamour tree.
Sing all a greene Willough:
Her hand on her bosome her head on her knee,
Sing Willough Willough Willough [Willough]
[Sing Willough Willough Willough Willough]
[Shalbe my Garland.]
The fresh Streames ran by her, and murmur'd her moanes
Sing Willough [Willough Willough]
Her salt teares fell from her, and softned the stones,
[Sing Willough Willough Willough]
[Sing Willough Willough Willough]
[Shalbe my Garland.]
Sing Willough, [willough willough]
Willough Willough [Willough]
Sing all a greene Willough must be my Garland.

This expansion and "reconstruction" of the lyrics in the 1623 Folio seems plausible enough, but setting them to the music in the manuscript requires some juggling of the melody. The manuscript-music as Cutts gives it (*Musique*, pp. 1 f.) consists of thirteen bars; but in order to make the expanded words of his reconstruction fit this music, Cutts (1957, pp. 21–23) arranges the melody as follows: the first nine bars of music ("The poore . . . Garland"), the same nine bars repeated ("The fresh . . . Garland"), and the song concluded with the last four bars of the music ("Sing . . . Garland").

On the other hand, if one supposes as Cutts does (1957, p. 19; *Musique*, p. 118) that the editors of the Folio "utilized the first version of the song that came into their hands, which was slightly corrupt and incomplete," then there is no reason why a "restoration" of the song should not be exactly modeled on the manuscript-song with its three refrains for each two-line stanza—if that is the melody it is intended to use. In such a restoration Desdemona would be supposed to sing two full choruses of the song, begin a third but then correct herself ("Nay, that's not next"), only to begin a third chorus again of two lines and one refrain before breaking off her song entirely. This is precisely the arrangement which Sternfeld (1963, pp. 43 f.) adopted.

In addition to the fragment of song in *Othello* and the more extended version in MS. 15,117, there exist at least five more willow songs from the late fifteenth and early sixteenth centuries. All of these have the anapestic tetrameter meter and one or more of the conventional refrains characteristic of the genre. All of them could conceivably have been sung to some variation of the "original" tune that was used for Desdemona's song on Shakespeare's stage—whether that tune was the one in MS. 15,117, the Dallis-Folger tune, or some melody that has long since been lost. The ballad which is closest in its lyrics to the songs in *Othello* and in the manuscript probably derives from the same original source as those two versions. It is to be found in the Roxburghe Collection, and has been reprinted in *RB* (1871–1899, I, 171–174); with a few variant readings, it also turns up in the Pepys Collection from which it was reprinted by Percy in *Reliques* (1765, I, 176–180). The four other willow songs, with the exception of their refrains, bear no verbal resemblance to these other ballads; but they are clearly analogous, and may have been written in imitation of the "original" willow song in an attempt to capitalize on its popularity or the popularity of the tune to which it was sung. The earliest of these is by John Heywood and it appears following John Redford's *Play of Wyt and Science* in B. M. Add. MS. 15,233; it has been reprinted by Halliwell (1848, pp. 86–88). The other analogues appear in *A gorgeous Gallery, of gallant Inuentions*, 1578 (ed. Rollins, 1926, pp. 83–86), in Thomas Howell's *H. His Deuises, for his owne exercise, and his Friends pleasure*, 1581 (sig. C₂), where it is immediately followed by another song titled "All of greene Lawrell," an obvious take-off on the type; and in Thomas Deloney's *The Gentile Craft. The second Part*, 1639 (ed. Lawlis, 1961, p. 206). Lawlis suggests (p. 369) that this last work may have been published as early as 1598, although there is no surviving record of that edition. The Willow Song refrain is imitated by Robert Jones in *The Muses Gardin for Delights*, 1610 (sig. D₁ᵛ), and also in a snatch of song from the Tudor period recently discovered in the binding of some part-books in the New York Public Library, MS. Drexel 4183 (Stevens, 1961, p. 426; Sternfeld, 1963, pp. 49–52, and J. Ward (1966, pp. 845 ff.).

The extant ballads clearly indicate the popularity of the song, a popularity which lasted for over a century. The earliest reference to a willow song for which a certain date can be assigned is probably "A ballett intituled I am not the fyrst that hath taken in hande/the wearynge of the Willowe garlande &c.," entered in the Stationers' Registers to Thomas Colwell for the year 1565/6 (Arber, 1875–1894, I, 270). There are numerous references to the genre in the literature of the time: Nicholas Breton's *Wits Trenchmour*, 1597 (ed. Grosart, 1879, II, b, 20), Thomas Middleton's *Blvrt Master Constable*, 1602 (ed. Bullen, 1885, I, 14), *Laugh and Lie Downe: Or, The Worldes Folly*, 1605 (sig. C₃), and in *The Two Noble Kinsmen* (ed. Kittredge, 1936, IV.i.80). There is an imitation of the ballad set by Pelham Humfrey during the Restoration (J. S. Smith, 1812, p. 171; Wooldridge, 1893; reprinted 1961, I, 108 f.), and a parody of the willow song in Playford's *Pleasant Musical Companion*, 1686 (pt. II, no. 17) attests its popularity in another way. Finally, after a long silence, the ghost of the genre rises again in the lyrics from Gilbert's and Sullivan's *Mikado* ([1885], p. 45), beginning

> On a tree by a river a little tom-tit
> Sang "Willow, titwillow, titwillow."

There are, of course, numerous songs and poems from the Renaissance bearing on the same theme and making explicit reference to the willow as the emblem of the forsaken lover; but not having the characteristic meter and not employing one or more of the conventional refrains, these cannot be considered representative of the true willow song genre.

DRAMATIC FUNCTION

Three times in *Othello* Shakespeare makes use of music to assist the drama. Iago's two songs are used to give an effect of drunken revel prior to the cashiering of Cassio, as well as to collapse the time that would be required for a realistic presentation of Iago's plot. The second occasion—not often noticed by readers of the play, since it is confined to a stage-direction—is the aubade played by the little band of musicians whom Cassio, the morning after his downfall, brings to the house of Othello. This music, as Granville-Barker points out (1947, II, 23), is Cassio's courteous way of making amends for the disturbances of the previous night; its further function is to ease the dramatic tension which has been built up. The dark events of the night before are past, and the morning has dawned bright with remedy and promise. Yet the happy augury of the music is touched with a bitter irony: it is on this very morning that Iago begins the conspiracy that ultimately leads to the tragedy. The next time music is heard in the play Desdemona is divesting for bed—and death.

Brennecke (1953, p. 37) appears to regard the willow song as a kind of psycho-analytic therapy for Desdemona; "what she cannot say," he remarks, "she sings . . . thereby revealing more of her subconscious awareness than any spoken words could indicate." But perhaps this point of view obscures the essential problem involved in the two scenes where Desdemona confronts Othello. If we can judge by her speech before the Venetian Council (I.iii.180–189, 249–260), Desdemona can speak well enough to the purpose when she understands the issues and feels the need. She is no shrinking Ophelia, no taciturn Cordelia. But in her first confrontation with Othello in the "Brothel Scene" (IV.ii.24–87) she simply does not understand what she is accused of; she is so conscious of her own innocence that Othello's words simply do not signify. It should furthermore be noted that in this scene Othello's accusations are couched in only the most general terms; he makes no circumstantial charge against his wife, he defines no specific crime; Cassio's name is never mentioned. Had Othello specified his accusations she might, at this point, have been able to prove her innocence; she certainly would have called for Cassio to give witness to it. But it was not Shakespeare's purpose to have a circumstantial accusation made until it became impossible of being disproved. Hence in the "Brothel Scene" he makes use of Desdemona's uncomprehending innocence and Othello's angry general charges as a bar to any real communication between husband and wife. When specific charges are made it is in the second confrontation of Othello and Desdemona (V.ii.23–83), and then it is too late. Her categorical denials of a relationship with Cassio (ll. 49, 58–61, 66–68, and 71) are meaningless; for if Cassio is dead, as they both believe, then in Desdemona's words, "Alas, he is betray'd and I undone."

If fault at all is to be found with Desdemona's inability to express herself, that fault should be found with her choice of language. Shakespeare makes of her a creature so pure of mind that she fails to realize that words may have less innocent senses than the ones she ordinarily attributes to them. A subtle irony Shakespeare has injected into her speeches is their unfortunate diction. Obvious examples are the reference she makes (IV.i.244) to "the love I bear to Cassio," where she means "friendship," but Othello takes the word in a more intimate sense, and (IV.ii.70) her use of "committed" denotatively when for Othello it has the sexual connotation of Edgar's "commit not with man's sworn spouse" (*Lear*, III.iv.84), a connotation that provokes Othello's outraged reiterations of the word.

Rather than serving such a complex purpose as Brennecke would attribute to it, Desdemona's willow song seems intended, as Bradley observes (1904, p. 61), to release and give vent to the painful tension that has been aroused, by the outflowing of a pathos that comes like the release of tears after some terrible sorrow.

King Lear

49

TEXT: Folio (1623), sig. 2q4ᵛ (I.iv.181–184).
TYPOGRAPHY: Unindented verse, roman face.

Fooles had nere leſſe grace in a yeere,
For wiſemen are growne foppiſh,
And know not how their wits to weare,
Their manners are ſo apiſh.

TEXTUAL COMMENTARY

1. **Fooles ... yeere**] Apparently a proverbial expression; see Tilley (1950, F-535).
grace] Q₁ (1608) and Q₂ (dated 1608, but 1619) read *wit*. Some modern editors follow the quarto readings and thereby destroy the meaning of the verse. *Wit* does not make much sense in the context; it was possibly the Q₁ compositor's error. His eye may have caught the word from the lines just preceding the song, "Thou hadst little wit in thy bald crown when thou gav'st thy golden one away," or from the third line of the song itself. For *grace NED* has "Favour or its manifestation . . . good-will." Compare *Much Ado* (II.iii.29 f.), "till all graces be in one woman, one woman shall not come in my grace." Malone (ed. 1790), however, argues for the quarto reading : In *Mother Bombie* . . . by [John] Lyly, 1594, we find [sig. D₂] "I thinke Gentlemen had neuer lesse wit in a yeere." I suspect therefore the original to be the true reading. ✦

1–2. **Fooles ... foppish**] Johnson (ed. 1765) : There never was a time when fools were less in favour, and the reason is, that they were never so little wanted, for wise men now supply their place. ✦

2. **foppish**] *NED*, citing this example, notes that the original meaning of the word was *foolish* or *silly*.

3. **And ... to**] The quartos read *And . . . doe.*

4. **apish**] *NED*: Foolishly imitative.

MUSIC

The original music for the Fool's song—if it is a song—is not known. Caulfield (n.d., II, 93) gives an anonymous tune, but there is no reason to suppose it is either early or authentic. Sternfeld (1964, *Songs*, p. 20) has set the words to the contemporary tune called "Robin" in the Ballet Lute Book. The only evidence that this is a song is Lear's immediately following remark: "When were you so wont to be full of songs, sirrah?" but his use of the term may be merely generic.

DRAMATIC FUNCTION

The Fool's rhyme serves both to characterize him as a "natural," and to illuminate the relationship in which he stands to Lear. He is the self-deposed king's better reason, and his impudent and riddling wit is meant to keep Lear aware of his own folly. The last two lines of the song are ambiguous; they may mean either that wise men in imitating fools are at a loss to manage the wit they should be using, or, that fools are getting so much competition from wise men that fools do not know what face to put on their own natural wittiness.

The Fool leads into his song in the quibbling fashion of his kind. To Lear's question, "Dost thou call me fool, boy?" he responds, "All thy other titles thou hast given away; that thou was born with." The acuteness of this rejoinder prompts Kent to remark, "This is not altogether fool [that is, altogether foolish] my lord." But the Fool takes Kent's words as literally applying to himself: he is no longer totally a fool because others are encroaching on his domain. I am no longer completely a fool because "lords and great men will not let me. If I had a monopoly out, they would have part on't."

Although the source of the Fool's song is not known, the phrase from Lyly's *Mother Bombie*, cited by Malone above, suggests that both Lyly and Shakespeare are echoing some popular song or rhyme of the day.

50

TEXT: Folio (1623), sig. 2q4ᵛ (I.iv.191–194).
TYPOGRAPHY: Mixed verse and prose, roman face.

[. . .] then they
For fodaine ioy did weepe,
And I for forrow fung,
That fuch a King fhould play bo-peepe,
And goe the Foole among.

TEXTUAL COMMENTARY

4. **play bo-peepe**] Steevens (ed. 1793) **:** Little more of this game, than its mere denomination, remains. It is mentioned, however, in [Thomas] Churchyard's [*A Musicall Consort of Heauenly harmonie . . . called Churchyards*] *Charitie* [1595, sig. C₁], in company with two other childish plays . . .

> Cold parts men plaie, much like old plain bopeepe
> Or counterfait, in dock out-nettle still. ◆

Douce (1839, pp. 104 f.) **:** In [Robert] Sherwood's *Dictionary* [1632] it is defined, "Jeu d'enfant; ou (plustost) des nourrices aux petits enfans; se cachans le visage, & puis se monstrant." The Italians say *far bau bau*, or *baco baco*, and *bauccare*; which shows that there must at some time or other have been a connexion between the nurse's . . . *boggle* or *buggy bo*, and the present expression. ◆ Arden (ind. ed. 1927) **:** Play silly pranks with, referring to the well-known nursery game. ◆ [The Arden editor directs attention to Sherwood (1632), the entry under *Faire les deux yeux*. There are two definitions for the term (sig. 2N₄), both applicable:

> *Faire les doux yeux.* To make it goodlie, counterfeit ciuilitie or modestie, seem coy; also, to winke, or smile pretily with the eyes; also, to be betweene sleeping and waking, or seeme to sleepe and see nothing. *Faire les doux yeux à.* To play at boe-peepe; or to winke lasciuiously, to looke flatteringly, or pitifully, at one, thereby to get somewhat.]

Kittredge (ind. ed. 1940) **:** *Should play bo-peepe*: should be so childish as to hide himself, i.e., renounce his royalty. Cf. Dekker, *Satiro-mastix* [1602] (Pearson ed. [1873], I, 257): 'Our vnhandsome-fac'd Poet does play at bo-peepes with your Grace, and cryes "all-hidde" as boyes do'; *Ballads from Manuscripts*, ed. Furnivall [1868–1873], I, 198: 'Thus youe make vs sottes [i.e., fools], And play with vs boopepe.' ◆ New Arden (ind. ed. 1959) **:** The implication is that Lear has blinded himself, hidden himself (i.e., abdicated), or played silly pranks. . . . The game seems to have been more like hide-and-seek than the modern bo-peep. ◆ [The metaphorical sense of the phrase was proverbial in Shakespeare's time; see Tilley (1950, B-540).]

5. **Foole**] Q$_1$ (1608) and Q$_2$ (dated 1608, but 1619) read *fooles*, and all the modern editors except Capell (ed. [1767–1768]) adopt this reading. But the emendation is unnecessary since *NED* gives an elliptical sense of the word *among*. Used adverbially it can mean "During this period, at the same time . . . betweenwhiles." Thus the meaning of the line in the Folio may be, "That such a king should play bo-peep, and betweenwhiles go about as a fool."

MUSIC

The original melody for this song may be preserved in two staves of manuscript music in the British Museum's copy (K.1.e.9) of *Pammelia. Mvsicks Miscellanie* (1609, sigs. A$_1$v–A$_2$). See Seng (1958, "Fool's Song," pp. 583–585) for a discussion and facsimile of the manuscript music. Sternfeld (1963, p. 176) reproduces the manuscript-staves with the words of the manuscript and the words of the Fool's song underlaid, with a note that a repeat sign occurs after bar 7 of the music. But (1964, *Songs*, pp. 20 f.) Sternfeld corrects his arrangement, setting the words and music as a round for three voices, and noting that the "repeat sign" is actually the signal for the next voice to enter.

According to Sternfeld (1963, p. 177, note; 1964, *Songs*, p. 22), another tune for the song may be "Flying Fame," to which he sets (1964) the Fool's lyrics. His evidence for doing so is a song in Thomas Heywood's *The Rape of Lvcrece* (see Source, below) which begins with two lines from a ballad sung to that tune, but concludes with two lines from the Fool's song or its source. But nearly all ballad-lyrics and ballad-tunes are interchangeable because they share a common form; moreover, the song in the Heywood play may be an *ad hoc* medley. It was probably sung on the stage to the tune of its opening lines, *viz.*, "Flying Fame," but this fact indicates nothing about the tune of the Fool's song in *Lear*. On the mobility of ballad-tunes see Music, song 10, above, and Sternfeld (1964, *SS*, pp. 220–222).

The words written underneath the staves of music in the British Museum's copy of *Pammelia* clearly connect it with either the Fool's song or with the ballad of "John Careless" which is the probable source of both:

> Late as I waked out of sleepe I harde a prety thinge
> some men for suddaine ioy do weepe, and some for
> 　　sorrow singe fa la la.

SOURCE

It seems likely that this song is a parody of the opening lines of a famous ballad in MS. Sloane 1896 (fols. 11–12^v), "A godly and vertuous songe or Ballade, made by the constant member of *Christe, John Carelesse*, being in prison in *kinges benche* for professing his word; whoe, ending his dayes therin, was throwen out and buryed most Ignominiously upon a donghill, by the aduersaryes of godes worde." The ballad is also printed in Miles Coverdale's *Certain most godly, fruitful, and comfortable letters of such true Saintes and holy Martyrs of God, as . . . gaue their lyues for the defence of Christes holy gospel* (1564, sigs. 2T₆ᵛ–2T₈ᵛ). In Coverdale's book the ballad follows twenty-two letters by Careless, and has four additional stanzas that are not found in the Sloane MS. The first three stanzas of the manuscript version of the ballad are as follows:

> Some men for sodayne joye do wepe,
>   and some in sorrowe synge;
> When as they are in daunger depe,
>   to put away mournyng.

> Betwene them both will I begyn,
>   being in joye and payne;
> With sighing to lament my synne,
>   and yet reioyce againe.

> My synfull lyfe doth still encrease,
>   my sorrowes are the more;
> From wickednesse I cannot cease,
>   woe is my heart therfore.

The first scholar to point out the connection between the Fool's song and the ballad of "John Careless" was Hyder E. Rollins; for a full discussion of Careless and his ballad see Rollins (1920, *Old English Ballads*, p. 48; 1920, *MLR*, pp. 87–89).

Although at first view it might seem likely that the Ballad of "John Careless" was a moralization of a popular song of the day, all the contemporary evidence goes against such a conclusion. The Careless ballad enjoyed considerable renown. Three entries in the Stationers' Registers—1 August 1586, 14 December 1624, 9 February 1635—attest its long-lived popularity. The fame of the ballad is further supported by contemporary references, parodies, and allusions. Thomas Nashe twice refers to it (ed. McKerrow, 1910, 1958, III, 104; V, 196), and one ballad, and possibly two, were sung to the tune of "John Careless" (see Rollins, *Old English Ballads*, p. 55, and *RB*, 1871–1899, III, 168–173). A song or medley in T. Heywood's *The Rape of Lvcrece* (1608, sig. C₁ᵛ) borrows two lines from it and combines them with two from "Sir Lancelot du Lake" (see song 10, above):

> When *Tarquin* first in Court began,
> And was approued King:
> Some men for sodden ioy gan weepe,
> And I for sorrow sing.

And the prefatory sonnet to the second part of "Christian Passions" in H[enry] L[ok's]. *Ecclesiastes* ([1597], sig. N₃) is also a clear allusion:

> Some men do mourne for suddeine ioy the[y] say.
> And some likewise in midst of sorrow sing.

DRAMATIC FUNCTION

The Fool's second song is closely related to the first, which precedes it by only a few lines. Where the earlier song had included the king in the roster of fools by implication—he is a man, and all men are fools from birth—this song, more audaciously, calls Lear by a title that he has earned for himself.

51

TEXT: Folio (1623), sig. 2r₂ᵛ (III.ii.74–77).
TYPOGRAPHY: Indented verse, roman face.

He that has and a little-tyne wit,
With heigh-ho, the Winde and the Raine,
Muſt make content with his Fortunes fit,
Though the Raine it raineth euery day.

TEXTUAL COMMENTARY

1. **little-tyne**] See song 34, l. 1, note.
2. **With . . . Raine**] Johnson (ed. 1765) : I fancy that the second line of this stanza
had once a termination that rhymed with the fourth; but I can only fancy it; for
both the copies [Folio and quartos] agree. It was once perhaps written, *With heigh
ho, the wind and the rain* in his way. The meaning seems likewise to require this
insertion. *He that has wit, however small, and finds wind and the rain in his way, must
content himself by thinking, that somewhere or other* it raineth every day, *and others are
therefore suffering like himself.* ✦
2–4. **With . . . day**] See relevant discussions, song 34, ll. 2, 4.

MUSIC

See Music, song 34, above.

DRAMATIC FUNCTION

The simplest explanation of the concurrence of this song and Feste's epilogue
song in *Twelfth Night* is probably that Shakespeare, finding the opening stanza of
Feste's song adaptable for his purposes at this point in *Lear*, simply transplanted it
from the earlier play, changing the first and third lines, and a single word in the
fourth, to make the song appropriate to the actual situation in which Lear and the
Fool find themselves; that is, out in the wind and the rain, and having by necessity
to content themselves with the fortunes which have befallen them. Whatever one
thinks of Feste's song, there is no reason to regard the inclusion of a varied stanza
of it here as an interpolation. This fragment of song, in position as well as sense, is
perfectly congruent with its surrounding text.

The scene in which the song occurs had opened with Lear contending against the
elements: "Blow, winds, and crack your cheeks; rage! blow!" But this first parox-
ysm of rage spends itself, leaving Lear free to turn from thoughts of his own
wrongs to consider the plight of the Fool (III.ii.68–73):

> Come on, my boy. How dost, my boy? Art cold?
> I am cold myself. . . .
> Poor fool and knave, I have one part in my heart
> That's sorry yet for thee.

The serener pathos which closes the scene is betokened in the quiet simplicity of the Fool's song, with its moral that "the rain it raineth every day," and that men must sometimes be content merely to endure the circumstances in which they find themselves. The Lear who can respond to this moral of the song by assenting, "True, my boy," is a Lear who fifty lines farther on in the play will be concerned about the "houseless poverty" of those

> Poor naked wretches, wheresoe'er you are
> That bide the pelting of this pitiless storm,
> How shall your houseless heads and unfed sides,
> Your loop'd and window'd raggedness, defend you
> From seasons such as these? O, I have ta'en
> Too little care of this!   (III.iv.26–33)

52

TEXT: First Quarto (1608), sig. G₃ᵛ (III.v.27–30).
TYPOGRAPHY: Mixed verse and prose, italic and roman face.

Edg.   [. . .] come ore the broome *Beſſy* to mee.
Foole. Her boat hath a leake, and ſhe muſt not ſpeake,
Why ſhe dares not come, ouer to thee.

GENERAL COMMENTARY

Kittredge (ind. ed. 1940) : Edgar, with a beckoning gesture, addresses the imaginary Goneril or Regan in the words of an old song in which a lover calls upon his sweetheart to come to him 'across the brook.' ◆ Sternfeld (1963, p. 170) : The second half of the stanza is sung by the Fool who, responding to Mad Tom's snatch, improvises his own version. . . . There is nothing delicate about the Fool's improvisation but this is only the obverse side of the coin . . . an oblique comment on the all-powerful emotion of love which ennobles the dying Lear and . . . softens the heart of the Macchiavellian Edmund as he lies dying.

TEXTUAL COMMENTARY

1. **broome**] Johnson (ed. 1765) : As there is no relation between *broom* and a *boat*, we may better read . . . *brook*. ◆ Malone (ed. 1790) reads *bourne*, citing the same song as it is quoted in William Wager's *A very mery and Pythie Commedie, called The longer thou liuest, the more foole thou art* (n.d. [1569], sig. A₃):

> Com ouer the Boorne Besse,
> My little pretie Besse,
> Com ouer the Boorne besse to me.

He notes further that a *bourne* in the north signifies a rivulet or a brook, and that from this many village names terminate in *burn*, as Milburn, Sherburn, and so forth.

Bessy] Malone (ed. 1790) : There is a peculiar propriety in this address . . . *Bessy* and poor *Tom* usually travelled together. The author [Richard West] of *The Court of Conscience Or Dick Whippers Sessions*, 1607, describing *beggars, idle rogues, and counterfeit madmen*, thus speaks of these associates [sig. F₃]:

> Another sort there is among you: They,
> Doe rage with furie as if they were so frantique,
> They knew not what they did but euery day,
> Make sport with stick and flowers, like an antique.
> Stowt roge and harlot counterfeted gomme,
> One calls her self poore Besse the other Tom. ◆

2–3. **Her . . . thee**] Kittredge (ind. ed. 1940), arguing from Edgar's remark following the song, "The foul fiend haunts poor Tom in the voice of a nightingale"
(III.vi.31 f.), maintains that the lines assigned to the Fool are an improvisation on
the original song, and not a part of it. [What Edgar's remark suggests even more
clearly is that he quotes the opening line of the original, as though addressed to an
"imaginary Goneril or Regan," and that the Fool then sings the lines assigned to
him. Since the original ballad survives only in a moralization, it is impossible to
know whether the Fool's lyric is a quotation or improvisation.]

MUSIC

The source of the Fool's lyric was evidently a popular song of Shakespeare's day
that survives now only in moralizations. The music for the song may be preserved
in either of two contemporary tunes. B. M. Add. MS. 5,665 (fols. 143ᵛ–144) contains
a musical setting for three voices of a moralization of the lost popular lyric. The
three-part song in the manuscript has been transcribed by Sternfeld (1963, pp.
181–183; 1964, *Songs*, pp. 26 f.). The words of the moralization run as follows:

> Come over the burne, Besse,
> Thou lytyll, prety Besse,
> Come over the burne, Besse, to me!
>
> The burne ys this worlde blynde
> And Besse ys mankynde;
> So propyr I can none fynde as she;
> She daunces and she lepys,
> And Crist stondes and clepys;
> Cum over the burne, Besse, to me.

According to Stevens (1961, p. 348) the song was a modified carol that was widely
current in the late fifteenth and sixteenth centuries. The first three lines of text
above seem to be a refrain, and are probably all that survives of the lyrics of the
original song.

The other contemporary tune is preserved in Cambridge University Library
MS. Dd.2.11 (fol. 80ᵛ) in lute tablature. This is apparently a later setting, and
unrelated to the music in MS. 5,665. It has been transcribed by Wooldridge (1893;
reprinted 1961, I, 121), Naylor (n.d., pp. 52–54) and Sternfeld (1963, pp. 185 f.). A
variant of this tune in the Weld Lute Book was noted by Wooldridge, and modern
transcriptions of it are given by Sternfeld (1963, p. 188; 1964, *Songs*, p. 28). He has
also provided settings of the Shakespeare words to the Cambridge MS. and Weld
Lute Book tunes (1963, p. 187; 1964, *Songs*, p. 28).

Other versions of the lyrics quoted from MS. 5,665 are to be found in the Trinity
College, Cambridge, MS. O.2.53 (fol. 55ᵛ), words only, 12 stanzas; and in MS.
Ashmole 176 (fol. 100), words only, 2 stanzas. Additional imitations or moraliza-
tions of the lost popular song are in Emmanuel College MS. 263 (fol. 1), B. M. MS.
Harl. 2252 (fol. 135), and in the library of the Society of Antiquaries, London (a
facsimile in *Transactions* of the Bibliographical Society. IV, 1898, 74). The moraliza-

tion by William Birche, "A songe between the Quenes maiestie and England," is a still later reworking of the popular song, being entered with the Stationers' Company in 1558/9, the year Elizabeth ascended the throne, and again in 1564 (see Arber, 1875, I, 96, 262).

DRAMATIC FUNCTION

Lacking the text of the original ballad, it is difficult to determine either the precise meaning of this fragment in *Lear* or its function in the episode where it occurs. But it seems likely that it may have been concerned with a lover and his leman who lived near to each other, but who were separated by a bourn running between them. The lover calls his mistress to come over to him, presumably to make love. Since the lost song was probably one of those "prophane" songs having to do with "synne and harlotrie" which pious ballad-makers like William Birche loved to moralize, Bessy very likely consented.

There is reason to believe that the words of the parody or improvisation sung by the Fool have an obscene sense: they suggest that Bessy declines the rendezvous because of either her *menses* or disease. If so, the song may have been intended to echo the "adultery theme" of the play, or to elaborate on the sexual repugnance of speeches such as those assigned to Edgar and Lear (III.iv.87–100, IV.vi.111–132).

53

TEXT: Folio (1623), sig. [2]x₆ (II.vii.118–123).
TYPOGRAPHY: Indented verse, italic face; s.d., *Muſicke Playes. The Song.*

Come thou Monarch of the Vine,
Plumpie Bacchus, with pinke eyne :
In thy Fattes our Cares be drown'd,
With thy Grapes our haires be Crown'd.
   Cup vs till the world go round,
   Cup vs till the world go round.

GENERAL COMMENTARY

Moore (1916, pp. 84 f.) remarks that the drinking songs in Shakespeare's plays often carried "powerful overtones of dramatic significance," and that they are often "prophetic of impending disaster." On the particular irony of this song he comments (p. 99) : The drinking song is rendered, with joined hands and drunken good fellowship, shortly before the final quarrel of the triumvirs. The forced air of conviviality but thinly covers the increasing animosity; the host of the evening is tempted to slay his guests and make himself lord of Rome, and the man who places the singers hand in hand for the song is no other than Enobarbus, who later deserts Anthony at his greatest need. ✦ Noble (1923, pp. 127 f.) : Following a hint from Plutarch as to the revels on Pompey's galley, Shakespeare caused a boy to sing . . . the while the three great men held hands. The song obviously partakes of the character of a hymn, a Bacchanalian equivalent of *Veni Creator*. The choice of the great Pentecostal Hymn . . . as the model . . . is remarkable, and is a tribute to the dramatist's exquisite judgment. . . . Shakespeare made his Pagan Romans sing on the stage as they might have done in real life, and thereby he showed that he understood the religious significance to a Roman of wine, how that it was a gift of the god to man, and that its influence was a divine inspiration, making men other than themselves. That he did not yield to the temptation to introduce on the occasion a merry drinking song, we may attribute to the force of his imagination which enabled him to realize the mentality of the characters with whose fortunes he was dealing. ♦ Granville-Barker (1947, I, 410) : The music for the revels on Pompey's galley is given to woodwind (the accompaniment of the song included), trumpets and drums reinforcing it occasionally. The clamor is insisted on [cf. II.vii.114, 136–138]. It is a soldiers' revel. But it never slips from the distinction of poetry; and the song itself—the boy's voice singing it—is like light beside the darkness of Menas' whisper to Pompey. ♦ Sternfeld (1963, pp. 86 f.) repeats Noble's contention that this song is a parody of the Pentecostal hymn. In support of his view he cites some English translations and imitations of the Latin hymn from Shakespeare's time. But the intriguing notion that Shakespeare may be indulging in parody here does not bear closer examination. There is no resemblance between the ninth-century hymn and Shakespeare's song except the opening words of both; and both medieval hymnology and Renaissance lyric poetry furnish numerous examples of poems beginning *Veni* or "Come." It is clear from the opening stanza of the ancient hymn that any resemblance to Shakespeare's song must be wholly fanciful:

> Veni creator Spiritus,
> Mentes tuorum visita,
> Imple superna gratia,
> Quae tu creasti pectora.

[Come, Creator Spirit, visit the minds of your [faithful], fill with heavenly grace the hearts which Thou hast created.] Indeed, if a parody is wanted, a much better example would be the twelfth-century hymn, sometimes attributed to Stephen Langton (Connelly, 1957, p. 111), which begins,

> Veni, sancte Spiritus,
> Et emitte caelitus
>   Lucis tuae radium:
> Veni, pater pauperum,
> Veni, dator munerum,
>   Veni, lumen cordium.

[Come, Holy Spirit, and send forth from heaven the ray of Thy light. Come, father of the poor; come, giver of gifts; come, light of hearts.] This later hymn resembles Shakespeare's song in stanzaic form, meter, and rhyme scheme. Even so, the resemblance is probably accidental. See Seng (1965, pp. 4–6).

TEXTUAL COMMENTARY

2. **pinke eyne**] Malone (ed. 1790) : [The expression also occurs] in a song sung by a drunken Clown in [Thomas Lodge's *The Wovnds of Ciull War. Liuely set forth in the true Tragedies of*] *Marius and Scilla*, 1594 [sig. G₃ᵛ]:

> Thou makest some to stumble, and many mo to fumble:
> And me haue pinkie nine, more braue and iolly wine. ♦

Hudson (ed. 1880–1881) : *Pink eyne* are *small eyes*. "Some haue myghty yies/and some be pynk yies. Quidam pergrandibus sunt luminibus/quidam peti." *Horman's Vulgaria*, 1519 [sig. E₆ᵛ]. The flower called a *pink* is in French *oeillet*, or *little eye*. ♦

New Arden (ind. ed. 1954) cites numerous examples of the expression from early texts, and concludes : Even the indefinite among these examples and others, point rather to smallness than redness. . . . [But] in two or three allusions to the colour of Bacchus' eyes which I have come upon, the word *red* is used. ✦ [*NED* is decisive on the point, defining the verb *pink* as "to shut the eyes, to wink, to leer." Hence pink eyes are probably the drooping eyes characteristic of drunkenness.]

3. **Fattes**] New Arden (ind. ed. 1954) : vats, which is the Southern form of the word.

MUSIC

The original music for the song is unknown. A setting of about 1750 by Thomas Chilcot is reprinted in Caulfield (n.d., I, 133–136), but without Chilcot's name. Sternfeld (1963, p. 87) suggests as an "apposite and attractive" contemporary setting, John Wilson's "Come thou father of the spring" in his *Cheerfull Ayres or Ballads*, 1660. He gives (1964, p. 31) an adaptation of this music arranged to fit the Shakespearean words.

DRAMATIC FUNCTION

Aside from the trumpets and flourishes, music occurs only twice in the play, but on each of these occasions it totally dominates the scenes in which it is played. The scene of revels aboard Pompey's galley opens with instrumental music which may have been played through most of the episode as an ironic counterpoint to the drunken wassail of the triumvirate, to the abortive conspiracy (and then defection) of Menas. This instrumental music is climaxed by the song to Bacchus, sung by a boy, but with all the revelers joining in the refrain. At the end of the scene the trumpets, drums and flutes are still sounding as the principals stagger off into the night. The second scene in which music occurs—and it is like a ghostly echo of the revels aboard the galley—is on a night shortly before Antony's last battle, when a company of common soldiers hear the music of hautboys sounding mysteriously in the air and from under the earth (IV.iii.). Disaster in *Antony and Cleopatra* is clearly portended by music. Music and song are symbolic of Alexandrian luxury and effeminacy as opposed to Roman sternness; and it is the pleasures of the East that pull Antony down.

The music and song convey a sense of uninhibited drunken revel, what Pompey calls "an Alexandrian feast," and Enobarbus "the Egyptian Bacchanals" (III.vii.101, 109). Significantly, it is Antony who wishes to join hands

> Till that the conquering wine hath steep'd our sense
> In soft and delicate Lethe.

But it is Caesar who puts an end to the revels:

> What would you more? Pompey, good night. Good brother,
> Let me request you off. Our graver business
> Frowns at this levity.

Cymbeline

54

TEXT: Folio (1623), sig. 3a₁ (II. iii.22–30).
TYPOGRAPHY: Unindented verse, italic face; s.d., *Song*.

Hearke, hearke, the Larke at Heauens gate ſings,
and Phœbus gins ariſe,
His Steeds to water at thoſe Springs
on chalic'd Flowres that lyes:
And winking Mary-buds begin to ope their Golden eyes   5
With euery thing that pretty is, my Lady ſweet ariſe:
Ariſe, ariſe.

GENERAL COMMENTARY

New Variorum (ind. ed. 1913) **:** This present 'Song' is the supreme crown of all aubades, and comes, by Shakespeare's consummate art, laden with the heaven's pure, refreshing breath, after the stifling presence of Iachimo in Imogen's chamber. ◆ Moore (1916, p. 88) quotes the New Variorum editor's remark and adds **:** The lark song . . . ushers in the full beauty of dawn, strangely contrasted with the scene just preceding. [Not only, according to Moore, does the song establish a mood, but it also affords Shakespeare an opportunity for character revelation, because, he continues (pp. 90 f.):] Cloten is bewrayed by his speech when he comments on the fresh lyric of love . . . which he has caused to be sung by Imogen's apartments, in the effort to win her from her absent lord. . . . [Prior to the song Cloten says (II.iii.12–14):] "I am advised to give her music a-mornings; they say it will penetrate." [And after the aubade he instructs the musicians (ll. 31–35):]

So get you gone. If this penetrate, I will consider your music the better; if it do not, it is a vice in her ears which horsehairs and calves' guts, nor the voice of unpaved eunuch to boot, can never amend.

This is language of the stable after the song of the lark—violent contrast, but surely vivid characterization. We are not surprised, shortly after, when the speaker plans a terrible revenge upon Imogen. ◆ Noble (1923, pp. 131 f.) **:** The previous trunk episode had created a heavy stifling atmosphere, which it was necessary to disperse; tragedy was the spirit present, by contrast music acted as relief. Further-more the music was otherwise required. Night was being transformed into dawn; on the modern stage . . . by means of artificial lights the gradual approach of dawn could be suggested. Shakespeare had no such aid to his hand, therefore he made Iachimo announce the time, and Cloten and his companions further to give prominence to the topic, and as a final resource he relied upon characteristically morning music to give the effect he desired. It is thus an interesting example of the manner in which the bare platform stage taxed the ingenuity of dramatists and of the effectual assistance that song rendered them in the attainment of their object. Song at this juncture was . . . absolutely indispensable.

[Noble also asserts (pp. 131 f.) that Shakespeare used this song, as he used "Who is Silvia" (song 3), as a vehicle for literary criticism:] The aubade introduces a whiff of comedy by reason of its criticism, but whereas in the case of the serenade to Silvia the point could only be discerned with difficulty, in *Cymbeline* the context makes the humour involved easily perceptible by any educated man in the audience. Just as was *Who is Silvia?*, so is *Hark, hark, the lark* in behalf of a dull and boorish suitor. . . . Consequently his demand for 'a very excellent good conceited thing' (this refers to the instrumental music to precede the song and the conceits would mean the imitations and other contrapuntal devices characteristic of that kind of composition), to be followed by 'a wonderful sweet air, with admirable rich words to it', is meant to be taken by the 'judicious' in the spirit of comedy. . . . As far as the literary part of the song is concerned, there is no doubt that Cloten's requirements have been very fully met, for it abounds in admirable rich words. ◆ W. M. Evans (1945, pp. 98 f.) **:** The "sett" effect of the song, together with the appearance of a special musician to perform it, showed that the aubade was by no means a spontaneous outpouring of Cloten's love. The calculated effect of the song, the well planned musical interlude, the aubade as a whole was symbolical of Cloten's well calculated plan of courtship. The artificial range of the singer's voice, whether genuine treble or male alto singing falsetto, intensified the effect of falseness in the musical protestations. Thus the presentation of the music reflected Cloten's nature—a nature truly "without the habite of honesty"—the appeal, Imogen's. ◆ [The validity of Evans' remarks depends in part on the question of the authenticity of the Bodleian manuscript setting. It is not certain that this was the "original" music; but see Music, below.] Granville-Barker (1947, I, 482) **:** Cloten's aubade will be sung by a man or boy, and most probably to the accompaniment of a consort of viols. . . . It might well have been sung by the actor of Arviragus. He, we find later, is ready enough to sing the dirge over Fidele. ◆ Auden (1957, p. 38) **:** Shakespeare shows us music being used with conscious evil intent . . . when Cloten serenades Imogen. Cloten is a lost soul without conscience or shame. He is shown, therefore, as someone who does not know one note from another. He has been told that music acts on women as an erotic stimulus, and wishes for the most erotic music that money can buy. ◆ B. Evans (1960, pp. 258 f.) **:** What has happened to Imogen as she slept has been a kind of rape; within our awareness, as within a dome, Cloten's triumphant morning song gathers a stunning resonance. . . . So glorious a hymn, within itself, would call up a response of pure joy. But the circumstances in which it is set prevent a simple response: it is sung at the behest of Cloten, a beast repugnant to Imogen; Imogen, though she will not immediately recognize the fact, has been undone during the night and cannot arise to the same world she left when she folded down the leaf of her book. ◆ Long (1961, pp. 51 f.) : This morning song, or hunts-up, has a counterpart in *The Two Gentlemen of Verona*— Thurio's song "Who is Sylvia?" ... The music in that case ... helped to characterize Thurio as an ineffectual lover. The same technique is used in *Cymbeline* to point up Cloten's nature—his petulance, grossness, and self-esteem—as revealed by his remarks about the music and his purpose in providing it and particularly by the obscene wordplay which introduces the music. ... The music also serves a strictly utilitarian purpose. It allows time for the actor playing the part of Imogen to make a costume change prior to his reappearance on the stage in the following scene, and it also provides time for the stage properties to be removed from the inner stage. ... Cloten's remarks on the music supply a description of the manner in which the music was performed in the original performances. As in the case of the aubade in *The Two Gentlemen* ... two pieces of music are played, one an instrumental "fancy" or fantasia ... followed by a song, a lutenist's ayre. ... Cloten and his company appear outside of Imogen's apartment, possibly in front of the curtains just previously drawn to close the bedroom scene. The musicians were doubtless three or four violists. ... The singer was most probably a singing boy. Cloten refers to the voice as that of an "unpaved," that is, beardless, eunuch; but the Italian *castrati* were rarities in the London of 1611. ◆ [There is no need even to consider the possibility of a *castrato* having been the singer; Cloten habitually speaks in scurrilous language, and this would be his characteristic way of referring to the unchanged voice of a boy. And "unpaved" means literally that—"without 'stones'."]

TEXTUAL COMMENTARY

1. **Hearke ... sings**] Malone (ed. 1790) cites parallels from Shakespeare's sonnet XXIX,

> (Like to the Larke at breake of daye arising)
> From sullen earth sings himns at Heauens gate,

from a song in Lyly's *Alexander and Campaspe* (1632, sig. K₄),

> None but the Larke so shrill and cleare,
> How [*sic* for *Now*] at heauens gats she claps her wings,
> The Morne not waking till shee sings,

and finds an echo in *Paradise Lost* (1667, sig. Q₂ᵛ),

> Joyn voices all ye living Souls, ye Birds,
> That singing up to Heaven Gate ascend,
> Bear on your wings and in your notes his praise.

2-3. **Phoebus ... Steeds**] Phoebus Apollo, the Greek sun-god who drove the chariot of the sun across the heavens.

3-4. **His ... lyes**] Warburton (ed. 1747) : The morning sun dries up the dew which lies in the cups of flowers. ◆

4. **Flowres that lyes**] Malone (ed. 1790) **:** There is scarcely a page of our author's works in which similar false concords may not be found.... Whether it is to be attributed to the poet or his printer, it is a gross offence against grammar. ◆ [Perhaps ungrammatical by eighteenth-century standards, but quite ordinary usage in Shakespeare. The singular number of the verb was used because the relative was felt to be singular. See Abbott (1884, pp. 167–169) who cites this example.]

5. **Mary-buds**] An elaborate controversy in *NQ* (XII, 1873, 243 f., 283 f., 363, 364; I, 1874, 24) about whether the word means marigold or daisy is settled by the *NED* which cites this occurrence as an illustration of the definition: the buds of the marigold, *Calendula officinalis*.

MUSIC

The earliest known music for the song is an anonymous setting in Bodleian MS. Don. c. 57 (fol. 78). Facsimiles of the manuscript are in W. M. Evans (1945, facing p. 95) and Long (1961, p. 136). Modern editions are given by Thewlis (1941, p. 34; reprinted by Long, 1961, p. 56), Cutts (1959, *Musique*, p. 6), Spink (1961, p. 55), and Sternfeld (1964, *Songs*, p. 29). Although the manuscript is an early one, there is no certainty that this music is the original tune for Shakespeare's song. Among the songs included in the collection, however, are works by John Hilton, John Wilson, and Robert Johnson, all of whom have connections with other Shakespearean songs (see Music for songs 17, 22, 45, 58–60, 63, 70). Spink (1961, p. 73) suggests that this setting of "Hark, hark, the lark" "may be by Johnson: no one seems more likely to have been the composer, all things considered. If so, its style suggests that it is an early song—as it would be if written for the first production in 1609." Cutts (1955, p. 113; 1959, *Musique*, p. 121) also asserts his belief that the song is Johnson's composition.

W. M. Evans (1945, p. 96) calls attention to the appropriateness of the manuscript music to the song in the play:

> In view of the preparations for a comment upon the song indicated in Shakespeare's text (1) Cloten's remark that the solo was sung by an "vnpaued Eunuch," (2) the introduction of special musicians to perform the aubade, and (3) the words of the song itself suggestive of a lark's high call and flight—it is not surprising that the score calls for a treble voice of a comparatively high range: middle F to high A.

Yet for all this the fact remains that the lyrics in the manuscript omit two lines from the text of the song as it appears in the play. It is to bridge this problem that Cutts (1959, *Musique*, p. 121) suggests repetition of bars 10–13 (plus a half-note), and Sternfeld (1964, *Songs*, p. 29) repeats bars 3–9 of the music in setting Shakespeare's words to the manuscript's tune. The solutions they propose work very well, but still do not preclude the possibility that the song in MS. Don. c. 57 is a composer's abridgement of the words of the Shakespeare song to make them fit his own melody—a melody which may be quite independent of the one used for the "original" rendition of the song on Shakespeare's stage.

The lyrics of the song as they appear in Don. c. 57 are as follows:

> Harke [harke, harke, harke,] the Larke
> > at heaven gate sings
> > [at heaven gate sings]
> & Phobus gins to rise
> The winking mary buds begin to ope theire golden eyes
> with ev'ry thing that pretty is
> my Lady sweet arise arise arise
> my Lady sweet Arise.

DRAMATIC FUNCTION

As early as 1597 Shakespeare had given his verdict on Cloten in the lines he wrote for *Merchant of Venice* (V.i.83–88):

> The man that hath no music in himself,
> Nor is not mov'd with concord of sweet sounds,
> Is fit for treasons, stratagems, and spoils;
> The motions of his spirit are dull as night,
> And his affections dark as Erebus.
> Let no such man be trusted.

That Cloten himself does not perform the aubade may be overlooked on the grounds that he is precisely the sort of courtier who would fastidiously observe the artificial rules of Renaissance etiquette which dictated that a gentleman should not sing in public. On the other hand, a gentleman was also expected to be knowledgeable about music and to have a cultivated taste and discernment concerning it. Thus for a Renaissance audience Cloten would have cut a sorry figure for his comments on the song.

55

TEXT: Folio (1623), sig. 3b₁ (IV.ii.258–281).
TYPOGRAPHY: Indented verse, italic face; s.d., *Song*.

Guid.   *Feare no more the heate o' th' Sun,*
Nor the furious Winters rages,
Thou thy worldly task haſt don,
Home art gon, and tane thy wages.
Golden Lads, and Girles all muſt,   5
As Chimney-Sweepers come to duſt.
Arui.   *Feare no more the frowne o' th' Great,*
Thou art paſt the Tirants ſtroake,
Care no more to cloath and eate,
To thee the Reede is as the Oake: 10
  The Scepter, Learning, Phyſicke muſt,
  All follow this and come to duſt.
Guid. *Feare no more the Lightning flaſh.*
Arui. *Nor th'all-dreaded Thunderſtone.*
Gui. *Feare not Slander, Cenſure, raſh.*   15
Arui. *Thou haſt finiſh'd Ioy and mone.*
Both. *All Louers young, all Louers muſt,*
  Conſigne to thee and come to duſt.
Guid. *No Exorciſor harme thee,*
Arui. *Nor no witch-craft charme thee.*   20
Guid. *Ghoſt vnlaid forbeare thee.*
Arui. *Nothing ill come neere thee.*
Both. *Quiet conſumation haue,*
  And renowned be thy graue.

GENERAL COMMENTARY

White (1854, p. 466) : Can anyone familiar with the cast of Shakespeare's thought, the turn of his expression, and the rhythm of his verse, believe that this Song is his ? It could not be at once tamer, more pretentious, or more unsuited to the characters than it is. What did Guiderius or Arviragus, bred from infancy in the forest, know about 'chimney sweepers' ? How foreign to their characters to philosophize on 'the sceptre, learning, physick'! Will anybody believe that Shakespeare, after he was out of Stratford Grammar School, or before, wrote such a couplet, as 'All

lovers young, all lovers must Consign to thee and come to dust'? Has he throughout his works given us reason to suspect him, on any evidence short of his own
hand and seal, of making these two lads, burying their adopted stripling brother
by the mouth of their cave in the primeval forest, close their dirge with such a
wish as, 'Quiet consummation have, And *renowned be thy grave*'?... The lines
are the production of some clumsy prentice of the muse. ✦ Halliwell (ed. 1853–
1865) : This truly beautiful dirge may safely be left to its own influences, yet it may
be worthy of note how exquisitely the fears dissipated by the hand of Death are
made to harmonize with the character of the wild district in which the speakers
were then living. ✦ New Variorum (ind. ed. 1913) quotes Staunton : "There is
something so strikingly inferior both in the thoughts and expression of the concluding couplet to each stanza ... that we may fairly set them down as additions
from the same hand which furnished the contemptible masque or vision that
deforms the last Act." [And Rolfe:] "The poor pun in *chimney sweepers* and *dust*
could hardly have been tolerated by Shakespeare in his later years; and the couplet
has no cohesion with the preceding lines. The same is true of those which end the
second and third stanzas. The final couplet is not so much out of place, but 'renowned' is a word out of place." [The editor of the New Variorum edition then
comments:] Staunton judiciously draws a distinction between the stanzas and the
couplets, which White does not, although the lines which White specifically con-
demns are only in the couplets. These it is which are by another hand than Shakespeare's, and are probably a continuation of the same trail which began with the
offensive references to 'rich left heirs' and 'lying priests' [IV.ii.225 f., 242]. The
stanzas themselves are Shakespeare's very own, and in their melody and sad
sweetness worthy of every exclamation of admiration which can be lavished on
them. ✦ Moore (1916, p. 87), instancing this song as an example, remarks : A
surprisingly large number of songs [in Shakespeare's plays] serve for what might
be called pagan ritual, a fact which is especially conspicuous because Christian
ritual is absent. ... No doubt it is due, in part, to the taste of the masque-loving
age. ... These passages must have been effective on the stage, however excrescent
they may seem to a modern reader. [Moore further observes (pp. 97 f.), that this
song serves to heighten the emotion of the scene in which it occurs:] The poignancy
of ... [the dirge for Imogen] is intensified by the fact that the singers are disguised
princes, her brothers, ignorant of her birth and theirs, and their supposed father is
a banished nobleman. ✦ Noble (1923, pp. 135 f.) : [The song's] couplets are objected
to because they contain far-fetched conceits and otherwise make no appropriate
sense. ... [The critics who make such charges] have approached the dirge from the
literary, the wrong, standpoint, and I venture to suggest they would do well to
examine the gruesome funeral games in which children love to indulge. ... It is
evident that Guiderius and Arviragus, with that zeal for ritual ever deeply en-
grained in the young, carry out their part without understanding very clearly the
meaning of the obsequies they are undertaking. ... That it is their special ritual is
made plainer by the fact that the dirge is identical, word for word, with the
exception of the names, with that performed for their reputed mother, before
they had the 'mannish crack'. Consequently there is nothing incongruous in the
introduction at the end of each stanza of nonsensical couplets. A curious habit to
which children are prone is to make such a string as 'the sceptre, learning, physic

must'... there is a characteristic Shakespearean touch in this addition. After all, the objection to the couplets is based on nothing more substantial than aesthetic grounds and such supports are usually very fragile. [Guiderius and Aviragus are hardly "children" by any standards—certainly not by seventeenth-century criteria. See commentary following Davies (1939, p. 167), below.] ♦ E. K. Chambers (1930, I, 486) : The song... has... been questioned, partly because it does not name Fidele, which is thought inconsistent with [IV.ii.237 f.]...

use like note and words
Save that Euriphile must be Fidele.

No doubt songs lend themselves to interpolation, but this is an exquisite one. Staunton distinguished himself by finding the last couplet of each stanza inferior to the rest. God knows why! Disintegration is a constant itch in some minds. ♦

Main (1951, item no. 36) endeavors to justify at least one of the "bad couplets," the first one with its "poor pun" on *chimney sweepers* and *dust*, by referring to what he believes is a pertinent passage in Frazer's *The Golden Bough*. See note to ll. 5-6, below. Nolan (1952, item no. 4) takes issue with Main, arguing that although the passage in Frazer may justify one couplet, it hardly can be used to defend the couplets which conclude the second and third stanzas of the song. Nolan writes : I think that all three couplets can be shown to have "natural cohesion with the preceding lines"—first, because they hark back to a theme which has been stated shortly before the dirge is sung; and, second, because the theme of the couplets develops naturally out of the theme stated in the other lines of the three stanzas. The theme of the couplets... is that Death comes to all.... No one escapes Death because of his appearance, rank, learning or age. The couplets, then, are connected by theme to the lines which immediately precede the dirge and in which the idea of Death the Great Leveler is first presented....

Though mean and mighty rotting
Together have one dust, yet reverence
(That angel of the world) doth make distinction
Of place 'tween high and low. Our foe was princely;
And though you took his life as being our foe,
Yet bury him as a prince. [IV.ii.246-251]

The point seems to be that the world makes a distinction between high and low, but that Death does not.... It is not strange, then, that the idea that Death is no respecter of persons should be in the brothers' minds when they sing the dirge a few minutes later. It keeps recurring in the couplets as a sort of chorus to the idea which they present in the first four lines of stanzas 1, 2, and 3. The first couplet develops quite logically from what is said in the lines preceding it. In these lines the idea that Death brings release from the troubles of life is set forth. Fidele is to fear no more the heat of the sun or the rages of winter. He has finished his worldly task; he has gone home and taken his wages. The couplet explains why he has gone home. He has suffered the universal lot of mankind: he has died. When their time comes "golden lads and girls" can no more escape Death than can chimney-sweepers.... In the first lines of the second stanza the singers return to the theme that Death brings release from the troubles of this life. Fidele is to fear no more the displeasure of the great or the stroke of the tyrant. He need not worry about clothing and food . . . there is no difference now between the weak and the strong (the reed and the oak). Then the couplet re-emphasizes that his experience is a universal one. . . . As Dr. Johnson puts it, ". . . All human excellence is equally subject to the stroke of death". . . . In the first four lines of the third stanza Guiderius and Arviragus again present the idea that Death has brought release to Fidele and in the couplet re-state that he is not alone in his dying. This time, to stress the universality of Death, the singers point out that all lovers must follow Fidele's example and "come to dust." . . . The last stanza rounds out the dirge and brings it to a close. . . . The singers have presented the ideas that Death has brought Fidele release from the temporal things of this life and that it is a universal experience. . . . Now they express the hope that nothing—exorcisor, witchcraft, ghost unlaid, or anything ill—may disturb his spirit. . . . It is true that Shakespeare does not shrink from a pun even in the most serious scenes, but it should be noted that in this dirge he uses "come to dust" in the second and third couplets, where no pun can possibly be involved. It may be, then, that the unsuspected [read *suspected*] pun in the first stanza is unintentional on his part. ◆

Davies (1939, p. 167) : Perhaps the most difficult stage in the [young] actor's life would be that during which he was neither boy nor man, but his training would dispose of the awkwardness which usually accompanies adolescence, and he would be able to play such parts as . . . Guiderius and Arviragus . . . who are unable to sing. Guiderius is the elder of the two, and Arviragus is sixteen, and probably would be played by a boy a year or so older. ◆ [Davies apparently bases his calculation of Arviragus' age on the boy's lament over the supposedly dead Imogen (IV.ii.198–201):

> I had rather
> Have skipp'd from sixteen years of age to sixty,
> To have turned my leaping time into a crutch,
> Than have seen this.

But "sixteen to sixty" sounds like a saying, and is not necessarily Arviragus' reference to his own age. A more likely calculation of the young men's ages can be based on a courtier's remarks in the opening scene of the play. He describes (I.i.57–62) how the infant boys were stolen from their nursery, and dates that event as having occurred "some twenty years ago," at a time when Guiderius was three and Arviragus was still in swaddling clothes. Unless the courtier's "some twenty" is meant to be taken very loosely, Guiderius must be about twenty–three and Arviragus about twenty at the time of the play's action, and they are fully grown young men by seventeenth-century standards. On these same grounds it is possible to explain the apparent makeshift by which the brothers decide to recite rather than to sing the dirge. A boy actor who could give a stage appearance of sixteen would probably have still preserved his voice; an actor who gave the appearance of twenty or older might, on the other hand, have a voice but recently "crack'd i' th' ring." Citing Cuthbert Kelly as an authority on Elizabethan and Jacobean music and voice-training, Davies remarks (p. 36) that "boy actors would be able to preserve their voices for singing until sixteen at least, and for speaking until nineteen or twenty." And it is worth noting, as Granville-Barker points out, that

Arviragus, the younger of the two, is ready enough to sing (IV.ii.236) until he is overruled by Guiderius.] Granville-Barker (1947, I, 482) : Guiderius' excuse for not joining [in singing the dirge] is so palpable and overcharged that we may well set it down to domestic difficulties supervening [*i.e.*, probably the inability of the actor playing the part to sing.]

TEXTUAL COMMENTARY

4. Home art gon] Corin (1959, pp. 173–179) argues against giving a Christian interpretation to the phrase. "Home," he remarks, is not heaven but the grave. He cites a number of examples from the *NED* in support of his contention, and points out that Bartlett's *Concordance to Shakespeare* gives no example of a Shakespearean usage where home means heaven.

5–6. Golden . . . dust] Tillyard (1943, p. 60) : They may be golden for more reasons than one, but one reason is that they are in perfect health, the elements being in them, as in gold, compounded in perfect proportion. ◆ Main (1951, item no. 36) calls attention to a passage in Frazer (1935, II, 82) to explain Shakespeare's "poor pun" : In his chapter on "Relics of Tree-Worship in Modern Europe" . . . where he discusses the festivities of spring celebrating the tree-spirit or the spirit of vegetation, Frazer cites this example:

> In England the best-known example of these leaf-clad mummers is the Jack-in-the-Green, a chimney-sweeper who walks encased in a pyramidal framework of wickerwork, which is covered with holly and ivy, and surmounted by a crown of flowers and ribbons. Thus arrayed he dances on May Day at the head of a troop of chimney-sweeps, who collect pence.

. . . The significant point here is that the chimney sweeper may be identified logically with the freshness and youth of "Golden lads and girls." And if this comparison is thus perfectly natural, then is the use of the pun on "dust" not only reasonable but also extremely precise for a dirge that laments the untimely death of a youth? . . . [There are] further associations of chimney sweeper and the Whitsuntide festivities. . . . "Chimney-sweepers," therefore, connotes the spirit of springtime. ◆ Nolan (1952, item no. 4) : It is difficult to fix the connotative values of "golden" in this context, but since Guiderius and Arviragus believe Fidele to be of gentle birth . . . perhaps a contrast between the station in life of the lads and the girls and that of the chimney-sweepers is intended. . . . Almost certainly there is implied a contrast between the inevitable connotation of fairness associated with "golden" . . . and the blackness which Shakespeare associates with chimney-sweepers. . . . To me, the significant point to be derived from the first couplet of the dirge is not that "the chimney sweeper may be identified logically with the freshness and youth of 'Golden lads and girls,' as Mr. Main believes, but rather that "golden lads and girls" and chimney-sweepers are actually thought of as two separate classes of people who, nevertheless, have one thing in common: they both must die. ◆ Phillips (1953, item no. 2) : Chimney-sweepers . . . did not begin . . . to be associated with springtime in the mind of the public until a century and a half after Shakespeare's death. The first references to their celebration of the return of spring on May-Day are apparently to be found in Grosley . . . [1772, I, 183 f.] and in the anonymous *May-Day: A Poem* . . . [1769, sigs. D₁–D₄] but during Shakespeare's lifetime and through the first half of the eighteenth century chimney-sweepers were no more thought of as votaries of the Goddess Flora than they were as bestowers of good luck, "sweep's luck." ¶ Yet Shakespeare undoubtedly chose chimney-sweepers to provide admirable contrast to the *Golden lads and girls*, thereby making the couplet coherent with the context: the soot-begrimed despised followers of Vulcan serving as foils for the fortune-favored children of Apollo. Chimney-sweepers in the seventeenth century, as well as in the nineteenth, were so despised for their fuliginous appearance and nauseating stench—the result of climbing chimneys and cleaning privies—that they were treated as pariahs. . . . No other laborers so familiar to the public and yet held in such low esteem by it could have served Shakespeare's purpose as well as the sooty sweeps when he was philosophizing upon the inevitability of death claiming all men, whether of good fortune or mean estate. ◆

17. **Louers**] Nolan (1952, item no. 4) **:** Perhaps the choice of the word "lovers" was suggested by the preceding line "Thou hast finish'd joy and moan," for the lot of young lovers is traditionally pictured as one of alternate joy and sorrow. ◆

18. **Consigne**] *NED*, quoting this example: To set one's seal, subscribe, agree to.

19. **Exorcisor**] Malone (ed. 1790) **:** An exorcisor . . . signified in Shakespeare's time, an enchanter or conjuror, not a person who had the power to lay spirits. ◆ [So in *Caesar* (II.i.323 f.),

> Thou like an exorcist hast conjur'd up
> My mortified spirit.

See also *NED*.]

23–24. **Quiet . . . graue**] Nolan (1952, item no. 4) disagrees with White (1854, p. 466) **:** This last wish is not an unnatural one. It does not seem strange that the brothers, who on short acquaintance have found Fidele to be a matchless youth and have come to love him more than their supposed father, should wish him to be remembered, his grave to be well-known.

MUSIC

The original music for this dirge is unknown. According to *A List* (1884, p. 11), Thomas Arne composed music for the song around 1740. Squire (1912, I, 71) notes that Arne's music is to be found in T. Billington's *A Second Set of Glees . . . to which is added Airs by Handel and Arne* [1790?], B. M. press mark G.805.5. Caulfield (n.d., II, 76–82) gives an anonymous composition dated about 1746. Long (1961, p. 60) has set the words to a tune from Gibbon (1930, p. 164) which he says is "a melody used by George Wither for a 'Lullabie' in his hymn collection *Halelviah* (1641)." Actually, the songs in Wither's collection do not have music printed with them, although some of the hymns have a tune-name assigned. But the "Rocking Song" which Gibbon reprints from Wither's book (sigs. E₅v–E₇) does not have any tune suggested in the original. Hence Gibbon's use of Luther's "Vater Unser" or the "Old 112th" rests on no authority but his own.

DRAMATIC FUNCTION

The inflated language of the funeral episode, the extravagant tone of the dirge and obsequies for Fidele, can be traced to two factors: an audience addicted to elaborate spectacles such as masques provided, and the unreality of the death of Fidele. Only the second point needs any explanation. This scene in *Cymbeline* is almost exactly comparable to the one in *Romeo and Juliet* (IV.iv), when Juliet is discovered, apparently dead, on the morning of her wedding day. The extravagant grief of Guiderius and Arviragus over the supposedly dead Fidele is exactly paralleled by the reaction of Juliet's family to her supposed demise. Since in both instances the audience knows that the decedent is *not* dead, a sincere outburst of grief—such, for instance, as surrounds the funeral services for Ophelia in *Hamlet*— would be out of place and a rude assault on the audience's feelings. With elaborately artificial funeral scenes Shakespeare obviates such difficulties. The hollow commonplaces of the language and sentiments he gives to his characters are in perfect propriety with the unreal events they adorn.

Samuel Johnson, perhaps, would be the best commentator on the dirge for Fidele. He would point out that the sentiments of the song are the universal maxims of every man's moral knowledge; that, though the dirge expresses them gracefully enough, it reveals nothing striking or new. He would say that the song "abounds with images which find a mirror in every mind, and with sentiments to which every bosom returns an echo." In short, it is quite good enough for the scene in which it occurs.

The Winter's Tale

56

TEXT: Folio (1623), sig. 2B₁ᵛ (IV.iii.1–12).
TYPOGRAPHY: Indented verse, italic and roman face; s.d., *Enter Autolicus singing.*

When Daffadils begin to peere,
With heigh the Doxy ouer the dale,
Why then comes in the ſweet o' the yeere,
For the red blood raigns in yᵉ winters pale.

The white ſheete bleaching on the hedge, 5
With hey the ſweet birds, O how they ſing:
Doth ſet my pugging tooth an edge,
For a quart of Ale is a diſh for a King.

The Larke, that tirra-Lyra chaunts,
With heigh, the Thruſh and the Iay: 10
Are Summer ſongs for me and my Aunts
While we lye tumbling in the hay.

GENERAL COMMENTARY

Moore (1916, p. 92) : In two successive scenes . . . [Autolycus] gives us no less than seven different songs or fragments, highly characteristic of his joyous roguery, which raises his whole-hearted rascality so far above the common level that it partakes of the out-door freshness of innocence. ♦ Noble (1923, p. 94) : [Autolycus'] entrance is one of the most effective in the comedies—the gay, careless, and unscrupulous character of the man is at once conveyed. . . . It is the song used as a soliloquy, whereby the audience can have intimate information as to Autolycus's point of view, and never has any man been limned more tersely and vividly than in the two opening songs. . . . From them we are led to suspect that, when the Clown enters, he is to be shorn some way or another. Robbed the Clown is and in

the meanest manner possible, but the songs deprive the theft of half its villainy. ✦
L. B. Wright (1927, p. 264) : Autolycus is a clown and only a clown. His performances are pure clownery; his songs are merely extraneous clown songs with
no dramatic value outside the clown scenes which are themselves extraneous. ✦
Bethell (n.d., pp. 45–47) : In rhythm and metre this is just another pleasant
Elizabethan lyric . . . its simplicity and traditional character are avouched in the
"heigh" of each second line, the monosyllabic language, the sparing use of
epithets. . . . Yet the song is startling enough . . . [for it] contrasts the poet's
countryside with the "low life" of the organised thieves. . . . We begin with the
daffodils, but the alliterative "doxy" in the second line signifies one of the women
held in common among the community of thieves. . . . The white sheet on the
hedge suggests the decent activity of cottage and farm, but a "pugging tooth," on
the analogy of a "sweet tooth," means a thievish tooth. . . . In the third stanza we
begin innocently again with the bird-songs . . . but "aunts" are women of loose
morals, paramours . . . presumably doxies. . . . We have a curious drawing together of quite different types of experience . . . [and] these strands of interest
interweave and produce a metaphysical lyric of wide significance. . . . Its primary
importance is in bringing the ideal world of romance into unmistakable relation
with contemporary life. . . . What Shakespeare supplies is a juxtaposition of
opposites, an association of natural beauty with the nasty sneak-thief and his
unlovely companions. As a character, Autolycus . . . is shown to have saving graces,
and his song expresses this same truth in metaphysical poetry where religious
vision penetrates beyond the over-simplified moral judgement of the world. ✦
Auden (1957, p. 42) : Autolycus . . . sings as he walks, because it makes walking
more rhythmical and less tiring, and he sings to keep up his spirits. His is a tough
life, with hunger and the gallows never very far away, and he needs all the courage
he can muster. ✦ Long (1961, pp. 71 f.) : The obvious use of the initial music . . . is
to change the character of the play from the tragic to the comic. . . . The scene
shifts from the palace of Polixenes to the countryside, and the new setting is
established by Autolycus, who paints a musical backdrop of spring flowers,
hedgerows, and convenient haymows. At the same time he reveals himself as a
rascal, but also a sympathetic rascal. That such a character can immediately enlist
the sympathy of the spectator is due, in large measure, to the fact that he is
singing a lilting song. . . . The song is a picaresque ballad filled with underworld
cant. It was sung, very likely, to a rather simple ballad tune.

TEXTUAL COMMENTARY

1. **When . . . peere**] That is, in earliest spring. Thus Perdita (IV.iv.118–120) remarks about the

> daffodils,
> That come before the swallow dares and take
> The winds of March with beauty.

2. **Doxy**] Arden (ind. ed. 1922) cites the definition in Cotgrave's *Dictionarie*, 1611:

Gueuse: f. A woman begger, a she rogue, a great, lazy and louzie quean; A Doxie, or Mort.

3-4. When ... pale] Warburton (ed. 1747) **:** I think this nonsense should be read thus,

> *Why, then* COME *in the sweet o' th' year;*
> *'FORE the red blood* REINS-*in the winter pale.*

i.e., Why then come in, or let us enjoy, pleasure, while the season serves, before *pale winter reins-in* the red or youthful *blood*; as much as to say, let us enjoy life in youth, before old age comes and freezes up the blood. ◆ Capell ([1779-1783?], II, part 4, p. 173) **:** i.e., for the red blood exercises dominion, begins to exert itself in a season which is within the pale or province of winter.... The daffodil's *peering* ... is at the latter end of winter where it joins the spring; and the *blood* ... is—his own blood; which then begins to excite him to cross the dale to his doxy. ◆ Malone (ed. 1790) **:** Autolicus, I think, calls the *spring* the *sweet of the year*, because in that season maidens put out their sheets to bleach on the hedges; and "his traffick" (as he afterwards tells us) is in sheets. ◆ Arden (ind. ed. 1922) **:** It is uncertain whether *pale* means (1) paleness, or (2) fenced area, enclosure.... Accepting the former meaning, we may interpret: "The red blood of spring reigns in place of winter's pallor." Accepting the latter ... "The red blood of spring has dominion over what was once the confines of winter." ◆ Noble (1923, pp. 94 f.) **:** The time of the year is sweet, for the blood now tingles that was lately within the pale (cf. 'English Pale' in Ireland) or under the influence of winter—the song serves for scene and indicates the season of the year. ◆ [For some reason or other, all the editors ignore the figure of double paronomasia, the puns on "pail" and "rain"; to secure these Shakespeare may have been content to leave the lines ambiguous.]

5. The ... hedge] Falstaff, speaking of his ill-clad, tatterdemalion troops in *1 Henry IV* (IV.ii.51 f.), says, "They'll find linen enough on every hedge." Cf. also song 4, l. 13, above.

7. pugging] Malone (ed. 1790) cites Steevens **:** "The word *pugging* is used by Greene in one of his pieces. And a puggard was a cant name for some particular kind of thief." ◆ Skeat (1906, pp. 342 f.) **:** Most commentators simply repeat a guess made by Nares, that "pugging" means "thievish." ... But this is extremely uncertain.... I have grave doubts as to "a thievish tooth"; for men do not usually use their teeth to steal with; neither does it suit the line which follows.... The sense is rather "my piercing tooth," or "tooth that cuts up my meat." And I take the general sense to be that Autolycus, seeing the white sheet ready to be taken, takes it as a matter of course; for another extra article added to his wares could easily be exchanged, at the nearest public-house, for a good solid meal, which, accompanied by a quart of ale, would naturally render him as happy as a king. I understand the whole sentence—"doth set my pugging tooth on edge"—to mean simply, "adds a new edge to my crumbling tooth." The object of having the new edge was to eat the more heartily and easily, not to assist him in lifting a white sheet from a hedge.... [In 1906, p. 391, Skeat corrects the misprint "crumbling" in his earlier note to the correct reading, "crunching," and adds that he finds further support for his interpretation in comments on this line made by Wise (1861, p. 106):] "All the commentators here explain 'a pugging-tooth' as a thievish

tooth, an explanation which certainly itself requires to be explained; but most
Warwickshire country-people could tell them that pugging-tooth was the same as
pegging or peg-tooth, that is, the canine or dog-tooth." ◆ Arden (ind. ed. 1922): In
Middleton's *The Roaring Girle* [1611, sig. L₂] . . . occurs the word *puggards* apparently
in the sense of thieves:

> Tempt him with gold to open the large booke
> Of his close villanies: and you your selfe shall cant
> Better then poore *Mol* can, and know more lawes
> Of cheaters, lifters, nips, foysts, puggers, curbers,
> Withall the diuels blacke guard, then it is fit
> Should be discouered to a noble wit.

. . . But in Devonshire dialect the word *pug-tooth* occurs in the sense of eye-tooth. ◆
Noble (1923, pp. 94 f.): 'Pugging' means thieving or cheating and the theft of the
sheets would provide the wherewithal to purchase a quart of ale. ◆ [*NED* gives a
1575 meaning of *pug*, "to pull or tug"; and "pugging" is what Autolycus does to
the sheets as he makes off with them.]

7. **an edge**] Almost all the modern editors emend *an* to *on*, perhaps needlessly,
since the line can be understood as a dative construction: "Doth set an edge to my
pugging tooth."

8. **dish**] Any hollow vessel of wood or metal used for drinking; hence the
modern Irish expression, "dish of tea." Cf. *NED*.

9. **tirra-Lyra**] Variorum (ed. 1821) cites a gloss by Malone: So, in an ancient
poem entitled, The Silke Worms and Their Flies, 1599:

> "Let Philomela sing, let Progne chide,
> "Let *Tyry-tyry-leerers* upward flie—."

In the margin the author explains *Tyryleerers* by its synonyme, *larks*. ◆ Douce
(1839, p. 217): The tire-lire was not, it seems, peculiar to the lark. In Skelton's
Colin Cloute [1545?, sig. C₇] we have,

> howe Cupyde shaked
> His darte and bent his bowe
> For to shote a crowe
> At her tyrly tyrlowe.

And in one of the Coventry pageants there is the following old song [ed. H. Craig,
1902, p. 31]:

> As I out rode this enderes night,
> Of thre ioli sheppardes I saw a sight,
> And all a-bowte there fold a star shone bright;
> *They sange terli terlow;*
> *So mereli the sheppards ther pipes can blow.* ◆

[Actually there is probably little connection, if any, between *tirra-Lyra* and *terly-
terlow*. Both words, of course, are echoic, but the latter seems to have been a

common song burden. Brougham ([1918], pp. 6 f.) cites a lyric in Balliol MS. 354 which has as its burden,

> Tyrle, tyrlow, tyrle, tyrlow
> So merrily the shepherds began to blow.]

Halliwell (ed. 1853–1865) : A fanciful combination of sounds, intended to imitate the note of the lark; borrowed from the French *tire-lire*, meaning the same. . . . It occurs in Dubartas ["La premiere sepmaine, le cinquiesme jour," ll. 615–617 (ed. Holmes, 1935–1940, II, 360)]:

> La gentille alouette avec son tire-lire
> Tire l'ire, à l'iré, et tire-lirant tire
> Vers la voute du ciel. ◆

Lever (1953, p. 82) suggests that the echo of Du Bartas in this line may have come from Shakespeare's reading of John Eliot's *Ortho-epia Gallica*, 1593, which quotes the above lines.

10. **With heigh**] The second folio (1632) corrects to *With heigh, with heigh*, a change adopted by all subsequent editors.

Iay] New Cambridge (ind. ed. 1931) suggests that this word is used with reference to "Aunts" in the line following. In a gloss the editors explain the word as alluding to women of "light character," citing *Merry Wives* (III.iii.42) and *Cymbeline* (III.iv.51 f.).

11. **Aunts**] Malone (ed. 1790) quotes Steevens : "*Aunt* appears at this time to have been a cant word for a bawd. In Middleton's . . . *A Tricke to Catch the Old-one* [1608, sig. B₄]:

> and was it not then better bestow'd vpon his Vncle then vpon one of his Aunts, I neede not say bawde, for euery owne knowes what Aunt stands for in the last Translation now sir.

MUSIC

The original melody for Autolycus' first song has apparently not survived. Ritson (1813, III, 281–283) gives both the words and a tune for the song. He remarks in a headnote: "This tune is not known to have been ever printed before, and was not obtained without some difficulty." The implication of the note and the title of his collection seems to be that he is reproducing the original music. I seriously doubt that he is. Since he also includes in his songbook the words and music to "When daisies pied," "When icicles hang by the wall," and "Under the greenwood tree," all in their late settings by Arne, there is no reason to suppose that the music he gives for Autolycus' song is "original." The earliest music recorded by *A List* (1884, p. 71) is a tune composed by William Boyce around 1759. It is reprinted in Caulfield (n.d., II, 49). Long (1961, p. 72) sets the words to a contemporary tune, "Row well, ye mariners," in Thomas Robinson's *Schoole of Musicke* (1603), from Wooldridge (1893; reprinted 1961, I, 127).

DRAMATIC FUNCTION

Obviously with comic intent, Shakespeare took the name of his rogue-peddler from a notorious character in Greek mythology; Autolycus was the maternal grandfather of Odysseus, and is recorded by Homer as being "the most accomplished thief and liar of his day" (*Odyssey*, XIX, 392–396; tr. Rieu, 1946, p. 308). Even more important than Autolycus' classical ancestry is the debt he owes to pre-Shakespearean drama. Moore (1922, p. 157) remarks that "He comes of an old theatrical family, and his ancestors must have sung and pilfered their way across the boards before Shakespeare was born."

But Shakespeare's Autolycus is more than a clowning peddler, ballad-singer, and rogue, and he is more than an incidental character in the play. The halting speech of Time as a Chorus at the beginning of the fourth act may advance the action of the play sixteen years, but it is not until Autolycus bursts onto the stage with song at the beginning of IV.iii. that the change in time—and mood—becomes believable. With his entrance the dark and tragic winter of Leontes' jealousy melts into a spring of promise and young love. Autolycus' first song is appropriately a *reverdie*, a song in which all of nature rejoices in the return of spring. Like all men Autolycus can celebrate the passing of winter and the return of warmer weather, but for him the spring has its own special—and professional—delights. The white sheets bleaching on the hedge, and perhaps maidens' smocks as well, are just waiting for this passing snapper-up of unconsidered trifles; and then there are always the more frankly Ovidian pleasures afield with some "aunt" or doxy.

When early in the play the little boy Mamillius sets out to tell his mother a story, he decides upon a sad tale, for

> A sad tale's best for winter. I have one
> Of sprites and goblins. . . .
> There was a man—. . .
> Dwelt by a churchyard. I will tell it softly;
> Yond crickets shall not hear it.   (II.i.25–31)

The boy's projected story symbolizes the first three acts of the play: it is the winter's tale of Leontes' jealousy, a story of a man whose soul is haunted by nameless sprites and goblins of fear and suspicion. The man who "dwelt by a churchyard" foreshadows the tragic effects of the king's jealousy on those around him: the deaths of Mamillius and Antigonus, and the supposed deaths, for sixteen years, of Hermione and her daughter.

To transform such materials into joyous comedy needs more than a lapse of time; what is needed is a new moral universe in which Leontes can find forgiveness for his sin, a new atmosphere where love and joy are again possible. The jocund herald of that new world is Autolycus with his torrent of song.

57

TEXT: Folio (1623), sig. 2B₁ᵛ (IV.iii.15–22).
TYPOGRAPHY: Indented verse, italic face.

But ſhall I go mourne for that (my deere)
the pale Moone ſhines by night:
And when I wander here, and there
I then do moſt go right.
If Tinkers may haue leaue to liue,
and beare the Sow-skin Bowget,
Then my account I well may giue,
and in the Stockes auouch-it.

GENERAL COMMENTARY

Noble (1923, p. 95) : [This song] informs us that [Autolycus] need not lament unduly the decline in his fortunes, for as there is only a pale light at night, he will be able to see sufficiently to carry on his petty larcenies and enjoy fair security and, if he wanders at random, well then he has the better luck. To be a tinker is a lawful calling, and accordingly he can carry a tinker's knapsack on his back and, if apprehended by the law, can plead such an occupation as a plausible explanation of the bag's contents. ♦ New Arden (ind. ed. 1963) : Like the Lincolnshire poacher's it was Autolycus' "delight on a shining night" to be out on the prowl. For a vagabond, since he has no specific destination, all directions are the right direction—no road is a wrong road. Dr Brooks cites Cade's comment [in *2 Henry VI*, IV.ii.199 f.]: "But then are we in order when we are most out of order" . . . anarchy is the mob's proper principle, and to travel without a destination is the vagabond's principle.

TEXTUAL COMMENTARY

1. that] A reference to his fallen fortunes. Just before the song he says, "I have serv'd Prince Florizel and in my time wore three-pile, but now I am out of service."

2. the . . . night] A better time for thievery; so in *1 Henry IV* (I.ii.15 f., 28–33) Falstaff says,

we that take purses go by the moon and the seven stars. . . . Let us be Diana's foresters, Gentlemen of the shade, Minions of the Moon; and let men say we be men of good government, being governed as the sea is, by our noble and chaste mistress the moon, under whose countenance we steal.

4. **go right**] That is, serve myself most profitably; with a play on "wandering" vs. "going in the right direction."

5. **If . . . liue**] Tinkers, peddlers, and petty chapmen shared a common unsavory reputation in medieval and Renaissance England, and the popular notions about their dishonesty extend down into modern times. They were apparently very little regulated by law, and their nomadic habits made it almost impossible for local magistrates to prosecute them for petty thieveries. Cf. Jusserand (1950, pp. 127 ff.) for an account of attempts to regulate their activities in the late middle ages.

6. **tbe**] An obvious typographical error for *the*, corrected by the Second Folio (1632).

Sow-skin Bowget] New Cambridge (ind. ed. 1931) : The bag in which the tinker carried the implements of his trade.

7–8. **Then . . . auouch-it**] New Arden (ind. ed. 1963) paraphrases the second stanza as follows: "If tinkers are allowed to trade and carry their pigskin bag— then I can account for myself and if they put me in the stocks can show my calling (i.e., that I am a tinker and not a vagabond and therefore should be released)." [But perhaps a more sardonic meaning is intended, *viz.*, Autolycus' disguise as a tinker may explain the contents of his sack, and so secure him from arrest as a thief, but it cannot guarantee him from arrest and punishment in the stocks as a vagrant.]

MUSIC

The original tune for the song is unknown. *A List* (1884, p. 72) records a setting by J. Lampe in 1748; it is in the B. M. sheet music collection (press mark G. 306, piece 251). There is an anonymous setting in Caulfield (n.d., II, 52). Long (1961, p. 73) has set the words to a tune titled "The Noble Shirve" in Wooldridge (1893; reprinted 1961, I, 126), a tune believed to date from at least the reign of James I.

DRAMATIC FUNCTION

The hint of roguery in Autolycus' first song is fully amplified in the second as he characterizes himself as a petty pilferer and irresponsible vagabond. Prior to this song he explains that he is now "out of service," and a little later in the same scene (ll. 94–96) explains why: he has been "whipp'd out of the court" for his vices, and has since then passed through the various declensions of knavery to have at last "settled only in rogue." Autolycus may be a notable liar, but he would probably be truthful about his vices, they being the "virtues" of his profession.

The rogue-peddler who cares not that he has been whipped out of honorable employment must have been a familiar figure in Shakespeare's day if Henry Chettle's pious and feeling account (*Kind-Harts Dreame* [1593], sig. C₁) is any evidence:

> I am giuen to vnderstand, that there be a company of idle youths, loathing honest labour and dispising lawfull trades, betake them to a vagrant and vicious

life, in euery corner of Cities & market Townes of the Realme singing and selling of ballads and pamphletes full of ribaudrie, and all scurrilous vanity, to the prophanation of Gods name, and with-drawing people from christian exercises, especially at faires markets and such publike meetings.

Autolycus' vices, such as they are, are fully atoned for by his exuberant joy in living. He is, as Professor Moore has observed (1922, p. 164),

a lover of existence, a man who laughs at the world's despite, until some critics have ventured the opinion that he will soon repent and turn to the paths of virtue. For they are unable to comprehend that curious work of nature, the singing rogue, even as the wisest of princes found it hard to understand the fellow who had so little feeling of his business that he sang at grave-making.

58

TEXT: Folio (1623), sig. 2B₂ (IV.iii.132–135).
TYPOGRAPHY: Indented verse, italic face; s.d., *Song*.

Iog-on, Iog-on, the foot-path way,
And merrily hent the Stile-a:
A merry heart goes all the day,
Your ſad tyres in a Mile-a.

GENERAL COMMENTARY

Halliwell (ed. 1853–1865) notes that there are two additional stanzas to this song in *An Antidote Against Melancholy: Made up in Pills* (1661); the three stanzas also appear, with slight variations, in *Catch that Catch can: or the Musical Companion* (1667, sig. M₃); see Music, below. Halliwell further remarks that "one of the old verses in the ballad of Robin Hood, Scarlet and John, commences with the [same] four first words." He is apparently referring to "Robin Hood and the Prince of Aragon" (Child, 1882–1898, V, 147) which begins,

'Jog on, jog on,' cries Robin Hood,
'The day it runs full fast.'

The expression is obviously a commonplace; cf. Pepys (II, 120).

TEXTUAL COMMENTARY

2. **hent**] White (ed. 1883) : Lay hold of; from *hentan*, A.S.= to take. ♦
3. **A merry ... day**] A proverbial expression; see W. G. Smith (1935, p. 50) and Tilley (1950, M-71); see also *2 Henry IV* (V.iii.50), and song 13, l. 2.

MUSIC

The original tune for this song may be preserved in a number of early versions. Under the title "Hanskin" it appears in the manuscript Fitzwilliam Virginal Book (ed. Fuller-Maitland, 1894–1899, II, 494–500) arranged in a set of variations by Richard Farnaby (ca. 1590?). Entitled "Jog on," this same tune appears in every edition of John Playford's *The English Dancing Master* from 1651 to 1698 (ed. Bridgewater, 1933, p. 53; ed. Dean-Smith, 1957, p. 45). The tune again turns up—this time as a song with three stanzas—in *An Antidote Against Melancholy: Made up in Pills* (1661, sigs. L₁–L₁ᵛ) and in Playford's *Catch that Catch can: or the Musical Companion* (1667, sig. M₃) in an arrangement by John Hilton for three voices. The

9+v.s.

basic tune also apparently circulated among ballads under the titles of "Sir Francis Drake" or "Eighty-eight."

There are many popular copies of the tune: Chappell (1840, II, 237; [1855–1859], I, 212), Wooldridge (1893; reprinted 1961, I, 159), Elson (1901, p. 248), Gibbon (1930, p. 104), Naylor (1931, p. 185), Pafford (1959, p. 173), and Kines (1964, p. 27). Hardy (1930, p. 77) gives both the Fitzwilliam and Playford versions of the tune. Long (1961, p. 74) reprints the Hilton setting as if the three parts were a single melody; actually they are intended to be sung in harmony. The "Hanskin" melody is preserved in the first part, though it is of course echoed in the two other harmonizing voices.

The fact that the names of Farnaby and Hilton are attached to the tune does not mean that either man was necessarily the original composer; the ascription is intended only to give credit for the particular arrangement or setting. Both the Fitzwilliam Book and Playford's *Dancing Master* preserve a great number of popular tunes from Shakespeare's time and earlier, set either as themes and variations for the virginal or as music for dancing. It is likely that Hilton simply took up the song sung by Autolycus and composed two more voices for it so that it could be sung as a three-part song.

While it seems fairly certain that "Hanskin" is the original melody, the authenticity of the additional stanzas in *An Antidote* and *Catch that Catch can* seems doubtful. They run as follows:

> Iog on, Jog on the Foot-path way,
>   and merrily hent the Stile-a,
> the Merry heart goes all day long,
>   the Sad tyres in a Mile-a:
>
> Your paltry Money Bags of Gold,
>   what need have we to stare for,
> when little or nothing soon is told,
>   and we have the less to care for:
>
> Cast care away, care away, let sorrow cease,
>   a fig for Melancholy,
> let's laugh and sing, laugh and sing, or if
>   you please,
> wee'l frolick with sweet *Molly*.   Jog on, &c.

The repetitions in the first and third lines of the third stanza are obviously an arranger's licenses, and when they are omitted the third stanza is in perfect metrical agreement with the others. It is barely possible that all three stanzas originally belonged to the song, and that Autolycus merely sang the opening one. On the other hand the second and third stanzas lack the simplicity and proverb-like quality of the first, and the fact that they turn up in a setting for three voices strongly suggests additions by an arranger who wanted the symmetry of three voices and three stanzas, with perhaps each voice carrying the main melody once. That the song is circular is suggested by the repetition of the opening words following the last stanza.

DRAMATIC FUNCTION

This song, even as the one which precedes it, is meant to characterize Autolycus, to illustrate his happy-go-lucky attitude toward life and responsibility. Moore (1922, p. 157 f.) compares Autolycus with Ariel in *The Tempest* and this song with "Where the bee sucks." In a single sentence he sums up the functions of these songs: "Ariel could sing more rapturously of the life of freedom yet to be, but none knew better than Autolycus the joys of the life that is."

59

TEXT: Folio (1623), sig. 2B₃ (IV.iv.220–231).
TYPOGRAPHY: Indented verse, italic face; s.d., *Enter Autolicus finging.*

> *Lawne as white as driuen Snow,*
> *Cypreſſe blacke as ere was Crow,*
> *Gloues as ſweete as Damaske Roſes,*
> *Maskes for faces, and for noſes:*
> *Bugle-bracelet, Necke-lace Amber,*   5
> *Perfume for a Ladies Chamber:*
> *Golden Quoifes, and Stomachers*
> *For my Lads, to giue their deers:*
> *Pins, and poaking-ſtickes of ſteele.*
> *What Maids lacke from head to heele:*   10
>   *Come buy of me, come: come buy, come buy,*
>   *Buy Lads, or elſe your Laſſes cry: Come buy.*

GENERAL COMMENTARY

Clemen (1951, p. 200) : The items from Autolycus' pedlar's pack are here compared to things which suggest the imagery of Elizabethan lyrics: white as driven snow, sweet as damask roses. And thus a romantic note is struck in this prosaic catalogue of trifles and petty stuff. But all this cheap knick-knackery . . . gives much colour and a homely and realistic flavour to this peasants' idyll. ◆ Long (1961, pp. 74–76) finds a tension between the music and song in the masque episode and the underlying drama having to do with Polixenes' wrath : The next scene presents the sheepshearing festival with full Arcadian flavor. Bucolic lads and lasses, wildly gamboling satyrs, the strains of bagpipes, pipe, and tabor, all form the background for the fresh, idyllic love of Florizel and Perdita. But this background contains somber colors both created and, ironically, accented by its music. The shadow of Polixenes' wrath, which gradually envelops the festival, is fed by the music. This parallel movement of music and action in the scene is made possible, apparently, by the use of pantomime while the music is being performed and by the particular songs and dances involved. . . . The growing anger of Polixenes, in opposition to the revelry of the scene, supplies the conflict of the little drama. . . . Under the festive sea moves a turgid undertow of anger actually nourished by the revelry, hence the irony of the episode. . . . If we may observe the thoughts of Polixenes as the songs and dances are performed, we may see that his thoughts seem to grow out of each piece of music, and that very likely he signals these thoughts by means of pantomime to the audience while the merrymaking is in progress. . . . When Autolycus sings his first peddler's cry, Polixenes is strengthened in his belief that Florizel is . . . interested in a light love that can be purchased with trinkets. ◆ [In similar fashion Long attempts to read Polixenes' mind about other songs and dances, and his reactions to them. A careful examination of his argument shows that it is mostly fanciful: there are few, if any, indications of pantomime in the text; Polixenes seems to be delighted with the sheepshearing festival until Florizel announces his refusal to consult his father about his marriage to Perdita, and this occurs long after the end of the masque-episode; and the "turgid undertow of anger" that Long finds in the "festive sea" is supported nowhere by the text of the scene. The textual evidence that Long adduces in support of his interpretation is mostly an *ex post facto* application of Polixenes' later angry speeches to the songs, music, and dances of the sheepshearing scene. No auditor of the play would ever be aware of such intricate tensions, and certainly would not apply Polixenes' sudden anger in ll. 428 ff. to a scene that occupies ll. 220–330.]

TEXTUAL COMMENTARY

2. **Cypresse blacke**] See commentary on *cypreffe*, song 31, l. 2.

3. **Gloues . . . Roses**] Halliwell (ed. 1853–1865) : The introduction of perfumed gloves is thus mentioned in Howes' edition of Stowe's Chronicle [(1631, sig. 4D₂)]:

> About the fourteenth or fifteenth yeere of the Queene . . . *Edward de vere*, Earle of Oxford, came from Italy, and brought with him Gloues, sweet bagges, a perfumed leather Jerkin, and other pleasant things, and that yeere the Queene had a paire of perfumed gloues . . . [and] tooke such pleasure in those Gloues that she was pictured with those Gloues upon her handes, and for many yeeres after, it was called the Earle of Oxford's perfume. ◆

[Shakespeare also refers to perfumed gloves in *Much Ado* (III.iv.62 f.). The fashion appears to have lasted well into the seventeenth century. James Howell in *Epistolae Ho-Elianae*, 1650 (sig. 2D₈ᵛ), Section III, in a letter to Captain Thomas Porter from Madrid, 10 July 1623, writes: "By the next oppotunity [*sic*] I will send you the Cordovan pockets and gloves you writ for of *Francisco* Morenos perfuming."]

4. **Maskes**] Worn by Renaissance ladies to ward off the effects of sun and elements. Smoothness and whiteness of skin was especially esteemed in Shakespeare's day. See *Two Gentlemen of Verona* (IV.iv.157–161), *Troilus and Cressida* (I.ii.286 f.), and *Othello* (IV.ii.9).

5. **Bugle-bracelet**] Arden (ind. ed. 1922) : A bracelet of black beads; compare "bugle eyeballs," *As You Like It*, III.v.47. ◆ [NED lists an example from 1579, and defines *bugle* as "A tube shaped glass bead, usually black, used to ornament wearing apparel."]

Amber] Malone (ed. 1790) : There should be only a comma after *amber* [for] . . . Autolycus . . . says that he has got among his other rare articles for ladies, some *necklace-amber* . . . commonly called bead-amber, fit to perfume a lady's chamber. ◆ [Actually *amber* has two meanings: it may refer to the perfume ambergris, or musk, as Malone thinks, or it may mean the fossil resin from which beads and ornaments were made. In *Taming of the Shrew* (IV.iii.58) there is a reference to "amber bracelets, beads." If the word in Autolycus' song merely means jewelry, then the "perfume" of the next line is not in apposition to *Amber*, but simply another one of the contents of his pack.]

9. **poaking-stickes**] Douce (1839, pp. 220 f.) : These implements . . . [were used] for stiffening the ruffs formerly worn by persons of both sexes . . . [and] this fashion being carried to a great extremity, became the subject of many satirical prints. . . .

MUSIC

The earliest known music for this song is an air printed in John Wilson's *Cheerfull Ayres or Ballads* (1660, sigs. I_4^v–K_1^v). There are facsimiles in the *New Variorum* (ind. ed. 1898, pp. 388 f.) and in Long (1961, pp. 142 f.). Reprints of the song or the tune are given by Vincent (1906, pp. 30 f.), Hardy (1930, pp. 78 f.), Gibbon (1930, p. 121), Pafford (1959, p. 174), Cutts (1959, *Musique*, pp. 20 f.), Long (1961, p. 80), and Kines (1964, pp. 29–31).

Wilson's version can hardly have been the original music for the song since he was only fifteen years old at the time of its first performance. Nosworthy (1958, p. 65) and Cutts (1959, *Musique*, p. 129) conjecture that Wilson, in publishing this song in *Cheerfull Ayres*, was merely giving his arrangement of the original tune by an earlier composer—possibly Robert Johnson, in Nosworthy's view. But there is no real evidence to support this notion.

ANALOGUES

Rimbault ([1864], p. 49) reprints a round by John Jenkins (b. 1592) that seems closely related to the words of Shakespeare's song. Jenkins' song is titled "Come, pretty maidens":

> Come, pretty maidens, what is't you buy ?
> See, what is't you lack ?
> If you can find a toy to your mind,
> Be so kind,
> View the pedler's pack.
> Here be laces and masks for your faces,
> Coral, jet and amber;
> Gloves made of thread, and toys for your head,
> And rich perfume for a lady's chamber.
> Come and buy, come, buy for your loving honey
> Some pretty toy to please the boy,
> I'll sell it you worth your money.

Another analogous peddler's song is reproduced by Sabol (1959, pp. 63–67) from the "Masque of Mountebanks" (1618) in B. M. Add. MS. 29,481 (fols. 17^v–19). It is also in the New York Public Library MS. Drexel 4175 (no. 29).

What is't you lack, what would you buy?
   What is is [*sic*] that you need?
Come to me, gallants; taste and try:
Here's that will do, here's that will do,
   Here's that will do the deed.

Here's water to quench maiden fires;
Here's spirits for old occupiers;
Here's med'cine to preserve ye long,
Here's oil will make weak sinews strong.

Is any deaf? Is any blind?
Is any fast or loose behind?
Is any foul that would be fair?
Would any lady change her hair?

Does any dream? Does any walk,
Or in their sleep affrighted talk?
I come to cure whate'er you feel,
Within, without, from head to heel.

Maids of the chamber or the kitchen,
If you be troubled with an itching,
Come give me but a kiss or two,
And I'll give that shall soon cure you.

Nor Galen nor Hippocrates
Did ever do such cures as these.

Is any so spent, that his wife keeps Lent?
   Does any waste in his marrow?
Is any a slug? Let him taste my drug,
   'Twill make him quick as a sparrow.

My powder and oil, extracted with toil,
   By rare sublime infusions.
I have proof they are good by my own dear blood,
   In many, many, many, many, many strange conclusions.

A third analogue occurs in Anthony Munday's *The Downfall of Robert, Earle of Huntington*, 1601 (sig. F₄ᵛ):

What lacke ye? what lacke yee? what ist ye wil buy?
Any points, pins, or laces, and laces, points or pins?
Fine gloues, fine glasses, any buskes, or maskes?
Or any other prettie things?
Come cheape for loue, or buy for money.
Any cony cony skins,

    For laces, points, or pins? faire maids come chuse or buy.
    I haue prettie poting sticks,
    And many other tricks, come chuse for loue, or buy for
        money.

Such similarities as exist among the words of the four songs may be a result of literary derivation, or may even point to the existence of a genre of Peddler's Songs at the time; but the most likely explanation of the similarities among these songs is that all of them are imitating the actual street-cries used by peddlers in Shakespeare's England.

DRAMATIC FUNCTION

Autolycus' song is largely extraneous, serving only to fill out the disguise he has adopted, that of a ballad-monger and peddler, a role which he takes off in caricature rather than character. His song perfectly portrays him as an itinerant hawker of ballads.

60

TEXT: Folio (1623), sig. 2B₃ (IV.iv.302–314).
TYPOGRAPHY: Indented verse, italic face; s.d., *Song*.

Song   *Get you hence, for I muſt goe*
Aut.   *Where it fits not you to know.*
Dor.   *Whether?*
Mop   *O whether?*
Dor.   *Whether?*   5
Mop.   *It becomes thy oath full well,*
       Thou to me thy ſecrets tell.
Dor: *Me too: Le⁚ me go thether:*
Mop   *Or thou goeſt to th' Grange, or Mill,*
Dor: *If to either thou doſt ill,*   10
Aut: *Neither.*
Dor: *What neither?*
Aut: *Neither:*
Dor: *Thou haſt ſworne my Loue to be,*
Mop   *Thou haſt ſworne it more to mee.*   15
       Then whether goeſt? Say whether?

GENERAL COMMENTARY

Capell ([1779–1783 ?], II, part 4, p. 176) : [This song] . . . is of wonderful sweetness, and musical without music, as are all the songs of this Poet in general.

TEXTUAL COMMENTARY

3. **Whether**] For *whither*. The spelling reflects a blurring of the pronunciation of short *i* and *e* in Shakespeare's day. See Kökeritz (1953, p. 212), and also the rhymes on ll. 5 and 12 of "Under the greenwood tree," song 20, above.

8. **Le⁚**] The letter *t*, perhaps pulled out of a loose chase by the inking balls during printing, re-inserted upside down. What is printed is the foot of a piece of type.

9. **Grange**] New Variorum (ind. ed. 1898) quotes Hunter: "Granges were the chief farm-houses of wealthy proprietors. The religious houses had granges on most of their estates. The officer who resided in them was called the *Grangiarius*. He superintended the farm, and at the grange the produce was laid up. . . . They

9*

were well-built stone houses, often of considerable extent and height, and . . . in a central position."

MUSIC

What may be the original music for this song, a composition probably by Robert Johnson, was discovered by Cutts (1956, *SS*, pp. 86–89) in a New York Public Library manuscript, Drexel 4175 (no. 59). Cutts gives the words and music here and in *Musique* (1959, pp. 17 f.). There is a fragmentary version of the same song for three voices in Drexel MS. 4041 (fols. 127–129), and Cutts also gives his edition of this in *Musique* (p. 19). Unfortunately there are at least six errors in transcription in Cutts's editions; persons using his book should be cautioned that the publishers have since issued a list of 109 *Addenda et Corrigenda* to the musical transcriptions (see Duckles, 1962). There is a more reliable edition by Spink (1961, pp. 62 f.), and an edition by Long (1961, pp. 82 f.), who also gives (pp. 138 f.) a facsimile of Drexel 4175.

The fragmentary version of the song in Drexel 4041 includes a second stanza which may have been part of Autolycus' original song:

> neuer more for lasses sake
> will I dance at fare or wake
> Ah mee   oh Ah mee   Ah mee
> who shall then ware a rated shooe
> or what shall the bagpipe doe
> recant or elce you slay mee
> recant or elce you slay me
> if thou leaue our Andorne greene
> where shall fill or frize be seene
> sleeping   what sleeping   sleeping
> no Ile warrant the sitting sadly
> or Idely walking madly
> in some darke   in some darke
> in some darke Corner weeping
> in some darke darke Corner weeping

As Autolycus finishes his song in Shakespeare's play (IV.iv.315 f.) he says, "We'll have this song out anon by ourselves," thereby implying that his version is not complete. But as Spink (1961, p. 74) points out, while the music for the first stanza fits the second "well enough down to bar 18 . . . thereafter verbal repetitions, false accentuation and other irregularities suggest that a different musical treatment was necessary." Although Cutts remarks that the second stanza is in perfect harmony with the episode in Shakespeare, he does not attempt to fit it to the music. New Arden (ind. ed. 1963) suggests an entirely different explanation for the additional stanza, that it is a post-1611 expansion of the song. The editor notes that "lyrics and stage songs were often expanded in broadsheets in the 17th century."

It is also Cutts's view that the words in Drexel 4175 give a better reading or ll. 14 f. than the text in the First Folio, because the manuscript version avoids the repetition of the word *sworne*. The comparable lines in the manuscript read,

> thou hast vow'de thy loue to mee,
> thou hast sworne my loue to bee.

There are no other important variations between the stanza in Shakespeare and those in the manuscripts.

It is curious that this setting for Autolycus' song has only recently been discovered. Both manuscripts were formerly owned by Edward F. Rimbault (1816–1876), a scholar who was especially concerned with Shakespeare songs.

The probable attribution of this song to Robert Johnson is based on his known association with the King's Men and its proximity in the manuscript to other theatrical songs composed by him for the King's Men.

DRAMATIC FUNCTION

The song sung by Autolycus, Mopsa, and Dorcas is a "three-men's song," or, as it was more frequently known in Shakespeare's day due to consonantal confusion, a "free-men's song." Classified under the heading were apparently all songs for three voices, whatever their other formal character may have been. Naylor (1931, pp. 82–84) discusses the form and (pp. 192 f.) gives some examples of it.

When Mopsa, after hearing Autolycus' account of a number of doleful ballads, calls for some merry ones, the peddler pulls out this song and says,

> Why, this is a passing merry one, and goes to the tune of 'Two maids wooing a man.' There's scarce a maid westward but she sings it. 'Tis in request, I can tell you.

Mopsa and Dorcas already know the tune. "We had the tune on't a month ago." And Mopsa points out that it is a tune "in three parts." No tune entitled "Two maids wooing a man" seems to have survived, though the Drexel MSS. versions of the song may preserve the melody of the original ballad. To modern ears that tune sounds more like a funeral march than a merry tune; if it sounded the same to a Shakespearean audience, Autolycus' selection of that ballad for singing may have been his joke on Mopsa and Dorcas.

Autolycus' songs so far in the play have revealed the two main facets of his character: his carefree love of life as it is, and his long-fingered ways with other people's property. This song may be intended to amplify a third feature of his personality only hinted at in the earlier songs. Part of his love for springtime comes from the opportunities the season affords him for tumbling in the hay with his "aunts" and doxeys. If his own mocking description of himself earlier in the play (IV.iii.102–105) is true—that he "compass'd a motion of the Prodigal Son, and married a tinker's wife," apparently only soon to abandon her—then his roguery is complete, for he is also revealed as a trifler with feminine hearts, even as the man in the song he sings with Dorcas and Mopsa.

61

TEXT: Folio (1623), sig. 2B₃ (IV.iv.322–330).
TYPOGRAPHY: Indented verse, italic face; s.d., *Song*.

Will you buy any Tape, or Lace for your Crpe?
My dainty Ducke, my deere-a?
Any Silke, any Thred, any Toyes for your head
Of the news't, and fins't, fins't weare-a.
Come to the Pedler, Money's a medler,   5
That doth vtter all mens ware-a.

GENERAL COMMENTARY

Long (1961, p. 85) : After the dialogue song, Autolycus, the Clown, and the "Wenches" move offstage to haggle over the peddler's wares. As our rascal exits, he sings another vender's cry . . . [which] belongs, as does "Lawne as white as driven Snow," to a genre frequently found in the early song books.

TEXTUAL COMMENTARY

1. **Crpe**] Corrected by the second folio (1632) to *Cape*.
2. **dainty . . . deere-a**] Apparently a conventional low-life term of endearment. Bottom, as Pyramus in *Midsummer Night's Dream* (V.i.286), addresses Thisby as "O dainty duck! O dear!"
4. **news't . . . fins't**] Noble (1923, p. 97) : Some editors omit the elision in "new'st" and "fin'st." The words, as they appear in the Folio, may be intended to mimic a salesman, and such a possibility must not be left out of account. Shopkeepers had then, as they have now, their peculiar little mannerisms. ◆ [The most plausible explanation of the elisions is simple metrical necessity. Without the elisions it is almost impossible to say—much less sing—the line smoothly.]
5. **medler**] Arden (ind. ed. 1922) : Meddler . . . usually spelt in modern editions with a single *d*; the meaning is, "a sharer in whatever is going on." ◆ [It seems possible that the word *medlar* is intended here, perhaps as a pun. Shakespeare explicitly puns on *meddler* and *medlar* in *Timon* (IV.iii.305–310) and seems to make a similar pun in *As You Like It* (III.ii.124 f.). Since the medlar is a fruit that is "rotten before it's ripe," the sense of these lines may be, "Come to the peddler and spend your money before, like the fruit, it's rotten on the tree; for money is only valuable as currency."]
6. **vtter**] Malone (ed. 1790) quotes Reed: "To *utter* is a legal phrase often made use of in law proceedings . . . and signifies, to vend by retail."

MUSIC

The original tune for Autolycus' final song is not known. The earliest recorded setting given by *A List* (1884, p. 75) seems to be one by William Boyce (1710–1779), composed about 1769, and reprinted in Linley (1816, II, 29). There is an anonymous setting in Caulfield (II, 58 f.) which might conceivably be one of the "traditional" stage versions which Caulfield says in his Preface that he is collecting; if this is the case, his setting may even be earlier than the one by Boyce, but Caulfield is not a reliable editor. Long (1961, p. 85) has set the song to a contemporary tune, "Sellenger's Round," from Wooldridge (1893; reprinted 1961, I, 256 f.).

DRAMATIC FUNCTION

Autolycus leaves the fourth scene of the penultimate act as he had entered it, true to his alias of peddler and ballad-monger, singing over his wares "as they were gods or goddesses." The bulk of this fourth scene is simply a pastoral masque, and Shakespeare briefly gives pause to the action of the play here for the sake of music, dance, and spectacle. The "language of flowers" poetry which dominates the first part of the scene is perfectly appropriate as dialogue for a masque. For the masque proper there is "a dance of Shepherds and Shepherdesses," and a short while later an antimasque "Dance of twelve Satyrs." To all this music and dance (a full performance would occupy a great deal more time than the written text and stage directions suggest) Autolycus' songs are a proper comic foil. Immediately after his last song the antimasque takes place, and then the action of the play resumes again. The hiatus in the action seems a deliberate device on Shakespeare's part to provide song, dance, and spectacle for an audience who loved those things.

The Tempest

62

TEXT: Folio (1623), sig. A₃ (I.ii.375–386).
TYPOGRAPHY: Indented verse, italic and roman face; s.d., *Ariel Song*.

Come vnto thefe yellow fands,
    and then take hands:
Curtfied when you haue, and kift
    the wilde waues whift:
Foote it featly heere, and there, and fweete Sprights beare   5
    the burthen.   *Burthen difperfedly.*
Harke, harke, bowgh wawgh: the watch-Dogges barke,
    bowgh-wawgh.
Ar. *Hark, hark, I heare, the ftraine of ftrutting Chanticlere*
    cry cockadidle-dowe.

GENERAL COMMENTARY

Moore (1916, p. 95) notes Shakespeare's use of song to incite characters to action. He remarks that "Ariel draws Ferdinand from the coast to Miranda's presence, by singing 'Come unto these yellow sands,'" and that in the second song Ariel "persuades the prince of his father's death, thus recalling his grief and preparing him for a new and unreserved affection." Noble (1923, p. 100): The laughing invitation [of this song] has drawn Ferdinand hither from the sea, and the illusion is given of terra firma by the noise of dogs barking and cocks crowing. An echo all round the stage is almost suggested. ◆ Davies (1939, pp. 165 f.): Large numbers of children are needed in . . . *The Tempest* as nymphs, dogs and spirits. . . . If the presentation of *The Tempest* was at celebrations attending the betrothal of Elizabeth of Bohemia (1613), there would be no difficulty in securing the services of royal choirboys for the masque. ◆ Cutts (1958, p. 348): It is not impossible to see in this song a counterpart to the Sirens' invitation to the wearied mariners to "Steer hither your winged pines" [in William Browne's 'Masque of the Inner Temple', 1614/15]. Ariel who sings the song has promised, as they did, peace and calm after the storm. . . . Of course . . . it is Ariel's music that has allayed the tempest, but the deeper significance of the return to order and harmony seems to have escaped attention. It seems to me that the legend of Circe and her island Sirens is being used as the basis of the plot's construction here, and that its evil aspect has been replaced by the benevolent power of Prospero. The sensual Sirens have given place to the "ayrie spirit," the celestial spirit, Ariel, working obedient to the divine will as represented by Prospero. ◆ Long (1961, pp. 97–99) : When [Ferdinand] wanders onto the stage, still dazed by his miraculous rescue, his attention has already been claimed by ethereal music performed by Ariel, whose song is accompanied by a distant barking of dogs and crowing of cocks. . . . Actually, this music is Prospero's magic made manifest. By his mysterious power Prospero has evoked the tempest. Once its purpose has been accomplished, Prospero calms the storm and enchants both Miranda and Ferdinand; so when they meet they immediately fall in love. The two songs and their instrumental support are the audible aspects of this gentler magic. ◆ R. Hunter (1965, p. 227) : Ariel is here issuing an invitation to the dance. It is addressed to Ferdinand. Miranda, the partner whose hands he will take, is onstage, but, having been enchanted by her father, is as yet unseeing and unseen. They will enter upon the dance, whose symbolic implications for the Elizabethans have been fully presented by Sir John Davies. . . . The result of Ferdinand and Miranda's dance will be the stilling—the "whisting"—of the wild waves, for the ultimate source of the tempest of the play is the hatred and evil of the older generation, and the result of strife between the fathers has been a chaos which will be reduced to order by the love and marriage of the children.

TEXTUAL COMMENTARY

3–4. **Curtsied . . . whist**] Dyce (ed. 1875–1876) : I believe that Steevens was right in considering the [fourth] line as parenthetical,—"The wild waves *being* whist;" the poet having had an eye to the ceremonies (the *court'sying* and *kissing*) which were formerly observed at the commencement of certain dances. ◆ C. A. Ward (1885, p. 105) : The passage seems to me to run thus: "Curtsied when you have and kissed"; the sad sea waves will *whist-le* their low dirge as you "foot it featly here and there." Certainly it is the same word as *hwis* and *hwistle*, and its first meaning is blowing; the second is by blowing *hist* to get silence. ◆ Noble (1923, p. 104) : The stops here are employed to achieve certain musical effects and 'the wild waves whist' is meant to succeed without pause on 'kissed', so as to suggest the stormy waves continually breaking in upon and receding again from the beach. ◆ New Arden (ind. ed. 1954) reviews the possible interpretations : "Kiss'd" each other? ("The wild waves whist" is then an absolute construction—"being silent", or "now being silent" after the storm.) Or, "kiss'd the wild waves into silence"? To take hands and curtsy (make a reverence) were the first two steps in all dances, but the kiss normally came when the dance was finished. . . . [Yet the notion that] "kiss'd" must govern "waves" . . . is disagreeable, being grotesque in a context which does not require grotesquerie. The syntax should perhaps be allowed to be ambiguous. Of course it was Ariel's music which allayed the tempest. ◆ Long (1961, p. 99) : By means of the song Ariel, in the form of a sea-spirit, directs his attendant spirits to curtsy and to kiss the "wilde waves whist." ♦ [The likelihood that this is an absolute construction is supported by a very close parallel in Milton's "Hymn on the Morning of Christ's Nativity" (ll. 64–66):

> The Winds, with wonder whist,
> Smoothly the waters kiss't,
> Whispering new joys to the mild Ocean.

But there is probably no way to resolve the ambiguity.]

5. **featly**] *NED*: Cleverly, deftly, nimbly.

5–6. **Sprights . . . burthen**] Capell ([1779–1783 ?], II, part 4, pp. 60 f.) comments on the stage direction "Burthen diſperſedly": There is a direction for a "*burthen,*" or chorus, but no words assign'd for it: it came in therefore at the words—"*Hark, hark;*" and consisted of a musick that seem'd to come from all parts of the stage, (for that is meant by the word—"*dispersedly*") imitative of the barking of dogs: and . . . Ariel . . . catches the first notes that usher . . . [these burthens] in, and accompanies them with his voice; as, in the next song, he does manifestly another wild air that makes the burthen of that. ♦ Noble (1923, p. 105) **:** If we examine the document that is our only authority for the text, we shall conclude that, had it not been for the accident of 'the burthen' being carried over for reasons of space from the previous line, 'Burthen dispersedly' would have appeared on the line by itself . . . [even as in a similar situation in "Under the greenwood tree"] the direction 'All together here' is placed above the line 'Who doth ambition shun', and there the context implies that the direction refers to the whole of the stanza. Accordingly one would say that 'Burthen dispersedly' applies to the song here until it is replaced by another direction, and such a direction occurs at l. 9, to which is prefixed 'Ar.', plainly signifying that Ariel at that point again takes up the song. ♦ Arden (ind. ed. 1926) **:** Chappell . . . tells us "The burden of a song, in the old acceptation of the word, was the base, foot, or under-song. It was sung throughout and not merely at the end of a verse." Here the burthen appears to be "Bow-wow," to which Ariel calls attention by his "Hark, hark." In the second stanza it is "Ding-dong," which he again prepares us for, and then begins or accompanies it. The burden in each case is taken up by the "sprites"—his meaner ministers . . . who imitated the barking of dogs or the ringing of a bell at different parts of the stage. But it is further probable that "Cock-a-diddle dow" is also a burthen, either introduced by Ariel when he uses the word "cry"; or taken up independently by the sprites, in which case "cry" should be regarded as a stage direction. ♦ J. D. Wilson (1930, p. 514) argues that, although all the editors since Dryden have inverted the word order of "beare the burthen," it is quite sufficient to allow the words "the burthen" to be a carryover to the next line, without, then, any need to distort the text. ♦ New Arden (ind. ed. 1954) **:** Properly a continuous undersong of the sort perhaps most familiar to the modern reader in certain carols. . . . Editors have rearranged this passage in many ways, but the F[olio] version . . . shows that the word *burthen* here means "refrain"; the animal- and bird-noises follow Ariel's verses. . . . I cannot follow Capell and most editors in reversing the order of words. ♦ [The modern editors' attempts to arrange these lines since Capell (ed. [1767–1768]), and their conjectural efforts to separate "stage directions" from the words of the song, are almost as numerous as the editors themselves. But against their attempts at emendation it is worth noting, according to E. K. Chambers (1951, I, 491), that *The Tempest* is one of the most carefully printed of all Shakespeare's plays, and that it is unusually good in punctuation and stage directions.]

7. **Harke ... barke**] Noble (1923, p. 106) **:** 'Hark, hark ... The Watch dogs bark' suggests that a rhyme out of a childish game is being employed, and the first part of the song, with its obvious reference to such games, strengthens the suggestion. ◆ [The "reference" Noble has in mind is presumably the taking of hands, curtseying, and kissing; but these are not restricted to "childish games"; it is far more likely that they are the formal preliminaries by adults dancing in a group. Nonetheless Noble may be right in suspecting an allusion to a lost jingle in this rhyme. A song in the *Westminster Drolleries* (ed. Ebsworth, 1875, II, 37), begins,

> Hark, hark, the Doggs do bark,
> My wife is coming in
> With Rogues and Jades,
> And roaring blades,
> They make a devilish din.]

bowgh wawgh] New Arden (ind. ed. 1954) **:** Probably derived from James Rosier's account of a ceremonial Virginian dance: "One among them, the eldest as he is iudged, riseth right vp, the others sitting still: and looking about, suddenly cried with a loud voice, *Baugh, Waugh* ... the men all together answering the same, fall a stamping round about the fire ... with sundrie out-cries" (*Purchas his Pilgrimage* [1613], p. 637 [sig. 3I₅]). ◆

10. **cockadidle-dowe**] Noble (1923, p. 106) argues that this cannot be part of the burthen **:** Presumably the burden would be expected to reproduce the cock-crow as naturally as possible, as in the case of the barks, and this might involve the song ending on a discord—a thing absolutely forbidden by all the rules, especially in Shakespeare's day when they were rather stricter than they are now. A burden which deals with musical instruments such as bells, whose key it is within the art of music to regulate, stands on a very different footing from that occupied by a burden whose subject is a noise of nature in a key uncontrolled by art. ... The ending of a song, such as the one we are considering, would sound exceedingly strange if the discord were not resolved. The crow accordingly does not belong to the burden but is completely within Ariel's power to regulate, and is therefore no more than suggested, it is not imitated. ◆ [But there is no evidence that the sound-effects available to Shakespeare's stage would not have been able to compass such difficulties.] Long (1961, p. 100) **:** The watchdogs' and the cocks' voices represent the outposts of human society to which Ferdinand is returning and the familiar order and peace which the weary traveler finds upon return to his home.

MUSIC

The earliest known music for Ariel's first song was composed by John Banister (1630–1679) for Dryden's and D'Avenant's adaptation of Shakespeare's *Tempest* in

1670. It is included in a collection of songs by Banister, J. Hart, and Pelham Humphrey, *The Ariels Songs in the Play call'd the Tempest* ([1670?], p. 2). A more famous setting of the same song is one composed by Henry Purcell for Elkanah Settle's adaptation of *A Midsummer Night's Dream* in his *The Fairy-Queen: An Opera* (1692). It is reprinted by Caulfield (n.d., I, 1–3). If the original music ever is discovered it will probably turn out to be by Robert Johnson (ca. 1583–1633), whose compositions for at least two other songs in *The Tempest* are extant. Long (1961, p. 115) has set the words to Dowland's "Now, o now I needs must part" (also known as "The Frog Galliard") from a Folger Library lute manuscript.

DRAMATIC FUNCTION

Lacking the original music it is impossible to tell how the song was meant to be performed, and whether its "burthen" was a continuous undersong, a chorus, or a refrain. Yet the text of the play seems to hint at a method of rendition that would be appropriate for music on an island that was "full of noises, sounds and sweet airs." The clearest suggestion is contained in Ferdinand's own words at the conclusion of the song (I.ii.387–389):

> Where should this music be? I' th' air, or
> th' earth?
> It sounds no more; and sure it waits upon
> Some god o' th' island.

And later Caliban comments on the unearthly music that fills the island (III.ii.144–149):

> Be not afeard. The isle is full of noises,
> Sounds and sweet airs that give delight and hurt not.
> Sometimes a thousand twangling instruments
> Will hum about mine ears; and sometime voices
> That, if I had wak'd after long sleep,
> Will make me sleep again.

Aside from the songs of Caliban, Stephano, and Trinculo, all the music in *The Tempest* seems to have this mysterious character, as though it were an emanation of the very air itself. Except for Ariel (III.ii.134) who goes "invisible" playing a catch on tabor and pipe, there are no directions in the play for instrumental music in the sight of the audience. Yet there are few of Shakespeare's plays which require so much music as *The Tempest*, and none of them puts so much emphasis on "dispersed" music, performed as if it came from all over the stage. The implications of such a manner of performing music would suggest that the burthens of Ariel's first two songs were performed in the same way: dispersedly, as if sounded by Ariel's subject spirits from all parts of the stage. As a matter of fact their burthen may have been a continuous undersong in the old acceptation of the term described by Chappell ([1855–1859], I, 222 f.).

A rendition of this song and the one that follows in this fashion would exploit fully Noble's suggestion that the first two songs are meant to give an illusion of *terra firma* after the sea-havoc of the tempest, and would also establish in the audience's mind the magical character of the island on which the shipwrecked noblemen find themselves. Prospero's island is to be the scene of fantastic marvels and music that seems to come from nowhere; but it is also to be the scene of an even more marvelous work, man's regeneration from evil.

63

TEXT: Folio (1623), sig. A₃ (I.ii.396–404).
TYPOGRAPHY: Indented verse, italic and roman face; s.d., *Ariell Song*.

> *Full fadom fiue thy Father lies,*
> *Of his bones are Corrall made:*
> *Thofe are pearles that were his eies,*
> *Nothing of him that doth fade,*
> *But doth fuffer a Sea-change*   5
> *Into fomething rich, & ftrange:*
> *Sea-Nimphs hourly ring his knell.*
>   Burthen: ding dong.
> *Harke now I heare them, ding-dong bell.*

GENERAL COMMENTARY

Warburton (ed. 1747): *Prospero* takes advantage of every favorable circumstance that the occasion offers. The principal affair is the Marriage of his daughter with young *Ferdinand*. But ... it was necessary they should be contracted before the affair came to ... the Father's knowledge. For *Prospero* was ignorant how this storm and shipwreck, caused by him, would work upon *Alonzo's* temper. It might either soften him, or increase his aversion for *Prospero* as the author. On the other hand, to engage *Ferdinand* without the consent of his Father, was difficult. For ... such engagements are not made without the consent of the Sovereign ... [and moreover] *Ferdinand* is ... of a most pious temper and disposition, which would prevent him contracting himself without his Father's knowledge. The Poet therefore ... has made *Ariel* persuade him of his Father's death to remove this Remora. ◆ Johnson (ed. 1765): *Ariel's* lays, however seasonable and efficacious, must be allowed to be of no supernatural dignity or elegance, they express nothing great, nor reveal anything above mortal discovery. The reason for which *Ariel* is introduced thus trifling is, that he and his companions are evidently of the fairy kind, an order of beings to which tradition has always ascribed a sort of diminutive agency, powerful but ludicrous, a humorous and frolick controlment of nature, well expressed by the songs of *Ariel*. ◆ Lamb (1808, p. 233) compares this song to the funeral dirge for Marcellus in Webster's *The White Divel*, 1612 (sig. L₁ᵛ):

> Call for the Robin-Red-brest and the wren,
> Since ore shadie groues they houer,
> And with leaues and flowres doe couer
> The friendlesse bodies of vnburied men.
> Call vnto his funerall Dole
> The Ante, the field-mouse, and the mole

> To reare him hillockes, that shall keepe him warme,
> And (when gay tombes are rob'd) sustaine no harme,
> But keepe the wolfe far thence: that's foe to men,
> For with his nailes hee'l dig them vp agen.

Lamb writes : I never saw anything like this Dirge, except the Ditty which reminds Ferdinand of his drowned Father in the Tempest. As that is of the water, watery; so this is of the earth, earthy. Both have that intenseness of feeling which seems to resolve itself into the elements which it contemplates. ◆ Noble (1923, p. 100) : The singing [of the first song] has hardly ceased when it recommences, but now in another strain and from the waters beyond the sands. Ferdinand is mocked into the belief that his father is drowned and the nymphs no more than formally grieve. The impression is given that Ariel has translated into song Ferdinand's imaginings and fears: one does not know whether the singing is real or a mere delusion of the senses. ◆ Cutts (1958, pp. 348 f.) : Ferdinand's comments on hearing the invitation song [62] indicate that the music which allayed the storm is now [in this song] drawing him almost against his will farther into the island by its power.... It seems to me that we have here the basic pattern of the approach to a Circean situation. The music has the power of Circean enchantment, guiding Ferdinand to Prospero's cave. It breaks off and begins again to suggest to Ferdinand a sense of direction and leads him to Miranda.... The essential difference is that Miranda, with whom Ferdinand now associates the music ("Most sure the Goddesse/On whom these ayres attend") is not Circe, lusting for wanton love. Her immediate love for Ferdinand is completely lawful. ◆ Long (1961, p. 116) : This poignant little elegy was apparently performed in the same manner as the first song. Ariel sings the first several lines solo. Upon Ariel's completion of the line *Into something rich, & strange*, the same echoing voices, only this time coming from the sea-nymphs, intone the repeated "ding dong" which form the burden to the final line. [And p. 100:] The voices that sing from the sea the lovely knell for Alonso ... are water-spirits (perhaps Plotinian) who, though apparently responsible for Alonso's death, yet make the separation of the King and his son as merciful as possible. Both the symbolism of the play and Shakespeare's plot require that Ferdinand should temporarily believe his father dead, but the symbolism also requires that Ferdinand should suffer no real harm in the process. He cannot know true harmony until he has experienced dissonance; hence, the tempest subsides to music, Ferdinand is returned to human society, his grief assuaged, and his love for Miranda evoked by divine music. ◆ Zimbardo (1963, pp. 50 f.) : The theme of *The Tempest* is not regeneration through suffering, but the eternal conflict between order and chaos, the attempt of art to impose form upon the formless and chaotic, and the limitations of art in this endeavor.... Without falling into an allegorical interpretation we can safely say that Prospero is an artist of a kind. He uses music, the very symbol of order, in creating his effects, he attempts to manipulate the other characters to the end of creating or preserving order and form.... Prospero at the beginning of the play is in a position in which he can take his enemies (who represent disordered mankind, since they are usurpers) ... out of the flux of life and into a kind of permanence, a change which Ariel describes [in his song]. The process is not one of regeneration into something more nobly human, and despite the interest of the Twentieth Century in Frazier's *Golden Bough*, there is nothing here that suggests fertility, rather the human and impermanent is transfixed into a rich permanence, but a lifeless one. Potentially corruptible bones and eyes become incorruptible coral and pearls; form and richness are fixed upon what was changing and subject to decay. Prospero takes the travellers out of the world of change and places them on his enchanted island, which is permeated with an ordering harmony. ◆ R. Hunter (1965, p. 228) : Ariel . . . reminds Ferdinand of his supposedly drowned father in words of puzzling but significant beauty. Alonso's corpse, the dirge tells us, lies at the bottom of the sea, where it is undergoing a marvelous transformation. Human flesh and bone fade and change from their mortal substance into the rich permanence of pearl and coral. A different but clearly analogous process does take place in the course of the play. Prospero will afflict his old enemy, Alonso, with a "heart-sorrow" so intense that it will drive him almost to suicide, yet it will finally result not in destruction, but in re-creation. Alonso will endure a psychological death of sorrow and remorse—a kind of sinking into the depths of his own mind. From this he will emerge regenerated, a new man, his psychological and spiritual substance transformed.

TEXTUAL COMMENTARY

2. **bones . . . made**] Atkinson (1949, p. 466) : It was too easy for a mere poet like Shakespeare to imagine such a sea-change. Coral, and the growth of coral islands, continued to be conveniently mysterious for a long time after his death. ◆ [The plural verb, a result of confusion by proximity to *bones*, is a frequent grammatical occurrence in Shakespeare; see Abbott (1884, pp. 298 f.). Shakespeare probably had in mind the red coral which is found in the Mediterranean, and which was given to infants in his day to teethe on. Whether by accident or accurate knowledge, his science is correct here. Both bone and coral are calcareous substances, and bone can be transmuted into coral by the action of the marine polyps which create coral deposits.]

4. **Nothing . . . fade**] Arden (ind. ed. 1926) : Every part of his body that is otherwise doomed to decay is transformed into some rich or rare sea-substance. ◆

7. **Sea-Nimphs**] The hyphen prints blind or only partially in some copies of the Folio.

8. **Burthen: ding dong**] Noble (1923, p. 107) : The effect which the burden had to convey was evidently that of a bell being rung by the waves—an effect absolutely necessary to the suggestion that the sea nymphs were ringing a watery knell. ◆

9. **Harke . . . bell**] Pattison (1948, p. 156) : The rime in the final couplet . . . suggests the last line was the work of the poet: it is clearly suitable for a choral refrain.

MUSIC

What is probably the original music for this song survives in two early manuscripts and one early song-collection. It is to be found in the Birmingham City

Reference Library MS. 57,316, in Folger Library MS. 747.1 (fols. 9ᵛ–13ᵛ), and in John Wilson's *Cheerfull Ayres or Ballads*, 1660 (sigs. B₃ᵛ–B₄). In both the Birmingham MS. and *Cheerfull Ayres* the song is assigned to Robert Johnson (158-?–1634?).

All of the modern popular copies or arrangements of the song derive from Wilson's 1660 edition, of which Long (1961, p. 144) gives a facsimile: Bridge (n.d., pp. 23–25), Elson (1901, pp. 187–189), Vincent (1906, pp. 28 f.), Hardy (1909, pp. 21–24), Gibbon (1930, p. 119), Bontoux (1936, pp. 326 f.), New Arden (ind. ed. 1954, 1958, p. 157), and Long (1961, p. 117).

There is a scholarly edition of Johnson's song in Spink (1961, pp. 24 f.); Cutts, who discovered the song in the Birmingham MS., gives (1959, *Musique*, p. 24) his transcription of that version. The words of the song, but not the music, are contained in New York Public Library MS. Drexel 4041 (fols. 64ᵛ–65).

Cutts (1959, *Musique*, p. 132) insists that this music is certainly the original composition for Shakespeare's play. Noting that some commentators have objected that the musical setting lacks the burthen "ding dong" of l. 8, he argues that this lack makes no difference since the music in the Birmingham MS. gives a clear indication of the way in which the burthen should be rendered by the bass in the appropriate passages. He observes that some notes in small characters near the end of the song indicate the part to be played by some instrument in imitating the sound of a bell. On the other hand Duckles (1962) has seriously questioned Cutts's reliability as a music editor, and Spink (1961) takes no notice of "des notes en petits caractères."

There are no significant variants between the words in Shakespeare and those in the manuscripts or printed version of the song.

DRAMATIC FUNCTION

Warburton's explanation of the part the song plays in the dramatic action is clear and convincing, and is cited by a number of the modern editors who followed him. But the song has also a symbolic function, perhaps vaguely glanced at by Arden (ind. ed. 1926) when he notes that every part of Alonso's body "that is otherwise doomed to decay is transformed into some rich or rare sea-substance." For this is precisely the point of the song. Alonso is not actually dead, yet he is to be transformed on the island. He is to achieve spiritual regeneration by means of the providential magic of Prospero, and it is this moral transformation that the song foreshadows.

64

TEXT: Folio (1623), sigs. A₄ᵥ–A₅ (II.i.300–305).
TYPOGRAPHY: Indented verse, italic face; s.d., *Sings in Gonzaloes eare.*

While you here do ſnoaring lie,
Open-ey'd Conſpiracie
His time doth take:
If of Life you keepe a care,
Shake off ſlumber and beware.
Awake, awake.

GENERAL COMMENTARY

Moore (1916, pp. 93–95) points to this song as an instance of Shakespeare's use of song to incite characters to action. He compares it with the song preceding Bassanio's choice of a casket in *Merchant of Venice*, Iago's drinking songs in *Othello*, and Bottom's song which awakes Titania in *Midsummer Night's Dream* (see songs 8, 9, 46, and 47, above). He remarks : Ariel's . . . song in Gonzalo's ear arouses the old man in time to save the king. . . . [Later] when the drunken conspirators [Stephano, Trinculo, and Caliban] come to seek the life of Prospero, they attempt to sing . . . [but their song is interrupted by Ariel's music and they] are led into a filthy pool. ◆ Long (1961, p. 102) : The "solemne Musicke" which lulls Alonso and Gonzalo to sleep serves a purpose similar to that of the elegy heard by Ferdinand; that is, it knits up the King's ravel'd sleave of care. . . . The slumber music is thus a merciful gesture made by Prospero. Since music induces the slumber, music must end it; and this is the purpose of the song, as Ariel carefully tells us.

MUSIC

The earliest known setting for the song is one by Thomas Arne, composed around 1746 and included in Caulfield (n.d., I, 18). Another setting by Thomas Linley, Jr., is included in Linley (1816, I, 7). Long (1961, p. 119) sets the words to a contemporary tune by John Bennet from Thomas Ravenscroft's *A Briefe Discovrse Of the true (but neglected) vse of Charact'ring the Degrees . . . in . . . Musicke* (1614).

DRAMATIC FUNCTION

The function of the song is evident from its context, and is adequately explained by the commentators.

65–66

TEXT: Folio (1623), sig. A₅ (II.ii.44 f., 48–56).
TYPOGRAPHY: Unindented verse, italic face; s.d., *Enter Stephano ſinging* and *Sings.*

[65]

I ſhall no more to ſea, to ſea, here ſhall I dye aſhore.

[66]

The Maſter, the Swabber, the Boate-ſwaine & I;
The Gunner, and his Mate
Lou'd Mall, Meg, and Marrian, and Margerie,
But none of vs car'd for Kate.   5
For ſhe had a tongue with a tang,
Would cry to a Sailor goe hang:
She lou'd not the ſauour of Tar nor of Pitch,
Yet a Tailor might ſcratch her where ere ſhe did itch.
Then to Sea Boyes, and let her goe hang.

GENERAL COMMENTARY

Moore (1916, p. 92) : The character of Stephano is outlined by his songs the moment he comes upon the stage. . . . His degrading influence upon Caliban is foreshadowed; it is only a step before the poor creature reels off the stage to attempt a murder, singing of new-found freedom. ◆ Noble (1923, p. 102) : The song, while hardly appropriate to a drawing-room, is in the thorough character of a good forecastle song, and it has the rough humour by which sailors, like soldiers, love their ditties to be pervaded. Stephano, be it noted, is not a sailor but a butler, and presumably would act as a kind of steward on board a ship. This class, as we know, is looked down upon by the navigating element, but its members frequently compensate themselves on shore by their swagger and by an exaggerated contempt for landlubbers, and in this song the tailor, who is no sort of a man in a sailor's eyes, is made to illustrate the contemptibility of Kate's depraved preference. ◆ Arden (ind. ed. 1926) : Shakespeare gives us (perhaps from some that he had heard sung) fragments of sailors' songs or "chanteys." These, which were in danger of passing away with the sailing ships, are now (May 1918) being revived by the U.S.A. Government. ◆ [Arden apparently refers to the Library of Congress' ballad collections.] ◆ L. B. Wright (1927, p. 263) : Comic diversion and clownery which have little organic relation to the play are furnished . . . by the singing of Stephano and Caliban. . . . Moore holds that Stephano's singing is for the purpose of delineating his character and foreshadowing Caliban's reaction to his influence. Such a statement presupposes that Shakespeare had a deeper meaning in the scene than mere entertainment and that it was necessary to delineate Stephano's character. The more sensible view seems to be . . . that the scene is mere clownery, and that the songs of both Stephano and Caliban are clown songs thrown in to help out the general comic effect. ◆ New Arden (ind. ed. 1954) : There is a theory that Shakespeare is here . . . recording or adapting some actual shanty. This is, on the whole, improbable, as the lines have not the marks of the working-song. ◆ [The later Arden editor fails to point out what the "marks" of a working-song are. There is nothing in the metrics of the song to suggest that a capstan could not be wound by them—it is a rising meter, the rhythm of effort—and the last line certainly sounds like a choral refrain to follow a song-leader's solo. Where the first three songs in *The Tempest* obviously have such intimate relations with their contexts and the actions of the play that it would seem likely they are Shakespeare's own compositions, the present song seems extraneous enough to have been an adaptation. The Gravedigger's Song in *Hamlet* is a comparable example; it shows the "marks" of working (see song 40, ll. 3–4); but the clown who takes the role in that play *is* working, at digging a grave. Stephano, on the other hand, is simply repeating a song he has heard in the fo'c'stle.] Long (1961, pp. 102 f.) : Stephano, reeling ripe with wine, staggers onto the scene . . . wherein he, Trinculo, and Caliban form their stupid and vicious alliance against Prospero. . . . Of course, Stephano sings because he is drunk, but the nature of both the singer and the song reveals symbolic connotations. In contrast to the spirit-music provided by Ariel, this is a "scurvy tune" sung by a carnal oaf much befuddled by drink. The bawdy song, the gross nature of Stephano, his drunkenness—all these reveal in the character of Stephano (and also, as we shall later discover, Trinculo and Caliban) the earthiness, sensuality, and disharmony personified by these opponents of Prospero's refined reign. We soon learn that all three are fit only for spoils and stratagems. They are parts of the inharmonious element of the island, and the sea-chantey accents their qualities.

TEXTUAL COMMENTARY

4. **Mall**] Chappell ([1855–1859], I, 289) points out that *Mall* is the old abbreviation of Mary.

8. **Tar . . . Pitch**] Both substances were extensively used aboard sailing ships. Tarpaulins and cordage were impregnated with them for protection against the corrosive action of salt-water, and ships' seams were caulked with pitch. From continued contact with these substances, sailors in Shakespeare's day must also have seemed to have been impregnated with them. Many sailors dressed their queues with pitch or tar to keep the hairs in order.

9. **Tailor**] A figure of ridicule in Shakespearean times, notorious for lack of manliness in figure and virility in character. The reputation was probably in part due to the fact that tailors performed a function believed naturally more suited to women, but also, possibly, because of a conventional image of them as diminutives; thus the tailor in *Midsummer Night's Dream* called Robin Starveling (but see com-

mentary on song 38) and the old proverb "It takes nine tailors to make a man" which Shakespeare alludes to in *Lear* (II.ii.60–62) and elsewhere.

itch] The word refers to venereal concupiscence; cf. *Antony* (III.xiii.6–8):

> Why should he follow?
> The itch of his affection should not then
> Have nick'd his captainship.

The lines refer to Antony's flight from the battle at sea in order to follow Cleopatra.

MUSIC

The original tunes for these songs are not known; the earliest settings are the anonymous ones in Caulfield (n.d., I, 16). An appropriate tune for 65 might be "Fortune, my foe," a melody that can easily be fitted to the words. In Shakespeare's day it was a tune used to march men to the gallows, and so is, indeed "a scurvy tune to sing at a man's funeral." An arrangement of this tune by Byrd is given in Fuller-Maitland (1894–1899, I, 254–257), and copies of it are also contained in Chappell (1840, II, 33 f.) and in Naylor (1931, p. 189). An equally lugubrious tune that will fit the words is "Walsingham" (see Music, song 35).

Stephano's sea-chantey has been happily set by Long (1961, p. 120) to a pre-Elizabethan tune called "The Leather Bottel," a melody which he has taken from Gibbon (1930, p. 44). It is also to be found in Chappell ([1855–1859], II, 514). Long notes that this tune fits the words and mood of the song perfectly, and adds that "if Shakespeare did not write or borrow the chantey with the tune of 'The Leather Bottel' in mind, he overlooked a most appropriate musical setting."

DRAMATIC FUNCTION

Both songs are obviously comic characterizations of Stephano. Even as Ophelia and Desdemona may have learned their bawdy songs at the knee of a nurse, so the butler Stephano may have picked up his chanteys from seamen in the ship's forecastle. The appropriateness of the first one is evident: spared from drowning and safe on land once more it is only natural that he should sing, "I shall no more to sea . . . here shall I die ashore." Yet fortuitously as well as fortunately he has floated to shore clinging to a butt of sack. With such a "comforter" in his possession all thoughts of death-by-water fly from his mind. Sack suggests parties; parties, a sailor's leave ashore; and shore-leave, those faithful girls of every port, Mall, Meg, Marrian, and Margerie—and a Kate who, inscrutably, prefers the shadow of a man.

67

TEXT: Folio (1623), sig. A₅ᵛ (II.ii.184–189).
TYPOGRAPHY: Indented verse, italic face; s.d., *Caliban Sings drunkenly.*

No more dams I'le make for fiſh,
Nor fetch in firing, at requiring,
Nor ſcrape trenchering, nor waſh diſh,
Ban' ban' Cacalyban
Has a new Maſter, get a new Man.

GENERAL COMMENTARY

Moore (1916, p. 86) : [At times Shakespeare uses song to mark] the conclusion of a change in one of the characters, as when Caliban has fallen completely under the influence of drink and the wiles of man. ♦ Long (1961, pp. 120 f.) : Caliban makes his first bow as a musician ... when he sings his drunken praise of what he thinks is freedom. .... The imagination is staggered by an attempt to re-create Caliban's vocal effects. Just how would such a monster sing, particularly when in his cups? Certainly the quality of his music would be very poor. Perhaps he did not really sing, but, as Trinculo remarks, howled his song. ... As for the tune of Caliban's song, we shall make no effort here to supply what is best left to the imagination.

TEXTUAL COMMENTARY

1. **No ... fish**] Lee (ed. [1910–1914]) : A reference to the artificial fish weirs, in making which the aborigines of Virginia were very skilful. Ralph Lane describes how, on his visit to Virginia in 1586, he set the Indians to make weirs or dams in order to provide supplies of fish for food. The English explorers were unable to master the intricate manner of construction and often expressed fear that disaffected Indians might destroy the fish-dams and imperil a chief source of the colonists' sustenance. Cf. Hakluyt's *Voyages* [ed. Hakluyt Society, 1903–1905, VIII, 334–336]. Lane's account is too scant to be regarded as the certain source of Shakespeare's knowledge about fish-dams, but even if it was not known to Shakespeare it is interesting in itself:

The King [of the Indians] was ... disposed ... to have assuredly brought us to ruine in the moneth of March 1586. himselfe also with all his Savages to have runne away from us ... which if he had done ... wee coulde [not] have bene preserved from starving. ... For ... wee had no weares for fish, neither coulde our men skill of the making of them. ... [But finally we] wanne this resolution of him, that out of hand he should goe about, and withall, to cause his men to set up weares foorthwith for us. ♦

3. **scrape trenchering**] Malone (ed. 1790) **:** In our author's time trenchers were in general use; and male domesticks were sometimes employed in cleansing them. "I have helped," (says Lilly . . . ad. an. 1620,) "to carry eighteen tubs of water in one morning, weed the garden; all manner of drudgeries I willingly performed; scrape trenchers &c." [*The Lives of those Eminent Antiquaries Elias Ashmole, Esquire, and Mr. William Lilly* (1774, p. 12)]. ✦ Douce (1839, p. 11) **:** In *The Life of a Satyrical Pvppy called Nim*, 1657 [sig. C₆] . . . a citizen describes "How long he bore the *water-Tankard*, scrapt *Trenchers*, and made cleane shooes." ✦ White (ed. 1883) **:** *Trenchering*. So the old text. Caliban is drunk, and his tongue is entangled with the fag-ends of *firing* and *requiring*. ✦ New Arden (ind. ed. 1954) **:** Almost always altered to "trencher" on insufficient grounds; it means "trenchers" collectively (Onions); cf. "clothing", "housing". ✦

4. **Cacalyban**] Malone (ed. 1790) **:** Perhaps our author remembered a song of Sir P. Sidney's [in *The Countesse of Pembrokes Arcadia* (1598, sigs. 2S₃–2S₄)]:

> Fa la la leridan, dan dan dan deridan;
> Dan dan dan deridan derida dei:
> For no faire signe can credit winne,
> If that the substance faile within.

[Actually Sidney is employing a conventional song burthen of his time.] ✦ Noble (1923, p. 103) **:** An interesting feature of the song is the "Ban Ban Cacaliban", which, as we know, is a characteristic of the triumphal chorus among aboriginal savages in its emphasis and repetition of parts of a name. . . . It is highly improbable that Shakespeare had knowledge of the music of man in a primitive state, but it is evident he had observed the impromptu musical efforts of young untrained boys, who like savages make a chorus by emphasizing and repeating parts of a name. ✦ Arden (ind. ed. 1926) **:** Note the effect of intoxication. ✦ Brooke (1929, p. 130) **:** It is doubtful whether Shakespeare meant to indicate anything more than that Caliban, whom the stage direction commands to "sing drunkenly," was having difficulty with his articulation.

MUSIC

The earliest surviving music for Caliban's song is a setting by John Christopher Smith, about 1756, reprinted in Caulfield (n.d., I, 8). It is from Smith's operatic version of *The Tempest*, same date.

DRAMATIC FUNCTION

Little needs to be added to the views of the commentators. The song signalizes Caliban's revolt from the wise Prospero, and thereby illustrates the inferiority of his nature; he rebels only to put himself under the authority of the clown Stephano. "No more dams" is a burlesque of a revolutionary song, but whatever hints of "liberté, égalité, fraternité" it evinces are contradicted by its culinary imagery. Its revolt is the revolt of a kitchen scullion.

68

TEXT: Folio (1623), sig. A₆ᵛ (III.ii.130–132).
TYPOGRAPHY: Indented verse, italic face; s.d., *Sings*.

Flout 'em, and cout 'em: and skowt 'em, and flout 'em,
Thought is free.

GENERAL COMMENTARY

Long (1961, p. 121) : In III, ii, the befuddled conspirators attempt a more complex form of music; they try to sing a catch together. . . . The catch is one of the most simple forms of part song, but even so the three rascals cannot manage it. Ariel, invisible to the three, has to correct them by playing the tune on his pipe and tabor. While he plays the Pied Piper, he leads the rats off the scene.

TEXTUAL COMMENTARY

1. **Flout ... skowt**] Welch (1911, pp. 186 f.) finds the word *flout* etymologically interesting because of its close association in the context of the play with Ariel's pipe (flute) and tabor : The [French] verb *flagorner*, to flatter, or wheedle, is believed by etymologists to be derived from *flagoler*; to flatter being to pour agreeable sounds into a person's ear. But to flatter is to deceive, and so to mock or make sport of, and thus in Dutch the word *fluiten* signifies both to play the flute and to mock. In our own language 'to flute' has the same double meaning; but we pronounce 'flute' differently in its two senses: when we refer to music, we speak of 'fluting', when we talk of mockery, we call it 'flouting'. 'Flout' is a Middle English form of 'flute'. ◆ [*NED* confirms this etymology. The words *flout* and *scout* are virtually synonymous. For *flout NED* has "to mock, jeer, insult; to express contempt for"; and for *scout*, "to mock at, deride," citing this example as the earliest occurrence. Shakespeare uses *flout* frequently, but *scout* is a nonce usage in his plays.]

cout 'em] The editors of the fourth folio (1685) and most of the modern editors since Pope (1728) read *scout 'em*. But Ridley (ind. ed. [1935]) remarks : The New Cambridge editors are perhaps right in retaining F's *cout* for the first occurrence. *Cout* is a variant of 'colt,' *i.e.*, 'make a fool of,' and the second time F reads *skowt*. ◆ New Arden (ind. ed. 1954) : This justification of F is impugned by M. Hunter in *R. E. S.* II [1926]. 347, where it is claimed that "scout" is more suitable to a catch, and that "cout" as a variant of "colt" does not occur before the nineteenth century. Tannenbaum also takes this view; but it is still possible that "cout" had a pre-literary history, or that it is a nonce- and nonsense-word. ◆

2. **Thought ... free**] Arden (ind. ed. 1926) : Probably the burden of a song, quoted by Maria in *Twelfth Night* (I.iii.73) in a way that points to its meaning of

unfavourable or critical or hypocritical thought; and the freedom of such thought, as we gather from the whole play, is assumed only by such irresponsible bondage as that of Caliban, or by such moral bondage as that of his associates. ♦ [The expression is also proverbial; it is one of the epigrams in John Heywood's *Woorkes*, 1587 (sig. C₆ᵛ), and has been collected by W. G. Smith (1935, p. 489) and by Tilley (1950, T-244).]

MUSIC

The original music for this round is not known. Long (1961, p. 121) reproduces the music of a catch by John Hilton as suitable, but he does not attempt to set Shakespeare's words to it. The setting given by Caulfield (n.d., I, 15) is from J. C. Smith (n.d., pp. 72 f.).

DRAMATIC FUNCTION

The catch sung by Stephano and Trinculo—and probably also by Caliban, since he says the others have taught it to him earlier—is a mockery of a revolutionary song. Its radical sentiments would have seemed especially anarchic in Shakespeare's day when thought—particularly revolutionary thought—was certainly not free. It is worth noting that the irresponsible freethinking of Caliban leads him nowhere but to plans for the murder of his former master, Prospero.

69

TEXT: Folio (1623), sigs. B₁v–B₂ (IV.i.106–117).
TYPOGRAPHY: Indented verse, italic and roman face; s.d., *They Sing*.

Iu. Honor, riches, marriage, bleſſing,
Long continuance, and encreaſing,
Hourely ioyes, be ſtill vpon you,
Iuno ſings her bleſſings on you.
Earths increaſe, foyzon plentie,   5
Barnes, and Garners, neuer empty.
Vines, with cluſtring bunches growing,
Plants, wtth goodly burthen bowing:
Spring come to you at the fartheſt,
In the very end of Harueſt.   10
Scarcity and want ſhall ſhun you,
Ceres bleſſing ſo is on you.

GENERAL COMMENTARY

Moore (1916, p. 87) remarks in connection with this song the "surprisingly large number" of songs in Shakespeare's plays which serve for "pagan ritual," but notes the rigid censorship which prohibited Christian representations on the secular stage. Arden (ind. ed. 1926) : As to the uncouth rhymes . . . they are perhaps a little more remarkable than anywhere else in Shakespeare; but . . . the poet was probably out of rhyming practice, and impatient of it, by this time; and the masque [had it been composed, as some critics have supposed,] by a lower hand than his would have had better rhyme—but worse reason. ◆ New Arden (ind. ed. 1954) : *Juno pronuba* pronounces a marriage-blessing on the couple; then Ceres, the bounteous, endows them with her abundance. Or so it is agreed. But possibly "They sing" the whole song together. The rough rhyming of these lines has often been remarked upon. They are not without parallel; compare the octosyllabics of [*Measure for Measure* (III.ii.275 ff.)], which some editors wish to dispose of; and also the disastrous conclusion of [*Richard II* (V.vi.30 ff.)], which persuaded E. M. W. Tillyard that "he [Shakespeare] was never very good at the couplet." (*Shakespeare's History Plays* (1944), p. 245.) In fact these lines are far from being the doggerel that an unsympathetic criticism has called them. Their movement is expertly and variously solemn. ◆ Cutts (1958, p. 355) : The masque is built into the general fabric of the idea that music symbolizes the harmony of macrocosmos and microcosmos alike; it is a straightforward portrayal of music's function in blessing an intended marriage union, with the gods descending to confirm that blessing, which as the instigators of harmony they have the right to confer.

TEXTUAL COMMENTARY

1. **Iu.**] The presence of Juno at a marriage was supposed to augur success and happiness; see commentary on l. 1, song 24. In her share of the song Juno appropriately wishes Ferdinand and Miranda joy, honor, and blessing. The presence of Ceres, goddess of grain, is intended to insure the young couple fertility. Lines 5–12, with their harvest imagery, are especially appropriate to her, and must originally have been headed with a speech-prefix assigning this part of the song to her.

3. **still**] That is, always, continuously.

5. **Earths . . . plentie**] All the modern editors since Theobald (ed. 1740) have inserted the speech-prefix *Cer.* at the beginning of this line.

Earths increase] Malone (ed. 1790) : Earth's *increase*, is the produce of the earth. The expression is scriptural [Ps. lxvii:6]: "Then shall the *earth* bring forth her *increase*, and God, even our God, shall give us his blessing." ◆

foyzon plentie] The expression may be read two ways: *foison-plenty* or *foison, plenty*. The latter reading is supported by Gonzalo's line earlier in the play (II.i.162 f.),

> but nature should bring forth
> Of its own kind, all foison, all abundance.

8. **wtth**] The obvious typographical error was corrected by the editors of the second folio (1632).

9–10. **Spring . . . Haruest**] Halliwell (ed. 1853–1865) : That is, let Spring come to you as soon as the harvest is over, so that no winter shall intervene. ◆ Keightley (1860, pp. 65 f.) : [This line] is pure nonsense. Spring come at the end of harvest! But read *Shall* instead of *Spring*, and we at once get grammar and sense. But *Shall* is not like *Spring*. All I can say is, that not long since I sent *he went*, very legibly written, to a printer's, and it came back to me *the local*. ◆ Hudson (ed. 1880–1881) : [Halliwell's] explanation is sustained . . . by Amos, ix:13 [*The Holie Bible*, 1572]:

> Behold, the dayes comme, saith the Lord, that the plowman shal touche the mower, and the treader of grapes hym that soweth seede.

Also in *The Fairie Queene*, iii.6.42:

> There is continuall spring, and haruest there
> Continuall, both meeting at one time. ◆

New Arden (ind. ed. 1954) : Almost certainly the expression of a conventional wish for a Golden Age of winterless years, in which spring and autumn are simultaneous, or consecutive. ◆

12. **Ceres**] The compositor's failure to italicize this name may be related in some way to a dropped speech-prefix at l. 5. The name of Juno is italicized both as a speech prefix (l. 1) and in the text of the song (l. 4).

MUSIC

The original music for the song is not known. Long (1961, p. 124) has set the first four lines "to what seems to be a masque song by William Lawes, as it appears in

10—v.s.

the New York Public Library MS. Drexel 4257." The earliest setting recorded by
A List (1884, p. 58) is one by Signorina de Gamberini, entitled "The friendly wish
from Shakespeare," doubtfully dated 1785; it is second in a collection of "Twelve
English and Italian Songs" by de Gamberini in the B. M. music library. More
easily available is the setting by Linley (1816, I, 18–21).

DRAMATIC FUNCTION

The masque song is largely extraneous to the action of the play except insofar as
it looks forward to the happy union of Ferdinand and Miranda, and to the successful fulfillment of Prospero's plans. Like Ariel's "Where the bee sucks," this song
looks beyond the time and island-setting in which it occurs to a future brave new
world which is to be founded in the love of a newer, younger generation.

For modern tastes the masque episode in the play may seem artificial and stilted;
yet by the same criteria the play itself would have to be rejected: it is as much a
masque as any play Shakespeare wrote. It is filled with song, dance, and spectacle;
its language is, for the most part, formal and elevated rather than naturalistic; its
plot is thin, its subject matter deals with magic and romance, and its theme is
moral, even allegorical. It is not surprising that modern critics tend to interpret
the play in symbological terms, or compare it with Milton's *Comus*. Hence it
hardly seems too much to regard the scene in which this song occurs as a masque
within a masque.

Shakespeare's increasing use of masque-like elements in his later plays is certainly
due in part to the popularity of the masque as a dramatic form in the Jacobean
period. The passion of James I and his queen for this sort of spectacle is well known.
But the introduction of such episodes into Shakespearean drama cannot be
attributed to the tastes of the Court alone. Shakespeare had used brief masques
in his plays long before the death of Elizabeth (for example, in *Midsummer Night's
Dream*, *Twelfth Night*, *Much Ado*, and *As You Like It*), and if the court-entertainments
after the accession of James influenced him, their influence was rather to increase
the importance of masques in his plays—as, for example, in *Cymbeline*, *Winter's
Tale*, and *The Tempest*—rather than merely to introduce the playwright to the
form. Finally, Shakespeare was fully aware, even as popular modern playwrights
are, of the importance of theatrical spectacle.

70

TEXT: Folio (1623), sig. B₃ (V.i.88–94).
TYPOGRAPHY: Indented verse, italic face; s.d., *Ariell ſings*.

> *Where the Bee ſucks, there ſuck I,*
> *In a Cowſlips bell, I lie,*
> *There I cowch when Owles doe crie,*
> *On the Batts backe I doe flie*
> *after Sommer merrily.*
> *Merrily, merrily, ſhall I liue now,*
> *Vnder the bloſſom that hangs on the Bow.*

GENERAL COMMENTARY

Capell ([1779–1783?], II, pt. 4, pp. 70 f.) : The pointing of Ariel's *song* . . . is . . . bad . . . in every edition . . . [but] under [the present editor's] punctuation, the *song* recovers its beauties and has perfect consistency. All the thoughts of it turn upon Ariel's approaching happiness, in that he should now be able to pursue the "*summer*," and live upon the more delicate productions of it; pleasures he had long been depriv'd of . . . and to paint his eager relish of them, he is made to express himself as if in actual possession. . . . [In using the word *couch* Shakespeare makes us] conceive more strongly the extream minuteness of this Being, which can thus nestle itself whole in the cup of such a small flower:—but when *winter* begins to come—here signify'd by the hooting of the owl, he makes the bat his post-horse to follow summer into some other land. ✦ Moore (1916, pp. 101 f.) : In at least one case [a song in Shakespeare's plays] projects our imaginations not merely into the next scene or act, but beyond the end of the play into the future which is yet unrevealed. Ariel . . . is allowed, after Prospero has again promised his freedom, to give us a glimpse of his fairy life in the years that are to come. ✦ Noble (1923, pp. 100 f.) : While he is attiring Prospero and just as he is about to be freed . . . [Ariel] sings of himself and as if to himself. Where the bee sucks, there Ariel derives the nectar which sustains him; he reposes in the cowslip safe from the owls; he rides on the bat after sunset in pursuit of summer and he lives under cover of the blossom that hangs on the bough. Such an ideal life in such a few words. It is this brevity and speed of development which distinguish Shakespeare's songs from all others. ✦ Stenberg (1927, p. 153) suggests that there is a parallel to this song-episode in Richard Edwards' *Damon and Pithias*, 1571. He quotes Damon's remark (sig. H₃) to his bondman Stephano, "Stephano, for thy good seruice, be thou free," and compares it with Prospero's words to Ariel, "Thou shalt ere long be free." With Ariel's song he juxtaposes Stephano's speech, beginning, "O most happie, pleasant, ioyfull, and triumphant day." But the commonplace situation of a master freeing a bondservant is enough to explain the equally commonplace parallels in statement and reply. ◆ Arden (ind. ed. 1926) **:** The purport of the song is, "I am bee-like; I can creep into a cowslip's bell, as I do if the owl is near; when the bat leaves at the end of summer, I go with him on his back; therefore I shall have eternal summer, and shall live ever among the flowers." ◆ New Arden (ind. ed. 1954) **:** There are no real difficulties in this song, but many have been invented. Ariel sings entirely as a fairy diminutive. . . . He sleeps, or shelters, in cowslips, and pursues the summer with the bat. Theobald prefers *sunset* to *summer*, on the ground that bats do not migrate, but . . . it is quite likely that the Elizabethans thought they did. ◆ Cutts (1958, p. 357) **:** The island's music, signifying the harmony from which the banishment from Milan in the first place had been a serious comic aberration, and signifying the harmony to which all discord, strife, disunion and evil intentions have been resolved, is finally dismissed in Ariel's paean of sheer joy at release for his service to Prospero.

TEXTUAL COMMENTARY

1. **suck**] Theobald (ed. 1740) emends to *lurk* **:** I have ventur'd to vary from the printed Copies here. Could *Ariel*, a Spirit of a refin'd aetherial Essence, be intended to want food? Besides, the sequent lines rather countenance *lurk*. ◆

2. **Cowslips**] The common name of *Primula veris*, a familiar pasture and meadow wildflower, bright yellow in color, and one of the earliest blooming spring flowers.

4–5. **On . . . merrily**] Theobald (ed. 1740) **:** Why, *after* Summer? Unless we must suppose, our Author alluded to that mistaken Notion of Bats, Swallows &c. crossing the Seas in pursuit of hot Weather. I conjectur'd, in my *Shakespeare restor'd*, that Sunset was our Author's word. . . . My Reasons for the Change were from the known Nature of the Bat. ◆ Warburton (ed. 1747) **:** Mr. *Theobald* has substituted *Sun-set*, because *Ariel* talks of riding on the Bat in his expedition. An idle fancy. That circumstance is given only to design the *time of night* in which fairies travel. . . . Ariel . . . was confined to the Island Winter and Summer. But the roughness of Winter is represented by *Shakespeare* as disagreeable to fairies, and such like delicate spirits, who on this account constantly follow Summer. ◆ Malone (ed. 1790) **:** Though the bat is "no bird of passage," Shakespeare probably meant to express what Dr. Warburton supposes. A short account, however, of this winged animal may perhaps prove the best illustration of the passage before us [Malone quotes Oliver Goldsmith's *An History of the Earth and Animated Nature* (1774, IV, 136 f.)]:

> This species of the bat is very common in England. It makes its first appearance early in summer, and begins its flight in the dusk of the evening. . . . It appears only in the most pleasant evenings. . . . At other times it continues in its retreat; the chink of a ruined building, or the hollow of a tree . . . never venturing out by daylight, nor in rainy weather; never hunting in quest of prey, but for a small part of the night, and then returning to its hole. But its short life is still more abridged by continuing in a torpid state during the winter.

¶ [And Malone continues:] When Shakespeare had determined to send Ariel in pursuit of summer, wherever it could be found, as most congenial to such an airy being, is it then surprising that he should have made the *bat*, rather than "the wind his post-horse"? ♦ Noble (1923, p. 101) **:** We may waive the fact that the bat is not a migratory creature; drama does not pretend to expound natural history with scientific exactitude, and moreover the island on which Ariel lived was not one where nature existed in its usual order.

MUSIC

What is probably the original music for the song survives in three early manuscripts and three early printed songbooks: Birmingham City Reference Library MS. 57,316, Bodleian Library MS. Don. c. 57 (fol. 139), Folger Library MS. 747.1 (fols. 9ᵛ–13ᵛ), John Playford's *Select Ayres and Dialogues for One, Two, and Three Voyces; to the Theorbo-Lvte or Basse Violl* (1659, sig. 2B₁ᵛ), John Wilson's *Cheerfull Ayres or Ballads* (1660, sigs. B₄ᵛ–C₁), and Playford's *Catch that Catch can: Or The Musical Companion* (1667, sigs. R₃ᵛ–R₄).

There is a scholarly modern edition of the song in Spink (1961, pp. 26 f.). Cutts (1959, *Musique*, p. 25) gives his transcription of the Birmingham MS. version which he discovered, and Long (1961, p. 127) prints his arrangement of the Bodleian MS. song and (p. 147) a facsimile of his source. The popular editions of the tune derive from the early printed texts, chiefly Wilson's *Cheerfull Ayres*: Bridge (n.d., pp. 21 f.), Elson (1901, pp. 184–186), Vincent (1906, pp. 27 f.), Kimmins (1928, pp. 33 f.), Hardy (1930, p. 19), Gibbon (1930, p. 120), Bontoux (1936, p. 328), and New Arden (ind. ed. 1954, 1958, p. 158).

Both of Playford's songbooks ascribe the song to John Wilson, as do the Bodleian MS. and (indirectly) the Folger MS. which is titled "John Wilson's Tempest music." Yet the song is certainly by Robert Johnson (158- ?–1634 ?), for his name is signed to it in the Birmingham MS., and Wilson himself attributes the song to Johnson in his own *Cheerfull Ayres*. The misascriptions to Wilson are easily explained. In publishing *Cheerfull Ayres* Wilson was reproducing Johnson's song, but with music for two additional voices composed by himself. To these he signs his own name. The attribution of the song to Wilson in the Playford books is doubtless due to nothing more than the fact that, when they were published at the Restoration, Wilson's name (he was Professor of Music at Oxford) had more commercial value than Johnson's.

DRAMATIC FUNCTION

Ariel's final song is a lyrical *coda* to the entire play. The tempest, moral as well as natural, is past. Miranda and Ferdinand are to be joined in marriage; father has been restored to son and son to father; Prospero has found that "the rarer action is In virtue than in vengeance," and, although his enemies were in his power, has chosen mercy rather than justice. If an epigraph may be borrowed from so unlikely a play as *Twelfth Night* (III.iv.419), "Tempests," indeed, "are kind, and salt waves fresh in love!"

For the brave new world of redeemed man which is to succeed on the old one of crime and punishment there could hardly be a better hymn of praise than Ariel's song of summer and freedom. It is not only Ariel who has been set free; in the symbolic message of the play man himself has been released from the fetters of his most ancient bondage.

BIBLIOGRAPHY

GENERAL INDEX

INDEX OF FIRST LINES

Bibliography

WORKS OF WILLIAM SHAKESPEARE

I. SIXTEENTH- AND SEVENTEENTH-CENTURY EDITIONS

The works below are arranged alphabetically by their modern short-titles; complete editions of the plays are followed by the separate editions of the plays and poems.

Comedies, Histories, & Tragedies, 1623, 1632, 1664, 1685; STC 22273, STC 22274, Wing S2914, Wing S2915.

Hamlet, 1603, 1604; STC 22275, STC 22276.
2 Henry IV, 1600, STC 22288.
King Lear, 1608, 1608 [1619]; STC 22292, STC 22293.
Love's Labor's Lost, 1598, STC 22294.
The Merchant of Venice, 1600, STC 22296.
The Merry Wives of Windsor, 1602, 1619; STC 22299, STC 22300.
A Midsummer Night's Dream, 1600, 1600 [1619]; STC 22302, STC 22303.
Much Ado about Nothing, 1600, STC 22304.
Othello, 1622, 1630, 1655; STC 22305, STC 22306, Wing S2939.
The Passionate Pilgrim, 1599, STC 22342.
Poems: written by Wil. Shake-speare, Gent., 1640 [the Cotes-Benson edition], STC 22344.
The Rape of Lucrece, 1594, STC 22345.
Romeo and Juliet, 1597, 1599; STC 22322, STC 22323.
The Sonnets, 1609, STC 22353.
The Two Noble Kinsmen, 1634, STC 11075.
Troilus and Cressida, 1609, STC 22332.
Venus and Adonis, 1593, STC 22354.

II. COMPLETE EDITIONS SINCE 1709

In the following list, complete editions of the works or plays by the modern editors are arranged by date of the final volume.

Rowe (1709). *The Works of Mr. William Shakespeare; In Six Volumes. Adorn'd with Cuts. Revis'd and Corrected, with an Account of the Life and Writings of the Author....* London: *Printed for Jacob Tonson, within Grays-Inn Gate, next Grays-Inn Lane*, ed. Nicholas Rowe. A seventh volume, of the poems, was printed for E. Curll and E. Sanger in 1710; the notes of this volume are by Charles Gildon.

Pope (1728). *The Works of Shakespeare. In Eight Volumes.... The Second Edition ... London: ... Printed for J. Tonson*, ed. Alexander Pope.

Theobald (1740). *The Works of Shakespeare: in Eight Volumes. Collated with the Oldest Copies, and Corrected: With Notes, Explanatory, and Critical.... The Second Edition....* London: *Printed for H. Lintott, C. Hitch, J. and R. Tonson, C. Corbet, R. and B. Wellington, J. Brindley, and E. New*, ed. Lewis Theobald.

Warburton (1747). *The Works of Shakespeare in Eight Volumes. . . . With a Comment and Notes, Critical and Explanatory. By Mr. Pope and Mr. Warburton. . . . London*, ed. William Warburton.

Johnson (1765). *The Plays of William Shakespeare in Eight Volumes*, ed. Samuel Johnson, London.

Capell ([1767–1768]). *Mr. William Shakespeare his Comedies, Histories, and Tragedies*, ed. Edward Capell, 10 vols. [London].

Hanmer (1770–1771). *The Works of Shakespeare. In Six Volumes. The Second Edition*, ed. Thomas Hanmer, Oxford.

Malone (1790). *The Plays and Poems of William Shakespeare, in ten volumes*, ed. Edmond Malone, London.

Steevens (1793). *The Plays of William Shakespeare. In Fifteen Volumes*, ed. George Steevens and Isaac Reed, London.

Reed (1813). *The Plays of William Shakespeare. In Twenty-one Volumes*, ed. Isaac Reed, London.

Variorum (1821). *The Plays and Poems of William Shakespeare. By the Late Edmond Malone*, ed. James Boswell, 21 vols., London.

Knight ([1838–1843]). *The Pictorial Edition of the Works of Shakespeare*, ed. Charles Knight [7 vols.], London. Issued as vols. I–II of Tragedies, I–II of Histories, and I–II of Comedies, with a final volume for remaining plays and index.

Staunton (1858–1860). *The Plays of Shakespeare*, ed. Howard Staunton, 3 vols., London.

Halliwell (1853–1865). *The Works of William Shakespeare*, ed. James O. Halliwell, 16 vols., London.

Cambridge (1863–1866). *The Works of William Shakespeare*, ed. William George Clark, John Glover, and William Aldis Wright, 9 vols., Cambridge and London.

Devrient (1873–1876). *Deutscher Bühnen und Familien Shakespeare*, ed. Eduard and Otto Devrient, 6 vols., Leipzig.

Dyce (1875–1876). *The Works of William Shakespeare*, ed. Alexander Dyce, 9 vols., London.

Collier (1878). *The Plays and Poems of William Shakespeare*, ed. John Payne Collier, 8 vols., London.

Hudson (1880–1881). *The Complete Works of William Shakespeare*, ed. H. N. Hudson, 20 vols., Boston.

White (1883). *Mr. William Shakespeare's Comedies Histories Tragedies and Poems*, ed. Richard Grant White [6 vols.], Boston. Issued as two volumes each of Comedies, Histories, and Tragedies.

Oxford ([1892]). *The Complete Works of William Shakespeare*, ed. W. J. Craig, Oxford.

Herford (1899). *The Works of Shakespeare*, ed. C. H. Herford, 10 vols., London.

Lee ([1910–1914]). *The Caxton Edition of the Complete Works of William Shakespeare*, ed. Sidney Lee, 20 vols., Caxton Publishing Co., London. This is a reissue of the *University Press Shakespeare, Renaissance Edition*, 40 vols., John Murray, London, 1906–1909.

Kittredge (1936). *The Complete Works of Shakespeare*, ed. George Lyman Kittredge, Ginn & Co., Boston.

Neilson (1942). *The Complete Plays and Poems of William Shakespeare*, ed. William Allen Neilson and Charles Jarvis Hill, Houghton Mifflin Co., Boston.

III. INDIVIDUAL EDITIONS OF THE PLAYS OR POEMS

The arrangement of the separate modern editions below is alphabetically and by date.

All's Well that Ends Well
  New Cambridge (1929), ed. A. Quiller-Couch and J. D. Wilson, Cambridge University Press, Cambridge, England.

Antony and Cleopatra
  New Arden (1954, 1956), ed. M. R. Ridley, Methuen & Co., Ltd., London; Harvard University Press, Cambridge, Mass.

As You Like It
  New Variorum (1890), ed. H. H. Furness, Philadelphia.
  Arden (1920), ed. J. W. Holme, Methuen & Co. Ltd., London.
  New Cambridge (1926), ed. A. Quiller-Couch and J. D. Wilson, Cambridge University Press, Cambridge, England.
  Kittredge (1939), ed. G. L. Kittredge, Ginn & Co., Boston.

Cymbeline
  New Variorum (1913), ed. H. H. Furness, J. B. Lippincott Co., Philadelphia.

Hamlet
  Arden (1928), ed. E. Dowden, Methuen & Co., Ltd., London.
  New Cambridge (1934), ed. A. Quiller-Couch and J. D. Wilson, Cambridge University Press, Cambridge, England.
  Kittredge (1939), ed. G. L. Kittredge, Ginn & Co., Boston.

2 Henry IV
  Arden (1923), ed. R. P. Cowl, Methuen & Co., Ltd., London.

King Lear
  Arden (1927), ed. W. J. Craig, Methuen & Co., Ltd., London.
  Kittredge (1940), ed. G. L. Kittredge, Ginn & Co., Boston.
  New Arden (1959), ed. K. Muir, Harvard University Press, Cambridge, Mass.

Love's Labor's Lost
  New Cambridge (1923), ed. A. Quiller-Couch and J. D. Wilson, Cambridge University Press, Cambridge, England.
  Arden (1930), ed. H. C. Hart, Methuen & Co., Ltd., London.
  New Arden (1951), ed. R. David, Methuen & Co., Ltd., London.

Measure for Measure
  New Cambridge (1950), ed. J. D. Wilson, Cambridge University Press, Cambridge, England.

The Merchant of Venice
  Arden (1927), ed. C. K. Pooler, Methuen & Co., Ltd., London.
  New Arden (1955), ed. J. R. Brown, Methuen & Co., Ltd., London.

A Midsummer Night's Dream
  Arden (1930), ed. H. Cunningham, Methuen & Co., Ltd., London.

Much Ado about Nothing
  Yale (1917), ed. C. F. T. Brooke, Yale University Press, New Haven, Conn.
  New Cambridge (1923), ed. A. Quiller-Couch and J. D. Wilson, Cambridge University Press, Cambridge, England.
  Arden (1924), ed. G. R. Trenery, Methuen & Co., Ltd., London.
  Kittredge (1941), ed. G. L. Kittredge, Ginn & Co., Boston.

Othello
  Arden (1928), ed. H. C. Hart, Methuen & Co., Ltd., London.
  New Arden (1958, 1962), ed. M. R. Ridley, Methuen & Co., Ltd., London; Harvard University Press, Cambridge, Mass.

The Poems
New Variorum (1938), ed. H. E. Rollins, J. B. Lippincott Co., Philadelphia.

Romeo and Juliet
New Variorum (1871), ed. H. H. Furness, Philadelphia.

The Sonnets
New Variorum (1944), ed. H. E. Rollins, 2 vols., J. B. Lippincott Co., Philadelphia.

The Tempest
New Cambridge (1921), ed. A. Quiller-Couch and J. D. Wilson, Cambridge University Press, Cambridge, England.
Arden (1926), ed. M. Luce, Methuen & Co., Ltd., London.
New Temple ([1935]), ed. M. R. Ridley, J. M. Dent and Sons, Ltd., London; E. P. Dutton & Co., New York.
New Arden (1954, 1958), ed. F. Kermode, Harvard University Press, Cambridge, Mass.

Troilus and Cressida
Arden (1922), ed. K. Deighton, Methuen & Co., Ltd., London.
New Variorum (1953), ed. H. N. Hillebrand and T. W. Baldwin, J. B. Lippincott Co., Philadelphia.

Twelfth Night
New Variorum (1901), ed. H. H. Furness, J. B. Lippincott Co., Philadelphia.
Arden (1929), ed. M. Luce, Methuen & Co., Ltd., London.
New Cambridge (1930), ed. A. Quiller-Couch and J. D. Wilson, Cambridge University Press, Cambridge, England.
Kittredge (1941), ed. G. L. Kittredge, Ginn & Co., Boston.

The Two Gentlemen of Verona
New Cambridge (1921), ed. A. Quiller-Couch and J. D. Wilson, Cambridge University Press, Cambridge, England.
Arden (1925), ed. R. W. Bond, Methuen & Co., Ltd., London.

The Winter's Tale
New Variorum (1898), ed. H. H. Furness, Philadelphia.
Arden (1922), ed. F. W. Moorman, Methuen & Co., Ltd., London.
New Cambridge (1950), ed. J. D. Wilson, Cambridge University Press, Cambridge, England.
New Arden (1963), ed. J. H. P. Pafford, Harvard University Press, Cambridge, Mass.

OTHER WORKS CITED IN THE COMMENTARY

Bibliographical Note

In the bibliography which follows, the works are arranged alphabetically by the last name of the author or editor. Multiple entries for a single author or editor are arranged chronologically under his name. Anonymous works are entered alphabetically under the first word (other than an article) of their title. Works signed only by initials are alphabetized according to the first initial. The spelling of *Shakespeare, Shakespeare's,* and

Shakespearean has been regularized throughout. The original orthography of titles has been preserved, with the exception of f and vv which have been normalized to s and w. The entries for rare books dating between 1475–1640 are followed by their STC number in Pollard and Redgrave's *Short-Title Catalogue*; books dating from 1641–1700 are followed by their number in Wing's *Short-Title Catalogue*. In a few instances rare books published after 1700 are further identified by their British Museum press marks.

Table of Abbreviations

B. M.	British Museum
DUJ	*Durham University Journal*
JAMS	*Journal of the American Musicological Society*
MLJ	*Modern Language Journal*
MLN	*Modern Language Notes*
MLR	*Modern Language Review*
NQ	*Notes and Queries*
PMLA	*Publications of the Modern Language Society of America*
RN	*Renaissance News*
SP	*Studies in Philology*
SQ	*Shakespeare Quarterly*
SS	*Shakespeare Survey*
TLS	*Times Literary Supplement*

A. A., 1859, "Ducdame.–As You Like It, Act II. Sc. 5," *NQ*, 8:284.
—— 1876, "King Stephen Was a Worthy Peer," *NQ*, 5:358.
A List. See Greenhill, J., et al., 1884.
Abbott, E. A., 1884, *A Shakespearean Grammar*, London.
Alexander, George, 1866, *Maver's Collection of Genuine Scottish Melodies*, 2 vols., Glasgow.
Allen, Percy, 1934, "Ducdame, Ducdame," *TLS*, 22 February, p. 126.
Andreas Capellanus, n.d. [*De arte amandi*], *Incipiunt tituli capitulorum tractatus amoris & de amoris remedio Andree Capellani pape jnnocencij quarti. Et habet iiij partes* [Strasburg, 1473/4 ?]. See also Parry, John J., ed. and tr., 1941.
Andrews, Hilda, ed., 1926, *My Ladye Nevells Booke*, J. Curwen and Sons, London and Philadelphia; n.d., New York.
An Antidote against Melancholy: Made up in Pills, 1661, London, Wing D66a.
Arber, Edward, ed., 1875–1894, *A Transcript of the Registers of the Company of Stationers of London (1554–1640)*, 5 vols., London.
Arkwright, G. E. P., 1954, "John Wilson," *Grove's Dictionary of Music and Musicians*, ed. Eric Blom, 9:311–313, Macmillan & Co., Ltd., London; St. Martin's Press, New York.
Armin, Robert, 1608, *A Nest of Ninnies*, London, STC 775. See also Collier, J. Payne, ed., 1842.
Atkinson, A. D., 1949, "Full Fathom Five," *NQ*, 194:465–468, 493–495.
Auden, Wystan H., 1957, "Music in Shakespeare, Its Dramatic Use in His Plays," *Encounter*, December, pp. 31–44. Also in The Dyer's Hand, Faber & Faber, Ltd., London; Random House, Inc., New York, 1957.
BB The Bagford Ballad Collection in the British Museum.
Bacchus Bountie. See Foulface, Phillip, *pseud.*, 1593.
Bacon, Francis, 1605, *The Two Bookes of Francis Bacon. Of the proficience and aduancement of Learning, diuine and humane*, London, STC 1164.
Baldwin, T. W., 1944, *William Shakespeare's Small Latine & Lesse Greeke*, 2 vols., University of Illinois Press, Urbana, Ill.

Banister, John, J. Hart, and Pelham Humphrey, n.d., *The Ariels Songs in the Play call'd the Tempest*, London [1670 ?], no Wing entry.

Bantock, Granville, and H. Orsmond Anderton, eds., 1916, *The Melvill Book of Roundels*, The Roxburghe Club, London.

Barber, C. L., 1959, *Shakespeare's Festive Comedy*, Princeton University Press, Princeton, N. J.

Barley, William, 1596, *A new Booke of Tabliture*, London, STC 1433.

Barrey, David Lodowick, 1611, *Ram-Alley: Or Merrie-Trickes*, London, STC 1502.

Bartlett, John, 1896, *A New and Complete Concordance or Verbal Index to Words, Phrases, & Passages in the Dramatic Works of Shakespeare, with A Supplementary Concordance to the Poems*, New York.

Barton, D. P., 1929, *Links between Shakespeare and the Law*, Faber and Gwyer, London.

Baskervill, Charles Read, 1921, "English Songs on the Night Visit," *PMLA*, 36:565–614.

—— 1923, "Bassanio as an Ideal Lover," *The Manly Anniversary Studies in Language and Literature*, pp. 90–103, University of Chicago Press, Chicago, Ill.

—— ed., 1929, *The Elizabethan Jig and Related Song Drama*, University of Chicago Press, Chicago, Ill.

Bateson, Frederick W., ed., 1930, *The Works of William Congreve*, Peter Davies, London.

Beaumont, Francis, and John Fletcher, 1613, *The Knight of the Burning Pestle*, London, STC 1674.

—— 1620, *Phylaster. Or, Love lyes a Bleeding*, London, STC 1681.

—— 1647, *Comedies and Tragedies*, London, Wing B1581. See also Waller, A. R., and Arnold Glover, eds., 1905–1912.

Beaumont, Joseph. See Grosart, A. B., ed., 1880.

Beck, Sydney, 1953, "The Case of 'O Mistresse mine'," *RN*, 6:19–23.

—— ed., 1959, *The First Book of Consort Lessons Collected by Thomas Morley 1599 & 1611*, New York Public Library, New York.

Beisly, Sidney, 1864, *Shakespeare's Garden*, London.

Belchier, Daubridgecourt, 1618, *Hans Beer-Pot His Invisible Comedie*, London, STC 1803.

Bennett, Josephine W., 1941, "Early Texts of Two of Ralegh's Poems," *The Huntington Library Quarterly*, 4:469–475.

Bethell, S. L., n.d., *The Winter's Tale: A Study*, Staples Press, London [1947].

Bible, The, 1572. See *The Holie Bible*.

Bidpai. See North, Thomas, tr., 1570.

Billington, Thomas, n.d., *A Second Set of Glees for Three, Four & Five Voices, Selected from the Scots Songs, to which is added Airs by Handel and Arne, harmonized by T. Billington*, London [1790 ?].

Birch, William, n.d., *The complaint of a sinner, vexed with paine, Desyring the ioye, that euer shall remayne. After W. E. moralized*, London [1563], STC 3076.

Bloom, J. Harvey, 1903, *Shakespeare's Garden*, Methuen & Co., London.

Blount, Edward, ed., 1632, *Sixe Covrt Comedies*, London, STC 17088.

Bond, R. Warwick, ed., 1902, *The Complete Works of John Lyly*, 3 vols., The Clarendon Press, Oxford.

Bontoux, Germaine, 1936, *La Chanson en Angleterre au Temps d'Élisabeth*, Oxford University Press, Oxford.

Boswell, James, ed., 1821. See *Works of William Shakespeare*, II, Variorum (1821).

Bourke, John G., 1891, *Scatalogic Rites of All Nations*, Washington, D. C.

Boyle, Robert, 1902, "Troilus and Cressida," *Englische Studien*, 30:21–59.

Bradley, A. C., 1904, *Shakespearean Tragedy*, Macmillan and Co., London.

—— 1916, "Feste the Jester," *A Book of Homage to Shakespeare*, ed. Israel Gollancz, pp. 164–169, Oxford University Press, Oxford.

Brand, John, 1870, *Observations on Popular Antiquities*, ed. and rev. W. Carew Hazlitt, 3 vols., London.

—— 1900, *Observations on Popular Antiquities*, with additions by Henry Ellis, Chatto & Windus, London.

Bremner, Robert, n.d., *Thirty Scots Songs for a Voice & Harpsichord*, Edinburgh [1757]. B. M. press mark G.802.b.

—— n.d., *Thirty Scots Songs Adapted for a Voice and Harpsichord*, 2 vols., London [ca. 1759, 1770 ?].

Brennecke, Ernest, Jr., 1939, "Shakespeare's Musical Collaboration with Morley," *PMLA*, 54:139–149.

—— 1952, "What Shall He Have That Killed the Deer ?," *The Musical Times*, 93:347–351.

—— 1953, "'Nay, That's Not Next!'," *SQ*, 4:35–38.

Breton, Nicholas, 1597, *The Arbor of amorous Deuises*, London, STC 3631. See also Rollins, Hyder E., ed., 1936.

—— 1597, *Wits Trenchmour, In a conference had betwixt a Scholler and an Angler*, London, STC 3713. See also Grosart, A. B., ed. [1879].

Bridge, J. Frederick, ed., n.d., *Songs from Shakespeare. The Earliest Known Settings*, London [1894 ?].

—— ed., 1923, *Shakespearean Music in the Plays and Early Operas*, J. M. Dent & Sons, London.

Bridgewater, Leslie, and Hugh Mellor, eds., 1933, *The English Dancing Master*, a photographic facsimile, H. Mellor, London.

Britten, James, and Robert Holland, 1886, *A Dictionary of English Plant-Names*, London.

Bronson, Bertrand H., 1948, "Daisies Pied and Icicles," *MLN*, 63:35–38.

Brooke, C. F. Tucker, ed., 1910, *The Works of Christopher Marlowe*, Clarendon Press, Oxford.

—— ed., 1929, *The Shakespeare Songs*, W. Morrow & Co., New York.

Brooks, Cleanth, 1948, "Irony and 'Ironic' Poetry," *The English Journal*, 37:57–63; *College English*, 9:231–237.

Brougham, Eleanor, ed., n.d., *Corn from Olde Fieldes*, John Lane, London [1918].

Brown, Carleton, ed., 1932, *English Lyrics of the XIIIth Century*, Clarendon Press, London.

Brown, James Walter, 1920, "An Elizabethan Song Cycle," *Cornhill Magazine*, 48:572–579.

—— 1921, "Some Elizabethan Lyrics," *Cornhill Magazine*, 51:285–296.

Brown, John R., 1959, "The Riddle Song in 'The Merchant of Venice'," *NQ*, 204:235.

Browne, William, n.d., *Britannia's Pastorals*, London [1613], STC 3914.

Brussel, Jack. See Wooldridge, H. Ellis, ed., 1893.

Bullen, A. H., ed., 1885–1886, *The Works of Thomas Middleton*, 8 vols., London.

Butler, H. E., ed. and tr., 1952, *Propertius*, Harvard University Press, Cambridge, Mass.

C. A. W., 1873, "Shakespeariana: Cymbeline, II.3: Mary-Buds," *NQ*, 12:363.

C. T., 1605, *Laugh and Lie Downe: Or, The Worldes Folly*, London, no STC entry.

Camden, William, 1605, *Remaines of A Greater Worke, Concerning Britaine*, London, STC 4521.

Capell, Edward, n.d., *Notes and Various Readings to Shakespeare*, 3 vols., London [1779–1783 ?].

—— n.d., *The School of Shakespeare: or, authentic extracts from divers English books, that were in print in that author's time*, London [1781–1783 ?]. Vol. III to *Notes and Various Readings*.

Castiglione, Baldassare, n.d., *Il Libro del cortegiano* [Venice, 1528]. See also Hoby, Thomas, tr., 1561.

Catch that Catch can, 1652. See Hilton, John, ed., 1652, and Playford, John, ed., 1667, 1673.

Catullus. See Cornish, F. W., ed. and tr. [1912], 1939.

Caulfield, John, n.d., *A Collection of the Vocal Music in Shakespeare's Plays, Including the Whole of the Songs, Duetts, Glees, Choruses, &c.*, 2 vols., London [1864].

Chambers, E. K., 1903, *The Medieval Stage*, 2 vols., Clarendon Press, Oxford.

—— 1930, *William Shakespeare. A Study of Facts and Problems*, 2 vols., Clarendon Press, Oxford.

—— 1947, *English Literature at the Close of the Middle Ages*, Clarendon Press, Oxford.

—— 1951, *The Elizabethan Stage*, 4 vols., Clarendon Press, Oxford.

Chambers, H. A., 1957, *A Shakespeare Song Book*, Blandford Press, London.

Chambers, Robert, 1862, 1890, *The Songs of Scotland Prior to Burns*, Edinburgh.

Chapman, George, 1605, *Al Fooles*, London, STC 4963.

—— *Works*. See Parrott, T. M., ed., 1910–1914.

Chappell, William, 1840, *A Collection of National English Airs*, 2 vols., London.

—— n.d., *Popular Music of the Olden Time*, 2 vols., London [1855–1859].

—— 1876, "King Stephen Was A Worthy Peer," *NQ*, 5:250.

—— ed., 1871–1880, *The Roxburghe Ballads*, 3 vols. [of 9], London. See also Ebsworth, J. W., ed., 1883–1899.

Chaucer, Geoffrey, *Works*. See Robinson, Fred N., ed., 1957.

Chettle, Henry, n.d., *Kind-Harts Dreame*, London [1593], STC 5123.

Chilcot, Thomas, n.d., *Twelve English Songs, with their Symphonies*, London [1750 ?].

Child, Francis James, ed., 1882–1898, *The English and Scottish Popular Ballads*, 10 pts., Boston, Mass.

Choice, Chance, and Change: Or, Conceites in their Colours, 1606, London, STC 5142.

Choyce Drollery: Songs & Sonnets, 1656, London, Wing C3916.

Churchyard, Thomas, 1595, *A Musicall Consort of Heauenly harmonie . . . called Churchyards Charitie*, London, STC 5245.

Clemen, Wolfgang H., 1951, *The Development of Shakespeare's Imagery*, Harvard University Press, Cambridge, Mass.

Coleridge, Samuel Taylor, Shakespearean criticism. See Raysor, Thomas M., ed., 1930,

Collier, J. Payne, ed., 1841, *Memoirs of Edward Alleyn*, London.

—— 1842, *Fools and Jesters: with a Reprint of Robert Armin's Nest of Ninnies 1608*. London.

—— 1845, "John Wilson, the singer, in 'Much ado about Nothing', a musical composer in Shakespeare's Plays," *Shakespeare Society's Papers*, 2:33–36.

—— 1853, *Notes and Emendations to the Text of Shakespeare's Plays, from Early Manuscript Corrections in a Copy-of-the-Folio, 1632*, London.

Collmann, H. L., ed., 1912, *Ballads and Broadsides, chiefly of the Elizabethan Period*, Roxburghe Club, Horace Hart, Oxford.

Ane compendious Buik. of Godly and Spirituall Sangis, 1600, Edinburgh, STC 2997. A later edition of *Gude and Godlie Ballatis*, 1567, Edinburgh; no STC entry.

Congreve, William, *Works*. See Bateson, Frederick W., ed., 1930.

Connelly, Joseph, 1957, *Hymns of the Roman Liturgy*, Newman Press, Westminster, Md.

Corin, Fernand, 1959, "A Note on the Dirge in Cymbeline," *English Studies*, 40:173–179.

Corkine, William, 1612, *The Second Booke of Ayres*, London, STC 5769.

Cornish, F. W., ed. and tr. [1912], 1939, *Catullus, Tibullus, and Pervigilium Veneris*, Harvard University Press, Cambridge, Mass.

Cotes-Benson, 1640. See Works of William Shakespeare, I, *Poems*.

Cotgrave, Randle, 1611, 1632, *A Dictionarie of the French and English Tongues*, London, STC 5830, STC 5831.

Coverdale, Miles, 1564, *Certain most godly, fruitful, and comfortable letters of such true*

Saintes and holy Martyrs of God, as . . . gaue their lyues for the defence of Christes holy gospel, London, STC 5886.

Craig, Alexander, 1606, *The Amorose Songes, Sonets, and Elegies*, London, STC 5956.

Craig, Hardin, ed., 1902, *Two Coventry Corpus Christi Plays*, Early English Text Society, Extra Series, vol. 87, London.

Cunliffe, J. W., ed., 1907–1910, *The Complete Works of George Gascoigne*, 2 vols., Cambridge University Press, Cambridge, England.

Cutts, John P., 1955, "Robert Johnson: King's Musician in His Majesty's Public Entertainment," *Music and Letters*, 36:110–125.

—— 1956, "An Unpublished Contemporary Setting of a Shakespeare Song," *Shakespeare Survey 9*, pp. 86–89, Cambridge University Press, Cambridge, England.

—— 1956, "The Original Music of a Song in *2 Henry IV*," *SQ*, 7:385–392.

—— 1957, "A Reconsideration of the *Willow Song*," *JAMS*, 10:14–24.

—— 1958, "Music and the Supernatural in *The Tempest*: A Study in Interpretation," *Music and Letters*, 39:347–358.

—— 1959, "A John Payne Collier Unfabricated 'Fabrication'," *NQ*, 204:104–106.

—— ed., 1959, *La Musique de scène de la troupe de Shakespeare: The King's Men sous le règne de Jacques Ier*, Centre National de la Recherche Scientifique, Paris.

Dale, J., n.d., *Dale's Collection of Sixty favorite Scotch Songs, Adapted for the Voice & Piano-Forte or Harpsichord*, 3 vols., London [1794].

Dart, R. Thurston, 1948, "Morley's Consort Lessons of 1599," *Proceedings of the Royal Musical Association*, 74:1–9.

—— 1954, "New Sources of Virginal Music," *Music and Letters*, 35:93–106.

—— and W. Coates, eds., 1955, *Jacobean Consort Music*, vol. 9 of *Musica Britannica, A National Collection of Music*, Stainer & Bell, London.

Dart, R. Thurston, ed., 1958, *Thomas Morley. The First Book of Airs* (1600), a revision of vol. 16 of Fellowes' *The English School of Lutenist Song Writers*, 1st ser.; Stainer and Bell, London.

—— ed., n.d., *Robert Jones. First Booke of Songes and Ayres* (1600), a revision of vols. 14 and 15 of Fellowes' *The English School of Lutenist Song Writers*, 2nd ser.; Stainer & Bell, London [1959].

—— ed., 1963, *John Bull Keyboard Music: II*, vol. 19 of *Musica Britannica, A National Collection of Music*, Stainer & Bell, London.

Davies, W. Robertson, 1939, *Shakespeare's Boy Actors*, J. M. Dent & Sons, London.

Davison, Francis, ed., 1602, *A Poetical Rhapsodie*, London, STC 6373. See also Rollins, Hyder E., ed., 1931–1932.

Day, Cyrus L., and Eleanore Boswell Murrie, 1940 (for 1937), *English Song-Books 1651–1702, A Bibliography with a First-Line Index of Songs*, printed for The Bibliographical Society, Oxford University Press, Oxford.

De Arte Amandi. See Andreas Capellanus [1473/4?] and Parry, John J., ed. and tr., 1941.

Dean-Smith, Margaret, ed., 1957, *Playford's English Dancing Master 1651*, a facsimile reprint, Schott, London.

Dekker, Thomas, 1602, *Satiro-mastix*, London, STC 6521.

—— and John Webster, 1607, *West-Ward Hoe*, London, STC 6540.

Dekker, Thomas, 1609, *The Gvls Horne-booke*, London, STC 6500.

—— *Works.* See Pearson, John, ed., 1873.

Deloney, Thomas, 1612, *Strange Histories*, London, STC 6568.

—— 1626, *The pleasant Historie Of John Winchcomb, called Iacke of Newberie*, London, STC 6560.

—— 1631, *The Garland of Good-Will*, London, STC 6554.

—— 1639, *The Gentile Craft. The second Part*, London, STC 6556.

Deloney, Thomas, 1678, *The Garland of Good-Will*, London, Wing D946. See also Dixon, James Henry, ed., 1851.

—— *Works*. See Mann, F. O., ed., 1912.

—— *Novels*. See Lawlis, Merritt E., ed., 1961.

Devrient, Eduard, and Otto Devrient, eds. and trs., 1873–1876. See Works of William Shakespeare, II.

Dixon, James Henry, ed., 1851, *The Garland of Good-Will, by Thomas Deloney*, London.

Dodoens, Rembert, 1578, *A Niewe Herball, or Historie of Plantes: wherin is contayned the whole discourse and perfect description of all sortes of Herbes and Plantes*, tr. Henry Lyte, London, STC 6984.

Dolmetsch, Mabel, 1949, *Dances of England and France from 1450 to 1600 with their Music and Authentic Manner of Performance*, Routledge & Kegan Paul, London.

Doni's Philosophie. See North, Thomas, tr., 1570.

Donne, John, *Poems*. See Grierson, H. J. C., ed., 1912.

Douce, Francis, 1839, *Illustrations of Shakespeare, and of Ancient Manners*, London.

Douce. The Francis Douce Ballad Collection in the Bodleian Library.

Dryden, John, and William D'Avenant, 1670, *The Tempest, or The Enchanted Island. A Comedy*, London, Wing S2944.

Du Bartas, Guillaume de Salluste, *Works*. See Holmes, Urban Tigner *et al.*, eds., 1935–1940.

Duckles, Vincent, 1954, "New Light on 'O Mistresse mine'," *RN*, 7:98–100.

—— 1954, "The 'Curious' Art of John Wilson (1595–1674): An Introduction to his Songs and Lute Music," *JAMS* 7:93–112.

—— 1962, a review of John P. Cutt's *Musique* in *JAMS*, 15:363–365.

D'Urfey, Thomas, ed., 1719, *Songs Compleat, Pleasant and Divertive*, 5 vols., London.

—— ed., 1719–1720, *Wit and Mirth: or Pills to Purge Melancholy*, 6 vols., London. A later issue of *Songs Compleat*, 1719.

—— ed., n.d., *Songs Compleat, Pleasant and Divertive*, 6 vols., n.p. [ca. 1876]. A modern reprint of vols. 2 and 6 from *Wit and Mirth*, and vols. 1, 3–5 from *Songs Compleat*. The title-page of each volume in this edition reproduces the title-page of the original volume from which the reprint was taken, including the original's place and date.

The Early English Carols. See Greene, Richard Leighton, ed., 1935.

Early English Christmas Carols. See Robbins, Rossell Hope, ed., 1961.

Ebsworth, J. W., ed., 1883–1899, *The Roxburghe Ballads*, 6 vols. of 9, London. See also Chappell, William, ed., 1871–1880.

—— ed., 1875, *Westminster Drolleries*, 2 pts., London.

Edwards, Edward, ed., 1903, *A Book of Shakespeare's Songs*, G. Schirmer, New York.

Edwards, Richard, 1571, *The excellent Comedie of two the moste faithfullest Freendes, Damon and Pithias*, London, STC 7514.

Eliot, John, 1593, *Ortho-epia Gallica. Eliots Frvits for the French*, London, STC 7574.

Ellacombe, Henry N., 1878, *The Plant Lore & Garden-Craft of Shakespeare*, Exeter.

Elson, Louis C., 1901, *Shakespeare in Music*, L. C. Page & Co., Boston.

Empson, William, 1947, *Seven Types of Ambiguity*, Chatto & Windus, London.

Englands Helicon, 1600. See Rollins, Hyder E., ed., 1935.

The English and Scottish Popular Ballads. See Child, Francis James, ed., 1882–1898.

Entwisle, Royle, 1873 [no title], *NQ*, 12:364.

Evans, Bertrand, 1960, *Shakespeare's Comedies*, Clarendon Press, Oxford.

Evans, Willa McClung, 1941, *Henry Lawes, Musician and Friend of Poets*, Modern Language Association of America, New York.

—— 1945, "Shakespeare's 'Harke Harke ye Larke'," *PMLA*, 60:95–101.

Exeter Book. See Krapp, George P., ed., 1936.

The Famovs Victories of Henry the fifth: Containing the Honourable Battell of Agin-court, 1598, London, STC 13072.

Fellowes, Edmund H., ed., 1922, *Philip Rosseter. Songs from Rosseter's Book of Airs*, 1601, vols. 8 and 9 of *The English School of Lutenist Song Writers*, 1st ser., Stainer & Bell, London.

—— ed., 1925, *Robert Jones. First Book of Songes and Ayres (1600)*, vols. 14 and 15 of *The English School of Lutenist Song Writers*, 2nd ser., Stainer & Bell, London.

—— ed., n.d., *Forty Elizabethan Songs*, 4 vols., Stainer & Bell, London [ca. 1921–1926].

—— ed., 1925–1927, *The English School of Lutenist Song Writers*, 2nd ser., 16 vols., Stainer & Bell, London.

—— ed., 1920–1932, *The English School of Lutenist Song Writers*, 1st ser., 16 vols., Stainer & Bell, London.

—— ed., 1932, *Thomas Morley. The First Book of Airs (1600)*, vol. 16 of *The English School of Lutenist Song Writers*, 1st ser.; rev. R. Thurston Dart, 1958; Stainer & Bell, London.

—— 1933, "It Was a Lover," *TLS*, 5 Jan., p. 9.

—— ed., 1937, *A Plaine and Easie Introduction to Practicall Musicke by Thomas Morley*, Shakespeare Association Facsimile no. 14, London.

—— ed., 1950, *The Collected Works of William Byrd*, vol. 20, "Keyboard Works (Part iii)," Stainer & Bell, London.

—— 1954 (rev. Eric Blom), "Thomas Ford," *Grove's Dictionary of Music and Musicians*, 3:427, Macmillan & Co., London; St. Martin's Press, New York.

Fifty Shakespeare Songs. See Vincent, Charles, ed., 1906.

Finney, Gretchen L., n.d., *Musical Backgrounds for English Literature 1580–1650*, Rutgers University Press, New Brunswick, N. J. [1962].

The Fitzwilliam Virginal Book. See Fuller-Maitland, J. A., and W. Barclay Squire, eds., 1894–1899.

Fleay, F. G., 1875, "On Certain Plays of Shakespeare of which Portions Were Written at Different Periods of His Life," *Transactions of the New Shakespeare Society 1874*, 2:285–304.

—— 1876, *Shakespeare Manual*, London.

Fletcher, John, and William Shakespeare, 1634, *The Two Noble Kinsmen*, London, STC 11075.

Fletcher, John, 1639, *The Bloody Brother*, London, STC 11064.

—— *The Maid in the Mill*. See Beaumont, Francis, and John Fletcher, 1647. See also Waller, A. R., and Arnold Glover, eds., 1905–1912.

Florio, John, 1598, *A Worlde of Wordes, Or Most copious, and exact Dictionarie in Italian and English*, London, STC 11098.

Flügel, Ewald, 1889–1903, "Liedersammlungen des XVI. Jahrhunderts, Besonders aus der Zeit Heinrich's VIII," *Anglia*, 12:225–272, 585–597; 26:94–285.

Folkard, Richard, Jr., 1884, *Plant Lore*, London.

Ford, C. Lawrence, 1900, "Shakespeariana," *NQ*, 6:5.

Foulface, Phillip, *pseud.*, 1593, *Bacchus Bountie; by Phillip Foulface of Ale-Foord*, London, STC 11208.

F[ox-] S[trangways], A. H., 1923, "Shakespeare's Songs," *TLS*, 12 July, p. 472.

Frankis, P. J., 1958, "The Testament of the Deer in Shakespeare," *Neuphilologische Mitteilungen*, 59:65–68.

Frazer, James G., 1935, *The Golden Bough: A Study in Magic and Religion*, 12 vols., Macmillan Co., New York.

Friedman, Albert B., 1953, "A New Version of 'Musselburgh Field'," *Journal of American Folklore*, 66:74–77.

Frost, Maurice, 1953, *English & Scottish Psalm & Hymn Tunes c. 1543–1677*, Oxford University Press, London.

Fuller-Maitland, J. A., and W. Barclay Squire, eds., 1894–1899, *The Fitzwilliam Virginal Book*, 2 vols., Leipzig; reprinted Ann Arbor, Mich., 1949.

Furnivall, Frederick J., ed., 1868–1873, *Ballads from Manuscripts*, 2 vols., London.

Garvin, Katharine, 1936, "A Speculation about 'Twelfth Night'," *NQ*, 170:326–328.

Gascoigne, George, *Works*. See Cunliffe, J. W., ed., 1907–1910.

Gaselee, Stephen, 1925, *An Anthology of Medieval Latin*, Macmillan & Co., London.

Genest, John, 1832, *Some Account of the English Stage from the Restoration in 1660 to 1830*, 10 vols., Bath.

Gerarde, John, 1597, *The Herball or Generall Historie of Plantes*, London, STC 11750.

Gibbon, John Murray, 1930, *Melody and the Lyric from Chaucer to the Cavaliers*, J. M. Dent & Sons, London.

Gilbert, W. S., n.d., *The Mikado, or The Town of Titipu*, London [1885].

Giraldi Cinthio, Giovanni Battista, 1565, *De Gli Hecatommithi, la seconda parte*, Mondovi.

Golding, Arthur, tr., 1567, *The. XV. Bookes of P. Ouidius Naso, entytuled Metamorphosis, translated oute of Latin into English meeter*, London, STC 18956.

Goldsmith, Oliver, 1774, *An History of the Earth and Animated Nature*, 8 vols., London.

Gordon, Philip, 1947, "The Morley-Shakespeare Myth," *Music and Letters*, 28 121–125.

A gorgious Gallery, of gallant Inuentions, 1578, London, STC 20402. See also Rollins, Hyder E., ed., 1926.

Granville-Barker, Harley, 1947, *Prefaces to Shakespeare*, 2 vols., Princeton University Press, Princeton, N. J.

Gray, Austin K., 1927, "The Song in *The Merchant of Venice*," *MLN*, 42:458 f.

Gray, Henry D., 1918, "The Original Version of 'Love's Labour's Lost'," *Leland Stanford Junior University Publications*, Stanford University, California.

Greenberg, Noah, ed., 1956, *An Elizabethan Song Book*, Doubleday & Co., Garden City, New York.

———— ed., 1961, *An English Songbook*, Doubleday & Co., Garden City, New York.

Greene, Richard L., ed., 1935, *The Early English Carols*, Clarendon Press, Oxford.

Greene, Robert, 1583, *Mamillia; A Mirrour or looking-glass for the Ladies of Englande*, London, STC 12269.

———— 1584, *Morando. The Tritameron of Loue*, London, STC 12276.

———— 1592, *A Qvip for an Vpstart Courtier*, London, STC 12300.

———— 1592, *Greenes, Groats-worth of witte, bought with a million of Repentance*, London, STC 12245.

Greenhill, J., W. A. Harrison, and Frederick J. Furnivall, eds., 1884, *A List of All the Songs & Passages in Shakespeare Which Have Been Set to Music*, New Shakespeare Society, London.

Greenlaw, Edwin, Charles G. Osgood, and Frederick M. Padelford, eds., 1932–1949, *The Works of Edmund Spenser. A Variorum Edition*, 9 vols. in 10, The Johns Hopkins Press, Baltimore, Md.

Greg, W. W., 1955, *The Shakespeare First Folio, Its Bibliographical and Textual History*, Clarendon Press, Oxford.

Greig, John, n.d., *Scots Minstrelsie: A National Monument of Scottish Song*, 6 vols., Edinburgh [1893–1895?].

Grierson, H. J. C., ed., 1912, *The Poems of John Donne*, 2 vols., Clarendon Press, Oxford.

Grindon, Leo H., 1883, *The Shakespeare Flora*, Manchester.

Grosart, A. B., ed., n.d., *Wits Trenchmour*, a privately printed facsimile edition [London, 1879].

———— ed., 1880, *Joseph Beaumont. The Complete Poems (1615–1699)*, 2 vols., Edinburgh.

Grosley, M., 1772, *A Tour to London; or, New Observations on England, and Its Inhabitants*, tr. Thomas Nugent, 2 vols., London.

Gude and Godlie Ballatis, 1567, Edinburgh, no STC entry. An earlier edition of *Ane compendious Buik. of Godly and Spirituall Sangis,* 1600, Edinburgh, STC 2997.

Hakluyt Society, ed., 1903–1905, *The Principal Navigations Voyages Traffiques & Discoveries of the English Nation,* 12 vols., Glasgow.

Hales, John W., and Frederick J. Furnivall, eds., 1867, *Bishop Percy's Folio Manuscript. Loose and Humorous Songs,* London.

—— eds., 1867–1868, *Bishop Percy's Folio Manuscript. Ballads and Romances,* 3 vols., London.

Hall, Joseph, 1597–1598, *Virgidemiarum, Sixe Bookes. First three Bookes, Of Tooth-lesse Satyrs. The three last Bookes. Of byting satyres,* London, STC 12716.

Halliwell, James O., ed., 1848, *The Moral Play of Wit and Science and Early Poetical Miscellanies,* London.

Hamilton, N. E. S. A., 1860, *An Inquiry into the Genuineness of the Manuscript-Corrections of Mr. J. Payne Collier's Annotated Shakespeare Folio, 1632,* London.

Hanford, James Holly, 1911, "Shakespeare and Raleigh," *The Nation,* 92:315 f.

Hardy, T. Maskell, 1909, *An Evening with Shakespeare,* Duffield & Co., New York.

—— 1930, *The Songs from Shakespeare's Plays,* 2 pts., Curwen & Co., London.

The Harleian Miscellany: a collection of scarce, curious, and entertaining pamphlets and tracts . . . found in the Late Earl of Oxford's library, 1808–1813, 10 vols., London.

Harting, James E., 1871, *The Ornithology of Shakespeare,* London.

Hawkins, John, 1776, *A General History of the Science and Practice of Music,* 5 vols., London.

Hazlitt, W. Carew, ed., 1868, *Inedited Tracts,* London.

—— 1870. See Brand, John, 1870.

A Health to the Gentlemanly profession of Seruingmen. See J. M., 1598.

Herford, C. H., and Percy and Evelyn Simpson, eds., 1925–1952, *Ben Jonson,* 11 vols., Clarendon Press, Oxford.

Heseltine, Philip [*pseud.,* Peter Warlock], ed., 1925, *Four English Songs of the Early Seventeenth Century,* Oxford University Press, London.

—— 1926, *The English Ayre,* Oxford University Press, London.

—— ed., 1928, *Pammelia and other Rounds & Catches By Thomas Ravenscroft (1609–1611),* Oxford University Press, London.

—— and Philip Wilson, eds., 1927–1931, *English Airs,* 6 vols., Oxford University Press, London.

Heywood, John, 1587, *The Woorkes of Iohn Heiwood Newly Imprinted,* London, STC 13288.

Heywood, Thomas, 1607, *The Fayre Mayde of the Exchange,* London, STC 13317.

—— 1608, *The Rape of Lvcrece. A True Roman Tragedie,* London, STC 13360.

Hickes, Georgius, 1705, *Linguarum vett. septentrionalium thesaurus,* 3 vols., Oxford.

Hill, Archibald A., 1951, "Towards a Literary Analysis," *English Studies in Honor of James Southall Wilson,* pp. 147–165, University of Virginia, Charlottesville, Va.

Hilton, John, ed., 1652, *Catch that Catch can, or A Choice Collection of Catches, Rovnds, & Canons for 3 or 4 Voyces, Collected & Published by John Hilton,* London, Wing H2036.

Hoby, Thomas, tr., 1561, *The Covrtyer of Covnt Baldessar Castilio, diuided into foure bookes,* London, STC 4778.

Holborne, Anthony, 1597, *The Cittharn Schoole,* London, STC 13562.

—— 1599, *Pavans, Galliards, Almains and other short Æirs,* London, STC 13563.

Hole, Robert, n.d., *Parthenia Inviolata, or Mayden-Musicke for the Virginalls and Bass-Viol,* London [1614?], STC 13567ᵃ. See also the facsimile published by the New York Public Library, New York, 1961.

The Holie Bible [Bishops' Version], 1572, London, STC 2107.

Hollander, John, 1959, "Twelfth Night and the Morality of Indulgence," *Sewanee Review,* 67:220–238.

—— 1961, *The Untuning of the Sky,* Princeton University Press, Princeton, N. J.

Holmes, Urban Tigner, Jr., John Coriden Lyons, and Robert White Linker, eds., 1935–1940, *The Works of Guillaume de Salluste, seigneur Du Bartas*, 3 vols., University of North Carolina Press, Chapel Hill, N. C.

Homer, *The Odyssey*. See Rieu, E. V., tr., 1946.

Horman, William, 1519, *Vulgaria*, London, STC 13811.

Hotson, Leslie, 1947, "Twelfth Night," *TLS*, 12 July, p. 351.

—— 1952, *Shakespeare's Motley*, Oxford University Press, New York.

—— 1954, *The First Night of Twelfth Night*, Rupert Hart-Davis, London.

Howell, James, 1650, *Epistolae Ho-Elianae. Familiar Letters Domestic and Forren. The second edition*, London, Wing H3072.

Howell, Thomas, 1581, *H. His Deuises, for his owne exercise, and his Friends pleasure*, London, STC 13875.

Howes, Edmund, ed., 1631, *Annales, or A Generall Chronicle of England*, London, STC 23340. Howes' continuation of John Stow's *The Annales of England*, 1592, STC 23334.

Hunter, Mark, 1926, "The Tempest, III.ii.121," *Review of English Studies*, 2:347 f.

Hunter, Robert G., 1965, *Shakespeare and the Comedy of Forgiveness*, Columbia University Press, New York.

Ing, Catherine, ed., 1951, *Elizabethan Lyrics*, Chatto & Windus, London.

J. D., 1640, *The Knave in Graine, New Vampt*, London, STC 6174.

J.M., 1598, *A Health to the Gentlemanly profession of Seruingmen: or, The Seruingmans Comfort*, London, STC 17140. See also Hazlitt, W. Carew, ed., 1868.

J. W. E., 1876, "King Stephen Was A Worthy Peer," *NQ*, 5:249 f.

Johnson, James, n.d., *The Scots Musical Museum*, 5 vols., Edinburgh [1787–1790].

Johnson, Richard, ed., 1620, *The Golden Garland of Princely pleasures and delicate Delights*, London, STC 14674.

Jones, Robert, 1600, *The First Booke of Songes and Ayres of foure parts with Tableture for the Lute*, London, STC 14732. See also Fellowes, E. H., ed., 1925, and Dart, R. Thurston, ed., n.d.

—— 1609, *A Mvsicall Dreame. Or the fovrth Booke of Ayres*, London, STC 14734.

—— 1610, *The Muses Gardin for Delights*, London, STC 14736.

Jonson, Ben, *Pans Anniversarie*. See Herford, C. H., *et al.*, eds., 1925–1952.

—— and George Chapman and John Marston, 1605, *Eastward Hoe*, London, STC 4971.

Jonson, Ben, 1616, *Works*. See Herford, C. H., *et al.*, eds., 1925–1952.

Jusserand, J. J., 1950, *English Wayfaring Life in the Middle Ages*, Ernest Benn Ltd., London.

Keats, John, 1820, *Lamia, Isabella, The Eve of St. Agnes, and Other Poems*, London.

Keightley, Thomas, 1860, "Are Critics Logicians?," *NQ*, 10:65 f.

Kidson, Frank, 1893, *Supplement to Chappell's Traditional Tunes*, London. An appendix to Wooldridge, H. E., ed. and rev., 1893.

Kilgour, Henry, 1876, "King Stephen Was a Worthy Peer," *NQ* 5:183 f.

Kimmins, G. T., 1928, *Songs from the Plays of William Shakespeare With Dances*, Novello and Co., London.

Kines, Tom, 1964, *Songs from Shakespeare's Plays and Popular Songs of Shakespeare's Time*, Oak Publications, New York.

The Knave in Graine, New Vampt. See J. D., 1640.

Knight, Charles, ed., [1838–1843], *The Pictorial Edition of the Works of Shakespeare*. See Works of William Shakespeare, II.

Knight, G. Wilson, 1953, *The Shakespearean Tempest*, Methuen & Co., London.

Kökeritz, Helge, 1953, *Shakespeare's Pronunciation*, Yale University Press, New Haven, Conn.

Krapp, George P., and E. v. K. Dobbie, eds., 1936, *The Exeter Book*, Columbia University Press, New York.

Lafontaine, Henry Cart de, ed., n.d., *The King's Musick. A Transcript of Records Relating to Music and Musicians (1460–1700)*, Novello & Co., London [1909].

Lamb, Charles, 1808, *Specimens of the English Dramatic Poets Who Lived About the Time of Shakespeare*, London.

Lamson, Roy, Jr., 1936, "English Broadside Ballad Tunes (1550–1700)," unpubl. diss., 3 vols., Harvard University, Cambridge, Mass.

Lane, Ralph. See Hakluyt Society, ed., 1903–1905.

Latham, Agnes M. C., ed., 1951, *The Poems of Sir Walter Ralegh*, Routledge & Kegan Paul, London.

Laugh and Lie Downe: Or, The Worldes Folly. See C. T., 1605.

Lawlis, Merritt E., 1956, "Shakespeare, Deloney, and the Earliest Text of the Arthur Ballad," *Harvard Library Bulletin*, 10:130–134.

———— ed., 1961, *The Novels of Thomas Deloney*, Indiana University Press, Bloomington, Ind.

Lawrence, William J., 1924, "Thomas Ravenscroft's Theatrical Associations," *MLR*, 19:418–423.

Leach, MacEdward, ed., 1961, *Pammelia, Deuteromelia, Melismata*, a facsimile edition, The Folklore Society, Philadelphia, Pa.

Lean, Vincent S., 1878, "Ducdame," *NQ*, 10:278.

LeComte, Edward S., 1960, "Ophelia's 'Bonny Sweet Robin'," *PMLA*, 75:480.

Lemnius, Levinus. See Newton, Thomas, tr., 1587.

Lever, J. W., 1953, "Shakespeare's French Fruits," *Shakespeare Survey 6*, pp. 79–90, Cambridge University Press, Cambridge, England.

The Life of a Satyrical Pvppy, Called Nim. See M[ay]., T[homas]., 1657.

Lily, William, and John Colet, 1566–1567, *A Short Introdvction of Grammar [Brevissima Institutio sev Ratio Grammatices]*, 2 pts., London, STC 15614.

Lilly, William. See *The Lives of those Eminent Antiquaries*, 1774.

Lindsey, Edwin S., 1924, "The Music of the Songs in Fletcher's Plays," *SP*, 21:325–355.

Linley, William, ed., 1816, *Shakespeare's Dramatic Songs*, 2 vols., London.

A List of All the Songs & Passages in Shakespeare Which Have Been Set to Music. See Greenhill, J., *et al.*, eds., 1884.

Littledale, H., and W. W. Greg, eds., 1921 [for 1920], *The Welsh Embassador*, Malone Society Reprints, London.

The Lives of those Eminent Antiquaries Elias Ashmole, Esquire, and Mr. William Lilly, 1774, London.

L[ok]., H[enry]., 1597, *Ecclesiastes, Otherwise Called The Preacher*, London, STC 16696.

Lodge, Thomas, 1590, *Rosalynde. Euphues golden legacie*, London, STC 16664.

———— 1594, *The Wovnds of the Ciuill War. Liuely set forth in the true Tragedies of Marius and Scilla*, London, STC 16678.

———— 1598, *Rosalynd. Euphues Golden Legacie*, London, STC 16667.

———— and Robert Greene, 1594, *A Looking Glasse for London and England*, London, STC 16679.

Long, John H., 1950, "Shakespeare and Thomas Morley," *MLN*, 65:17–22.

———— 1953, "Music for the Replica Staging of Shakespeare," *Studies in Shakespeare*, eds. Arthur D. Matthews and Clark M. Emery, pp. 88–95, University of Miami Press, Coral Gables, Fla.

———— 1954, "Beck's 'The case of "O Mistresse mine"'," *RN*, 7:15 f.

———— 1955, *Shakespeare's Use of Music: A Study of the Music and Its Performance in the Original Production of Seven Comedies*, University of Florida Press, Gainesville, Fla.

———— 1961, *Shakespeare's Use of Music. The Final Comedies*, University of Florida Press, Gainesville, Fla.

Loose and Humorous Songs. See Hales, John E., and Frederick J. Furnivall, eds., 1867.

Lucas, F. L., ed., 1927, *The Complete Works of John Webster*, 4 vols., Chatto & Windus, London.

Lumsden, David, 1954, *An Anthology of English Lute Music*, L. Schott, London.

Lyly, John, n.d., *Euphves. The Anatomy of Wyt*, London [1578], STC 17051.

——— 1580, *Euphues and his England*, London, STC 17054.

——— 1591, *Endimion, The Man in the Moone*, London, STC 17050.

——— 1594, *Mother Bombie*, London, STC 17084.

——— *Alexander and Campaspe*. See Blount, Edward, ed., 1632.

——— *Works*. See Bond, R. Warwick, ed., 1902.

Lyte, Henry, tr., 1578, *A Niewe Herball, or Historie of Plantes: wherin is contayned the whole discourse and perfect description of all sortes of Herbes and Plantes*, by Rembert Dodoens, London, STC 6984.

McCullen, Joseph T., Jr., 1952, "The Functions of Songs Aroused by Madness in Elizabethan Drama," *A Tribute to George Coffin Taylor. Studies and Essays, Chiefly Elizabethan, by His Students and Friends*, ed. Arnold Williams, pp. 185–196, University of North Carolina Press, Chapel Hill, N. C.

McKerrow, R. B., ed., 1910, *The Works of Thomas Nashe*, 5 vols., Sidgwick & Jackson, London; 1958, Basil Blackwell, Oxford.

MacSweeney, Joseph J., 1918, "Shakespeare and the Ballad," *NQ*, 4:40 f.

Main, W. W., 1951, "Shakespeare's 'Fear No More the Heat o' th' Sun'," *Explicator*, vol. 9 (March), item no. 36.

Mann, F. O., ed., 1912, *The Works of Thomas Deloney*, Clarendon Press, Oxford.

Marder, Louis, 1950, "Shakespeare's Musical Background," *MLN*, 65:501–503.

Marlowe, Christopher, and Thomas Nashe, 1594, *The Tragedie of Dido Queene of Carthage*, London, STC 17441.

Marlowe, Christopher, 1633, *The Famous Tragedie of The Rich Iew of Malta*, London, STC 17412.

——— *Works*. See Brooke, C. F. Tucker, ed., 1910.

Marston, John, 1602, *The History of Antonio and Mellida. The first part*, London, STC 17473.

Martin, W. Keble, 1965, *The Concise British Flora in Colour*, Ebury Press and Michael Joseph, London.

The Maske of Flowers, 1614, London, STC 17625.

Massinger, Philip, and Nathaniel Field, 1632, *The Fatall Dowry*, London, STC 17646.

Massinger, Philip, 1636, *The Great Dvke of Florence. A Comicall Historie*, London, STC 17637.

M[ay]., T[homas]., 1657, *The Life of a Satyrical Pvppy, Called Nim*, London, Wing M1411.

May-Day: A Poem, In Four Parts, 1769, London. B. M. press mark 11632.b.34.

The Maydes Metamorphosis, 1600, London, STC 17188.

Metcalfe, J. Powell, and Edward F. Rimbault, eds., n.d., *The Rounds, Catches and Canons of England*, London [1864].

Middleton, Thomas, 1602, *Blvrt Master Constable. Or The Spaniards Night-walke*, London, STC 17876.

——— 1608, *A Tricke to Catch the Old-one*, London, STC 17896ª.

——— and Thomas Dekker, 1611, *The Roaring Girle. Or Moll Cut-purse*, London, STC 17908.

Middleton, Thomas, *Works*. See Bullen, A. H., ed., 1885–1886.

Miller, Frank Justus, ed. and tr., 1951, *Metamorphoses* [Ovid], 2 vols., Harvard University Press, Cambridge, Mass.

Milton, John, 1667, *Paradise Lost*, London, Wing M2136.

Mirth in Abundance, 1659, London, Wing M2227.

Montemayor, Jorge de. See Young, Bartholomew, tr., 1598.

Moore, John Robert, 1916, "The Function of the Songs in Shakespeare's Plays," *Shake-*

speare Studies by Members of the Department of English of the University of Wisconsin, pp. 78–102, Madison, Wis.

—— 1922, "Ancestors of Autolycus in the English Moralities and Interludes," *Washington University Studies,* Humanistic Series, vol. IX, no. 2, pp. 157–164, St. Louis, Mo.

—— 1939, "A Reply and a Symposium," *PMLA,* 54:149–152.

—— 1950, "Shakespeare and Morley Again," *MLN,* 65:504 f.

Morley, Thomas, 1597, *A Plaine and Easie Introduction to Practicall Musicke,* London, STC 18133. See also Fellowes, E. H., ed., 1937.

—— 1599, 1611, *The First Booke of Consort Lessons,* London, STC 18131, STC 18132. See also Beck, Sydney, ed., 1959.

—— 1600, *The First Booke of Ayres. Or Little Short Songs, to Sing and Play to the Lvte,* London, no STC entry. See also Fellowes, E. H., ed., 1932, and Dart, R. Thurston, ed., 1958.

—— 1601, *Madrigales The Triumphes of Oriana, to 5. and 6. voices: composed by diuers seuerall aucthors,* London, STC 18130.

Morris, Harry, 1958, "Ophelia's 'Bonny Sweet Robin'," *PMLA,* 73:601–603.

Munday, Anthony, and Henry Chettle, 1601, *The Death of Robert, Earle of Hvntington,* London, STC 18269.

Munday, Anthony, 1601, *The Downfall of Robert, Earle of Huntington,* London, STC 18271. Reprinted by The Malone Society, 1964 (1965).

Musique. See Cutts, John P. ed., 1959, *La Musique.*

NED. See *A New English Dictionary.*

Nashe, Thomas, 1600, *A Pleasant Comedie, called Summers last will and Testament,* London, STC 18376.

—— *Works.* See McKerrow, R. B., ed., 1910.

Naylor, Edward W., 1905, *An Elizabethan Virginal Book,* J. M. Dent & Co., London.

—— n.d., *Shakespeare Music (Music of the Period),* J. Curwen & Sons, London [1912].

—— 1931, *Shakespeare and Music,* J. M. Dent & Sons, London.

A New English Dictionary on Historical Principles, 1888–1933, eds. James Murray, Henry Bradley, William A. Craigie, and C. T. Onions, 10 vols. and supplement, Oxford University Press, London.

Newton, Thomas, tr., 1587, *An Herbal for the Bible.* . . . *Drawen into English by Thomas Newton,* London, STC 15454.

A New Variorum Edition of Shakespeare. See appropriate entries under Works of William Shakespeare, III.

Nicholson, B., 1873, "Shakespeariana: Cymbeline II.3: Mary-Buds," *NQ,* 12:283 f.

—— 1874, "Shakespeariana: Mary-Buds," *NQ,* 1:24.

Nicoll, Allardyce, ed., n.d., *The Works of Cyril Tourneur,* Fanfrolico Press, London [1930].

Nixon, Anthony, 1606, *The Blacke yeare,* London, STC 18582.

Noble, Richmond, 1923, *Shakespeare's Use of Song with the Text of the Principal Songs,* Oxford University Press, London.

—— 1930, "A Song in As You Like It," *TLS,* 5 June, p. 478.

—— 1930, "Feste's Epilogue Song," *TLS,* 10 July, p. 576.

—— 1933, "It Was a Lover," *TLS,* 12 January, p. 24.

Nolan, Edward F., 1952, "Shakespeare's 'Fear No More the Heat o' th' Sun'," *Explicator,* vol. 11 (October), item no. 4.

North, Thomas, tr., 1570, *The Morall Philosophie of Doni* [Bidpai], London, STC 3053.

Nosworthy, J. M., 1958, "Music and Its Function in the Romances of Shakespeare," *Shakespeare Survey* 11, pp. 60–69, Cambridge University Press, Cambridge, England.

Nott, George Frederick, ed., 1815–1816, *The Works of Henry Howard, Earl of Surrey, and of Sir Thomas Wyatt the Elder,* 2 vols., London.

Osborn, James M., 1958, "Benedick's Song in 'Much Ado'," *The Times*, London, 17 November, p. 11.
———— 1958, "Shakespeare Verse Traced to Source," *The New York Times*, 18 November, p. 39.
Oswald, James, n.d., *The Caledonian Pocket Companion. In Seven Volumes, Containing All the Favourite Scotch Tunes with Variations For the German Flute with an Index to the Whole*, London [1750–1760?]. B. M. press mark Hirsch M. 1443.
———— n.d., *The Caledonian Pocket Companion In Ten Volumes*, London [1760?]. B. M. press mark e.1290.a.
———— n.d., *The Caledonian Pocket Companion, Containing A favourite Collection of Scotch Tunes*, 2 vols., London [1770?]. B. M. press mark e.1290.b.
Overbury, Thomas, 1614, *A Wife Now the Widdow of Sir Thomas Overbvrye. Being A most exquisite and singular Poem of the choice of a Wife. Wherevnto Are Added many witty Characters, and conceited Newes*, London, STC 18905.
Ovid. See Golding, Arthur, tr., 1567. See also Miller, Frank Justus, ed. and tr., 1951.
P. P. C., 1873, "Shakespeariana: 'winking Mary-buds'," *NQ*, 12:243 f.
PB See Rollins, Hyder E., ed., 1929–1932.
Padelford, Frederick M., and Allen R. Benham, 1908, "The Songs in Manuscript Rawlinson C. 813," *Anglia*, 31:309–397.
Pafford, J. H. P., 1959, "Music and the Songs in 'The Winter's Tale'," *SQ*, 10:161–175.
Pammelia. Mvsick's Miscellanie. See Ravenscroft, Thomas, 1609.
Parrott, Thomas Marc, ed., 1910–1914, *The Plays and Poems of George Chapman*, 2 vols., G. Routledge & Sons, London.
Parry, John J., ed. and tr., 1941, *The Art of Courtly Love By Andreas Capellanus*, F. Ungar Publishing Co., New York.
Patrick, J. Max, 1953, "The Problem of Ophelia," *Studies in Shakespeare*, ed. Arthur D. Matthews and Clark M. Emery, pp. 139–144, University of Miami Press, Coral Gables, Fla.
Patterson, Frank Allen, 1916, "Shakespeare and the Medieval Lyric," *Shakespearean Studies by Members of the Department of English and Comparative Literature in Columbia University*, pp. 431–452, Columbia University Press, New York.
Pattison, Bruce, 1948, *Music and Poetry of the English Renaissance*, Methuen & Co., London.
Pearson, John, ed., 1873, *The Dramatic Works of Thomas Dekker*, 4 vols., London.
Peele, George, 1593, *The Famous Chronicle of king Edward the first*, London, STC 19535.
———— 1595, *The Old Wiues Tale*, London, STC 19545.
———— 1607, *The Merrie Conceited Iests of George Peele*, London, STC 19541.
Pepys The Pepys Ballad Collection in the library of Magdalene College, Cambridge, England.
Percy, Thomas, ed., 1765. See *The Reliques*.
Percy Folio MS. See Hales, J. W., and Frederick J. Furnivall, eds., 1867–1868.
Petronius Arbiter, 1587, *Satyricon. Adiecta sunt veterum quorundam poetarum carmina non dissimilis argumenti*, Paris.
Pettie, George, n.d., *A petite Pallace of Pettie his pleasure*, London [1576], STC 19819.
Phillips, George L., 1953, "Shakespeare's Fear No More the Heat o' th' Sun," *Explicator*, vol. 12 (October), item no. 2.
Playford, John, ed., 1651, 1686, *The English Dancing Master*, London, Wing P2477, Wing P2473. See also Bridgewater, Leslie, and Hugh Mellor, eds., 1933, and Dean-Smith, Margaret, ed., 1957.
———— ed., 1652, *Select Musicall Ayres, and Dialogves, For one and two Voyces, to sing to the Theorbo, Lute, Or Basse Violl*, London, Wing P2502.
———— ed., 1653, *Select Musicall Ayres and Dialogues, In Three Bookes*, London, Wing P2503.

Playford, John, ed., 1659, *Select Ayres and Dialogues For One, Two, and Three Voyces; To the Theorbo-Lvte or Basse-Violl*, London, Wing P2500.

—— ed., 1666, *Musick's Delight on the Cithren*, London, Wing P2491.

—— ed., 1667, 1673, *Catch that Catch can: or the Musical Companion*, London, Wing P2456, Wing P2490.

—— ed., 1669, *The Treasury of Musick*, London, Wing P2504.

—— ed., 1686, *The Second Book of the Pleasant Musical Companion: Being A New Collection of Select Catches, Songs, and Glees, for Two and Three Voices*, London, no Wing entry. This work is no. 85 in Day, Cyrus L., and Eleanore Boswell Murrie, 1940 (for 1937).

Pleasant Sonnets, 1566, London, no STC entry. This is a one-leaf fragment of the 1566 edition of Robinson, Clement, 1584.

Poems. See Works of William Shakespeare, III.

A Poetical Rhapsody. See Davison, Francis, ed., 1602; see also Rollins, Hyder E., ed., 1931–1932.

Pollard, A. W., 1917, *Shakespeare's Fight with the Pirates and the Problems of the Transmission of His Text*, Cambridge University Press, Cambridge, England.

—— and G. R. Redgrave, 1926, *A Short-Title Catalogue of Books Printed in England, Scotland, and Ireland, And of English Books Printed Abroad 1475–1640*, The Bibliographical Society, London.

Pope, Alexander, 1728, *The Dunciad*, London.

Porter, Cole. See Spewack, Samuel, 1953.

Potter, Frank Hunter, 1915, *Reliquary of English Song*, G. Schirmer & Co., New York.

Propertius. See Butler, H. E., ed. and tr., 1952.

Purchas, Samuel, 1613, *Pvrchas his Pilgrimage*, London, STC 20505.

RB The Roxburghe Ballad Collection in the British Museum.

RB The Roxburghe Ballads, 1871–1899. See Chappell, William, ed., 1871–1880, and Ebsworth, J. W., ed., 1883–1899.

Rabelais, Francis, 1904, *Master Francis Rabelais. Five Books of the Lives, Heroic Deeds and Sayings of Gargantua and His Son Pantagruel Translated into English by Sir Thomas Urquhart of Cromarty and Peter Antony Motteux*, 3 vols., A. H. Bullen, London.

—— n.d., *Les Cinq libres de Rabelais, avec notes et glossaire*, 2 vols., Flammarion, Paris [1906].

Ralegh, Walter. See Latham, Agnes, ed., 1951.

Ramsay, Allan, ed., 1724, *The Tea Table Miscellany*, Edinburgh.

—— ed., 1793, *The Tea-Table Miscellany: A Collection of Choice Songs Scots and English*, 4 vols., Berwick.

Ramsbottom, John, 1953, *Mushrooms & Toadstools, A Study of the Activity of Fungi*, William Collins Sons & Co., London.

Randolph, Thomas, *The Drinking Academy*. See Tannenbaum, Samuel A., and Hyder E. Rollins, eds., 1930.

Ravenscroft, Thomas, 1609, *Deuteromelia: or The Second part of Musicks melodie*, London, STC 20757. See also Leach, MacEdward, ed., 1961.

—— 1609, *Pammelia. Mvsicks Miscellanie*, London, STC 20759. See also Heseltine, Philip, ed., 1928, and Leach, MacEdward, ed., 1961.

—— 1611, *Melismata. Mvsicall Phansies. Fitting the Covrt, Citie, and Covntrey Hvmovrs*, London, STC 20758. See also Leach, MacEdward, ed., 1961.

—— 1614, *A Briefe Discovrse Of the true (but neglected) vse of Charact'ring the Degrees ... in ... Musicke*, London, STC 20756.

Raysor, Thomas M., ed., 1930, *Coleridge's Shakespearean Criticism*, 2 vols., Harvard University Press, Cambridge, Mass.

Redford, John. See Halliwell, J. O., ed., 1848.

Reed, Edward Bliss, ed., 1932, *Christmas Carols Printed in the Sixteenth Century*, Harvard University Press, Cambridge, Mass.

Reese, Gustave, 1954, *Music in the Renaissance*, W. W. Norton & Co., New York.

The Reliques of Ancient English Poetry, 1765, ed. Thomas Percy, 3 vols., London.

The Retvrne from Pernassvs: Or The Scourge of Simony, 1606, London, STC 19309.

Rieu, E. V., tr., 1946, *The Odyssey*, Penguin Books, Harmondsworth, Middlesex, England.

Rimbault, Edward F., 1846, *Who Was "Jack Wilson," the Singer of Shakespeare's Stage?*, London.

—— 1850, *Musical Illustrations of Bishop Percy's Reliques of Ancient English Poetry*, London.

Ritson, Joseph, 1794, *Scottish Songs*, 2 vols., London.

—— 1813, *A Select Collection of English Songs with Their Original Airs*, 3 vols., London.

—— 1869, *Scotish Songs*, 2 vols., Glasgow.

Robbins, Rossell Hope, ed., 1952, *Secular Lyrics of the XIVth and XVth Centuries*, Clarendon Press, Oxford.

—— 1959, "Middle English Carols as Processional Hymns," *SP*, 56:559–582.

—— ed., 1961, *Early English Christmas Carols*, Columbia University Press, New York.

—— ed., 1966, "The Bradshaw Carols," *PMLA*, 81:308–310.

Robin Good-fellow, his Mad Prankes and Mery Iests, 1628, London, STC 12016.

Robin Hood's Garland, n.d., London [1663], Wing R1637.

Robinson, Clement, 1584, *A Handefull of pleasant delites*, London, STC 21105. See also Rollins, Hyder E., ed., 1924.

Robinson, Fred N., ed., 1957, *The Poetical Works of Geoffrey Chaucer*, Houghton Mifflin Co., Boston, Mass.

Robinson, Thomas, 1603, *The Schoole of Musicke*, London, STC 21128.

Rohde, Eleanour S., 1935, *Shakespeare's Wild Flowers*, The Medici Society, London.

Roffe, Alfred, 1878, *The Handbook of Shakespeare Music*, London.

Rollins, Hyder E., 1919, "The Black-Letter Broadside Ballad," *PMLA*, 34:258–339.

—— 1919, "Concerning Bodleian MS. Ashmole 48," *MLN*, 34:340–351.

—— 1920, "'King Lear' and the Ballad of 'John Careless'," *MLR*, 15:87–89.

—— ed., 1920, *Old English Ballads 1553–1625, Chiefly from Manuscripts*, Cambridge University Press, Cambridge, England.

—— 1920, "William Elderton: Elizabethan Actor and Ballad-Writer," *SP*, 17:199–245.

—— ed., 1922, *A Pepysian Garland, Black-Letter Broadside Ballads of the Years 1595–1639*, Cambridge University Press, Cambridge, England.

—— 1924, "An Analytical Index to the Ballad-Entries (1557–1709) in the Registers of the Company of Stationers of London," *SP*, 21:1–324.

—— ed., 1924, *A Handful of Pleasant Delights (1584) By Clement Robinson and Divers Others*, Harvard University Press, Cambridge, Mass.

—— ed., 1926, *A Gorgeous Gallery of Gallant Inventions (1578)*, Harvard University Press, Cambridge, Mass.

—— ed., 1928–1929, *Tottel's Miscellany 1557–1587*, 2 vols., Harvard University Press, Cambridge, Mass.

—— ed., 1929–1932, *The Pepys Ballads*, 8 vols., Harvard University Press, Cambridge, Mass.

—— ed., 1931–1932, *A Poetical Rhapsody 1602–1621*, 2 vols., Harvard University Press, Cambridge, Mass.

—— ed., 1935, *England's Helicon 1600, 1614*, 2 vols., Harvard University Press, Cambridge, Mass.

—— ed., 1936, *The Arbor of Amorous Devices 1597 by Nicholas Breton and Others*, a facsimile edition, Harvard University Press, Cambridge, Mass.

—— ed., 1938, *The Poems*. See Works of William Shakespeare, II.

Rollins, Hyder E., ed., 1944, *The Sonnets*. See Works of William Shakespeare, III.

Rosier, James. See Purchas, Samuel, 1613.

Rosseter, Philip, 1601, *A Booke of Ayres*, London, STC 21332. See also Fellowes, E. H., ed., 1922.

Rowley, William, 1633, *A Match at Midnight*, London, STC 21421.

Roxburghe. The Roxburghe Ballad Collection in the British Museum.

The Roxburghe Ballads. See Chappell, William, ed., 1871–1880; Ebsworth, J. W., ed., 1883–1899.

Rushton, W. L., 1873, "Parallel Passages," *NQ*, 12:304.

SQ (1951). *Shakespeare Quarterly*, 2:280.

Sabol, Andrew, 1959, *Songs and Dances for the Stuart Masque*, Brown University Press, Providence, R. I.

Savage, F. G., 1923, *The Flora & Folk Lore of Shakespeare*, E. J. Burrow & Co., Cheltenham and London.

Scott, Walter, 1852, *The Heart of Midlothian* (vol. VII of the Waverly Novels), Edinburgh.

Seccome, Thomas, 1922, "John Wilson," *Dictionary of National Biography*, eds. Leslie Stephen and Sidney Lee, 21:574–576, Oxford University Press, London.

Seng, Peter J., 1955, "The Dramatic Function of the Songs in Shakespeare's Plays: A Variorum Edition," unpubl. diss., Harvard University.

———— 1958, "Music in Shakespeare," *Encounter*, March, pp. 67 f.

———— 1958, "The Riddle Song in 'Merchant of Venice'," *NQ*, 203:191–193.

———— 1958, "The Earliest Known Music for Desdemona's 'Willow Song'," *SQ*, 9:419 f.

———— 1958, "An Early Tune for the Fool's Song in *King Lear*," *SQ*, 9:583–585.

———— 1959, "The Foresters' Song in *As You Like It*," *SQ*, 10:246–249.

———— 1962, "Songs, Time, and the Rejection of Falstaff," *Shakespeare Survey 15*, pp. 31–40, Cambridge University Press, Cambridge, England.

———— 1964, "Ophelia's Songs in *Hamlet*," *Durham University Journal*, 56:77–85.

———— 1964, "Pandarus' Song and Lily's Grammar," *Modern Language Journal*, 48:212–215.

———— 1965, "Shakespearean Hymn-Parody?," *RN*, 18:4–6.

Settle, Elkanah, 1692, *The Fairy-Queen: An Opera*, London, Wing S2681.

Shaaber, M. A., ed., 1957, "*The First Rape of Faire Hellen* by John Trussell," *SQ*, 8:407–448.

The Shakespeare Vocal Album, 1864, London.

Sherwood, Robert, 1632, *Dictionaire Anglois et François, pour l'vtilité de tous ceux, qui sont desireux de deux Langues*, London, STC 5831. Part 2 of Cotgrave, Randle, 1632.

Sidgwick, Frank, ed., 1908, *The Sources and Analogues of 'A Midsummer-Night's Dream'*, Duffield & Co., New York; Chatto & Windus, London.

Sidney, Philip, 1598, *The Covntesse of Pembrokes Arcadia*, London, STC 22541.

Simpson, Claude M., 1966, *The British Broadside Ballad and Its Music*, Rutgers University Press, New Brunswick, N.J.

Simpson, Percy, 1911, *Shakespearean Punctuation*, Clarendon Press, Oxford.

Singer, S. W., 1852, "On a Passage in 'Cymbeline', Act IV. Sc. 2," *NQ*, 5:556.

Singleton, Esther, 1922, *The Shakespeare Garden*, Century Co., New York.

Skeat, W. W., 1906, "A Pugging Tooth," *NQ*, 6:342 f., 391.

Skelton, John, n.d., *Here after foloweth the Boke of Phyllyp Sparowe*, London [1545?], STC 22594.

———— n.d., *Here after foloweth a litel boke called Colin Cloute*, London [1545?], STC 22601.

Smith, Charles G., 1963, *Shakespeare's Proverb Lore: His Use of the Sententiae of Leonard Culman and Publilius Syrus*, Harvard University Press, Cambridge, Mass.

Smith, John Christopher, n.d., *The Tempest. An Opera*, London [1756].

Smith, John Stafford, ed., 1812, *Musica Antiqua*, 2 vols., London.

Smith, William G., 1935, *The Oxford Dictionary of English Proverbs*, Clarendon Press, Oxford.

Songes and Sonettes, 1557, London, STC 13860. See also Rollins, Hyder E., ed., 1928–1929.

Sonnets. See Works of William Shakespeare, III.

Sowerby, John E., illustrator, 1914, *British Wild Flowers*, by C. Pierpont Johnson, Gurney & Jackson, London.

Spencer, Robert, 1960 [for 1958], "The Weld Lute-Book," *The Lute Society Journal*, 1:121–131.

Spencer, Theodore, 1942, *Shakespeare and the Nature of Man*, Macmillan & Co., New York.

Spenser, Edmund. See Greenlaw, Edwin, *et al.*, eds., 1932–1949.

Spewack, Samuel, and Bella Spewack, 1953, *Kiss Me Kate, A Musical Play*, lyrics by Cole Porter, Alfred A. Knopf, New York.

Spink, Ian, ed., 1961, *Robert Johnson: Ayres, Songs and Dialogues*, vol. 17 of *The English School of Lutenist Song Writers*, 2nd ser., Stainer & Bell, London.

Squire, W. Barclay, ed., 1912, *Catalogue of Printed Music Published Between 1487 and 1800 Now in the British Museum*, 2 vols., British Museum, London.

STC See Pollard, A. W., and G. R. Redgrave, 1926.

S[tafford]., W[illiam]., 1581, *A Compendious or briefe examination of certayne ordinary complaints*, London, STC 23133.

Stenberg, Theodore, 1927, "'Damon and Pithias' and 'The Tempest'," *NQ*, 152:153.

Stenhouse, William, ed., 1839, *The Scots Musical Museum by James Johnson*, 6 vols., Edinburgh.

—— ed., 1853, *The Scots Musical Museum . . . originally published by James Johnson*, 4 vols., Edinburgh and London.

Stephens, F. G., 1872, "Cuckoo Song," *NQ*, 10:368 f.

Sternfeld, Frederick W., 1952, "Troilus and Cressida: Music for the Play," *English Institute Essays*, pp. 107–137, New York.

—— 1958, "Lasso's Music for Shakespeare's 'Samingo'," *SQ*, 9:105–116.

—— 1959, "Shakespeare's use of Popular Song," *Elizabethan and Jacobean Studies Presented to Frank Percy Wilson*, ed. H. Davis, pp. 150–166, Clarendon Press, Oxford.

—— 1963, *Music in Shakespearean Tragedy*, Routledge & Kegan Paul, London; Dover Publications, Inc., New York.

—— 1964, "Music and Ballads," *Shakespeare Survey 17*, pp. 214–222, Cambridge University Press, Cambridge, England.

—— ed., 1964, *Songs from Shakespeare's Tragedies*, Oxford University Press, London.

—— 1964, "Ophelia's Version of the Walsingham Song," *Music and Letters*, 45:108–113.

Sternhold, T., I. Hopkins and others, 1562, *The Whole Booke of Psalmes, collected into Englysh metre*, London, STC 2430.

Stevens, John, 1961, *Music and Poetry in the Early Tudor Court*, Methuen & Co., London.

—— ed., 1962, *Music at the Court of Henry VIII*, vol. 18 of *Musica Britannica, A National Collection of Music*, Stainer & Bell, London.

Stow, John. See Howes, Edmund, 1631.

Sullivan, Paul R., 1948, "Untheological Grace," *College English*, 10:164 f.

Surrey, Henry Howard, Earl of, *Works*. See Nott, G. F., ed., 1815–1816.

Swan, John, 1635, *Specvlvm Mundi or A Glasse Representing the Face of the World*, Cambridge, STC 23516.

T. Y., 1850, "Folk Lore of South Northamptonshire," *NQ*, 2:164.

Tannenbaum, Samuel, and Hyder E. Rollins, eds., 1930, *The Drinking Academy*, Harvard University Press, Cambridge, Mass.

The Tea Table Miscellany. See Ramsay, Allan, ed., 1724, 1793.

Thewlis, George A., 1941, "Some Notes on a Bodleian Manuscript," *Music and Letters*, 22:32–35.

Thomson, George, n.d., *Thomson's Collection of the Songs of Burns, Sir Walter Scott, and Other Eminent Lyric Poets Ancient and Modern, United to the Select Melodies of Scotland and of Ireland & Wales*, 6 vols., London and Edinburgh [1825].

Thurston, Herbert, ed., 1926–1938, *The Lives of the Saints, Originally Compiled by the Rev. Alban Butler*, 12 vols., Burns, Oates & Co., London.

Tilley, Morris Palmer, 1926, *Elizabethan Proverb Lore in Lyly's Euphues and in Pettie's Petite Pallace with Parallels from Shakespeare*, University of Michigan Publications, Language and Literature, vol. 2, New York.

—— 1950, *A Dictionary of the Proverbs in England in the Sixteenth and Seventeenth Centuries*, University of Michigan Press, Ann Arbor, Mich.

Tillyard, E. M. W., 1943, *The Elizabethan World Picture*, Chatto & Windus, London.

—— 1944, *Shakespeare's History Plays*, Chatto & Windus, London.

Topsell, Edward, 1607, *The Historie of Foure-Footed Beastes*, London, STC 24123.

—— 1608, *The Historie of Serpents*, London, STC 24124.

Tottel, Richard, "Miscellany." See *Songes and Sonettes*, 1557. See also Rollins, Hyder E., ed., 1928–1929.

Tourneur, Cyril. See Nicoll, Allardyce, ed. [1930].

Transactions of the Bibliographical Society, 1898, vol. 4, London.

Tregeagle, 1878, "Ducdame," *NQ*, 10:55.

The Triumphes of Oriana. See Morley, Thomas, 1601.

The Troublesome Raigne of John, King of England, 1591, London, STC 14644.

Trussell, John. See Shaaber, Maurice A., ed., 1957.

Turberville, George, 1567, *Epitaphes, Epigrams, Songs, and Sonets*, London, STC 24326.

The Two Noble Kinsmen. See Fletcher, John, and William Shakespeare, 1634. See also Works of William Shakespeare, II, Kittredge (1936).

van Wijk, H. L. Gerth, 1911, *A Dictionary of Plant Names*, 2 vols., Martinus Nijhoff, The Hague, Holland.

Vernon, Joseph, n.d., *The New Songs in the Pantomime of the Witches: the Celebrated Epilogue in the Comedy of Twelfth Night . . . Sung by Mr. Vernon at Vaux Hall, composed by J. Vernon*, London [1772]. B. M. press mark G.378.a.

Vincent, Charles, ed., 1906, *Fifty Shakespeare Songs*, Oliver Ditson Co., Boston, Mass.

Vlasto, Jill, 1954, "An Elizabethan Anthology of Rounds," *Musical Quarterly*, 40:222–234.

Vyvyan, John, 1959, *The Shakespearean Ethic*, Chatto & Windus, London.

—— 1960, *Shakespeare and the Rose of Love, A Study of the Early Plays in Relation to the Medieval Philosophy of Love*, Chatto & Windus, London.

—— 1961, *Shakespeare and Platonic Beauty*, Chatto & Windus, London.

W. N., gent., 1607, *Barley-breake, Or, A Warning for Wantons*, London, STC 18336.

Waddell, Helen, ed., 1935, *Medieval Latin Lyrics*, Constable & Co., London.

Wager, William, n.d., *A very mery and Pythie Commedie, called The longer thou liuest, the more foole thou art*, London [1569], STC 24935.

Walker, Andrew Jackson, 1934, "Popular Songs and Broadside Ballads in the English Drama, 1559–1642," unpubl. diss., Harvard University.

Waller, A. R., and Arnold Glover, eds., 1905–1912, *The Works of Francis Beaumont and John Fletcher*, 10 vols., Cambridge University Press, Cambridge, England.

Walther, Hans, 1959, *Initia Carminum ac Versuum Medii Aevi Posterioris Latinorum, Alphabetisches Verzeichnis der Versanfänge mittellateinischer Dichtungen*, Vandenhoeck & Ruprecht, Göttingen.

Walton, Isaac, 1653, *The Compleat Angler or the Contemplative Man's Recreation*, London, Wing W661.

Ward, C. A., 1885, "Whist, 'Tempest', I, ii.," *NQ*, 12:104 f.

Ward, John, 1951, "The Dolfull Domps," *JAMS*, 4:111–121.

—— 1954, *The Dublin Virginal Manuscript*, Wellesley College, Wellesley, Mass.

—— 1957, "Music for *A Handefull of pleasant delites*," *JAMS*, 10:151–180.

—— 1966, "*Joan qd John* and Other Fragments at Western Reserve University," *Aspects of Medieval & Renaissance Music: A Birthday Offering to Gustave Reese*, ed. Jan LaRue, pp. 832–855, W. W. Norton Co., New York.

Warlock, Peter, *pseud*. See Heseltine, Philip.

Watson, Thomas, 1590, *An Eglogve Vpon the death of the Right Honorable Sir Francis Walsingham*, London, STC 25121.

Webster, John, 1612, *The White Divel*, London, STC 25178.

—— *Works*. See Lucas, F. L., ed., 1927.

Weiss, John, 1876, *Wit, Humor and Shakespeare*, Boston.

Welch, Christopher, 1911, *Six Lectures on the Recorder and Other Flutes in Relation to Literature*, Henry Frowde, London.

The Welch Embassadour, or the happie Newes his Worship hath brought to London, 1643, London, Wing W1314.

The Welsh Embassador. See Littledale, H., and W. W. Greg, eds., 1921.

Wells, Evelyn, 1950, *The Ballad Tree, a study of British and American Ballads, their folklore, verse and music, together with sixty traditional ballads and their tunes*, Ronald Press, New York.

West, Richard, 1607, *The Court of Conscience Or Dick Whippers Sessions*, London, STC 25263.

Westminster Drolleries. See Ebsworth, J. W., ed., 1875.

Whetstone, George, 1578, *The Right Excellent and famous Historye, of Promos and Cassandra*, London, STC 25347.

White, Richard Grant, 1854, *Shakespeare's Scholar: being historical and critical studies of his text, characters, and commentators, with an examination of Mr. Collier's folio of 1632*, New York.

The Whole Booke of Psalmes. See Sternhold, T., *et al.*, 1562.

Wilson, J. Dover, 1930, "Textual Points in *As You Like It* and *Twelfth Night*," *TLS*, 19 June, p. 514.

—— 1947, "Twelfth Night," *TLS*, 26 July, p. 379.

Wilson, John, 1660, *Cheerfull Ayres or Ballads*, Oxford, Wing W2908.

Wing, Donald, 1945–1951, *Short-Title Catalogue of Books Printed in England, Scotland, Ireland, Wales, and British America, and of English Books Printed in Other Countries, 1641–1700*, 3 vols., The Index Society, New York.

Wise, John R., 1861, *Shakespeare: his Birthplace and its Neighborhood*, London.

Wither, George, 1641, *Halelviah or, Britans Second Remembrancer*, London, Wing W3162.

Witlim, Rawligh, 1760, "Passages in Shakespeare Explained," *The Gentleman's Magazine and Historical Chronicle*, 30:276 f.

Woodfill, Walter L., 1953, *Musicians in English Society from Elizabeth to Charles I*, Princeton University Press, Princeton, N. J.

Woodward, Marcus, ed., 1928, *Gerard's Herball*, Houghton Mifflin Co., Boston, Mass.

Wooldridge, H. Ellis, ed. and rev., 1893, *Old English Popular Music by William Chappell*, 2 vols., London. There is a modern reprint, two volumes in one, by Jack Brussel, New York, 1961.

Wright, Louis B., 1927, "Extraneous Song in Elizabethan Drama after the Advent of Shakespeare," *SP*, 24:261–274.

Wright, Thomas, ed., 1860, *Songs and Ballads*, London.

Wyatt, Thomas, *Works*. See Nott, F. G., ed., 1815–1816.

A Yorkshire Tragedy, 1608, London, STC 22340.

Young, Bartholomew, tr., 1598, *Diana of George of Montemayor: Translated out of Spanish into English by Bartholomew Yong*, London, STC 18044.

Young, Thomas, 1617, *Englands Bane: or, The Description of Drunkenesse*, London, STC 26116.

Zimbardo, Rose Abdelnour, 1963, "Form and Disorder in The Tempest," *SQ*, 14:49–65.

General Index

Index of First Lines

SONGS, SOURCES, ANALOGUES AND RELATED LYRICS
